"So many of us have learned about neo-Calvinism through one thinker such as Abraham Kuyper or Herman Bavinck or J. H. Bavinck or Klaas Schilder, but here we are presented with it as a whole tradition with many rich variations and dimensions. This introduction is highly readable and perfect for the theological student. But it is also eminently practical. The chapter on Revelation and Reason alone is bristling with insights and implications for the evangelist, apologist, and missionary. Highly recommended."

—**Timothy Keller,**
pastor emeritus, Redeemer Presbyterian Church, New York City;
author of *The Reason for God*

"This is an indispensable primer on the most generative and influential version of 'neo-Calvinism,' the modern Dutch version that stems from the theological writings of Abraham Kuyper and Herman Bavinck. Comprehensive yet concise, it is the best place to start for those who need an introduction to the orthodox yet modern, theological yet secular work of the most important Calvinist intellectuals of the last two centuries."

—**Douglas A. Sweeney,**
Beeson Divinity School Samford University

"While some might imagine the theologian as a lonely soul on a lonesome path, theology's true nature is communal and convivial. It is nothing less than the communion of saints pondering the faith together. As a tradition larger than any of its individual stellar figures, neo-Calvinism is an example of this. In this outstanding book, Brock and Sutanto offer the reader a lucid, insightful, and fresh introduction to that tradition's core claims, whilst also modeling the power of thinking theologically together for the benefit of others. It is essential reading for all students of Reformed theology."

—**James Eglinton,**
Meldrum Senior Lecturer in Reformed Theology, University of Edinburgh

"Dutch neo-Calvinism is one of the most influential iterations of the Reformed tradition. Its importance lies in its all-encompassing vision of Christianity that touches and transforms every aspect of the life of faith. In this short, clear, and engaging work Gray Sutanto and Cory Brock provide readers with a state-of-the-art introduction to the theological agenda of this movement. I highly recommend it."

—**Oliver Crisp,**
principal of St. Mary's College;
head of the School of Divinity, University of St. Andrews

"Neo-Calvinism has won overwhelmingly by spreading its reach to a truly global audience and stretching its concerns to virtually every field. Too often, therefore, serious understanding of neo-Calvinism's animating impulses—the theological principles found predominantly in the writings of Kuyper and Bavinck—has been a lost cause. Cory Brock and Gray Sutanto serve as able guides in reintroducing the witness and wisdom of those two theological giants and the catholic force of their effort to take every thought captive to Christ. Take and read of what they saw and said and of what we may be called to hear and herald, too."

—Michael Allen,
John Dyer Trimble Professor of Systematic Theology,
Reformed Theological Seminary

"This book is a milestone in the new reception of Dutch neo-Calvinism currently under way in the English-speaking world. This reception will be greatly boosted by Cory Brock and Gray Sutanto's admirably clear and comprehensive introduction to the central theological insights of neo-Calvinism's founding figures. A great virtue of the book is that, while the authors' interpretive grip on the texts is clear throughout, they allow Kuyper and Bavinck to speak in their own words, thus enticing readers to delve into the primary sources themselves. Those sympathetic to the movement will discover, perhaps for the first time, the depth, range, and rigor of theological wisdom that launched it, and that alone can sustain and renew it today. Those unfamiliar with the movement, or perhaps suspicious of it, will encounter a remarkable and distinctive articulation of Reformed theology that compels serious critical attention, even when some of its particular claims may need to be superseded."

—Jonathan Chaplin,
member of the Centre for Faith in Public Life at Wesley House, Cambridge;
author of *Herman Dooyeweerd: Christian Philosopher of State and Civil Society*

"A timely and important contribution to the study of neo-Calvinism! This well-researched and well-referenced book by Cory C. Brock and N. Gray Sutanto prove that, despite its Dutch origin, neo-Calvinism offers a distinctive-yet-eclectic theological vision for the church worldwide. As such, it will continue to be a 'fruitful dialogue partner' for other traditions to enrich the ongoing constructive theological discussions that in turn will benefit the church globally."

—Yuzo Adhinarta,
president, Reformed Theological Seminary of Indonesia

"Considerable attention has been paid over the years to the social, political, and cultural components of the neo-Calvinist movement, relatively little to its theological component. Yet the founders of the movement, Abraham Kuyper and Herman Bavinck, were primarily theologians, and what they had to say on other matters always had theological roots. The authors, Sutanto and Brock, focus squarely on the theology of the two founders, highlighting the fact that their theology was thoroughly engaged with the modern world while yet being distinctly catholic, and bringing to light the theological roots of their thinking on social, political, and cultural matters. What emerges from their discussion is how learned and creative Kuyper and Bavinck were, and how extraordinarily comprehensive and integrated was the theology that they produced. They were systematic theologians—in the best sense of the word 'systematic.' This is a book that has long been needed. Finally, it's here!"

—**Nicholas Wolterstorff**,
Noah Porter Professor Emeritus of Philosophical Theology, Yale University

"This is an outstanding and much needed volume! At last we have a thoroughly theological introduction to neo-Calvinism! Those who are new to this stream of thought could have no better guide. Those who are acquainted with neo-Calvinism will find this sure-footed account of key loci in Kuyper and Bavinck to be a richly helpful resource. But this volume is not simply a valuable distillation of their theology—it also points the way toward a continuing, constructive neo-Calvinist theology for today."

—**Suzanne McDonald**,
professor of systematic and historical theology, Western Theological Seminary

"This book is long overdue. Now that studies of Bavinck and Kuyper are booming and their influence is spreading across the globe, this accessible overview of neo-Calvinism's original theology fills an important gap in the literature. It will definitely serve both the church and the scholarly community for decades to come. Preventing us from walking away with our own preferred images of Bavinck and Kuyper, the authors insightfully trace back the orthodox-yet-modern attitude of both Dutch theologians to its dogmatic roots. These roots are explored here with great skill and care. Therefore, Brock and Sutanto have put us greatly in their debt with this remarkable synthesis. The fact that neither of them is from Dutch descent clearly demonstrates that neo-Calvinism's influence has by now spread way beyond its native soil."

—**Gijsbert van den Brink**,
professor of theology, Vrije Universiteit Amsterdam

"Good introductions are worth their weight in gold. Sutanto and Brock's *Neo-Calvinism: A Theological Introduction* is a superb addition to their ranks. Measured, sympathetic, and lucid, it is a first-class piece of writing and a complete pleasure to read—a triumph that could not have come along at a better time!"

—Jon Balserak,
senior lecturer in early modern religion, University of Bristol

"We have long known that we needed a proper theological treatment of neo-Calvinism, but with this volume we have been blessed with far more. Sutanto and Brock have not only provided a truly valuable guide to a notoriously unwieldy and complicated program; they have done so in a way that captures something of neo-Calvinism's abiding theological freshness, culturally attuned wisdom, and refreshingly candid commitment to Jesus Christ as Lord of all. A uniquely important, invigorating book that should be read and reread for many years to come."

—Mark Garcia,
associate professor of systematic theology, Westminster Theological Seminary

"Neo-Calvinism, which has found a wide variety of expressions since its inception, is a multidimensional way of understanding the world and being in but not of the world. In this book, Cory Brock and Gray Sutanto focus on Abraham Kuyper and Herman Bavinck to outline for us the central theological themes and motifs that provide unity to the diverse dimensions of neo-Calvinism as a worldview that cannot be reduced to theology. The authors authoritatively demonstrate that neo-Calvinism is 'eclectically orthodox yet modern, self-consciously holistic, and organic and not mechanical,' and they do so by being such in their own writing. This is a much-needed reintroduction to neo-Calvinism in our day and age, when misunderstandings, misinterpretations, and misapplications of neo-Calvinism abound in Christian as well as non-Christian communities worldwide."

—Alex Shao Kai Tseng,
research professor, School of Philosophy, Zhejiang University

Neo-Calvinism

A Theological Introduction

Neo-Calvinism

A Theological Introduction

Cory C. Brock

and

N. Gray Sutanto

LEXHAM
ACADEMIC

Neo-Calvinism: A Theological Introduction

Copyright 2022 Cory C. Brock and N. Gray Sutanto

Lexham Academic, an imprint of Lexham Press
1313 Commercial St., Bellingham, WA 98225
LexhamPress.com

Print ISBN 9781683596462
Digital ISBN 9781683596479
Library of Congress Control Number 2022940303

Lexham Editorial: Todd Hains, Claire Brubaker, Erin Mangum, Mandi Newell
Cover Design: Joshua Hunt, Brittany Schrock
Typesetting: Abigail Stocker

For Heather and Indita

Contents

Abbreviations

BR	*The Bavinck Review*
CG	Abraham Kuyper. *Common Grace: God's Gifts for a Fallen World*. Translated by Nelson D. Kloosterman and Ed M. van der Maas. Edited by Jordan J. Ballor and Stephen J. Grabill. 3 vols. Bellingham, WA: Lexham, 2015–2020.
CCC	Herman Bavinck. "The Catholicity of Christianity and the Church." Translated by John Bolt. *Calvin Theological Journal* 27 (1992): 220–51.
CTJ	*Calvin Theological Journal*
CW	Herman Bavinck. *Christian Worldview*. Translated by James Eglinton, Nathaniel Gray Sutanto, and Cory C. Brock. Wheaton, IL: Crossway, 2020.
Encyclopedia	Abraham Kuyper. *Encyclopedia of Sacred Theology: Its Principles*. New York: Charles Scribner's Sons, 1898.
GD	Herman Bavinck. *Gereformeerde Dogmatiek*. 3rd ed. 4 vols. Kampen: Kok, 1918.
GE	Herman Bavinck. *Gereformeerde Ethiek*. Utrecht: Kokboekcentrum, 2019.
KGHG	Herman Bavinck. "The Kingdom of God, the Highest Good." Translated by Nelson Kloosterman. *BR* 2 (2011): 133–70.
Lectures	Abraham Kuyper. *Lectures on Calvinism*. Peabody, MA: Hendrickson, 2008.

PoR	Herman Bavinck. *Philosophy of Revelation: A New Annotated Edition*. Edited by Cory Brock and Nathaniel Gray Sutanto. Peabody, MA: Hendrickson, 2018.

Pro Rege	Abraham Kuyper. *Pro Rege: Living under Christ's Kingship*. Translated by Albert Gootjes. Edited by John Kok and Nelson D. Kloosterman. Bellingham, WA: Lexham, 2016.

RD	Herman Bavinck. *Reformed Dogmatics*. 4 vols. Translated by John Vriend. Edited by John Bolt. Grand Rapids: Baker Academic, 2003–2008.

RE	Herman Bavinck. *Reformed Ethics: Volume 1: Created, Fallen, and Converted Humanity*. Edited by John Bolt. Grand Rapids: Baker Academic, 2019.

SG	Hans Boersma. *Seeing God: The Beatific Vision in the Christian Tradition*. Grand Rapids: Eerdmans, 2018.

"Tract"	Abraham Kuyper. "Tract on the Reformation of the Church." Pages 75–280 in *On the Church*. Edited by John Halsey Wood Jr. and Andrew M. McGinnis. Abraham Kuyper Collected Works in Public Theology. Bellingham, WA: Lexham, 2016.

WWG	Herman Bavinck. *Wonderful Works of God: Instruction in the Christian Religion according to the Reformed Confession*. Edited by Carlton Wynne. Glenside, PA: Westminster Seminary Press, 2019.

Foreword

George Harinck

O NE CAN STUDY neo-Calvinism or employ neo-Calvinist notions without being acquainted with its theology. Neo-Calvinist jurist Herman Dooyeweerd developed a philosophical system in which theology is not the ground-laying structure or the queen amid other sciences, but merely one of the academic disciplines. And Abraham Kuyper himself stressed in his Stone Lectures that the Calvinist worldview was not reducible to theology or the confessions as such. Neo-Calvinism is appreciated by many for its engagement with culture and society, where theology seems to play a minor role and where the public role of the institutional church is limited or absent. Kuyper's and Herman Bavinck's ideal notion of society is formulated in nontheological terms: it is a place of freedom for every worldview.

Still, the fact cannot be denied that both founding fathers of neo-Calvinism, Kuyper and Bavinck, were theologians, that their keyworks were of a theological nature—Kuyper's *Encyclopedia of Sacred Theology* and of Bavinck's *Reformed Dogmatics*—and that the academic institutions they shaped were theological in the first place. Basically, all well-known notions in neo-Calvinism that may seem nontheological at first glance, such as sphere sovereignty, democracy, pluralism, and worldview, are deeply rooted in theology. Their employment is possible without knowledge of the theology that sustains them, but if one wants to understand their dimensions and direction, one has to go back to their theological roots.

Such is the concern in this book: it focuses on the theology of Kuyper and Bavinck, the founders of neo-Calvinism. In a way this introduction by Cory Brock and Gray Sutanto is a return to theology. For whatever Kuyper and Bavinck accomplished in society and academia—it is well-known that they were politicians, journalists, professors, and leaders in the school struggle[1]—their activities and research began as a theological enterprise. The need of the church for an up-to-date Reformed theology was their primary motive. The first dissertations on Kuyper and Bavinck were defended around the Second World War. They too were mainly theological in nature. Theology was the central focus, even when it was not the primary topic under investigation.

Some other examples noting this theological core are S. J. Ridderbos's dissertation *De theologische cultuurbeschouwing van Abraham Kuyper* (Abraham Kuyper's theological view of culture), defended in 1947 at Vrije Universiteit Amsterdam, and E. E. Rosenboom's dissertation *Die Idee einer christlichen Universität im theologischen Denken von Abraham Kuyper* (The idea of a Christian university in Kuyper's theology), defended at the Georg-August Universität of Göttingen in 1950. Later on, the research on Kuyper's and Bavinck's works and activities took on a philosophical, sociological, and historical dimension, and to such an extent that the theological and more specifically dogmatic dimension of neo-Calvinism was somewhat left behind. When the research of neo-Calvinism developed internationally in the beginning of the twenty-first century, theologians from global contexts were often in the lead, but what they lacked was a theological overview of and reflection on the neo-Calvinist tradition.

How did such theological neglect happen? I would point the reader to several reasons. Maybe the oldest stems from the theological conflict that accompanied the rise of neo-Calvinism in the Netherlands. The confrontations of Kuyper and Bavinck against modern theology, ethical theology, and traditional and experientialist Reformed theology were real clashes,

---

1. See the 2017 publication by Craig G. Bartholomew, *Contours of the Kuyperian Tradition: A Systematic Introduction* (Downers Grove, IL: IVP Academic, 2017).

and they caused divisions and alienations that had not existed before their times. Kuyper was a polemical theologian; but Bavinck, too, contributed to the conflicts, disputes, and tension that molded the new and independent position of neo-Calvinist theology. Of course, their opponents added their bit to heated controversy and a polluted atmosphere. This was especially the case with the loci of revelation (Scripture), creation, and the covenant. Kuyper never restored his broken relationships with the modern, ethical, and Reformed theologians, though Bavinck did try to mend the fragmented connections, reaching out to the modern theologians and keeping a good personal relationship with ethical theologian J. H. Gunning Jr. Even though he tried to build theological bridges or at least to initiate conversations with other theological schools or traditions, his efforts were not very successful. The relation with experiential Reformed theology, for example, did not lead to significant confrontation, but has stayed uncomfortable until the present day. These theological controversies were transplanted to the domain of the church, especially in the tensions between the Gereformeerde Kerken in Nederland (neo-Calvinist), on the one side, and the Nederlandse Hervormde Kerk (modern, ethical, and traditional Reformed) and smaller, experiential Reformed denominations, on the other side. It was not until the 1960s that the first two denominations were on speaking terms. They reduced their differences to a "domestic dispute"[2] and finally merged in 2004 as the Protestantse Kerk in Nederland (also including the Lutherans). In ecclesial life the main sharp edges have been smoothed, but in the Dutch theological landscape these late nineteenth and early twentieth century divisions lingered on, in such a way that led neo-Calvinist dogmatician Cornelis van der Kooi to speak of ongoing "Balkanization."[3]

A second reason for the neglect of the theological frame is the presence of an autarkic trait in neo-Calvinism. Its theological tradition had a flying start in the last decades of the nineteenth century due to its quality.

---

2. So *hervormde* theologian A. A. van Ruler in George Puchinger's interview with him on 7 June 1969. G. Puchinger, *Hervormd-gereformeerd, één of gescheiden* (Delft: W. D. Meinema, 1969), 381.

3. Kees van der Kooi, "Over kerk en samenleving. Enkele opmerkingen bij de verschijning van Kuypers *Commentatio,*" *Documentatieblad voor de Nederlandse Kerkgeschiedenis na 1800* 65 (November 2006): 21.

No other tradition could match the breadth and depth of Kuyper's *Encyclopedia* and Bavinck's *Dogmatics*, and after the turn of the century the Gereformeerde Kerken and the Vrije Universiteit, along with the neo-Calvinist Kampen Theologische School, were flourishing like no other church or theological department. This situation gave way to the neo-Calvinists' impression that they covered the theological discipline in its entirety and had no need to interact with other theological traditions. They, and no one else, were *issu de Calvin*. This imbalance between identity and connectivity has been a hallmark of neo-Calvinist theology, explaining why ethical theology was rejected completely and why the theology of Karl Barth met a cold reception in neo-Calvinist circles until the 1950s. Theologically, the neo-Calvinists thought they had everything they needed. Barth was welcome as a friend and ally only if he aligned his Reformed theology with Kuyper's and Bavinck's. These were the years Gerrit C. Berkouwer characterizes as a time of principled "isolation."[4] Because of this attitude, neo-Calvinist theology for a long time had a negative connotation in the theological world. This may explain the relative disinterest in this theological tradition in the past few decades in the Netherlands.

The third reason for the neglect may include a general spirit or implicit conviction that neo-Calvinists ought not agree to disagree dogmatically within their own circle. Historically, every minor point of difference had to be solved, for a variety of opinions would weaken the disputed position of neo-Calvinist theology. The pretended cohesiveness and completeness of this theology was incompatible with theological disagreements. In at least three cases this zeal for uniformity led to a church split: in 1924 on common grace (in the United States), in 1926 on the historical character of Scripture, and in 1944 on baptism, the covenant, and church polity. These incidents did not contribute to the popularity of neo-Calvinist theology.

A final reason neo-Calvinist theology has been neglected is the philosophizing of the notion of worldview. This notion is related to neo-Calvinism through its philosophical tradition, more so than via its theological branch. In the 1930s Herman Dooyeweerd and Dirk Vollenhoven developed a neo-Calvinist philosophy, rooted in the works of Kuyper and

---

4. G.C. Berkouwer, *Het probleem der Schriftkritiek* (Kampen: J.H. Kok, [1938]) ch. 7, esp. 383–84.

Bavinck. This philosophy was highly influential in North America, where it was introduced at Calvin College after the Second World War as part of the Kuyperian heritage. The notion of worldview was on the rise in evangelical circles in the United States from the mid-nineteenth century on, when these groups started their systematic opposition against modernism in their country. The Calvinist philosophy of Dooyeweerd and Vollenhoven fit very well in this intellectual climate and helped the small group of neo-Calvinists in the United States to fortify this worldview-thinking intellectually. Kuyper and Bavinck were mostly studied through this lens, and hence worldview, understood as a philosophical concept, became the distinguishing mark of neo-Calvinism, more so than its dogmatics.

In the Netherlands, this theological backlash has not been overcome yet, and neo-Calvinist theology is not *en vogue*, but internationally the interest in neo-Calvinist dogmatics is on the rise. A new generation of theologians from all over the world, and often without historical connections with the Dutch neo-Calvinist tradition, came into contact with its theology through the translations of Bavinck's *Reformed Dogmatics*, Kuyper's Stone Lectures on *Calvinism*, and many other publications they wrote. Since about 2000 this translation got a new and decisive impulse and developed into an industry, thanks to many, but especially through the efforts of John Bolt (Bavinck) and Rimmer De Vries (Kuyper). Translations in English, French, German, Portuguese, Korean, Russian, Chinese, and other languages are available or on their way. At present a young generation of international researchers has a plethora of texts at their disposal to revive and explore neo-Calvinist theology and open new avenues.

This introduction to neo-Calvinist theology is an excellent specimen of this revival, for two reasons. In the first place, Brock and Sutanto are scholars who have been educated in neo-Calvinist theology solidly, in places such as Edinburgh and Kampen (and in Pasadena, Amsterdam, and Grand Rapids). They are well acquainted with neo-Calvinist theology and give an excellent overview of Kuyper's and Bavinck's theology in this new introduction by going *ad fontes*, back to its sources, and by combining and summarizing their views. They represent the energy of a new generation, eager to discover, develop, and apply this theology in our present world. In order to do this, a balanced overview of the basics of neo-Calvinist theology is the indispensable starting point. The main concern of the authors is not to contextualize or historicize this theology, but to present its structure and architecture as envisioned by Kuyper and Bavinck. They bring Kuyper and Bavinck into conversation with recent international studies of their work. Interestingly, such an overview did not yet exist. We were in need of this book.

Second, by doing this work they also offer a state of the art of neo-Calvinist theological research plus an introduction to recent debates in the international theological community, such as on the beatific vision and on common grace and natural theology. It is most interesting for a Dutch neo-Calvinist scholar such as me to read this introduction so independent of the Dutch context, which limited and stifled its theological influence, as described above. In this book, Brock and Sutanto open the windows and hopefully also eliminate the barriers that still seem to limit the development of neo-Calvinist theology in its Dutch context.

I welcome this introduction as a milestone in the history of neo-Calvinist theology. It marks the transition of this theology from a Dutch specialty into an international flavor. The Dutch source and stream of neo-Calvinism was, is, and will be relevant, but this book is the sign that its theology has now passed beyond the Dutch fairway. It has reached the international waters. Fit for all seasons, it is now at open sea, where, as far as Kuyper and Bavinck was concerned and Brock and Sutanto demonstrate, it is meant to be.

Kampen, the Netherlands
July 2021

Acknowledgments

THE IDEA FOR this book first came during our time studying together at New College, University of Edinburgh, 2015–2018. We continue to be thankful for the friendship of like-minded neo-Calvinists there. Further, we are grateful for the continual encouragement from James Eglinton and George Harinck. We are also grateful to Lexham Press and to Jesse Myers, Brannon Ellis, and Todd Hains for taking on this project. Indeed, it was a lively conversation with Jesse and Brannon in particular over breakfast at the Biola Cafeteria during the 2019 LA Theology Conference that spawned the idea for this book.

I (Gray) would like to thank my colleagues, friends, and students at Reformed Theological Seminary for their support and hospitality. Many of the ideas in this book were formed through conversations both in and outside the classroom. In particular, my thanks to Thomas Keene, Scott Redd, Peter Lee, Jennifer Patterson, Timo Sazo, William Ross, D. Blair Smith, and Michael Allen, for the streams of thoughtful conversation as I wrote the bulk of this book in quarantine from Jakarta and Bali, Indonesia. Thanks as well are due, of course, to my wife, Indita, whose patience made the writing of this book possible.

I (Cory) was able to write this book during my time ministering at First Presbyterian Church in Jackson, Mississippi. I am grateful for space given me to both pastor and do research as a theologian in that season. Likewise, I am ever thankful for my wife and family for lovingly putting up with the seasons of book writing that coexist alongside the many other aspects of life. Last, Gray and I have both had countless conversations about the topics in this work with so many in Edinburgh, Reformed Theological Seminary, and the churches in which we have served, and we are indebted to their thoughts. In particular, Bruce Pass and George Harinck read through the entire manuscript and offered invaluable feedback. This book is a better work because of their attention. We would also like to thank Jon Huff for forming the bibliography, and Wilson Sugeng for the index.

I

Introduction

Academically, Kuyper was first and foremost a theologian. However, because he was involved in so many areas of life, his public work has often received far more attention than his work as a theologian. In recent years the Kuyperian tradition has been developed in philosophy and politics, but far less so in theology. This is a mistake. The theology of Kuyper, Bavinck, and Berkouwer, to mention the three major figures, is exceptionally rich and needs to be retrieved and updated for today.

— *Craig G. Bartholomew,* Contours of the Kuyperian Tradition

B ARTHOLOMEW'S OBSERVATION HERE, which marks the beginning of his chapter on theology in his fine introduction to the Kuyperian tradition, continues to ring true. Studies on neo-Calvinism carry on apace, and this is a cause for celebration. However, despite both the rigorous dogmatic output and the details of the theology that functions in its center and heart, studies that focus directly on neo-Calvinistic theology in particular are scant by comparison. In addition, as Bartholomew points out, the neo-Calvinist tradition is not developing as dogmatics. Though the studies that explore the implications of neo-Calvinism on public theology, politics, and philosophy are exciting, worth investigating on their own right, and intertwined with the work of dogmatics, this imbalance is unfortunate. This is the case not least because the dogmatic output of Kuyper and Bavinck is so rich but also because their work seems to promise substantial yields for contemporary dogmatics.

In a neglected essay by George Hunsinger written in 1996 (and republished in 1999), for example, he predicts that Kuyper and Bavinck will mark a decisive middle way forward for generative dialogue between evangelicals and postliberals on the doctrine of Scripture and its interpretation specifically: "The views of Abraham Kuyper and Herman Bavinck offer a greater possibility for fruitful evangelical dialogue with postliberal *theology* than the tendency represented by Carl Henry."[1] Consider also Joshua Ralston's 2016 editorial in the *International Journal of Systematic Theology*. Ralston, working with Brian Gerrish's *Christian Faith*, locates Gerrish closer to Friedrich Schleiermacher than either Barth or Bavinck, which locates Bavinck shoulder to shoulder with other giants in the modern theological landscape.[2] Indeed, Bavinck is recognized now as a choice that stands between the two giants of modern theology.

The theologies of Kuyper and Bavinck not only contain promising possibilities for contemporary dogmatics, but are also a significant but sometimes silent influence behind many theological trajectories today: the theological interpretation of Scripture, redemptive-historical hermeneutics, theological retrieval, Christian missiology, apologetics, and eschatology. This book seeks to fill this need by providing a theological introduction to the unique dogmatic contributions of the first generation neo-Calvinists, especially Kuyper and Bavinck. Three further impulses prompt the writing of this book.

First, as mentioned above, much literary output has been focused on the political and philosophical deliverances of neo-Calvinism, to the neglect of its dogmatic creativity. When the theology of neo-Calvinism is treated within these works, it is discussed as a prelude to the political or philosophical program under discussion. To be sure, political theology is a dogmatic enterprise. Yet, in many of the works under consideration, the emphasis lands on cultural discipleship rather than political theology. The five-volume *Kuyper Center Review*, for example, while having individual chapters on particular theological loci, focuses self-consciously on *Reformed Theology and Public Life* and has covered topics such as politics,

---

1. George Hunsinger, *Disruptive Grace: Studies in the Theology of Karl Barth* (Grand Rapids: Eerdmans, 1999), 340.

2. Joshua Ralston, "Editorial," *International Journal of Systematic Theology* 18.3 (July 2016): 257.

religion, and public life (vol. 1), Calvinism and culture (vol. 3), Calvinism and democracy (vol. 4), and the church and academy (vol. 5). Even its most explicitly theological volume, the second, written on the doctrines of revelation and common grace, was divided into two parts: revelation and philosophy, and common grace with interreligious dialogue.[3] There are many monographs and edited volumes that treat specific histories and applications of neo-Calvinism: neo-Calvinism and worldview (Heslam), neo-Calvinism and Christian philosophy (Goheen and Bartholomew), neo-Calvinism and culture (Edgar), the political theology of Herman Dooyeweerd (Chaplin), and the history and life of Kuyper and Bavinck (Dordt, Bratt, Bolt, Harinck, and Eglinton).[4] Yet, a single volume that treats their distinctive dogmatic theology in an introductory yet summative and textually grounded way is yet to be written. Bartholomew's excellent introduction to the Kuyperian tradition devotes much of its attention to neo-Calvinism's contribution to philosophy, culture, politics, and education, with only a few chapters on explicitly dogmatic topics (Scripture, creation and redemption, and theology). The point here is not to demean these efforts (and we have benefited very much from all of them) but merely to establish the focused dogmatic lacuna.

Second, there is a major diversity on what passes as neo-Calvinism or neo-Calvinistic in the present day. To quote Kuyper quoting Plato, "Plato does not say in vain: 'To teach a thing rightly it is necessary first to define its name.'"[5] What does the name "neo-Calvinism" mean? While the answer is manifold, for our purposes, we want to define historic neo-Calvinism as a nineteenth- and early twentieth-century movement in the Netherlands.

---

3. John Bowlin, ed., *Kuyper Center Review*, vol. 2, *Revelation and Common Grace* (Grand Rapids: Eerdmans, 2011).

4. Peter Heslam, *Creating a Christian Worldview: Abraham Kuyper's Lectures on Calvinism* (Grand Rapids: Eerdmans, 1998); Jonathan Chaplin, *Herman Dooyeweerd: Christian Philosophy of State and Civil Society* (Notre Dame, IN: University of Notre Dame Press, 2011); Chaplin, *On Kuyper: A Collection of Readings on the Life, Work, and Legacy of Abraham Kuyper*, ed. Steve Bishop and John H. Kok (Sioux Center, IA: Dordt College Press, 2013); Craig Bartholomew and Michael Goheen, *Christian Philosophy: A Systematic and Narrative Introduction* (Grand Rapids: Baker Academic, 2013); George Harinck and James Eglinton, eds., *Neo-Calvinism and the French Revolution* (London: Bloomsbury T&T Clark, 2014); John Bolt, *Herman Bavinck on the Christian Life* (Wheaton, IL: Crossway, 2015); William Edgar, *Created and Creating: A Biblical Theology of Culture* (Downers Grove, IL: IVP Academic, 2017); James Eglinton, *Bavinck: A Critical Biography* (Grand Rapids: Baker Academic, 2020).

5. *Encyclopedia*, 229.

Neo-Calvinism was a revival of Reformed confessionalist theology in the Netherlands roughly beginning with the rise of Kuyper as a theologian, with the founding of the Vrije Universiteit in 1880, the formation of the Gereformeerde Kerken in 1892, and its systematization in the theological output of Herman Bavinck. Its most mature distinctive was not first in political theology, Reformational philosophy, or public-theological models for the relation between the church and social order, but in its careful, nuanced, and unique marriage between classical, Reformed confessionalist dogmatics and modern philosophy and theology that allowed it to speak Reformed dogmatics to a particular European, modern world. By modern, we mean that age beginning with the fall of the Bastille (1789), with the metaphysics and epistemology of Kant, and spanning all the way through the long nineteenth century into the Great War. The public-theological models birthed in the neo-Calvinist age in the Netherlands, while having political-theological derivatives important for today, were for the Netherlands in a particular time and place. Yet, what historic neo-Calvinism offers foremost today is both its material dogmatic reflections and a model for adapting and updating orthodox, confessional dogmatic reasoning for each generation and in each culture. Springing from its roots, there is indeed a neo-Calvinist tradition that blossomed in all manner of directions over the last century. Yet, in defining the essential dogmatic contributions, it is important to first speak of historic neo-Calvinist theology, and here we focus on the first-generation of neo-Calvinism.

At a popular level, the term "neo-Calvinism" has now become associated, even as a synonym, with transformationalism (a public theology defining the mission of the church as social as much as evangelical). This ought not to be so. In other instances, some associate the term with a more recent cohort of public Christians. Daniel Knauss provides a clear example: "From Herman Dooyeweerd to Francis Schaeffer and Nancy Pearcey, [neo-Calvinism] is confessionally partisan, [where] self-legitimizing history is told, apparently in total ignorance of and complete contradiction to established historical and theological scholarship of at least the past three decades."[6] For Knauss, neo-Calvinism is a movement dissociated

---

6. Daniel Knauss, "Neocalvinism … No: Why I Am Not a Neocalvinist," *Comment*, June 1, 2006, https://www.cardus.ca/comment/article/neocalvinism-no-why-i-am-not-a-neocalvinist/.

from the church, and one that began in the 1950s. It is the philosophy of Dooyeweerd and the worldviewism of Pearcey. Knauss goes on to suggest that neo-Calvinism ignores the best of scholarship and includes what he calls a "killing of the fathers."[7] This version and common level understanding of neo-Calvinism is impossible to find if one looks to its origins. Historic neo-Calvinism was a Dutch enterprise for the sake of the whole church under the theological minds of Kuyper and Bavinck that included at its core an immense ecclesiological movement, a return to the "fathers" and to a catholic, confessional faith in a modernist context.

In this vein, there are also tendencies in studies on Kuyper and Bavinck that are driven by the desire to append them to particular movements or ideological traditions relating to intramural theological debate. The use of Kuyper and Bavinck within the contemporary dichotomy between Thomism and Van Tilianism, for example, exemplifies this in a rather stark manner. The desire to distance or append Kuyper or Bavinck to these movements often produces a rather lopsided reading of the primary sources, such that particular passages are emphasized while others are ignored, reducing these first generation neo-Calvinists to either preludes or formidable critics of Thomism or Van Tilianism. In our judgment, this debate has gradually become counterproductive, and for these reasons we have set aside this debate entirely in this present volume in order to unveil the dogmatic distinctives of Kuyper and Bavinck in their own milieu. Further, neo-Calvinism need not be genetically overassociated with either of these traditions—their work is too capacious, eclectic, and distinctive to be appended to another "ism" other than on their own terms. While we do not deny that neo-Calvinism remains a fruitful dialogue partner for these and other traditions, whether past or present, this is not our interest to pursue in this book.

Third, there is an exciting amount of English translations on Kuyper and Bavinck today that span across many different publishers. This includes the initiatives of the Acton Institute, publishing Kuyper's works with Lexham Press; Baker Publishing Group's English editions of Bavinck's *Reformed Dogmatics* and *Essays on Religion, Science, and Society*; and, more

---

7. Knauss, "Neocalvinism ... No."

recently, Bavinck's previously unpublished *Reformed Ethics*, Hendrickson's
new editions of Bavinck's *Philosophy of Revelation* and the *Sacrifice of Praise*,
Westminster Seminary Press's new edition of Bavinck's *Magnalia Dei* (*The
Wonderful Works of God*), and Crossway's English translation of Bavinck's
Christian Worldview and other volumes on the way. With this renaissance
of translations, however, comes a degree of intimidation. How should
one begin to explore this staggering amount of newly translated material?
Again, this book aims to fill that need.

There is, of course, an exciting amount of new scholarship that attends
to the theological works of Bavinck and Kuyper, but these monographs
are highly specialized in nature, exploring a particular doctrine within
either Kuyper or Bavinck in a niche and highly detailed way. These include
studies on Kuyper's doctrine of the Spirit (Bacote), Scripture (van Keulen
and Henk van den Belt), and ecclesiology (Wood); and Bavinck's eschatology (Mattson), Trinitarian theology (Eglinton), Christology (Pass), and
our own work on Bavinck's epistemology and use of Romantic sources,
among others.[8] The downfall of the two-Bavinck thesis, particularly, frees
the student of neo-Calvinism to give more sustained attention to positive presentations of the whole project, rather than being encumbered
in deconstructing previous dichotomizing readings. We have also contributed to this trajectory of Bavinck scholarship. Sutanto's monograph,
God and Knowledge, sought to locate the classical and modern sources
of Bavinck's theological epistemology, and argues that the organicism
that structures Bavinck's epistemology showcases a principled eclecticism. Brock's monograph, *Orthodox yet Modern: Herman Bavinck's Use
of Schleiermacher*, proves Bavinck's eclectic theological method by establishing that Bavinck appropriated the modern-theological turn to the self,

---

8. Vincent Bacote, *The Spirit of Public Theology: Appropriating the Legacy of Abraham
Kuyper* (Grand Rapids: Baker Academic, 2005); Henk van den Belt, *The Authority of Scripture in
Reformed Theology: Truth and Trust* (Leiden: Brill, 2008); Dirk van Keulen, *Bijbel en Dogmatiek:
Schriftbeschouwing en schriftgebruik in het dogmatisch werk van A. Kuyper, H. Bavinck en G.C. Berkouwer*
(Kampen: Kok, 2003); Brian Mattson, *Restored to Our Destiny: Eschatology and the Image of God in
Herman Bavinck's Reformed Dogmatics* (Leiden: Brill, 2011); James Eglinton, *Trinity and Organism:
Toward a New Reading of Herman Bavinck's Organic Motif* (New York: Bloomsbury T&T Clark, 2011);
John Halsey Wood Jr., *Going Dutch in the Modern Age: Abraham Kuyper's Struggle for a Free Church
in the Netherlands* (Oxford: Oxford University Press, 2013); Bruce Pass, *The Heart of Dogmatics:
Christology and Christocentricism in Herman Bavinck* (Göttingen: Vandenhoeck & Ruprecht, 2020).

particularly in Schleiermacher. No longer is the researcher now forced to choose between a "modern" or "classical" Bavinck. With Bavinck's (and, by extension, neo-Calvinism's) eclecticism firmly in place, the reader can get a sense of the unity behind the occasional deployment of particular ideas from both classical and modern milieus. This book follows this research trajectory and presupposes the established consensus on the eclectic character of Bavinck's thought.

Hence, this particular introductory volume provides a panoramic overview of the distinctive dogmatic contributions of neo-Calvinism. In that regard, while we are broadly sympathetic with many of the claims of Kuyper and Bavinck, the purpose of this book is *descriptive* rather than prescriptive. That is, we aim to present what Kuyper and Bavinck themselves offered as the distinctive marks of their own theological work (even while we may agree or disagree with some of their theological judgments) precisely because a close reading of the primary texts demands them. The chapters of this present book represent that aim, as we cover differing theological loci. Moreover, while we do at times draw from second- or third-generation neo-Calvinists to press a particular point, Kuyper and Bavinck remain the focus of this book. We also try to include minimal forays into the secondary literature, seeking only to do so if it illumines a salient feature of some theological description. Our main goal here is exposition and summation of key dogmatic developments. The decision to focus on these loci rests on what Kuyper and Bavinck explicitly regarded as the main loci that needed further work and clarification—that there is no chapter focusing solely on the doctrine of God and Trinity (although these doctrines are present in every chapter), for example, indicates that, while there were interesting creative insights from Kuyper and Bavinck on the doctrine, they did not regard it as a doctrine to be rearticulated anew but rather were largely content with a retrieval of classical statements of the same.[9]

---

9. On the salient and creative aspects of the doctrine of God from the neo-Calvinist tradition specifically, see especially Gayle Doornbos, "Herman Bavinck's Trinitarian Theology: The Ontological, Cosmological, and Soteriological Dimensions of the Doctrine of the Trinity" (PhD thesis, University of Toronto, 2019), and Cameron D. Clausing, "'A Christian Dogmatic Does Not Yet Exist': The Influence of the Nineteenth Century Historical Turn on the Theological Methodology of Herman Bavinck" (PhD thesis, University of Edinburgh, 2020).

While the chapters focus on distinct theological loci, there are at least three binding themes that thread them together, and we take these to be distinctive neo-calvinistic modes of the thinking operation. The neo-Calvinists are methodologically and eclectically (1) orthodox yet modern, (2) self-consciously holistic, and (3) organic, not mechanical. Let us summarize these briefly in turn.

First, neo-Calvinism conveyed that the heritage of classical Reformed orthodoxy can engage fruitfully with the insights of modern theology and philosophy. Along with Kuyper, Bavinck often conceived his own neo-Calvinist position as that between conservatism and modernism. While conservatism decried the present in a nostalgic call for the past, Bavinck argued that the present age remains a remarkable opportunity to recommunicate the Christian faith in fresh ways. Instead of shying away from the modern debates and arguing that orthodox theology should bypass the academic discussions of the day, Bavinck and Kuyper often sought to incorporate as many contemporary insights as possible within the boundaries of orthodox Calvinism. Indeed, James Eglinton rightly notes that Bavinck often "fought modern with modern."[10] These inclinations led the neo-Calvinists to be critiqued by modernists and conservative thinkers alike. Modernists argued that Bavinck and Kuyper were merely redressing fundamentalism in modern idiom, while conservatives often accused them of capitulating to the allure of the modern age. Indeed, Bavinck's 1911 oration "Modernism and Orthodoxy," as we will see, addressed these charges directly all the while arguing that modernism and orthodoxy may exist fruitfully together. Hence, just as the Reformed orthodoxy of the early modern period was eclectic in its deployment of medieval philosophies for dogmatics, so were Kuyper and Bavinck self-consciously eclectic in their use of classical and modern insights for the sake of constructive theological work.

Second, neo-Calvinism argued for the holistic and leavening implications of the Christian faith. Aware of the totalizing nontheistic ideals of the 1789 French Revolution and later of Nietzsche's thoroughgoing nihilism, Bavinck, like Kuyper, saw that it was necessary to present Christianity

---

10. Eglinton, *Bavinck: A Critical Biography*, 138.

as a full-orbed alternative. It was no longer viable simply to assume that Christianity was relevant for public life in these modern conditions, which increasingly argued that faith belonged within the ecclesial and private spheres alone. This realization led Bavinck and Kuyper to call confessional theology to awaken to Christianity's ability to speak of reality (of self, world, and God) and to offer reasons for its necessity not merely in the church, but for every area of life. However, while Kuyper argued for this in a deductive and perhaps at times inflated way, Bavinck's method was more reserved and inductive. He argued that Christianity remained the inescapable conclusion if one patiently sifted through the data that contemporary arguments presented.

Finally, neo-Calvinism enfolded the organic language ubiquitous in Romantic philosophy into its own confessional Calvinism. The organism idea includes the claim that God created the world, that God created natures, and that the world is a unity-in-diversity of parts existing for a purpose, as God defines them. While organic imagery was often invoked to argue for the union between subject and object, between God and human affection, in a way that sometimes denigrated the necessity and authority of Scripture in theology, Kuyper and Bavinck utilized theological organicism in order to convey the richness of the orthodox Christian worldview. Neo-Calvinistic organicism includes the idea of inductively drawing together all the facts explained by the reality of the Triune God. If nontheistic worldviews are reductionist, neglecting one phenomenon by reducing it to the other (as seen in naturalism or pantheism), which is a mechanical move, Christianity preserved the Creator-creature distinction and argued that the world exists in a pluriform way. The mechanistic tendency is, for Kuyper and Bavinck, a one-sided reduction, a reference to a false or forced uniformity, or sometimes used to describe the human devolution of an organic reality, fighting against the world as God created it to be. It is to take that which is living and whole by divine command, and cut it into isolated parts and set those against the others. For example, to suppose one particular ethnic people group more aligned with the image of God than another (the sin of ethnic partiality) would be mechanical, dividing the human organism that God has created as one. The mechanical pushes against nature as God made it.

Yet, by the logic of the Christian faith, psychology and spirituality, the physical and the immaterial, can coexist as each diverse part is united under the single idea of creation, which all points back to the archetypal unity-and-diversity of the Triune God. The principle of organism refers, then, to a unity of parts that arises precisely from God the Creator, possessing both nature and purpose. In a simple sense, the organic is the natural. And while the organic is indeed a common Romantic concept within the modern world, Kuyper and Bavinck appeal to its presence in Scripture, in the imagery and metaphor of the garden, the tree of life, the body, and the vine, among others, which God chooses to use to describe creation, Eden, the church, and the eschatological kingdom. It is critical to remember too that the language and concept of organism appears widely in classical philosophy, especially in Plato, which is precisely the origin from which modern Romantic philosophy derives the idea. The ubiquitous presence of the idea in both name and metaphor across philosophies and theologies is evidence of a reality, that God created the world, the cosmos, to be one in many.

Neo-Calvinists of later generations took these holistic insights in a number of fascinating though at times mutually conflicting directions. This is seen in the works of diverse figures, including the likes of Bavinck's missiologist nephew, Johan Bavinck (1895–1964); philosopher Herman Dooyeweerd (1894–1977); and theologians Klaas Schilder (1890–1952) and G. C. Berkouwer (1903–1996). Indeed, the neo-Calvinist tradition remains lively and diverse, yet united in these ideals of a publicly engaged Reformed theology, inheriting a penchant against any form of separatism and dualism for the sake of holism, and the desire to communicate a capacious Christian faith for the contemporary world. As such, this book serves not merely as an introduction, but also as an invitation to this generative theological trajectory.

OVERVIEW OF CHAPTERS

This book has organized the chapters in accordance with the order of presentation common in Reformed dogmatics: from prolegomena, to creation, salvation, and ecclesiology. As such, reading the chapters in subsequent order would provide an organic and logical dogmatic ordering.

However, readers who seek to dip to a particular locus that interests them most can also do so fruitfully. Although other chapters are occasionally referenced, each chapter is a relatively self-contained study of the dogmatic locus under discussion.

The second chapter seeks to trace out the way in which the term "neo-Calvinism" began to be used in the Netherlands of the nineteenth century but more particularly by Kuyper and Bavinck. What did this term mean, exactly, and what did the "neo-" in neo-Calvinism refer to? Cognizant of the ways in which "Calvinism" has taken on a life of its own in twentieth- and twenty-first-century scholarship, we seek to distinguish Bavinck's and Kuyper's usage of "neo-Calvinism" from these contemporary definitions. Particularly, the chapter argues that Kuyper and Bavinck considered their projects to be inspired by the holistic impulses of John Calvin and used "Calvinism" specifically to refer to a full-orbed vision of the implications of Christ's lordship for every sphere of life. Hence, while there were shifting attitudes toward the helpfulness of the term to identify their own theological and public projects, Kuyper and Bavinck continued to maintain that Reformed theology resulted in a holistic responsibility.

The third chapter observes the way in which Kuyper and Bavinck charted a path between what they considered to be a dead conservatism, on the one hand, and a forgetful liberalism, on the other. True catholicity involves the recognition not only that orthodoxy is rooted in the past, but also that it labors for the future. In this regard, Kuyper made a distinction between the form and essence of Christianity—the forms of Christianity might look different from age to age, and from place to place, but the essence remains the same. Conservatism clings to a dead form while forgetting that the essence can live on through new cultural, linguistic, and philosophical dresses. It mistakes the forms for the essence. Thus, the Christian theologian must be conservative without conservatism. Liberalism, on the other hand, substitutes the essence of Christianity and supplants it with an entirely new root—it forgets that Christianity is based on a historical revelation and has been developing through the catholic church across time. Bavinck argues that the catholicity of the church, therefore, means recognizing the culturally and philosophically pliable character of Christianity. Precisely because the Christian faith is truly universal, it can utilize and reshape any culture, philosophy, and place, and is not tied down to any one culture, philosophy, or place.

The fourth chapter explores the relationship between revelation and reason, particularly focusing on Kuyper's and Bavinck's understanding of general revelation. While Kuyper and Bavinck follow the classical Reformed articulation of revelation, they preferred the terms "general and special revelation" over the terms "natural and supernatural theology" in order to highlight humanity's dependence on God for every point of theological knowledge, though they recognize the relative usefulness of the latter terms. This chapter also notes that Kuyper and Bavinck nuance this doctrine in a decisively romantic direction, arguing that revelation is perceived by human beings in a pre-theoretical fashion, resulting in unconscious affections, a feeling of absolute dependence. Due to the systematic and philosophically nuanced ways in which Bavinck in particular articulated these ideas in his writings, this chapter (along with the chapter on common grace) involves more technical exposition of the relevant writings.

The fifth chapter studies the doctrine of Scripture in a twofold way: the authority and usefulness of Scripture in relation to the other sciences, on the one hand, and the organic inspiration of Scripture, on the other. While Bavinck and Kuyper argue that Scripture is a book for humanity and is authoritative over and for the other sciences, they articulate this in a nuanced fashion. They resist a biblicist impulse that argues that the Bible is the sole source of knowledge for all of the other disciplines. They argue that the Bible has a soteriological and religious aim and is not a manual for the other sciences. Nonetheless, due to the organic character of all reality and subsequently of all knowledge, the Bible remains relevant and authoritative for the other disciplines. Further, both Kuyper and Bavinck argue that an organic account of the inspiration of Scripture is needed to do justice to the interface between divine and human agency in the authorship of Scripture. The key distinctions between center and periphery, between differing modes of inspiration, Scripture's attributes, and the analogy of Christ's dual nature with Scripture's divine and human origins are noted in this chapter.

The sixth chapter deals with the organic unity between creation and re-creation. The relationship between creation and salvation is one of the most prominent and tenacious matters appearing in the whole of the neo-Calvinist theological tradition. This is often referred to as the nature-grace relation. In brief, neo-Calvinism accents an essential theological commitment: that the *goal* of salvation is not an entirely new idea, even post fall, because the goal of re-creation is the end of creation, yet by different means. Re-creation's end is creation's original end: that God would make his dwelling place with humankind, the Immanuel principle. The organic unity in the nature-grace relation, or that grace restores nature, is perhaps the key insight and emphasis of neo-Calvinist dogmatics that gives shape to all else.

The seventh chapter observes the holistic character of Bavinck's and Kuyper's theological anthropology. In particular, Bavinck argues for what we have termed an "organic whole federalism" view of corporate humanity. The image of God, he argues, refers not merely to individuals as psychosomatic unities, but also singularly to the corporate human race taken as a whole. Rooted in the classical conviction that the perfections of God can only be reflected in finite creation in a manifold way, no single human individual can manifest the fullness of the image of God, and hence the diversity of individuals is involved together in imaging God. The unity of this organism of humanity is founded in the federal headship of Adam or in Christ. Kuyper likewise emphasizes the unity of humanity in both Adam and Christ. Kuyper also builds a narrative anthropology, or one shaped by the nature-grace relation, arguing that humanity's royal calling in Adam is fulfilled and recommissioned in its union with Christ.

The eighth chapter defines the doctrine of common grace in relation to the gospel and ends by noting the key differences between common grace and the natural-law tradition. Kuyper believed that common grace required a separate treatment as a locus in dogmatics and that it had been neglected since Calvin. For Kuyper and Bavinck, God's common grace is God's general favor that sustains the creation order despite sin. Common grace is distinct from special grace. God's special grace restores, renews, and recreates creation order as the kingdom of God. The former serves and anticipates the latter. In brief, God's common grace is the fact of his loving patience in preserving both humanity and the creaturely cosmos despite human rebellion and its polluting corruption for the sake of redemption, while also offering the possibility of human development, of progress in the richness of human life and civilization. Common grace marks an era between the curse of the world and the second advent of Christ, wherein God gifts moral, epistemic, and natural goods to the world, maintaining in high degree an organic creaturely unity despite the curse.

The ninth chapter, finally, identifies Bavinck's and Kuyper's understanding of the church as both institute and organism, and discusses the relation between these terms with the invisible and visible church. Kuyper and Bavinck were both churchmen and ecclesial theologians. Neo-Calvinism is an ecclesial movement, forming a new denomination and providing a robust theology of institute and organism that has guided Reformed ecclesiology for a century. The chapter finally moves to a discussion of the relationship between the church and the world, and sketches a neo-Calvinistic political theology in brief.

By sketching the dogmatic roots and contours of neo-Calvinism, we hope to reground the neo-Calvinist tradition in its own catholic roots and also to invite nonspecialists from other backgrounds to draw on this tradition for their own work. We have pulled from many sources in both the corpuses of Kuyper and Bavinck, and yet there are many more not explored in this work. We also hope that readers will be provoked to read these theologians for themselves.

II

Calvinism and
Neo-Calvinism

*To repristination I am as averse as any man; but in order to place
for the defense of Christianity, principle over against principle, the
worldview over against worldview, there lies at hand, for him who
is a Protestant in bone and marrow, only the Calvinistic principle
as the sole trustworthy foundation on which to build. ... What, then,
are we to understand by this return to Calvinism? Do I mean that
all believing Protestants should subscribe the sooner the better to the
Reformed symbols, and thus all ecclesial multiformity be swallowed
up in the unity of the Reformed church organization? I am far from
cherishing so crude, so ignorant, so unhistorical a desire.*

—Abraham Kuyper, Lectures on Calvinism

*One forgets thereby that the doctrine of God in Christian theology
is not built on singular disparate statements but on the whole of
revelation in Scripture, and that Calvinism as it was revived in the
previous century deserved to be judged not after a single work but in
its entirety and compared with the doctrine of the Reformer of Geneva.
Positioning oneself at this impartial standpoint, one shall soon make
the surprising discovery that the alleged contrariety does not exist
between the Scriptures and contemporary theology, and neither does
it exist between the old and the new Calvinism, but it appears in*

15

Scripture itself and is encountered in every theologian. I do not thereby
deny that it has at the present time adopted a more acute form for the
reasons mentioned above.

—*Herman Bavinck, "Modernism and Orthodoxy"*

RECENT SCHOLARSHIP ON Calvin and Calvinism emphasizes that Calvin was simply one major figure of the Reformation among many, that he neither intended to be the defining standard for Reformed orthodoxy, nor was he ever treated as such until the late nineteenth century.[1] Rather, the Reformation is more appropriately characterized as a plural historical theological movement that encompassed multiple countries, taking on various trajectories, and represented a broad confessional unity that bound together a diversity of theologians. The term "Calvinist," used in a positive sense to identify someone's commitment to, say, predestinarianism or unconditional election, or the so-called five points, is thus a contemporary heuristic. Indeed, the earliest usage of the term itself was actually as a pejorative against Protestants.[2]

Bavinck himself argued that the term "Reformed" is to be preferred "far above orthodox but also that of Calvinistic and of Neo-Calvinistic," precisely because "Reformed" signals a clear dependence upon the orthodoxy of the past.[3] Yet, Kuyper and Bavinck did draw much inspiration specifically from Calvin and his theological work and efforts at reforming the city of Geneva. While they insisted on their dependence on Reformed orthodoxy, Bavinck and Kuyper were self-conscious that their retrieval of Calvin signaled something new, as they were motivated by the distinct questions of the modern age. Their influence is no doubt, at least in part, a reason why the term gained positive ascendancy in contemporary Reformed thought. They produced a retrieval of "Calvinism," as seen in

---

1. A section of this chapter is adapted from N. Gray Sutanto, "Bavinck's Christian Worldview: Classical Contours, Context, and Significance," *Reformed Faith and Practice* 5.2 (2020): 28–39.

2. Bruce Gordon, *Calvin* (New Haven: Yale University Press, 2009), 185. See also Ryan McGraw, *Reformed Scholasticism: Recovering the Tools of Reformed Theology* (London: Bloomsbury T&T Clark, 2019), 118.

3. Herman Bavinck, "Modernism and Orthodoxy," in *On Theology: Herman Bavinck's Theological Orations*, trans. Bruce Pass (Leiden: Brill, 2021), 82.

works such as Kuyper's *Lectures on Calvinism* and Bavinck's article "The Future of Calvinism," or "Calvin and Common Grace," presenting Calvin's thought in a more acute form in their contemporary day, as the opening citations indicate.

Observing particular passages in Bavinck's *Certainty of Faith*, for example, Gijsbert van den Brink contrasts Bavinck with B. B. Warfield, an Old Princeton theologian, precisely because "Bavinck was critical of what he saw as subtle theological changes occurring in the transition from Calvin and other Reformers toward post-Reformation Reformed orthodox theology," where "evidences became more and more important as rational underpinnings of the Christian scheme." While Warfield appealed to the Reformed orthodox scholastics more favorably, Bavinck prefers to invoke "the Reformation:" "no doubt having in mind the theology of Reformers like Luther and Calvin." In doing so, van den Brink argues that Bavinck does not stand in the current model of interpretation that sees a fundamental continuity between Calvin and the Reformed orthodox, which is "forcefully advanced and elaborated today by Richard Muller and his school."[4] Craig Bartholomew, likewise, observes that "Bavinck, for example, consciously distances himself from the scholasticism of seventeenth- and eighteenth-century theology."[5]

While van den Brink may be overstating Bavinck's distancing of himself against the Reformed orthodox—Bavinck indeed sought to stand upon their work[6]—Bavinck did see some salient discontinuities between the Reformation and the Protestant scholastics (as van den Brink observes) in passages such as this: "The faith of the sixteenth century became the orthodoxy of the seventeenth. People no longer confessed their beliefs, but they only believed their confessions. Among most of the people

---

4. Gijsbert van den Brink, "On Certainty in Faith and Science: The Bavinck-Warfield Exchange," *BR* 8 (2017): 82–83. Van den Brink cites Bavinck's *The Certainty of Faith*, trans. Harrie der Nederlanden (Ontario: Paideia, 1980), 85.

5. Bartholomew, *Contours of the Kuyperian Tradition*, 285. Bartholomew is discussing Bavinck's (and Kuyper's) view of the use of Scripture in theology, and cites particularly Bavinck's *RD* 1:180–83.

6. As seen in his editing of the *Leiden Synopsis* and other passages within his *RD*. See, for example, Bavinck, *RD* 1:83–84. Bartholomew also nuances his remark on Bavinck in *Contours of the Kuyperian Tradition*, 286–87.

this orthodoxy prepared the road for rationalism."[7] A distinctive of the Reformation, Bavinck argued, was its concern for the reformation of every area of life, whether family, science, or art, and hence reason itself had to be located in an economy of grace. Kuyper, too, argues that Calvin uniquely propounded a doctrine of *common grace* that was declining in the centuries after him:

> People may exaggerate when they say of the Anabaptists that they like to sit "with my book in a quiet nook," but there is still some truth to it. Calvinists always had another viewpoint, and praise may be not be withheld from them for how they excelled in general human development by their confession of common grace. Even so, it can hardly be denied that, after their decline in the late seventeenth and eighteenth centuries, they too showed a remarkably increasing tendency to separate themselves in groups, withdrawing from general human life.[8]

These comments indicate that while Bavinck and Kuyper saw a fundamental continuity between Calvin and the Reformed orthodox, the two were not simply identified in their minds. This prompts several questions. What, exactly, did they desire in their retrieval of Calvin? Specifically, what theological role or function did the term signify for them? What did the "neo" in "neo-Calvinism" mean, theologically?

The oldest found use of the word "neo-Calvinist" was in 1887 as a pejorative, discovered by George Harinck, in a review of W. Geesink's work *Calvinisten in Nederland* (Geesink was an ethicist at the Vrije Universiteit of Amsterdam).[9] The usages of the term "neo-Calvinism" (*Neo-Calvinisme*), between 1897 and 1910 in the Netherlands were markedly polarizing, as the term was used either by critics or admirers of Kuyper's and Bavinck's ideals. While Kuyperian thinkers such as Anne Anema extolled the term, associating it with "perfect peace" (*volmaakten vrede*), others argued that

---

7. Bavinck, *Certainty of Faith*, 41; see also RD 2:78.

8. *Pro Rege* 1:169–70.

9. George Harinck, "Herman Bavinck and the Neo-Calvinist Concept of the French Revolution," in *Neo-Calvinism and French Revolution*, ed. James Eglinton and George Harinck (London: Bloomsbury, 2016), 21n43. See also Eglinton, *Bavinck: A Critical Biography*, 157–58.

it signified nothing more than a "revival of Clericalism in a new form" (*eene herleving van het Clericalisme in een nieuwen vorm*).[10] Indeed, this latter work, titled *The Fall of Dr. A. Kuyper*, associated neo-Calvinism with a political project that smuggled in the clerical principles of Calvin. It was considered nothing more than Kuyper's desire to "*rule the state on Calvin's Dogma*."[11] Another study on Calvin's influence in the Netherlands indicated a consciousness that Kuyper's neo-Calvinism was different from past emphases: neo-Calvinism was "something other than Dordt" (*iets anders dan het Dordstsche*).[12] Newspaper articles also tethered neo-Calvinism to Kuyper's political project rather than a mere theological outlook per se and were similarly scathing in their criticisms. A 1901 article from the liberal anti-Kuyperian newspaper *Algemeene Handelsblad* argued that Kuyper's antirevolutionary project was becoming increasingly narrow-minded precisely because it was commending "Calvinism" as the only power against revolutionary principles for Dutch society.[13] It further argued that one must make a distinction between Groen van Prinsterer's evangelical antirevolutionary party and Kuyper's Calvinistic one.[14]

Bavinck's *Dogmatics*, of course, stood out as the representative theological work of neo-Calvinism. While one particular newspaper article identifies Bavinck's *Reformed Dogmatics* as proof that "neo-Calvinism" was becoming more influential among younger theologians, the journalist is rather scathing about what he considered to be the authoritarian character of Bavinck's dogmatic starting point, denouncing Bavinck as a "modern scholastic!"[15] The article goes on to argue that "the starting point and determination of the object of Bavinck's dogmatics are both

---

10. Anne Anema, *Calvinisme en rechtwetenschap: een studie* (Amsterdam: Kirchner, 1897), xvi; M. Beversluis, *De val van Dr. A. Kuyper: een zegen voor ons land en volk* (Oud-Beierland: W. Hoogwerf Az., 1905), 10.

11. Beversluis, *De val van Dr. A. Kuyper*, 10, emphasis original. Dutch original: "Dr. Kuyper wilde den staat regeeren naar Calvins dogma's."

12. A. J. Hoogenbirk, *Heeft Calvijn ooit bestaan?: kritisch onderzoek der Calvijn-legende* (Nijkerk: Callenbach, 1907), 36.

13. "De toekomstige regeering," *Algemeen Handelsblad*, August 1, 1901.

14. Kuyper himself was aware of this difference between his party and Groen van Prinsterer's Reveil party. See Wood, *Going Dutch in the Modern Age*, 13.

15. "Vergadering van Predikanten en Gemeenteleden der Evangelische richting," *Provinciale Overijsselsche en Zwolsche Courant*, June 1, 1899. Dutch original: "Moderne Scholastiek!"

condemnable."[16] The author is referring to the fact that Bavinck locates
the authority of dogmatic logic in the authority of Scripture by identifying it with the word of God, arguing that the Christian ought to follow
it simply because God has spoken: *"Deus Dixit."* The article goes on to
contrast Bavinck's scriptural starting point with a christological one. The
message is clear: either one begins with the Bible or begins with Christ.
Neo-Calvinism's detractors, then, rejected Bavinck's project because they
believed that it was simply reviving a kind of biblicism, along with antiquated orthodox beliefs, while pretending to be modern by using new
idioms. This was the case in both the political and theological realms of
reception.

   While these books and newspaper articles use the term as a pejorative against Kuyper and Bavinck, charging them with a kind of prudish
clericalism that desired to subdue the state under outdated theological
principles, Kuyper and Bavinck themselves did not see this as a weakness, but rather as a strength of Calvinism. For them, these principles
confessed not outdated notions but enduring truths. Kuyper and Bavinck
used the term "Calvinism" to refer to the Protestant principles that serve
as the bulwark for political and civil liberties, and the majority of media
attention during their era unsurprisingly focused on this political dimension.[17] However, this chapter explores their *theological* use of the term, not
by seeking to provide a singular concise definition but rather by way of
canvassing a description.

   In the remainder of this chapter, we argue that Kuyper and Bavinck
identify Calvinism with the development of a Christian world- and life-
view, a theology of God's sovereignty, and the doctrine of common grace
(concomitant with a radical doctrine of sin) as that which undergirds
natural life. These, in turn, motivate the Kuyperian emphases on the
leavening powers of Christianity. The term "neo-Calvinism," then, refers
to their development of Calvin's theology into a holistic worldview that

   16. "Vergadering van Predikanten." Dutch original: "Het uitgangspunt van B.'s dogmatiek en de
bepaling van het voorwerp daarvan, zijne beide verwerpelijke."
   17. B. B. Warfield's introduction to the English translation of Kuyper's *Encyclopedia* also comments
that the publications on Kuyper's life then would "naturally" be devoted largely to "Dr. Kuyper's
political program as leader of the Anti-revolutionary party." "Introductory Note," in *Encyclopedia*, xiii.

had a particularly God-centered orientation toward all things within the context of the modern consciousness. A number of theological claims are at the forefront of neo-Calvinism: the absolute sovereignty of God, the unity of humanity as God's image bearers, the radicality of sin, the restraining power and provision of common grace, the church's mission to engage in every sphere of life, and the kingdom of God as a kingdom of renewal.[18] What the detractors saw as an antiquated dogmatism, Kuyper and Bavinck regarded as a firm framework from which one could restore a more united vision of life.

KUYPER: CALVINISM AS A THEOLOGICAL WORLD- AND LIFE-SYSTEM

Perhaps the most obvious place to observe the theological meaning of Calvinism according to Kuyper and Bavinck is in the former's 1898 *Lectures on Calvinism*. The first lecture in particular, "Calvinism as a Life System," offers arguably the clearest presentation of Kuyper's Calvinistic theology.[19]

Kuyper begins the lecture by distinguishing between four different senses of Calvinism.[20] The first use is pejorative, associating Calvinism with a sectarian spirit that separates itself from the broader culture. The second use is confessional, defining Calvinism as a theological commitment to God's absolute sovereignty and predestinarianism. Though Kuyper is fundamentally in agreement with this use, he notes that the confessional sense of Calvinism is often associated too with a kind of "dogmatic narrowness," and that theologians such as Charles Hodge prefer

---

18. Hence Bratt's comment about the intersection between Kuyper's theology and cultural analysis remains apt: "He made cultural engagement a strategic priority for his followers in the context of their times. And he deployed that effort along the lines of his two key theological innovations: the doctrine of common grace and the epistemology of worldview." James Bratt, *Abraham Kuyper: Modern Calvinist, Christian Democrat* (Grand Rapids, Eerdmans, 2013), 194. See also 192–93, 198, 261–63.

19. "Kuyper developed his view of neo-Calvinism as a life-system relatively late in his career, in the 1890s, culminating in the full presentation of his view in the Stone Lectures. The word neo-Calvinism was coined after Kuyper's publication of the first volume of his *Encyclopaedie* in 1894" (Harinck, "Herman Bavinck and the Neo-Calvinist Concept," 21). To clarify, while the oldest use of the term "neo-Calvinist" was used by a critical review of Geesink in 1887, as noted above, the appropriation of the term by circles congenial to Kuyper's own ideas was in 1896.

20. *Lectures*, 4–6.

to speak of "Augustinianism" rather than Calvinism in order to avoid the strong stigma attached to it. The third use refers to the denominational title, as utilized by some Baptists and Methodists, referring to themselves as "Calvinistic Baptists" or "Calvinistic Methodists." Here, Kuyper registers concerns that reveals his catholic sentiments: "Without doubt this practice would have been most severely criticized by Calvin himself. During his lifetime, no Reformed church ever dreamed of naming the church of Christ after any man."[21]

The fourth use is one that Kuyper espouses and elaborates on the most. It refers to Calvinism in a *scientific* sense, with historical, philosophical, and political connotations. Philosophically, it refers to those ideas that have lodged themselves into the imagination of various life spheres that arise from Calvin's writings, including science, art, education, and politics. Politically it refers to the recognition of the "liberty of the nations," which stems from a deep grasp of the equality of all humanity before a sovereign God.[22] In espousing this holistic understanding, Kuyper insists that the "domain of Calvinism is indeed far broader than the narrow confessional interpretation would us to suppose."[23] Its basic principles are so far-reaching and wide that any branch of Christianity that roots itself in the Protestant Reformation is inevitably leavened with Calvinism.

Calvinism conceptually presents a world- and life-order that competes not with particular philosophies or theologies but with the other "great complexes of human life, known as paganism, Islamism, and Romanism."[24] Beginning with a religious consciousness and revealed theology, it proceeds to construct an entire cosmological vision:

> Calvinism is rooted in a form of religion which was peculiarly its own, and from this specific religious consciousness there was developed first a peculiar theology, then a special church-order, and then a given form for political and social life, for the interpretation of

---

21. *Lectures*, 5.

22. *Lectures*, 6. See also Abraham Kuyper, "Calvinism: Source and Stronghold of Our Constitutional Liberties," in *Abraham Kuyper: A Centennial Reader*, ed. James Bratt (Grand Rapids: Eerdmans, 1998), 277–322.

23. *Lectures*, 7.

24. *Lectures*, 8.

the moral world order, for the relation between nature and grace, between Christianity and the world, between church and state, and finally for art and science; and amid all these life utterances it remained always the self-same Calvinism, insofar as simultaneously and spontaneously all these developments sprang from its deepest life principle.

In short, "Calvinism made its appearance, not merely to create a different church form, but an entirely different form for human life, to furnish human society with a different method of existence, and to populate the world of the human heart with different ideals and conceptions."[25]

Kuyper went on to elaborate on those distinctly Calvinistic theological principles in three ways: the relationship between humans and God, humans among one another, and humans to the world.

The first of these three relationships is the most important. It is the "mother-idea." In relation to God, Calvinism "does not seek God in the creature, as paganism; it does not isolate God from the creature, as Islamism; it posits no mediate communication between God and the creatures, as does Romanism; but proclaims the exalted thought that, although standing in high majesty above the creature, God enters into immediate fellowship with the creature, as God the Holy Spirit." This, along with the Reformed emphasis on the absolute sovereignty of God, places humanity in general and the church in particular before the presence of God at every point: "The persuasion that the whole of a man's life is to be lived as in the divine Presence has become the fundamental thought of Calvinism. By this decisive idea, or rather by this mighty fact, it has allowed itself to be controlled in every department of its entire domain. It is from this mother-thought that the all-embracing life-system of Calvinism sprang."[26]

From this first relationship, the other two follow. All of humanity enjoys equality and liberty precisely because God is the sovereign one above them and they are all his image bearers. Despite Kuyper's unfortunate comments on race elsewhere, here he argues that Calvinism opposes a hierarchy of human worth, and consequently slavery, because it confesses

---

25. *Lectures*, 8–9.
26. *Lectures*, 12, 16.

that God is the authority who defines the unity of humanity. Also, all of humanity is called to engage the whole world for God's glory, and Kuyper juxtaposes this idea with the dualisms he finds within Islam, which "makes sport" of the world, and with Rome, which places an antithesis between the holiness of the church and the cursedness of the world. The doctrine of common grace becomes important for Kuyper here: Calvinism "has at once placed to the front the great principle that there is a particular grace which works salvation, and also a common grace by which God, maintaining the life of the world, relaxes the curse which rests upon it, arrests its process of corruption, and thus allows the untrammeled development of our life in which to glorify himself as Creator."[27] James Bratt articulates the relationship between common grace and worldview in this way:

> A worldview embraces the whole world, the same claim Kuyper was now making for Calvinism among his followers. Worldview thus established a mandate for critical Christian comprehensiveness. Believers had to extend the logic of faith to sites they had heretofore ignored, had to test anew every theory and practice to see if it was of God, had to reconceptualize every place they had taken for granted or had visited on other terms. If common grace could baptize whole cultures as "Christian," worldview analysis delved beneath the surface of every project to ferret out its animating faith.[28]

Though a sustained focus on neo-Calvinism's theology of common grace is the subject matter of another chapter, it is hard to overemphasize its significance here, especially as both Kuyper and Bavinck trace their understanding of the doctrine back to Calvin.[29] The doctrine of common grace is a distinctly Calvinistic doctrine because it addresses a specific problem particular to Reformed theology: How can our confession of the

---

27. Lectures, 18–20.

28. Bratt, Abraham Kuyper: Modern Calvinist, 208. To clarify Bratt's point, it is not that common grace baptizes whole cultures as Christian per se, but that common grace renders whole cultures dependent on the gracious operations of the Christian God.

29. Hence Bratt: "This was the doctrine of common grace, the 'seed' of which he located in some words of Calvin but whose 'manifestation' he elaborated much further than any predecessor had ever tried" (Abraham Kuyper: Modern Calvinist, 192–93).

radical depravity of post fall humanity comport with our experience of the apparent goodness of so many people outside Christianity and the joy and benefits of the world itself? How can regenerate and spirit-indwelled Christians continue to labor in and for the world, and often ally with the world, for the common good? Common grace presupposes the Reformed doctrine of total depravity and loses its significance when detached from it. Kuyper's emphasis on this elsewhere is lucid:

> If we see in sin a cause of spiritual and physical weakening, but not a deadly quick-acting poison that if unrestrained immediately leads to spiritual, temporal, and eternal death, then there is certainly no restraining of sin—a conclusion to which Calvin was the first to point, and on which the entire doctrine of common grace is built. This is why the Reformed confession has continuously placed full emphasis on the deadly character of sin and has seriously combated any weakening of the concept of sin.[30]

Indeed, the doctrine of common grace allows Kuyper to (1) sketch a world- and life-view that pushes the church outward to participate within every sphere of life (2) without compromising the radical confession that humanity and the world is totally depraved and cursed, at enmity with God, and is a servant of unrighteousness. In order to articulate the exact relationship between the two claims of this paradox, Kuyper insists on retrieving Calvin's theology in particular. Here he is worth citing in full:

> In his *Institutes,* Calvin formulated the profound understanding of this *common grace* most clearly when he answered the question of how we can explain the fact that uprightness and nobility excelled among the pagans and unbelievers so often to such a high degree. Most people who expressed their views always made it appear as though this fact provided proof against the deep and pervasive depravity to which our human nature had sunk through sin. "You slander our human nature," so they argued, "if you confess that through sin we are inclined to all evil and incapable of any good. Those many excellent pagans, who do not know Christ and who

---

30. *CG* 1:299–300.

nevertheless often put us to shame, prove the opposite. And unbelievers as well who live among us often surpass many a child of
God in quiet, sober devotion to duty."
    Calvin protested against this view. Their claim would indeed
be valid if these people were like that in and of themselves. But
precisely this must be refuted, and the explanation sought rather in
the claim that "amid this corruption of nature there is some place
for God's grace; not such grace as to cleanse it, but to restrain it
inwardly." [Kuyper is citing *Institutes* 2.3.3.] ... Here lies the root
of the doctrine of common grace, together with the explanation
of why it forms such an indispensable part of the Reformed confession. It arose not from philosophical invention, but from the
confession of the deadly character of sin.[31]

One should note that these distinct retrievals of Calvin should not
eclipse Kuyper's catholic sensibilities. He was well aware that Calvin is
but one figure among the Reformation, having written on the ecclesiolo-
gies of Calvin and Polish Reformer John á Lasco even in his early days as
a graduate student at Leiden University. An appeal to Calvinism should
not discard other voices within the Christian tradition.[32] "Luther can be
interpreted without Calvin, but not Calvin without Luther." Surely, for
Kuyper, Calvin had a "cosmological" vision that Martin Luther lacked,
but Calvin was dependent on the hero of Wittenberg. Furthermore, in a
logical sense, Kuyper argued that Calvinism was already resident within
Augustine, and "long before Augustine, [Calvinism was] proclaimed to
the city of the seven hills by the apostle in his Epistle to the Romans;
and from Paul goes back to Israel and its prophets, yea to the tents of
the patriarchs."[33] Hence, though Kuyper does single out Calvin among
the Reformers and the Reformation, the theology of Calvinism should
be set within a fundamental reciprocal relationship and dependence on

---

31. CG 1:7–8.

32. For more on this, see Jasper Vree, "Historical Introduction," in *Abraham Kuyper's Commentatio
(1860): The Young Kuyper about Calvin, a Lasco, and the Church* (Leiden: Brill, 2005), 7–66.

33. *Lectures*, 13, 23.

the confessional traditions of the Reformation and the broadly catholic Christian tradition that traces itself back to biblical revelation.

BAVINCK ON CALVINISM AND
A CHRISTIAN WORLDVIEW

Bavinck's retrieval of Calvin echoes Kuyper in several significant respects. He discusses the importance of Calvin, Calvinism, and worldview in three specific texts that we will now briefly survey in chronological order: "The Catholicity of Christianity and the Church" (1888), "The Future of Calvinism" (1894), and finally *Christian Worldview* (1904). As we will see, before his 1904 lectures on worldview, Bavinck argued more specifically that Calvinism in particular, over against other Christian theologies on offer, provides a holistic world- and-life-view that encompasses every sphere of life. However, upon the emergence of the more thoroughgoing forms of unbelief in the wake of Friedrich Nietzsche, Bavinck emphasized that it was the Christian, *organic* worldview that could best answer the perennial questions of the world and provide unity between the self, world, and God. There was thus a shift in emphasis in Bavinck's writings on worldview, from a *Calvinistic* worldview as an alternative to other forms of Christian or religious worldviews (as in, say, Lutheranism or Roman Catholicism), to a *Christian* worldview over against unbelief.[34]

Bavinck echoes the same emphases in Kuyper even relatively early in his writing career, utilizing Calvin to denote a cosmological theology all the way back in 1888 on his article on catholicity. There he juxtaposes Luther's exclusively ecclesial reformation with Calvin's pervasive and truly catholic (universal) understanding of the Reformation. Indeed, Bavinck charges Luther and Zwingli with committing themselves to a dualism that fails to extricate theology fully from the nature-grace dualism of Roman Catholicism. Luther frees the earthly realm from the spiritual but "speaks as though the external is a matter of complete indifference and not capable

---

34. See Harinck, "Herman Bavinck and the Neo-Calvinist Concept," 25–28. This is not to suggest that Bavinck considered Calvinism to be insignificant after 1904. See, for example, his *Johannes Calvijn: Eene lezing ter gelegenheid van den vierhonderdsten gedenkdag zijner geboorte, 10 July 1509–1909* (Kampen: Kok, 1909), and "Calvin and Common Grace," in *Calvin and the Reformation: Four Studies*, trans. Geerhardus Vos, ed. William Park Armstrong (London: Revell, 1909), 99–130.

of ethical renewal." Luther continues to argue, Bavinck supposes, that re-creation only extends to the inward person and not to creation itself. While Huldrych Zwingli tried to overcome this dualism too, he did not do so in the way Calvin did. Bavinck argues that Calvin overcame "this dualism completely."[35] He goes on to praise Calvin in no uncertain terms:

> Nonetheless, it is Calvin whose labors completed the Reformation and saved Protestantism. He traces the operation of sin to a greater extent than did Luther, and to a greater depth than did Zwingli. It is for that reason that the grace of God is more restricted by Luther and less rich in Zwingli than it is in Calvin. In the powerful mind of the French Reformer, recreation is not a system that supplements Creation, as in Catholicism, not a religious reformation that leaves Creation intact, as in Luther, much less a radically new creation as in Anabaptism, but a joyful tiding of the renewal of all creatures. Here the Gospel comes fully into its own, comes to true catholicity. There is nothing that cannot or ought not to be evangelized. Not only the church but also home, school, society, and state are placed under the dominion of the principle of Christianity. Calvin established this dominionism in Geneva with an iron will and implacable rigor. ... All of this results from the fact that the Bible is, for Luther, only a source of salvation truth, whereas for Calvin it is the norm for all of life.[36]

A few themes that will be further fleshed out throughout this book have already emerged in this salient passage. A pervasive sketch of God's grace of re-creation is God's response to the radicality of sin. The scope of God's redemptive grace itself is unsatisfied with the renewal of individuals or the spiritual life of humanity, but has to do with the whole cosmos. The universality and catholicity of Calvin is set against the dualisms of Lutheranism, Rome, and Zwingli (and later Anabaptism).

If the 1888 article singles out Calvin for his strongly cosmological and catholic insights, his 1894 lecture, "The Future of Calvinism," shows

---

35. CCC, 237.
36. CCC, 237–38.

how Bavinck moves from using Calvin frequently to the deployment of "Calvinism" as a holistic vision. Though he argues that the two terms are theologically intertwined, in 1894 he begins to draw a clear distinction between the terms "Reformed" and "Calvinist." Perhaps in a counterintuitive way to the contemporary reader, Bavinck argues that the latter is cosmological in scope while the former is "purely theological."

> Calvinism is a specific type among the Protestant Churches and confessions. Frequently this type is designated by the name of Reformed. The words Reformed and Calvinistic, however, though cognate in meaning, are by no means equivalent, the former being more limited and less comprehensive than the latter. Reformed expresses merely a religious and ecclesiastical distinction; it is a purely theological conception. The term Calvinism is of wider application and denotes a specific type in the political, social and civil spheres. It stands for that characteristic view of life and the world as a whole, which was born from the powerful mind of the French Reformer. Calvinist is the name of a Reformed Christian in so far as he reveals a specific character and a distinct physiognomy, not merely in his church and theology, but also in social and political life, in science and art.[37]

Notice first that Bavinck identifies the term "Reformed" with a religious and theological concept, much more akin to Kuyper's second use of "Calvinism" as a confessional term. Second, while marking that Calvinism and Reformed theology are connected, Calvinism goes beyond theological confession with its cosmological dimensions, rooted specifically in the holistic vision of Calvin. Moving beyond Calvin as an individual, Calvinism now denotes an extension of Reformed theology to all aspects of human life.

If the 1888 article emphasizes specifically a unified vision of nature and grace, the 1894 article also fleshes out the theological doctrines that undergird Calvinism's holism. The "root principle" of Calvinism is none

---

37. Herman Bavinck, "The Future of Calvinism," trans. Geerhardus Vos, *The Presbyterian and Reformed Review* 17 (1894): 3.

other than the absolute sovereignty of God, from which all of the other distinctive theological emphases of the Reformed tradition are "derived and explained." This includes the typical Reformed emphases on the authority of the Scriptures, the unconditional nature of election, and thus "the doctrine of the absolute dependence of the creature, as it is expressed in the Calvinistic confessions in regard to providence, foreordination, election, the inability of man." Calvinists bear a consistent theological method that "distinguishes [them] from Romanist and other Protestant theologians." Unsatisfied with bare phenomena, Calvinism calls one to look through appearances in order to push toward the invisible and divine realities that undergird them. Taking a posture that submits to God's primacy, then, Calvinists develop eyes that reorient all things in the light of their "relation with and subordination to God."[38]

Such a theological starting point not only sets Calvinists apart, however, but also provides them with a principle that is "too rich and fruitful to allow its influence to be confined to the production of a specific type in the sphere of religion and theology."[39] Here, while appealing to the historical examples of Calvinism's world-encompassing productivity, Bavinck argues specifically that Calvinism is not just a theology but also a *world-and life*-view, providing its own distinct philosophy, ethical injunctions, political theory, and a particular view of science and art:

> [Calvinism] produces a specific view of the world and life as a whole; so to speak, a philosophy all its own. The moral life also that grows upon the soil of Calvinism bears a distinct physiognomy. ... In close connection with this, Calvinism has developed its own political system and political life. ... In the same manner the principles of Calvinism bear in themselves the germ of a specific type in science and art, though it must be admitted that this germ has not as yet been fully developed.[40]

---

38. Bavinck, "Future of Calvinism," 4–5.
39. Bavinck, "Future of Calvinism," 5.
40. Bavinck, "Future of Calvinism," 5–6.

This last comment on the germ of Calvinism not yet being developed in science and art is key. Bavinck echoes the same point toward the end of the article, emphasizing that Calvinism seeks progress without prescribing a uniform way of life. Calvinism, in other words, provides the seeds and principles that can take root in multiple nations, with each of those nations developing according to distinctions in culture, in history, and among its various people groups. "Calvinism wishes no cessation of progress and promotes multiformity. It feels the impulse to penetrate ever more deeply into the mysteries of salvation, and in feeling this honors every gift and different calling of the Churches."[41] Perhaps in a counterintuitive fashion, Bavinck argues that the priority on the sovereignty of God actually protects the freedom of the nations—God is sovereign, and thus no human being is. Hence, the theologian's work too is mere approximation to reality grounded on an external authority, and God could guide the churches and Christians in ways that might be surprising to some particular group. Calvinism's commitment to the absolute sovereignty of God is thus a freeing, rather than a constricting, reality.

Bavinck anticipates his turn to the *Christian* worldview in his claim in that article that Calvinism is "catholic in the best sense of the word."[42] Indeed, his 1904 work *Christian Worldview* largely leaves behind the intra-Christian polemics and focuses on Christianity as a holistic alternative against unbelief itself. Here, one finds no citation of Calvin, but the imprint of Bavinck's earlier work is still apparent: Christianity is a holistic, world-encompassing faith that generates enduring answers to perennial questions. It produces a coherent unity in response to the discord that one feels in the modern age; a discord that itself arises from the rejection of the Christian faith. "In reality, there are only two worldviews, the theistic and the atheistic," he writes.[43]

Why did Bavinck shift his emphasis? At the turn of the twentieth century, Bavinck realized that a new kind of thoroughgoing unbelief was emerging. He was no longer fighting theological battles within Christianity,

---

41. Bavinck, "Future of Calvinism," 23.
42. Bavinck, "Future of Calvinism," 6.
43. *CW*, 73.

whether with Lutherans, Catholics, or theological liberalism. Rather, Bavinck was encountering followers of a more radically consistent kind of unbelief in the wake of the philosophy of Nietzsche. Nietzschean nihilists did not say that one could still believe in the basic goodness of Christian teachings despite disbelieving in God. Rather, they argued that because God is dead, one has to revise all of Western civilization and all of what one believes. If God is dead, why should there be truth, goodness, or beauty? Hence, the rise of nihilism created a discord between humankind and the world: What meaning do I have here? Can I even know the world? What does it mean to be good? Notice Bavinck's allusion to Nietzschean nihilism in the introduction to *Christian Worldview*.

> We no longer need God. There is no place for him in our world. Let the old hermit in the forest continue to worship God. We, the youth of Zarathustra, know that God is dead and will not be resurrected.
>   The convergence of this rejection of Christianity and the inner discord that disturbs us in modern life gives occasion to the question whether the two phenomena exist in a causal relation.[44]

In response to this, Bavinck suggests that there is a causal link between the "inner discord" that one feels in the modern world, on the one hand, and the rejection of Christianity that is becoming increasingly pervasive, on the other. He wanted to show that Christianity provided a more thoroughgoing and satisfying alternative to the unbelief in his day for the needs of both the head and the heart.

CHRISTIANITY AND AN ORGANIC WORLDVIEW

How, exactly, did Bavinck construct a Christian worldview? Here is a key passage for understanding his work:

> Just as sense perception is the basis of all science, the results of science are and remain the starting point of philosophy. Yet it is incorrect that philosophy should be no more than the summary of the results of the various sciences and that they should be set

---

44. *CW*, 25.

together only as the wheels of a clock. Wisdom is grounded on science but is not limited to it. It aims above science and seeks to press through to "first principles" [*prima principia*]. It already does this if it makes a special group of phenomena—religion, ethics, law, history, language, culture, and so on—into the object of its reflection [*denkende beschouwing*] and tries to trace the leading ideas. But it does this, above all, as it seeks for the final grounds of all things and builds a worldview thereon.

If this is the nature and task of philosophy, then it is presupposed—to an even greater degree than sense perception and science—that the world rests in thought and that ideas control all things. There is no wisdom other than that which is in and out of the faith in a realm of unseen and eternal things. It is built on the reality of ideas because it is the "science of the idea" and because it seeks the idea of the whole in the parts and of the general in the particular. It tacitly proceeds from the Christian faith, which states that the world is grounded in wisdom in its whole and in all its parts (Ps. 104:24; Prov. 3:19; 1 Cor. 1:21).[45]

Notice three key terms first of all: science, philosophy, and wisdom. Contrary to some contemporary criticisms against worldview thinking, worldview building is not an armchair, merely intellectual exercise for Bavinck.[46] Instead, he argues that to build a worldview, one has to begin with science—that is, with the deliverances of sense perception. This is the methodological starting point: begin with the inductive deliverances of all of the different sciences.

This is why in the editorial introduction to our translation of *Christian Worldview* we use the analogy of building a map as a way of depicting how to build a Christian worldview, rather than the common analogy of using spectacles. While the latter analogy often communicates that a Christian worldview can be put on rather quickly, building a map communicates that

45. *CW*, 50–51.
46. See especially the work of James K. A. Smith's Cultural Liturgies series: *Desiring the Kingdom: Worship, Worldview, and Cultural Formation* (Grand Rapids: Baker Academic, 2009), *Imagining the Kingdom: How Worship Works* (Grand Rapids: Baker Academic, 2013), and *Awaiting the King: Reforming Public Theology* (Grand Rapids: Baker Academic, 2017).

constructing a worldview takes progressive and inductive work, which can then be revised as new information arises.[47] Building a Christian worldview has Trinitarian parameters and principles, to be sure, but organization and construction are open to empirical evidences that promise the correction and enlargement of the maps by which we investigate the world. There is thus a reciprocal relationship between the maps we use and the world investigated. As we explore the deliverances of the sciences, we can reorganize our map, but as we reconfigure the map we revisit new terrain with the map as our guide.

Philosophy pursues the summary of these deliverances, and then, following the guidance of wisdom, pursues the unity behind the sciences into the first principles therein. A worldview, then, is built on the "final grounds of all things," after discovering that "the world rests in thought and that ideas control all things." The empirical phenomena we encounter in daily life and in science, which includes the many academic disciplines, actually lead us to invisible and indeed divine realities. Bavinck is here appealing to the classical doctrine of divine ideas, where creation reflects ectypally the diverse perfections and wisdom of the Triune God.[48] Reality is thus grounded in divine wisdom, and thus there is a whole that undergirds the sum of its parts. For Bavinck then, a world- and life-view allows the parameters of religion to bear on the discoveries of philosophy and the sciences.

Bavinck argues that Christianity offers an organic worldview according to which justice is given to the realities of both unity and diversity, the one and many. The Christian worldview brings the multiformity of being, particulars, into a conceptual unity, corresponding to a metaphysical unity, under the first principle of being: the Triune God. In his words:

47. See James Eglinton, Nathaniel Gray Sutanto, and Cory C. Brock, "Introduction," in CW, 21–29.

48. On the classical contours of Bavinck's organicism, see Nathaniel Gray Sutanto, God and Knowledge: Herman Bavinck's Theological Epistemology (Edinburgh: T&T Clark, 2020), especially ch. 2, and Sutanto, "Divine Providence's Wetenschappelijke Benefits," in Divine Action and Providence, ed. Fred Sanders and Oliver Crisp (Grand Rapids: Zondervan, 2019), 96–114. See also the fruitful interaction with Bavinck's account in Steven J. Duby, God in Himself: Scripture, Metaphysics, and the Task of Christian Theology (Downers Grove, IL: IVP Academic, 2020), 112–13.

It is only when we exchange the mechanical and dynamic world-view for the organic that justice is done to both the oneness and diversity, and equally to being and becoming. According to this organic worldview, the world is in no sense one-dimensional; rather, it contains a fullness of being, a rich exchange of phenomena, a rich multiplicity of creation. ... There are lifeless and living, inorganic and organic, inanimate and animate, unconscious and conscious, material and spiritual creations, which differ, respectively, in character but are still taken up in the oneness of the whole.[49]

How does Bavinck then apply this worldview and its metaphysics to particular issues? We will take a look here at two specifically nineteenth-century issues he addressed. The first is epistemology, and the second is ethics.

One of the most pervasive issues discussed in nineteenth-century epistemology is the connection between subjects and objects. That is, how do the mental representations in our minds actually give us an accurate access to extramental physical objects? The ideas in our mind, for example, have no weight, mass, or physicality to them, whereas objects in the world are tangible things that we bump up against. Consider a hypothetical black chair standing before us. The chair itself is quite heavy. It has a mass, a substance to it. One might presume that it is the presence of this chair that created the mental idea of the chair inside your mind. But the idea of the chair, notice, is quite different from the chair itself. The idea is not in space and time in the same manner that the chair is, having no weight, substance, or mass. How do these two heterogenous realities actually correspond?

Empiricism, which places the weight of knowledge on the sense perception of the external object, and rationalism, which places the weight of knowledge on the ideas within us, cannot seem to make sense of this connection between subjectivity and object. So, Bavinck:

Empiricism trusts only sensible perceptions and believes that the processing of elementary perceptions into representations and

---

49. *CW*, 71–72.

concepts, into judgments and decisions, removes us further and further from reality and gives us only ideas [*denkbeelden*] that, though clean and subjectively indispensable, are merely "nominal" [*nomina*] and so are subjective representations, nothing but "the breath of a voice" [*flatus vocis*], bearing no sounds, only merely a "concept of the mind" [conceptus mentis]. Conversely, rationalism judges that sensible perceptions provide us with no true knowledge; they bring merely cursory and unstable phenomena into view, while not allowing us to see the essence of the things. ... In both cases and in both directions, the harmony between subject and object, and between knowing and being is broken.[50]

In short, empiricism begins with objects, but then argues that the ideas in our mind are merely nominal and subjective representations of those objects, having no intrinsic connection to them, thereby separating our thoughts from the truth contained in the objective world. Rationalism, on the other hand, begins with ideas, but can only infer from one idea the presence of another idea, not the things outside the mind, much less the "essence of the things." By way of contrast, Bavinck argues that the knowability of external reality has to be acknowledged from the very beginning of our scientific investigation, "but this presupposition is of such a great significance that it must be considered and ought to be justified."[51]

How, then, does he justify the knowability of the world? Here the argumentation is complex but for our present purposes can be simplified to a few moves. First, appealing to the classical doctrine of divine ideas, Bavinck argues that the physical objects in the world can be represented by the ideas of the mind only if the world itself is rooted in ideas, that is, in the divine ideas: "The doctrine of the creation of all things by the Word of God is the explanation of all knowing and knowing about [*kennen en weten*], the presupposition behind the correspondence between subject and object." Appealing to Hebrews 11:3 and Romans 1:18, Bavinck argues,

---

50. *CW*, 32. For a more detailed analysis of Bavinck's account of perception, see Nathaniel Sutanto, "Herman Bavinck and Thomas Reid on Perception and Knowing God," *Harvard Theological Review* 111 (2018): 115–34.

51. *CW*, 40.

"The world becomes, and can only become" our spiritual property, if "it is itself existing spiritually [geestelijk] and logically and resting in thought."[52]

Second, Bavinck argues that the world is created with a diversity of parts. There are bodies and ideas, spirits and physical objects, yet all of these parts are united by a divine wisdom into a single organic unity: "It is the same divine wisdom [Goddelijk wijsheid] that created the whole organically into a connected whole and planted in us the urge for a 'unified' [einheitliche] worldview. If this is possible, it can be explained only on the basis of the claim that the world is an organism and has first been thought of as such." In the final analysis, Bavinck argues that it is distinctly Christian, Trinitarian metaphysics that epistemically justifies the reliability of our knowledge of external realities: "The Christian—that is, the organic—view gives the answer that thinking proceeds from being, word precedes deed. All things are knowable because they were first thought. And because they are first thought, they can be distinct and still one. It is the idea that animates and protects the organism's distinct parts."[53] In short, Bavinck uses the fact that the Logos (as Son of God) mediated all creation to argue for a justified certainty of objective knowledge. It is because the Son of God mediates both object and subject that a unity between the two is possible.

Bavinck's argument leads him to a broad, holistic kind of vision. He does not reject the deliverances of the rationalist or empiricist philosophers, but rather takes them seriously and tries to accommodate both. He begins with sense perception. But this does not negate ideas. Sense data corresponds to subjective ideas because God the Son upholds the relation and God the Spirit gives knowledge to sentient creatures. The Christian worldview, in Bavinck's hands, leads us to a capacious vision that allows us to accommodate the best insights of the current debates.

Second, Bavinck's argument concerning ethics is particularly potent, especially considering that he wrote it decades before the Second World War. Here Bavinck is wrestling once again with the nonbelieving thesis that ethics as an investigation of goodness and value is not grounded in

---

52. CW, 46.
53. CW, 51, 74. On the organic motif in general, see Eglinton, Trinity and Organism.

a divine source outside us. The main alternative considered in the nineteenth century, then, was to argue that ethics and norms were grounded in history. However, Bavinck argues, the moment one suggests that the good is determined not by the fact of transcendent norms but rather in immanent history, one has to answer the question, Which history? Or, perhaps more pertinently, Whose history?

Bavinck argues that rejecting transcendent norms means absolutizing our own preferences and, by extension, the preferences of our own people group in the present. The history of *our* culture, nation, and people will be judged the absolute standard by which we adjudicate between other histories, cultures, and people groups. Having done away with divine ideas, we will inevitably seek stability elsewhere: "Because a person always needs some form of stability, however, the grave and in no sense imaginary danger quickly arises that through this one-sided historical viewpoint, he is led to a counterfeit nationalism, to a narrow chauvinism, to a fanaticism about race and instinct."[54]

Hauntingly, Bavinck traces this to the German nationalist philosophies arising in his day. Writing in 1904, Bavinck was terrifyingly prescient regarding the tragedies that would arise just a few decades later:

> "The German spirit shall heal the world" [some people say]. But that is how the so called pure historical view turns into the most biased construction of history. If the theory or the system requires it, then the primal human is a wild animal, then the most uncivilized peoples are the representatives of the original human race ... then Jesus did not come from Israel but from the Aryans.[55]

Rejecting transcendent norms, in other words, does not lead to a humble position that allows us to appreciate the diversities of the different peoples and cultures. Rather, the German philosophers with whom Bavinck interacted showed that a diseased nationalism was the inevitable result. Germany became the standard by which many were judging the other nations as less developed, primitive, and so on: "Relativism appears,

54. *CW*, 100.
55. *CW*, 101.

then, to be impartial, as it wants to know of no fixed norms and claims to be concerned with and to speak of only the concrete, the historical. But it makes the relative itself into the absolute and therefore exchanges true freedom for coercion, real faith for superstition."[56]

In a provocative fashion (the application of which is not difficult to see in a racially polarized twenty-first century), Bavinck argued in 1904 that rejecting the Christian faith leads to the terrible consequence of racism or ethnocentrism. What appears to be the most humble and relativistic view turns out to be the most triumphalist and imperialist. By getting rid of the transcendent, we end up absolutizing one particular historical people group.

But how exactly, then, do we do justice to both the transcendent and the historical? Bavinck insists that ethics has to be based on the transcendent God himself. The true, good, and beautiful subsists in the one God. The God whose ideas are reflected in the world, and through whom we then know all things, is the same God who created the norms we encounter within reality. By God's thought, God granted "reality to things and truth to our intellect," and, likewise, God determined "the norms for our knowing, willing, and acting." But this one God does not just elevate these moral norms for us. He also entered into human history. The Logos became flesh, and so the transcendent ethical ideal became historical in Jesus. As the Logos enters into flesh, he too invites us to partake in his divine wisdom in Christ: "But just as the wisdom of God became flesh in Christ, so should the truth also enter us."[57]

CONCLUSION

It is appropriate to close this chapter by returning to the epigraph above. For what reason, specifically, did Bavinck argue that the retrieval of Calvinism was more "acute" than its original counterparts? Bavinck argues that this "new Calvinism" adopted "a more acute form" because the modern "conception of the world has definitely undergone significant change, and our knowledge of the connection between cause and effect

---

56. *CW*, 102.
57. *CW*, 108, 110, 132–33.

in nature and history has increased appreciably." Yet, "The question has always been there, and it comes down to this: how is it possible that the God that science recognizes and the God that religion requires is one and the same God? How can the infinite, eternal being that is the power in all power and the life of all life be at the same time the loving, the gracious, and the caring Father of his children?"[58]

The retrieval of Calvin and the acute representation of him in the modern era, in other words, was motivated by the desire to seek a holistic relationship between the various scholarly disciplines (or the so-called natural life) and the God of Christianity. What is the relationship between our faith and the world? While the search for unity reflects the perennial character of this question and debate, the neo-Calvinists were seeking to assert this unity as a result of the numerous discoveries and enhancements within the modern era while subverting its existential devolutions.[59] Bavinck was fundamentally seeking to avoid "the fatal separation between world and church, between science and faith, between scientific and ecclesial theology."[60] Hence, as this chapter demonstrated, neo-Calvinists sought a fully orbed vision and application of theology to other areas of life within the modern age, and they turned specifically to the Reformer of Geneva for help and inspiration.[61]

This chapter has surveyed in brief the particular deployment of Calvin and Calvin's Geneva in the Kuyperian imagination, and it showed the way in which they deployed the term to refer precisely to that sort of holistic theological vision. The "neo" in "neo-Calvinism," then, can be summarily described in these two interconnected ways. The first refers to the way in which Bavinck and Kuyper saw Calvin as a signal to Reformed theology's holistic implications. They contrast this holism not only with other forms of Christianity (such as Roman Catholicism and Lutheranism), but also, ultimately, as a full-orbed alternative to the more thoroughgoing forms of unbelief that arose at the turn of the twentieth century. As

---

58. Bavinck, "Modernism and Orthodoxy," 96.

59. In "Modernism and Orthodoxy," Bavinck also argues that the modern scholarship requires neo-Calvinists to consider the historical and psychological dimensions of revelation (105–7).

60. Bavinck, "Modernism and Orthodoxy," 99.

61. Bavinck, "Modernism and Orthodoxy," 106–7.

such, though they did emphasize the importance of Calvin and his work in Geneva as an inspiration to offer a well-rounded worldview, neo-Calvinism ultimately argues that Christianity in itself provides a more capacious vision that can satisfy the questions of the mind and the longings of the heart, and especially so amid the individualism and ideologies of the modern world.

The second is that Calvin's vision, in the first-generation neo-Calvinistic imagination, provided a holistic model according to which Reformed theology ought to be organically related to the deliverances of the modern sciences. While Bavinck did, for example, pick out salient examples of modern research that neo-Calvinism sought particularly to address, such as the epistemological connectedness between subjects and objects and the relationship between history and ethics, he also emphasized that the relationship between the enduring truths of the past and the consciousness of the contemporary day, once again, is a perennial issue to which theologians of every generation must attend.

If this chapter has emphasized the ways in which Kuyper and Bavinck had sought to draw resources from Calvin and paleo-Calvinism, it will become clearer as the book progresses that their work was a creative and critical retrieval rather than one of regurgitation or repristination. Indeed, as the next chapter shows, Kuyper and Bavinck thought that some reshaping of their Calvinist roots was necessary to meet the questions and demands of the modern age. This is at times present (as already intimated above) in their explicit critiques of Calvin and Reformed orthodoxy—Kuyper himself argues that, "by choosing in favour of liberty of religion, we do not pick up the gauntlet for Calvinism, but that we directly opposed it." In context, Kuyper was referring to the way in which the Reformation's leaders took up the "fatal after effect of a system grey with age" as reflected in their presumed Constantinian perspective, which unified church and state and hence led to criminal charges that were instituted by religious authorities (as seen especially, in Kuyper's mind, by "the fire of Servetus").[62] Kuyper would have been critical of what he deemed to be Geneva's ecclesial overreach into political legislation, or to what Scott Amos has observed in reference to

---

62. Kuyper, *Lectures on Calvinism*, 86.

a text like Martin Bucer's *De Regno Christi*, which "regarded Constantine's reign as the golden age to which Christendom should return."[63] Whether this critique is fair is a different issue, but it clearly shows that Kuyper's retrieval of Calvin was not uncritical.

This conviction that the church "could express itself only in one form and as one institution" is in contradiction, in Kuyper's judgment, to the seeds of multiformity found in other emphases within Reformational Calvinism that emphasized the freedom of conscience.[64] Richard Mouw rightly notes that, for Kuyper, "the proper correctives to this regrettable pattern can be found in a unique and compelling way within Calvinism's own theological resources."[65] In contrast to the established church model, Kuyper advocates for sphere sovereignty, according to which Christ's lordship reigns in each sphere in its own way, which will be further explored in following chapters. The result will be a kind of Christian pluralism that envisions a state that recognizes the rights and freedoms of other worldviews to pursue their own directions in the multiple structures of society:

> For an example, consider the social service that was the most important to the Christian pluralists of the nineteenth century—public education. Kuyper and the Christian pluralists argued that the state should provide equal funding to all schools, regardless of their faith orientations. The pluralists argued that state funds should come with some basic limits and expectations. For example the state could expect that subjects like math, reading, and writing be taught. That said, the state could not dictate the philosophical spirit in which those subjects would be taught. The basics of this pluralistic model of church-state partnership would soon be extended to the Dutch systems of healthcare, charity, arts, media, and more. The basic principle was that the free association—not the coercive state—would direct and provide social services.[66]

---

63. Scott Amos, "Martin Bucer's *Kingdom of Christ*," in *The Oxford Handbook of Reformed Theology*, ed. Michael Allen and Scott R. Swain (Oxford: Oxford University Press, 2021), 199.

64. Kuyper, *Lectures on Calvinism*, 87.

65. Richard Mouw, "Abraham Kuyper's *Lectures on Calvinism*," in Allen and Swain, *Oxford Handbook of Reformed Theology*, 336–37.

66. Matthew Kaemingk, *Christian Hospitality and Muslim Immigration* (Grand Rapids: Eerdmans, 2018), 131–32.

These differences on the relationship between church and state, however, are rooted in further theological judgments about redemptive history, common grace, and the church's pluriformity and catholicity. The latter, in particular, informed Kuyper's and Bavinck's vision of the relationship between modernity and orthodoxy. If the church is truly catholic, then it is a leavening and organic agent that will be manifested in a diversity of ways and in a diversity of cultures. The result is a canvassing of the church catholic as a developing and pluriform kingdom: a unity-in-diversity rather than uniformity or cacophony. It is to this subject that the next chapter in particular turns.

III

Catholic and Modern

So too those who profess the Reformed religion can and must, as long as they remain true to their origins, never give the impression that for them orthodoxy per se is the highest truth. However high we may estimate the confessions of the church, they are a "standardized norm," subservient to Holy Scripture, and thus always remain subject to revision and expansion.

—Herman Bavinck, "Modernism and Orthodoxy"

NEO-CALVINISM, BY DEFINITION, stands on the doctrinal history of Reformed theology and the codification of that orthodoxy in the confessional traditions of the Reformation. Furthermore, the movement fought to retrieve Reformed orthodoxy in response to the rise of the various modernisms, including both social and theological, as manifested particularly in theological liberalism and public unbelief. Kuyper famously argued that modernism (in the form of theological liberalism) was a beautiful façade that dressed itself in the guise of Christianity, attracting elite intellectuals because of its surface-level aesthetics.[1] Despite this external allure, however, Kuyper argued that theological liberalism offered no real substance underneath its splendor and hence would necessarily fail to satisfy the longings of the human heart. Kuyper was uncompromising in

---

1. Abraham Kuyper, "Modernism: A *Fata Morgana* in the Christian Domain," in Bratt, *Abraham Kuyper: A Centennial Reader*, 87–125.

his denouncement of the liberal project, which reduced the Christ of faith to a merely human Jesus of history, and revelation to mere anthropological expression, arguing that it is an illusion based on the whims of human projection: "*Their God is an abstraction* and has no actual existence."[2] In the preface to the English translation of the *Encyclopedia of Sacred Theology*, Kuyper further denounces attempts at constructing a theology that mediates between the rationalism of modernism and the older Reformed faith: "In this *Vermittelungs-theologie* [mediation theology] there is no stability of starting point, no unity of principle, and no harmonious life-interpretation on which a worldview, based on coherent principles, can be erected."[3]

Yet, as we will see, Kuyper's and Bavinck's insistence on being rooted in the orthodoxy of the past represents no facile desire for mere historical regurgitation. Indeed, instead of merely arguing for the necessity of orthodox conservatism per se, they distinguished between true and false forms of theological preservation. While false conservatism forcefully applies uniformity, true conservation takes the shape of a unity-in-diversity, distinguishing between proper orthodoxy and the generational forms in which that orthodoxy might be dressed.

This chapter outlines Kuyper's and Bavinck's understanding of the catholicity of the church and her faith as a unity-in-diversity. The universal unity of the church generates and undergirds an organic multiformity that emerges out of the personalities of the church's differing locations in space and time. Hence, it further clarifies that though Kuyper and Bavinck stood on the orthodoxy of the past, they made a clear distinction between the *essence* of that orthodoxy and its external forms. While the former must be preserved, the latter changes with each passing generation and local reception. Multiformity, then, is not a threat but a *good*, and so one must distinguish between true and false kinds of conservation.

---

2. Kuyper, "Modernism," 107, emphasis original.

3. *Encyclopedia*, viii.

KUYPER ON UNITY, MULTIFORMITY, AND ORTHODOXY

Unity is not uniformity. This is an axiomatic principle for Kuyper's theological, political, and philosophical outlook. While unity is organic and manifests itself as a diverse multiformity, uniformity is mechanical, artificial, manufactured, and externally opposed to stifle natural life. Indeed, Kuyper argued in an 1869 lecture that uniformity is the curse of modern life—he finds it taking hold in the way in which the modern age imposes one particular fashion, philosophy, and ethos on the people, as seen in the rationalistic hegemony arising from the French Revolution or the emerging materialism of late modern thought that reduces all phenomena to the merely physical. Over against what he considers to be this deadening force of uniformity in the different spheres of life, Kuyper argues that Christians need to recover multiformity: "If multiformity is the undeniable mark of fresh and vigorous life, our age seeks to realize its curse in its quest for uniformity."[4]

Kuyper also argues that uniformity leaks into the church and its theology, contrary to the clear teachings of Scripture concerning the diversity of God's intended creational design. Appealing to Genesis, for example, Kuyper claims that God created everything according to its own kind, "after its own, unique, given character. ... [This is] the royal law of creation which applies to more than seed-bearing herbs." Creation testifies to this revealed intent, as it displays an "infinite diversity, an inexhaustible profusion of variations that strikes and fascinates you in every domain of nature, in the ever-varying shape of a snowflake as well as in the endlessly differentiated form of flower and life."[5]

This unity-in-diversity is also the mark of the church. Kuyper describes this unity in a characteristically poetic fashion, connecting it to the biblical themes of the ecclesial body, the event of Pentecost, and the new-creation worship anticipated in John's apocalyptic vision:

---

4. Abraham Kuyper, "Uniformity: The Curse of Modern Life," in Bratt, *Abraham Kuyper: A Centennial Reader*, 25.

5. Kuyper, "Uniformity," 34.

Yet just as it was one in origin, so for all its diversity and dispersion its ideal unity for the future still holds in the promised Messiah, the head of humanity, who is coming. That unity, however, is not based on the sameness of a *model* but on the oneness of a *body* in which every member retains its own place. Not like a drop of water in a stream or piece of gravel in a pit but like branches grafted into the one vine, the members of the human race must find their unity in Christ. In the unity of the kingdom of God diversity is not lost but all the more sharply defined. On the great day of Pentecost the Holy Spirit did not speak in one uniform language; instead, everyone heard the Spirit proclaiming the mighty works of God in his own tongue. Though the wall of *separation* has been demolished by Christ, the lines of *distinction* have not been abolished. Someday, before the throne of the Lamb, doxologies will be sung to him who conquered, not by a uniform mass of people but by a humanity diversified in peoples and tribes, in nations and tongues.[6]

Where, then, does uniformity leak into the life of the church? Kuyper describes this as "the problem of *unity in diversity*," precisely because the church, in his assessment, always struggles to maintain the balance between christological unity and Spirit-empowered personal diversity. This struggle manifests itself chiefly in Roman Catholicism and in the national churches produced by the Reformation.

Roman Catholicism, Kuyper observes, imposes a forced uniformity in a mechanical fashion, decreeing to every church everywhere its styles, message, and behavior. "[Rome's] belief system had to be uniform, its government uniform, its liturgy uniform, its message to all regions of the world carried in *one* language, and life everywhere shaped by one model."[7] Rome produces no multiformity.

The Reformation, however, "broke up that false unity in two ways," but relocated it within a different context. These two ways include the "*national* and *individual* resistance" that the Protestant Reformation produced. However, Kuyper argues that this resistance relocated an imposed

---

6. Kuyper, "Uniformity," 35, emphases original.
7. Kuyper, "Uniformity," 37, emphasis original.

uniformity to the sovereign states and national churches, such that the Reformed movement had done nothing "but restore the uniformity of Rome in their own bosom and in a different way." While arguing for liberty, each Reformed nation had its own uniform confession, piety, liturgy, and government: "Here again, as in Rome before, unity did not develop organically but was imposed by force."[8]

Kuyper, however, is not suggesting that each church should be free to create novel dogmas, creeds, or an ecclesial life untethered from a united past and shared confession. He argues that such a position would mean the "destruction of the church." "One who speaks of doctrinal liberty in a church contradicts himself and nullifies the church's essence."[9] Kuyper insisted that an historic, creedal orthodoxy has to be preserved.

Nonetheless, Kuyper makes plain that orthodoxy is not identical with repristination, in what is perhaps one of his clearest statements on the dangers of hyperconfessionalism:

> Then what? Shall we recall the days of old and, as confessionalists in the worst sense of the word, press the people of our generation into a form that has not arisen from their own convictions? But that is to try the impossible! The past does not return; all repristination is nonsensical; every attempt at reaction is condemned to fail inasmuch as it denies the claims of the present. That way one becomes a confessionalist, zealous for the form but without the courage of the confession. That does not help us move forward but takes us back to a failed uniformity.[10]

Hence, Kuyper argues against two opposite extremes. The first involves a kind of theological liberalism that states that the church should have no unifying dogma, sacramental practice, or confession. The second extreme is a form of clericalism that insists on maintaining the older forms of the past for the sake of the confessions and institutions themselves, a kind

---

8. Kuyper, "Uniformity," 37–38.

9. Kuyper, "Uniformity," 38.

10. Kuyper, "Uniformity," 38. Later on, Kuyper repeats this sternly: "I detest all clericalism. All clericalism is the same, all confessionalism is the same. The life of a free church community can manifest itself only where that life finds its own form" ("Uniformity," 39).

of conservatism that maintains tradition for tradition's sake. This dead conservativism does not recognize the demands generated in each generation: new questions and grammars that require fresh forms and answers.

What, then, is the alternative? Rather than a national resistance that seeks a localized ecclesial uniformity, Kuyper argues that the only solution is to "accept—freely and candidly, without any reservations—a free multiformity."[11] A free and multiform church eschews any externally imposed uniformity, whether from a state, national church, or magisterium.[12] Gathering on the basis of personal convictions arising from the authority of revelation, churches form organically as gatherings and institutions from the desires of a worshiping people:

> If there are people of good will who are one in mind and spirit, let them join together and courageously confess the faith of their hearts, but let them not claim any greater unity than that which is really their common possession. Thus, with complete autonomy let groups and circles unite who know what they want, know what they confess, and possess an actual, not merely a nominal, unity. If here and there such circles exist which share a common life-trait, let them become conscious of their unity and display it before the eyes of the world, but let it be only that feature and no other bond that unites them.[13]

Kuyper proposes that within each nation, there ought to be manifestations of "common life-traits" that arise spontaneously, and no less within ecclesial circles. A common faith is that which binds together differing ethnicities and cultures, and is thus internally emerging rather than externally (and mechanically) imposed. Kuyper then applies this to the Dutch occupation of Indonesia. He desires "not to make them 'Dutch' but to make them Javanese Christians in whose domestic and social life

---

11. Kuyper, "Uniformity," 39.

12. In context, of course, this argument proved to be particularly useful for Kuyper's desire to form the Doleantie as a new denomination that provided an alternative to the established Netherlands Reformed Church. The formation of new denominations does not threaten religious stability precisely because it recognizes the freedom of conscience and pluriformity. For more on this, see Wood, *Going Dutch in the Modern Age*, 112–13.

13. Kuyper, "Uniformity," 39.

a spiritual life will flow according to its own character and form."[14] James Bratt's observation that this speech "was a catalogue of Romantic values, celebrating the wild over the tamed, the free-forming over the calculated, the unique individual over the standardized type, above all the organic over the mechanical" rings true.[15] It follows naturally, then, that Kuyper also argues that modern theological liberalism cannot represent the truth—not simply because it contradicts creedal Christianity but also because it fails to satisfy the longings of the human heart. In doing so, "Kuyper meets Modernism on its own grounds."[16]

While this lecture clarified the multiformity Kuyper thought should be a mark of the church, it still left lingering questions. What, exactly, is the difference between a true preservation of orthodoxy and a bad conservatism? What did Kuyper mean when he argued that there was a difference between the *form* of the church's faith and the *confession* underlying it?

While, as we will see, Bavinck did offer more precise answers, Kuyper explored these ideas directly in his Utrecht farewell sermon, delivered a year later, appropriately titled "Conservatism and Orthodoxy: False and True Preservation."[17] Here he articulated the necessary relationship between Christianity and conservatism, but then continues to distinguish between true and false conservatisms, returning once again to his distinction between form and confession, or between form and essence.

Kuyper offers at least two reasons why Christianity and conservatism stand in relation. First, Christianity proclaims a reformation rather than a revolution. By its story of redemption, Christianity seeks to reform that which exists rather than tearing it apart to anticipate something wholly new. "Conservatism is so integral to the core of its being that it even refuses to abandon the human body to death but in the article concerning the 'resurrection of the body' prophesies complete salvation." Second, Christianity is an *"historical phenomenon,"* and as such it stands on the

---

14. Kuyper, "Uniformity," 41.

15. Bratt, *Abraham Kuyper: Modern Calvinist*, 72.

16. James Bratt, "Introduction to Modernism: A *Fata Morgana* in the Christian Domain," in Bratt, *Abraham Kuyper: A Centennial Reader*, 88.

17. Abraham Kuyper, "Conservatism and Orthodoxy: False and True Preservation," in Bratt, *Abraham Kuyper: A Centennial Reader*, 65–85.

historical events of God's redemptive work, which climaxed in the incarnate person and work of Christ. Standing on the past, Christianity anticipates the future realization of God's eschatological reformation of the new cosmos. While false conservatism frustrates God's plans by insisting on the status quo of the present, true conservatism anticipates the march of the future as it stands on the past. In Kuyper's words: "The conservatism we must condemn wants to hold on to what is *as* it is. True conservatism seeks to preserve what is in terms of what it will become in Christ, that is, resurrected from the dead."[18]

Kuyper targets a specific kind of false conservatism that manifests itself in Reformed circles particularly. He observes that conservative confessionalists tend to romanticize the Reformation and thus seek to retrieve its purity in a shifting present age:

Is it any wonder, then, that the past gradually begins to attract them so powerfully, that their imagination is increasingly fascinated by the manly strength so brilliantly displayed by the heroes of the Reformation? There they see what they are looking for: an unbroken unity encompassing the whole of life, a single-minded devotion to the cause that possessed their soul, a total poise resulting from an unassailable faith. ... If only they could have lived then! ... They try again for that fullness of light even if the shadows have to be painted all the darker for it. "Return! Return!" they cry to the age of our ancestors. Matching the deed to their cry they gird themselves for imitation and set out to reconstruct what the hands of their ancestors had fashioned.[19]

Kuyper condemns this attitude in no uncertain terms. These attempts at imitation are doomed to failure, he reckons, because "they wanted to *repristinate* and because *repristination* is an undertaking that is self-condemned."[20] This kind of construction seeks to do the impossible by turning away from the present, seeking to embody a time that no longer exists.

18. Kuyper, "Conservatism and Orthodoxy," 71, 78, 80, emphasis original.
19. Kuyper, "Conservatism and Orthodoxy," 73.
20. Kuyper, "Conservatism and Orthodoxy," 73.

It creates further fragmentation and division while failing to address the live questions. It can feed bitterness and perpetuate fatigue with failed attempts to preserve the past. As John Halsey Wood also comments, Kuyper regarded repristination as a representation of what "killed inner religious life."[21]

Kuyper's suggestion, in contrast to this false conservatism, is a return toward a distinction between form and essence, and he uses different words to refer to these twin concepts. While forms fade with each passing generation, the essence remains: true orthodoxy preserves the essence and is uninterested in conserving fading forms. So Kuyper: "First seek to have for yourself the life your fathers had and then hold fast what you have. Then articulate that life in your own language as they did in theirs." Preservation of essence also demands the anticipation of the emergence of forms not yet predicted: "One can aim at preserving either that which has so far emerged from that principle or the principle itself. Conservatism does the former; genuine orthodoxy must do the latter. It must be concerned to keep not just a few blossoms that have budded on the plant but the plant itself, along with the formative power present in its roots, that plant along with its promise of the innumerable blossoms of its life brings us."[22]

Kuyper's line of reasoning leads to clear imperatives. The church preserves a living faith that persists through time, but the forms of that faith come and go in its confessions, liturgies, and subcultures, among many other variations. The responsibility of its ministers and theologians, then, is to present that essence in the forms of their own time and location. True preservation holds on to both continuity and discontinuity with the past. Kuyper articulates this responsibility by appealing again to the concepts of form and essence:

> A life without a firmly defined form cannot exist in this finite world. Accordingly, you can only hold on to the eternal in the form that real life manifests it in and around you. Naturally that form must be taken from this life and so must change with the alterations through

---

21. Wood, *Going Dutch in the Modern Age*, 62.

22. Kuyper, "Conservatism and Orthodoxy," 74, 81.

which life passes. Certainly it must have continuity with the form it had for our fathers, for we know no other life than that in which they rejoiced and which has been passed on to us in their forms. Still it is our calling to hold fast what we have in Christ *in our time*, not in theirs, and so it is from our own time that we must take the material which to prepare that form today. That labor is enormous, Congregation, especially where so much of it has been neglected.

The upshot is clear: "Therefore let us not complain if in church life too the old forms become ever less useful. Let us rather recognize our duty to search for new ones. You are all members of that church; in that church everyone has a place. Show in that church only the eternal that *you* have."[23]

Let us take stock. For Kuyper, true unity arises not mechanically but organically. As the Spirit works in the personalities of God's people, the true and living faith of that people will manifest itself in a diversity of ways. True orthodoxy, therefore, stands on the essence of that faith, a faith in God built on the historic events of God's redemptive work in Christ, while anticipating a future in which the present cosmos will be wholly transformed. Orthodoxy, therefore, preserves a past that anticipates a surprising future. As such, the responsibility of the church is to articulate that faith in its own location and generation, while anticipating the realization of God's work of reformation in the eschaton. Kuyper's rallying call toward the end of his Stone Lectures rings the same message: he desires "the development of the principles of Calvinism in accordance with the needs of our modern consciousness and their application to every department of life."[24]

In Kuyper's mind, multiformity leads to *disharmony* only because of the entrance of sin. Hypothetically speaking, Kuyper projects the possibility of each nation and time producing differing forms of theological and world-conceptions that lead not to disunity but rather to a greater harmonious whole, with each nation and time accenting a different aspect of the truth. Multiformity, then, and the need of each generation and place to produce their own form of theological confession, does not entail an

---

23. Kuyper, "Conservatism and Orthodoxy," 82–83, emphasis original.
24. Kuyper, *Lectures on Calvinism*, 177.

endorsement of theological relativism or of cultural snobbery that states that the present must intrinsically render the past forms obsolete, but a desire to preserve the insight that the truth is greater than any one time or place or one *apprehension* of that truth. Hence, "in the absence of a disturbance [due to sin], this multiformity would have been as *harmonious*, as now it works *unharmoniously*."[25]

A CATHOLICITY THAT CONSISTS IN DIVERSITY: UNITY-IN-DIVERSITY AND THE ORGANIC MOTIF IN BAVINCK

As we turn now to Bavinck, we will see that the same Kuyperian motifs are present. In Bavinck, however, there is greater precision with regard to the character and implications of this unity-in-diversity model of the church, as he considers that the free, organic churches will manifest themselves in very different ways in each place and time.

The diversity Bavinck desires is not meant to contradict an underlying unity. Indeed, the very connotations of the word "catholicity" would demand a recognition of unity. Invoking the organic language according to which the whole is larger than the parts and the whole is necessary for the parts to be understood, Bavinck argues that catholicity refers "to the church as a unified whole in contrast to the dispersed local congregations that make up the whole and are included in it." It involves, second, contrasting global catholicity with a national catholicity as exemplified, say, in the nation of Israel: "the unity of the church as inclusive of all believers from every nation, in all times and places." As such, and finally, a fuller definition of catholicity "embraces the whole of human experience." Christianity as the work of the Spirit is a catholic work, permeating the divisions of the self and decompartmentalizing human life. These defining features of catholicity presuppose the all-encompassing and universal character of the Christian religion precisely as a "world religion that should govern all people and sanctify all creatures irrespective of geography, nationality, place, and time."[26]

---

25. *Encyclopedia*, 90.
26. CCC, 221.

This argument, presented in Bavinck's 1888 address "The Catholicity of Christianity and the Church," partners well with his discussion on the attributes of the church in the fourth volume of *Reformed Dogmatics*. There Bavinck articulates this unity in theologically concrete terms. The unity of the church is constituted by the "headship" of Christ, the "communion" of believers in the Spirit with their head, and the uniting virtues of faith, hope, and love, sanctified by a single baptism. Succinctly stated, the invisible, spiritual, yet real and partially manifested bond that "unites all true Christians is always more than that which separates them."[27]

Bavinck's 1888 address included extensive discussions on the *leavening* power of Christianity as part of its catholicity. Indeed, true catholicity recognizes that the powers of the Christian religion have influence in every sphere of life. As such, Christianity, precisely because it is not tethered to a particular nation, culture, or perennial *Sitz im Leben*, has the capacity to embrace and leaven any society with which it comes into contact, thereby producing a multiformity in unity. In Bavinck's words, Christianity "can enter into all situations, can connect with all forms of natural life, is suitable to every time, and beneficial for all things, and is relevant in all circumstances. It is free and independent because it is in conflict only with sin and in the blood of the Cross there is purification for every sin."[28] In this last claim, Bavinck is echoing his oft-quoted axiom that Protestantism "traded the quantitative antithesis of the natural and the supernatural for the qualitative, ethical antithesis of sin and grace."[29] Christianity is only against sin, not culture as such. We will explore this claim extensively in later chapters.

If this is the case, catholicity is expressed not *in spite* of diversity but precisely *in* diversity. Catholicity consists not in mechanical uniformity but in a "richness," a "many-sidedness" and in "pluriformity."[30] Continuing on the claim that Christianity is a world religion and thus for every time

---

28. CCC, 249. Bavinck's understanding of common grace and the universal character of the Christian vocation also grounds these claims. See especially his "Calvin and Common Grace," in Armstrong, *Calvin and the Reformation*, 99–130. "[Calvin's] ethics is diametrically opposed to all ascetism, it is catholic and universal in scope" ("Calvin and Common Grace," 128).

29. *RD* 4:410. See also Eglinton, *Trinity and Organism*, 40–41, 96.

30. CCC, 250.

and place, Bavinck argues for the inherent desirability of confessional and international diversity on distinctly Reformed grounds in this way:

> That church is most catholic that most clearly expresses in its confession and applies in its practice this international and cosmopolitan character of the Christian religion. The Reformed had an eye for it when in various countries and churches they confessed the truth in an indigenous, free, and independent manner and at the Synod of Dort invited delegates from all over Reformed Christianity.[31]

This train of thought explains in part Bavinck's claim that "free churches undoubtedly have the promise of the future," that is, "provided they preserve the catholicity of the Christian faith and the Christian church."[32] The churches, free from state coercion and national allegiances, express this catholicity in the culturally and confessionally diverse expressions of the faith. The qualifier, however, is important, as Bavinck carefully guards himself against the misunderstanding that he is advocating for a kind of principled separatism. He is aware of the tendency of some free churches toward sectarianism and fragmentation in the guise of defending the freedom of conscience.[33] The qualifier maintains that free churches must be vigilant in preserving the catholic dimensions of proper ecclesial existence.

Nonetheless, for Bavinck, Reformed Christianity is the bedrock on which true catholicity and diversity flourishes. The 1888 address anticipates Bavinck's 1894 article "The Future of Calvinism," which effectively intensifies Bavinck's claims concerning Reformed Christianity and focuses them on the catholic nature of Calvinism.[34] While the Lutheran Reformation had a more purely religious and theological character, Calvinism nurtured a universality that extended beyond the religious sphere. "Calvinism," Bavinck writes, "has a world-encompassing tendency,

---

31. *RD* 4:323.

32. *CCC*, 250.

33. This secures Bavinck from the charge of triumphalism: "In the Protestant principle there is indeed a dissolving element as well as a church-reforming one. The one Christian church has been fragmented into innumerable sects and small churches, assemblies, and conventicles" (*CCC*, 249).

34. Bavinck, "Future of Calvinism." See ch. 1 in this present volume on Bavinck's use of Calvin and Calvinism.

being catholic in the best sense of the word. The Calvinist is fully conscious of this far-reaching tendency, and, borne on by this principle, he
aims with calm and unswerving determination at the end, which God
himself pursues in every creature, the glorification of his name."[35] The
universal impulse of Calvinism manifests itself in its international reception, generating various confessions of faith that reflect the contextual
absorption of its principles. Bavinck contrasts Calvinism further from
Lutheranism accordingly:

> Lutheranism, strictly speaking, has produced but a single Church
> and a single Confession. Calvinism on the other hand has found
> entrance into many nations and founded many multiform churches.
> It created not one but a number of Confessions. And yet the latter
> are all but copies of one another. The Zwinglian Confessions bear a
> different character from those of Calvin. The Catechism of Geneva
> differs considerably from that of Heidelberg. The Belgic Confession
> is quite distinct from the Westminster Standards. The Episcopal
> Church has been recognized as a Reformed Church as much as the
> Presbyterian Churches. This remarkable fact shows that Calvinism
> has room for the display of individuality, for that difference in char-
> acter which must exhibit itself among the various nationalities.[36]

The diversity of confessions that Calvinism generated, in correspondence with the various cultures and nations that absorbed it, indicates its
inherent propensity toward producing theological plurality in the search
for a deeper penetration of the riches of God's truth. "Calvinism wishes
no cessation of progress and promotes multiformity." Recognizing the distinct callings and gifting of the variety of ecclesial branches and identities,
Calvinism does not "demand for itself the same development in America

---

35. Bavinck, "Future of Calvinism," 6. Bavinck remained aware of the various ways in which
the Reformed have failed to live up to this ideal. A few pages later he says this about the Reformed
religion that often arose after the Reformation era of which Calvin was representative: "The Reformed,
who had once stood at the head of every movement and been the liberals and radicals of their time,
now became conservative, reactionary, panegyrists of the old, and the despisers of the new times. ...
It was no longer the old, high-minded, radical Calvinism, but a Calvinism that had become rough,
harsh, unpolished, without splendor and fire, cold and dry and dead" ("Future of Calvinism," 11).

36. Bavinck, "Future of Calvinism," 22.

and England which it has found in Holland." This claim grounds his conviction that American theologians need not deem it necessary to seek theological education from foreign lands such as Germany and should instead embrace the freedom for themselves to develop their "Reformed Church" in a manner that fits "in accordance with [their] own nature." In short, Bavinck argues that just as every nation "honors its independence, so it is the calling of the Church to guard and preserve its individual character, and, instructed by the teachings of history, to labor for the Church and theology of the future."[37]

It is worth noting at this point that these are the kind of remarks that led George Harinck to comment that it was Bavinck's "openness to cultural relativism [that] reveals [him] as a modern man."[38] When Bavinck's concluding reflections on the distinctive character of America's religion and Christianity are taken into consideration, which culminated in the controversial statement that "Calvinism is not the only truth," Harinck's comment that Bavinck had a sanguine attitude in relation to relativism is apparent.[39] However, one should temper these observations with Bavinck's own words concerning the unique character of Calvinism. It is, Bavinck argued, "the richest and most beautiful form of Christianity, but it is not coextensive with Christianity." The manifestation of Christianity in its fullest and most developed form can only be achieved by the unity of its diverse parts coming together, each proclaiming different sides of the body. Calvinism, in other words, "allows of various minor shades" and "in the application of its theological and ecclesiastical principles avoids all mechanical uniformity." The confessional diversity that marks Reformed Christianity witnesses to the proclivity for Calvinism to appreciate plurality, but this confessional diversity, for Bavinck, signals Calvinism's openness to other branches of Christianity *outside* the Reformed tradition as

---

37. Bavinck, "Future of Calvinism," 23.

38. George Harinck, "Calvinism Isn't the Only Truth: Herman Bavinck's Impressions of the USA," in *The Sesquicentennial of Dutch Immigration: 150 Years of Ethnic Heritage; Proceedings of the 11th Biennial Conference of the Association for the Advancement of Dutch American Studies*, ed. Larry J. Wagenaar and Robert P. Swierenga (Holland, MI: Joint Archives of Holland, Hope College, 1998), 154.

39. This is not to be mistaken with strong relativism, the claim that there is no truth. Rather, Bavinck is suggesting that each culture will appropriate and approximate the truth in its own particular ways. Hence, though truth is one, the expressions of that truth as culturally located will be diverse.

well: "Calvinism though laying claim to being the purest religion, and to having most thoroughly purified Christianity of all Romish admixture, has never pretended to be the only true Christian religion."[40] Therein is the paradox of Bavinck's conception of Calvinism: it is the purest theological position, but its purity consists precisely in the relativizing of its importance. The truth of Calvinism is vindicated when it sees good in the existence of other branches of the church that might disagree with its own theological position.

At this point, Bavinck's use of the organic motif in his treatise on the catholicity of Christianity is pertinent. When issues regarding theological plurality are discussed, there is a tendency to deploy a distinction between fundamental and nonfundamental articles of the faith. The fundamental articles, one might argue, are those that ground the unity of the Christian church, whereas the nonfundamental articles are those convictions about which different branches of the church can disagree. Bavinck objects to the mechanical ways in which this distinction was deployed in the past. Here, it is worth citing Bavinck at length.

> Theologians in a previous era distinguished between fundamental and nonfundamental articles of faith. That distinction was often understood in very mechanical ways with two sets of articles loosely placed next to each other. This distinction was also a strictly confessional designation: Fundamental was defined in terms of the contents of one's own confession. However, understood in an organic way, the distinction does have validity. In the same way that the one universal Christian church comes to more or less purity of expression in individual churches, in the same way the one universal Christian truth comes to more or less pure expression in the various confessions of faith. There is no universal Christianity present *above* the confessional divisions but only *in* them. No one church, no matter how pure, is identical with the universal church. In the same way no confession, no matter

---

40. Bavinck, "Future of Calvinism," 22–24.

how refined by the Word of God, is identical with the whole of Christian truth.[41]

Bavinck's argument is as follows: a mechanical way of construing the distinction between fundamental and nonfundamental articles tends to relegate the nonfundamental articles as unimportant, as if the matters on which the confessions differ are not considered by those respective confessions to be issues that are absent from divine revelation.[42] An organic way of construing this distinction would instead see them each as providing different shades to the singular and multiform ecclesial faith that they claim to express, while respecting the historical, cultural, temporal, and contextual features that contribute to their emergence. In that way, the secondary articles within a particularly theological orientation are of immense importance because they are born of an exegetically revealed system as interpreted in a particular space and time.[43] As Bavinck argues in his 1911 address "Modernism and Orthodoxy": "The whole of Christian theology is even built on the assumption, that it cannot consist in a literalistic reproduction of the Holy Scriptures but that it, taking a position in special revelation, independent and free, bound only to its object, must develop itself and thereby conjoin itself to the consciousness and life of the times, in which it appears and labors."[44]

An organic construal of the unity-in-diversity expressed in the confessional diversities of the church is thus not merely an ideal to be recognized: it is also an inevitability, the eclipsing of which betrays an inadequate grasp of the finitude that attends the church's absorption of

---

41. CCC, 251, emphasis original. See also the discussion in James Eglinton, "Vox Theologiae: Boldness and Humility in Public Theological Speech," *International Journal of Public Theology* 9 (2015): 5–28, especially 24–25.

42. RD 1:612–13.

43. Relevant here, too, is Bavinck's "Essence of Christianity," in *Essays on Religion, Science, and Society*, trans. Harry Boonstra and Gerrit Sheeres, ed. John Bolt (Grand Rapids: Baker Academic, 2008), 33–47.

44. Herman Bavinck, *Modernisme en Orthodoxie: Rede gehouden bij de overdracht van het rectoraat aan de Vrije Universiteit op 20 october 1911* (Kampen: Kok, 1911), 35. Dutch original: "Heel de Christelijke theologie is zelfs op de onderstelling gebouwd, dat zij niet in een letterlijk nasspreken van de H. Schrift bestaat of bestaan kan, maar dat zij, in de bijzondere openbaring positie nemend, zelfstandig en vrij, alleen door haar object gebonden, zich ontwikkelen mag en zich daarbij heeft aan te sluiten aan het bewustzijn en leven van den tijd, waarin zij optreedt en arbeidt."

divine revelation. Given that this is the case, the second point follows from the first: Christianity is flexible and pliable enough to accommodate and leaven any culture. Observing this second point also necessitates attending to Bavinck's charge against Roman Catholicism that it is in itself a logical contradiction.

CALVINISM AS FLEXIBLE AND PLIANT AND THE CONTRADICTION OF ROMAN CATHOLICITY

Bavinck proclaims that Calvinism is "thoroughly intellectual"; it "possesses a far-reaching principle, a consistent system," and, as such, "involves a comprehensive view of the world and life." Calvinism "produces a specific view of the world and life as a whole; so to speak, a philosophy all its own."[45] Bavinck, paradoxically, argues that Calvinism is adaptable to any culture because it is an all-encompassing worldview. Bavinck's argument is a response to those orthodox theologians who sought to escape the modern worldview in its entirety.[46] Calvinism, he writes, "is sufficiently pliant and flexible to appreciate and appropriate what is good in our age." Its all-encompassing character means that the philosophies and social values of every age inevitably, though often unwittingly, produce tenets that are organically found in Calvinism. Turning to the philosophic systems of his century, Bavinck argues that the central lines of Calvinism are still echoed in the "moral principles of Kant," the "pessimistic philosophy" of Arthur Schopenhauer, and, indeed, in "almost every system" of the nineteenth-century that denies the "indeterminism of the will."[47]

In other words, Calvinism is uniquely suited to encounter eighteenth- and nineteenth-century philosophies precisely because Calvinism can accommodate and appropriate the philosophical truths of any age. Although Christian theology has used Plato and Aristotle as the primary

---

45. Bavinck, "Future of Calvinism," 5, 21. Bavinck reiterates that theology can "fashion for herself a philosophy" or appropriate any preexisting one with little difficulty in "The Theology of Albrecht Ritschl," trans. John Bolt, BR 3 (2012): 123.

46. In Bavinck's words, it is the temptation "to return simply a distant past as the solution for the ills of the present." See Herman Bavinck, "The Catholicity of Christianity and the Church," trans. John Bolt, Calvin Theological Journal 27 (1992): 245.

47. Bavinck, "Future of Calvinism," 21–22.

philosophical handmaidens, one must remember that "theology is not in need of a specific philosophy. It is not per se hostile to any philosophical system and does not, a priori and without criticism give priority to the philosophy of Plato or Kant or vice versa. But it brings along its own criteria, tests all philosophy by them, and takes over what it deems true and useful."[48] There is no perennial or natural philosophy to which Christianity must be attached, and it is for that reason that it can make use of any philosophy it encounters.

It is in this context that Bavinck's charge against (pre–Vatican II) Rome is intelligible, especially in light of Pope Leo XIII's encyclical *Aeterni Patris*.[49] Contrary to Calvinism's capacity to critique and yet accommodate the modern worldview, Roman Catholicism, he argues, involves a retrieval of "Scholasticism."[50] On one side, Protestant Christians, "we ourselves," Bavinck argues, "are influenced by" the "modern worldview." "Our view of things is quite different from that of previous generations."[51] Protestants participate in modern culture, affirming its democratic values, its efforts to reduce crime and to increase the comforts of life, and affirm "the freedom of religion and conscience." Reformed theologians, in other words, "do not scorn the good things which God in this age has given them; forgetting the things that are behind, they stretch forward to the things that are before. They strive to make progress, to escape from the deadly embrace

---

48. *RD* 1:609.

49. Bavinck critiques Roman Catholicism for expressing an inadequate vision of catholicity. An important point within his critique that we cannot unpack here is his claim that Rome fails to be catholic because it does not see the Christian faith as a transforming or leavening agent. "Rome thus maintains the catholicity of the Christian faith in the sense that it seeks to bring the entire world under the submission of the church. But it denies catholicity in the sense that the Christian faith itself must be a leavening agent in everything. In this way an eternal dualism remains, Christianity does not become an immanent, reforming reality" (CCC, 231). Geerhardus Vos echoes the same critique: "One can also take the catholicity of the Church intensively; that is to say, from the religious life of a Christian, insofar as it is manifested in the church, an influence must proceed in every area of life, so that everything is Christianized in the noblest sense of the word. Where religion is reduced to a matter of secondary importance, as something for Sunday, then that is the opposite of catholicity. ... For Rome, catholic = Roman Catholic." See Vos, *Reformed Dogmatics*, vol. 5, *Ecclesiology, the Means of Grace, Eschatology*, trans. and ed. Richard Gaffin (Bellingham, WA: Lexham, 2016), 23. See, however, the qualifications Vos gives for these claims on page 9 of the same volume.

50. Despite Bavinck's use of "scholasticism" as a pejorative in this context, he was aware that, in itself, scholasticism signifies a pedagogical method rather than doctrinal content. See, in this respect, *RD* 1:83–84.

51. CCC, 245.

of dead conservatism, and to take their place, as before, at the head of every movement."[52] In contrast, Rome opposes the modern worldview, at least as exemplified by the contemporary movements Bavinck encountered, in the form of the neo-scholastic revivals and the reaffirmation of neo-Thomistic philosophy. "The Middle Ages remain the ideal to which all Roman Catholics aspire. The restoration of Thomistic philosophy by the encyclical of August 4, 1879, seals this aspiration."[53] Rome's 1864 *Syllabus of Errors*, too, was a sign that they were "making no concession to the modern worldview"; it "declared that the methods and principles of Scholasticism were adequate to meet the needs of the day and the further development of science."[54]

Bavinck's argument against pre-Vatican II Roman Catholicism also emphasizes that the conjunction of the modifier to the noun in "Roman Catholicism" displays a contradiction: "mutually contradictory are the terms 'Roman' and 'Catholic.'"[55] In the Roman Catholic claim that communion is to be defined by an association with a particular location (Rome) and in a person (the papacy), it fails to account for the growing number of genuine believers outside their jurisdiction. "Unity and catholicity are claims of Rome that cannot undo the fact that millions of Christians live outside of its communion. There is not just one church but many churches, not one of which embraces all believers." The contradiction in the union of "Roman" and "catholic," then, is by virtue of the former's designation of a particular expression and institution of the faith, and the universal scope of the latter. As such, Roman catholicity must acknowledge a perennial philosophy, location, line of succession, and institution. "By its very nature, therefore, Rome has to be intolerant. It cannot acknowledge any churches other than itself. It is itself the only church, the bride of Christ, the temple of the Holy Spirit." In short, the Roman view of unity "is obligated to now anathematize over half of the whole of Christendom."

---

52. Bavinck, "Future of Calvinism," 13.

53. CCC, 231. Bavinck is referring to Pope Leo XIII's encyclical *Aeterni Patris*.

54. CCC, 245.

55. *RD* 4:322. For an analysis of Bavinck's construal of the nature-grace relationship vis-à-vis Henri de Lubac's contributions, see Gregory W. Parker Jr., "Reformation or Revolution?: Herman Bavinck and Henri de Lubac on Nature and Grace," *Perichoresis* 15 (2017): 81–95.

In Bavinck's judgment, then, it is more accurate to designate the papal view simply with the predicate "Roman" or the "papal church," for these "express its nature much more accurately than 'Catholic.'"[56]

What would Bavinck make, then, of the charge from Roman Catholic apologists that Protestantism has nurtured division, whereas Catholicism has preserved unity? Bavinck was evidently frustrated by this charge, as he claims with uncharacteristic sarcasm: "External unity does have an immediate appeal and seems more attractive. Rome lets no opportunity pass to parade its glorious unity in contrast to the divisions of Protestantism."[57] He responds in no uncertain terms:

> Yet under this external unity Rome hides the same differences and oppositions that the Protestant principle allows to develop alongside each other. For this reason it is not a curse but a blessing that the Reformation refused all false, inauthentic forms of unity and permitted external differentiation of that which did not internally belong together. It is a sad fact of life that the State Churches are still poisoned with this Roman leaven and seek to marshall their forces against Rome by externally uniting faith and unbelief in a way that blunts consciences and corrupts character, resulting in a church life that is thoroughly unhealthy.[58]

Note the mechanical language with which Bavinck describes the Roman Catholic construal of unity. Institutional unity is an imposed and external unity that veils the real theological differences within. As Geerhardus Vos claims, "arrogating to oneself an external name is not true catholicity."[59] Protestantism, with its spiritual rather than political or institutional articulation of unity, can account for the freedom of conscience and is not surprised by the diversity it now encounters. In a sense, Bavinck is arguing that diversity is inevitable: diversity is the result of the church's current location in varying contexts and generations, and a consequence of its finitude. The Roman Catholic claim, then, is not only dishonest, for

---

56. *RD* 4:309, 311, 320, 323.
57. CCC, 250.
58. CCC, 250.
59. Vos, *Reformed Dogmatics* 5:27.

it veils the divisions within its institutional unity, but is also naïve. It is dependent on an overrealized eschatology concerning the achievability of a fully united body in this life. As such, Bavinck argues that the existence of the full, spiritual, and visible manifestation of the church remains an object of faith—hoped for but not yet seen until the eschaton. "The one, holy, universal church that is presently an object of faith, will not come into being until the body of Christ reaches full maturity. Only then will the church achieve the unity of faith and the knowledge of the Son of God, and only then will she know as she is known."[60]

Bavinck argues that catholicity describes the God-ordained organism of both church and cosmos. The unity consists in a spiritual bond and communion through the Spirit, with Christ as head. That diversity consists in the confessional plurality that emerges from the various contexts in which churches reside. Calvinism, in particular, articulates a catholicity that accounts for this diversity, and in fact gives an intellectual and ecclesial structure that makes it possible. Hence, Calvinism, with its all-encompassing worldview, is in no need of a perennial culture, location, or philosophy, and for that reason can accommodate any culture, location, or philosophy. We come now to the final point: not only is diversity a goal that Calvinism desires and accommodates, but Calvinism also recognizes diversity as an inevitable reality.

CALVINISM RECOGNIZES
THE INEVITABILITY OF DIVERSITY

As noted above, Bavinck recognized that the Protestants of his era possessed distinct intellectual dispositions from those that come before them. They, more than before, believed in the freedom of conscience, the equality of all creatures in God's image, the democratic right of the people, and so on. These changes were to be embraced, and a rejection of them with a preference for the traditions and lifestyles of the past, Bavinck thought, revealed a naivete with respect to how one's social-temporal locations always condition one's mode of being. As we saw, in the 1911 address on "Modernism and Orthodoxy," Bavinck was disputing the charges that the

---

60. CCC, 251.

neo-Calvinistic movement adopted a double-mindedness that revealed a fickleness of commitment between the two poles. The modern worldview might be antithetical to orthodoxy, Bavinck responded, but it is impossible to disregard its achievements, no less because its existence arose from the Christian orthodoxy of the past. The orthodox, however, were also wrong insofar as they considered themselves to be unaffected by their contemporary culture. "Just as modern theology, in general, thinks and lives out of the Christian tradition much more than they themselves suppose, so is orthodoxy also—unless it entirely shut itself off from the environment—in [a] stronger or weaker degree under the influence of the spiritual currents of this century."[61]

Bavinck's analysis goes two ways, then, and both involve claims concerning the parasitic character of modernism and orthodoxy. Modernism can only exist because it is dependent on the orthodoxy of the past, out of which it arose. Orthodoxy, likewise, must exist within the benefits produced by the modern, scientific culture as a gift of common grace. Both are wrong when they treat the other as a mere fiend to oppose. The neo-Calvinistic movement recognizes this inevitability in gratitude: "because we are children of this time, we gratefully receive every good gift which the Father of lights bestowed on this era."[62] As such, Bavinck would also admit that the search for the "essence of Christianity first arose in modern times."[63]

Kuyper, likewise, argued for this reciprocal relationship between modernism and orthodoxy in 1871. While demonstrating the radical differences between modernism's liberal theology from Christianity's creedal and confessional tradition, Kuyper argues that modernism continued to depend on the very orthodoxy it rejects:

---

61. Bavinck, *Modernisme en Orthodoxie*, 15. Dutch original: "Trouwens, niemand, die meeleeft met zijn tijd, kan in elk opzicht tegen al het moderne gekant zijn. Zooals de moderne theologie over het algemeen nog veel sterker uit de Christelijke traditie denkt en leeft dan zij zelve vermoedt, zoo staat ook de orthodoxie, tenzij zij zich geheel van hare omgeving afsluit, in zwakker of sterker mate onder den invloed van de geestesstroomingen dezer eeuw."

62. Bavinck, *Modernisme en Orthodoxie*, 13. Dutch original: "Want wij zijn kinderen van dezen tijd, en nemen dankbaar elke goede gave aan, welke de Vader der lichten in deze eeuw ons schenkt."

63. Bavinck, "Essence of Christianity," 37.

The reproach goes too far, however, if it is taken to mean that Modernism might have come equally well had there never been a Christian church. On the contrary, as little as the reflection of a beech tree could quiver on the surface of a stream if that tree had not actually struck its roots in the bank, so Modernism would never have conjured up its images had there been no Christian church in our age. Granted that it never brought its light to bear on real Christianity and only taught its image in the camera obscura of its own pagan premises. Nevertheless also in its transparencies you can discern the main outline of the Christian faith, however vague and shadowy it may be. ... It is therefore safe to say that, however far it has wandered down pagan roads, Modernism still belongs to the sphere of Christianity, for shadows cannot be separated from the trees which case them.[64]

Kuyper goes on to draw an analogy between the ancient heresy of Arianism and the theology of modernism. Both movements were significant and influential in their own respective periods and were considered threats to the Christian faith. Nonetheless, orthodox Christianity should be thankful for the emergence of these heresies, for their birth forced the orthodox to reconnect with their past and to sharpen their thinking. In effect, Kuyper argues that attending to the real challenges of modernism affords the orthodox with the opportunity to purge themselves from false conservatism in order to defend true orthodoxy. Likening theological liberalism with a kind of poisonous vaccine that awakens the immune system with the proper dosage, Kuyper even argues that modernism, in that sense, saved true orthodoxy: "In short, when I say that without the Modernists we would still be groaning under the leaden weight of an all-killing Conservatism, you will understand in what sense I dare state openly that, both in reality and morally, Modernism has saved orthodoxy in the church of Jesus!"[65]

---

64. Kuyper, "Modernism," 101.
65. Kuyper, "Modernism," 119.

LOOKING FORWARD

This chapter has explored the way in which Kuyper and Bavinck conceived of the catholicity of the church as a multiformity, indeed, a unity-in-diversity that is organic rather than mechanical. Though the church confesses the same Christ as its head, the various cultures, times, and personalities that make up the church create a diversity of expressions and characters that cannot be merely flattened for the sake of uniformity. Every generation requires new forms of the same confession, and this means that it is the responsibility of the theologians of every age to rethink and present orthodoxy in fresh ways. Bavinck's foreword to *The Wonderful Works of God* bears this imprint explicitly, as he self-consciously seeks to present an introductory-level theological text that addresses the needs of his generation. The turn to the twentieth century saw the decline in interest in the "mysteries of the kingdom of God," Bavinck observes, and increasingly more see their faith as "irrelevant to life, having little or nothing to do with the present."[66] These conditions generate the need to present theology in fresh ways. A quote from the introduction to this book is worth revisiting. Note the way in which Bavinck echoes Kuyper's distinction between form and essence:

> We are children of a new time and live in a different era. And the desire to maintain these older forms, and to persist with the old simply because it is old, is troublesome and pointless.
>
> But not only is this desire useless, it also contradicts our own confession. It is precisely because the Christian faith is the recognition of a work of God—a work that began in the dawn of time and continues in *this* era—that its essence is a fruit of the ages, while its form is the fruit of *this* age. However much good Francken's *Kern*, Marck's *Merg* and Brakel's *Reasonable Service* affected in former days, they can no longer be brought to new life. They do not speak to the younger generation, and they involuntarily give rise to the thought that Christianity no longer fits in this present era. Thus, there is an urgent need for a work that takes the place of these works of the fathers and brings forth old truth in a form that corresponds with the demands of this era.[67]

---

66. *WWG*, xxxii.
67. *WWG*, xxxii.

Bavinck, like Kuyper, appreciated the works of their "fathers," which referred not just to the patristic, medieval, and Reformed orthodox but also the divines of their preceding nineteenth-century generation. But this appreciation generated no desire for repristination. While maintaining the same faith, Bavinck and Kuyper sought to dress that faith in new forms in order to meet the needs of their day. This, too, is a product of their convictions concerning the catholicity and multiformity of the church. The universal faith expresses itself in diverse ways in each place and generation.

This does create lingering questions: Is not truth unchangeable? Are they compromising the clarity and objectivity of the truth when they admit that each generation requires a new form of expression? On what basis can one distinguish clearly between form and essence? How does one maintain the freedom of the organic spirit of the church's personalities without imposing external unity?[68] Bavinck comes closest to defining that essence of Christianity in his direct discussion of the matter in his 1906 essay on this topic. He suggests that three core claims are indisputable within that essence: (1) that there is a distinction between the truths Christ revealed and our reception of the truth, (2) true Christianity is revealed in the Scriptures, and (3) Christ is not only historically but doctrinally authoritative. Bavinck further suggests that this essence is much broader than Christology, though one finds the center there: "We cannot stop with Christ. Just because he is the subject and the object, the core and the center of the gospel, he is not its origin nor its final destination."[69]

These are pressing questions worth pondering, especially when we consider that scholars following Bavinck and Kuyper applied the distinction between form and content not to the expression of orthodoxy per se but to the nature of Scripture itself. That is, is there a distinction to be made "between the form and content of the Bible [*tussen vorm en inhoud van de bijbel*]"?[70] Such a distinction opens the possibility of claiming that

---

68. Questions such as these stand behind Wood's identification of certain tensions in Kuyper's thought: "the tensions of [Kuyper's] theology appeared in topics such as the role of doctrinal confessions, democratic church polity, and his experience with American revivalism, which Kuyper dealt with on an ad hoc basis" (*Going Dutch in the Modern Age*, 73).

69. Bavinck, "Essence of Christianity," 42–43, 47.

70. Van Keulen, *Bijbel en Dogmatiek*, 243. See also Bruce Pass, "Upholding *Sola Scriptura* Today: Some Unturned Stones in Herman Bavinck's Doctrine of Inspiration," *International Journal of Systematic Theology* 20 (2018): 517–36.

though the form of Scripture might contain errors, it is the spiritual or soteriological essence that ought to be preserved. We will come back to this question and questions like these in chapter 5, after considering the relation between God's revelation and human reason in neo-Calvinism.

IV

Revelation and Reason

As the flower was already present in the seed, and unfolded itself from it by a lawful development, so does the clear conception spring slowly from a process in our world of thought, which primarily at least went on altogether outside our consciousness. ... From that unconscious substrata of our life germinates first of all impression. This impression is first defined by the word by which it is expressed. The idea which impels us springs from it but gradually.

—Abraham Kuyper, Encyclopedia of Sacred Theology: Its Principles

Natural theology is not taken by us in that worn-out sense in which, at the close of the seventeenth century, a barren scheme of individual truths was framed, which was made to stand as natural theology alongside of the supernatural. Natural theology is with us no scheme, but the knowledge of God itself, which still remains in the sinner and is still within his reach, entirely in harmony with the sense of Rom. 1:19 and Rom. 2:14.

—Abraham Kuyper, Encyclopedia of Sacred Theology: Its Principles

THIS CHAPTER OUTLINES the neo-Calvinistic account of general revelation. We argue that the neo-Calvinists affirmed the classical Reformed doctrine of general revelation, according to which image bearers of God have the rational capacity to receive God's revealing work in creation, history, and the human conscience. Alongside this emphasis on the classical account, the neo-Calvinists *also* provide a romantic emphasis on the *affective* dimensions of revelation's reception. We do not merely know God's existence by way of *cognition*. God's revelation is deeply implanted within the human soul, such that it is *felt* prior to reasoning or willing. This knowledge is not only intuitive or preratiocinative, but also affective and felt. Indeed, for the neo-Calvinists, affections, or feeling, in this context, is less about emotion and is actually considered a subset of knowledge, a "knowledge without concepts." Reasoning occurs within this context of affective knowledge.

This rendering is the result of a theological reinterpretation of philosophical tools in both Romanticism and phenomenology. The conceptual implications of this reinterpretation are as follows: (1) There is a strong distinction between the ubiquity of general revelation and its reception, on the one hand, and an epistemological or cognitive response and articulation of it, on the other. (2) The affirmation that there is a universal knowledge of God implies that image bearers are aware of God prior to the activity of constructing a natural theology. This does not mean that natural theology is impossible, but that natural theology is always a second moment that reflects on the implanted and affective knowledge that is already given by general revelation. Human beings both possess the capacity to receive God's revelation and are always under the exposure of the impressions (*indrukken*) that stem from general revelation. This revelation is an implanted, while not innate, and precognitive attunement (though suppressed), by virtue of God's dynamic acting in the world, and not by virtue of humanity's intellectual articulation of God. General revelation and suppression, then, in accordance with Romans 1, has to do first with matters pertaining to the soul (or psyche), before epistemology.[1]

Because Herman Bavinck in particular has articulated the importance of general revelation more systematically across his corpus, from his 1897 *Beginselen der psychologie* to his 1908 *Philosophy of Revelation*, this chapter

---

1. J. H. Bavinck, *The Church between Temple and Mosque* (Grand Rapids: Eerdmans, 1966), 121. See also Paul Visser, "Religion, Mission, and Kingdom: A Comparison of Herman and Johan Herman Bavinck," *Calvin Theological Journal* 45 (2010): 124–26.

begins with Bavinck in order to lay out the basic contours of this neo-Calvinistic account of general revelation and reason, while also paying attention to the works of J. H. Bavinck and Abraham Kuyper where they are most relevant.[2] First, we show how these neo-Calvinists characterize general revelation and its reception as an unconscious, affective, and felt knowledge. Second, we show that a theologically appropriate account of natural theology therefore involves recognizing that it is a second moment of reflection and response to that pretheoretical general revelation. Finally, we draw this chapter to a close by noting some salient implications of their doctrine. Due to the philosophically contextualized character of these discussions that are highly attuned to nineteenth-century debates, this chapter will also involve more technical forays into the philosophical vocabulary from which Bavinck draws.

AN ENTRYWAY: *THE WONDERFUL WORKS OF GOD* ON GENERAL REVELATION AND THE FEELING OF DEPENDENCE

Before we get to the more technical writings of Herman Bavinck, his *Wonderful Works of God* (1909) is a helpful entryway into the neo-Calvinistic understanding of general revelation. Indeed, this book condenses much of the themes laid out in his more technical work into an accessible form. There are three aspects of his description of general revelation worth noting that anticipate the fuller discussion below.[3]

First, Bavinck argues that an external revelation of God in nature has to be joined with an internal revelation of God to humanity. This insight was instigated by his psychological studies on religion:

And so too the revelation of God in all the work of His hands would be quite unknowable to man if God had not planted in his soul an inerasable sense of His existence and being. The indisputable fact is, however, that God Himself has added to the external

2. For Herman Bavinck's influence on J. H. Bavinck, see Visser, "Religion, Mission and Kingdom," and his "Introduction," in *The J. H. Bavinck Reader*, trans. James De Jong, ed. John Bolt, James Bratt, and Paul Visser (Grand Rapids: Eerdmans, 2008), 35.

3. A section of this chapter is adapted from Nathaniel Gray Sutanto, "Neo-Calvinism on General Revelation: A Dogmatic Sketch," *International Journal of Systematic Theology* 20.4 (2018): 495–516.

revelation in nature an internal revelation to man. The historical and psychological investigation of religion disclose again and again that religion cannot be explained except on the basis of such an increated sense. Always the investigators return at the end of their study to the proposition they repudiated at its beginning, namely, that man is at bottom a religious creature.[4]

As such, Bavinck emphasizes that while "God reveals Himself *outside* of man; He reveals Himself also *within* man."[5] In other words, both internally and externally, God's revelation is pervasive.

Second, Bavinck links this to the classical Reformed emphases on an inner capacity or *habitus* to see the revelation of God in nature and Calvin's sense of divinity. Thus, within humanity there exists "a drive to find out God in His works and to understand His revelation." Appealing to Paul's language in Romans 1, Bavinck argues that humans have the "ability to see the invisible things of God."[6]

Third, this sense of divinity has two elements. The first element involves a "feeling of absolute dependency"[7] that lies behind all conscious thinking and action:

In the first place, a sense of absolute dependency is characteristic of it. Underneath the mind and will, underneath our thought and action, there is in us a self-consciousness which is interdependent with our self-existence and seems to coincide with it. Before we think, before we will, we *are*, we *exist*. We exist in a *definite* way, and in indissoluble unity with this existence we have a *sense* of existence and a sense of existing *as* we are. And the core of this near identity of self-existence and self-consciousness is the feeling of dependency. In our inmost selves, we are immediately, without benefit of reasoning, that is, and prior to all reasoning—conscious of ourselves as created, limited, dependent beings. ... Man is a "dependent" of the universe. And, further, he is dependent, *together*

---

4. *WWG*, 26.
5. *WWG*, 26.
6. *WWG*, 26.
7. *WWG*, 26–27.

with other created things, and dependent this time in an absolute sense, on God, who is the one, eternal, and real being.[8]

The internal revelation of God thus manifests itself, particularly as a *feeling* of absolute dependence, an affection that lies beneath all of our cognitive and volitional activity. The second element, Bavinck argues, is that which drives us not to discouragement but precisely to a religious affection. This feeling's object is not a generic sense of deity but precisely of the power of God, the "Godhead" himself, that is "of the absolute perfection of God."[9] This sense of the divine causes human beings to desire God in worship. Attending humanity's existence, therefore, is an inescapable feeling of our dependence on the absolute God.

These broad strokes—of (1) the pervasiveness of God's revelation both internal and external to our psyches, (2) the creation of human beings with the capacity to receive divine revelation, and (3) the result that human beings always feel their dependence on God and are stirred toward religious affection—are further codified in much of the neo-Calvinist writings.

REVELATION AND AFFECTION:
A KNOWLEDGE WITHOUT CONCEPTS

Herman Bavinck's most sustained reflections on the role of consciousness and its relation to revelation are found in his *Philosophy of Revelation* and his *Beginselen der Psychologie* (Foundations of Psychology). This focus on consciousness and the role of the psyche was triggered by what he considered to be "the trend" of modern theology, which centers on the issue of "*how* revelation has come about" rather than on its specific content.[10]

---

8. *WWG*, 26–27.

9. *WWG*, 27.

10. *PoR*, 21. As James Bratt comments, the "*Philosophy of Revelation* lectures, delivered on his second trip [to America] registers the maturation of [Bavinck's turn to the subject]," a movement "from without to within," which would "become increasingly characteristic of Bavinck's approach to biblical hermeneutics, to theological reflection, and to cultural commentary." See Bratt, "The Context of Herman Bavinck's Stone Lectures: Culture and Politics in 1908," *BR* 1 (2010): 4. The phrase "from without to within [*van buiten naar binnen*]" is taken from George Harinck, "'Land dat ons verwondert en betoovert.' Bavinck en Amerika," in *Ontmoetingen met Bavinck*, ed. George Harinck and Gerrit Neven (Barneveld: De Vuurbaak, 2006), 35–46. See also Cornelis van der Kooi, "On the Inner Testimony of the Spirit, Especially in H. Bavinck," *Journal of Reformed Theology* 2 (2008), especially 107–9.

New investigations have led theologians to think more carefully about the psychological mediation of revelation's reception.

In the third chapter of the *Philosophy of Revelation*, Bavinck argues that one mistake with subjective idealism is its conflation of psychology and logic. Subjective idealism correctly observes the phenomena internal to the psyche and consciousness, but mistakenly argues that the existence of reality must be deduced from that internal phenomena. In his words: "The mistake of idealism lies in confounding the act with its content, the function with the object, the psychological with the logical nature of perception."[11] By conflating logic and psychology, subjective idealists, Bavinck argues, end up with a radical skepticism that verges on solipsism: one is only ever sure of the contents of consciousness and not of the external world.

In opposition to this process, Bavinck argues that the knowledge of the external world is simply a given feature of human knowing and existence. An awareness of one's finitude and contingency is a definite aspect of creaturely being. In the depths of self-consciousness, "we find at its very root the sense of dependence [*afhankelijkheidsgevoel*]."[12] "In our self-consciousness we are not only conscious of being, but also of something definite, of being the very thing we are."[13] Creatures primordially feel their dependence on external objects (relatively) and God (absolutely). As Bavinck writes explicitly, Schleiermacher was quite right in his claim that consciousness of self involves a consciousness of one's dependence:

And this definite mode of being, most generally described, consists in a dependent, limited, finite, created being. Before all thinking and willing, before all reasoning and action, we are and exist, exist in a definite way, and inseparable therefrom have a consciousness of our being and of its specific mode. The core of our self-consciousness is, as Schleiermacher perceived much more clearly than Kant, not autonomy, but a [feeling] of dependence. In the act of becoming conscious of ourselves we become conscious of

---

11. *PoR*, 56.

12. Herman Bavinck, *Wijsbegeerte der openbaring: Stone-lezingen* (Kok: Kampen, 1908), 64–65, 121.

13. *PoR*, 57.

ourselves as creatures. ... We feel ourselves dependent on everything around us; we are not alone.[14]

What Bavinck maintains, and what subjective idealism rejects, is the
claim that there is something "immediate" about the "existence of both the
world and God." Indeed, "in self-consciousness both the existence and
the specific mode of existence of the self and ego, are revealed." Bavinck
is here arguing that there is a bond between self and reality, between
the self and its knowledge of the self as a unified whole, that is obtained
prior to all thinking. This is a knowledge in consciousness not reducible to the conscious entertaining of propositions that are believed—it
is an assumed consciousness that is part and parcel of one's existence in
the world. Bavinck grounds these claims in the reality of divine revelation: "revelation, is the secret of the mind; in our self-consciousness, independently of our co-operation and apart from our will, the reality of our
ego and of the world is revealed to us."[15] Evoking Acts 14 and 17, Bavinck
ties self-consciousness to the general revelation of God: "God, the creator
of all nature, has not left himself without witness, but through all nature,
both that of man himself and that of the outside world, speaks to him. ...
Revelation alone accounts for the impressive and incontrovertible fact
of the worship of God. In self-consciousness God makes known to us
man, the world, and himself."[16] In his treatment on the unconscious life,
Bavinck relates these moves to Kant's notion of intuition with Augustine's
inner sense of the self:

[In consciousness, there is] observing, remembering, judging, knowing; but also feelings, both sensory and spiritual. ...

14. *PoR*, 57. The older edition's English translation of the word *afhankelijkheidsgevoel* into "sense
of dependence" veils the allusion to Schleiermacher, and hence the word "feeling" is to be preferred.
Schleiermacher's influence on Bavinck has been gradually recognized in the recent literature. See
especially Brock, *Orthodox yet Modern*; Cory Brock and Nathaniel Gray Sutanto, "Herman Bavinck's
Reformed Eclecticism: On Catholicity, Consciousness, and Theological Epistemology," *Scottish Journal
of Theology* 70.3 (August 2017): 319–24.

15. *PoR*, 57–59. Thus Schleiermacher: "If man is not one with the Eternal in the unity of intuition and feeling which is immediate, he remains, in the unity of consciousness which is derived,
forever apart." See Schleiermacher, *On Religion: Speeches to Its Cultured Despisers*, trans. John Oman
(Louisville: Westminster John Knox, 1994), 40.

16. *PoR*, 66.

Consciousness is knowledge, and awareness, "knowing" what goes on inside of me. And second, it is an immediate awareness. It is a knowledge obtained not through external sense organs or through deliberate research and serious study but directly through immediate experience, through an "inner sense' [inneren Sinn], as Kant called it, in imitation of the *sensus interior* of Augustine and the Scholastics. ... This immediate awareness, which is part of and is produced by certain psychic phenomena, has an attendant character: it is a direct and concomitant consciousness.[17]

Bavinck had already elucidated many of these claims in his treatment of the knowing faculty in *Beginselen der Psychologie*. There Bavinck argues that feeling is not a separate faculty, but a specific activity within the knowing faculty in the human psyche. After summarizing the contemporary positions that describe the faculty of feeling (*gevoelvermogen*), Bavinck argues that one of the primary mistakes in the discussion is locating feeling as a separate, individual faculty that runs alongside other faculties (of knowing and desiring): "feeling ... taken in the subjective sense and as an immediate sensation or consciousness of agreeable or unagreeable states, is not a particular faculty, nor can it be." Rather, "As sensation or consciousness [feeling] belongs with all intuitions [beseffen], impressions [indrukken], perception, concepts, and so on, to the knowing faculty [kenvermogen].[18] Feeling considers the same objects of knowledge as the intellect, but knows them in a different mode—again, a knowledge prior to thinking and willing. Appealing to Schopenhauer, Bavinck makes the significant move in *locating feeling as a function of the knowing faculty*. In his words:

17. Herman Bavinck, "The Unconscious," in Bolt, *Essays on Religion*, 176. The gloss for the original German is included in the translation cited. It should be clear here that Bavinck's sense of the word "immediate," as reflected in these passages, does not refer to the acceptance of the notion that creatures can know God in his essence. Bavinck accepts that creatures know God immediately in the sense that this knowledge of God obtains directly because of God's revealing action, but mediately in the sense that revelation never grants us unmediated knowledge of God's essence. "Even in cases where he reveals himself internally in the human consciousness by his Spirit, this revelation always occurs organically and hence mediately. The distance between the Creator and creature is much too great for human beings to perceive God directly" (RD 1:309–10). Where most relevant, we draw the original texts from GD.

18. Herman Bavinck, *Beginselen der Psychologie* (Kampen: Bos, 1897), 55.

Through feeling, we indicate, as Schopenhauer rightly said, all immediate and direct knowing that precedes thinking and reflection, which is in contrast to knowledge in abstract concepts and in the state of reasoning. Just as when something is told, we feel instinctively whether [that which is said] is true or untrue. From here it is decisive that feeling in this sense is not a special [separated] faculty, but a special activity within the knowing faculty.[19]

This articulation of feeling as an immediate awareness, however, should not be mistaken to be a detached contemplation on the truth of propositions. Drawing from nineteenth-century German Romanticism, it is more akin to the type of knowledge derived from our sense of touch or of the inner states of the soul, and to the unconscious ways in which we inhabit the world. This knowledge may obtain apart from conscious reflection, and it is here that he specifies that feeling indicates an inner certainty because it is a knowledge without concepts: "This way of taking cognizance is of the highest significance. ... It is not less certain than [reasoning and thinking], but exceeds far above them in certainty. But it is indeed less clear and conscious, *precisely because it is not a knowledge in concepts [juist omdat zij geen kennis in begrippen]*, and is not the fruit of deliberate reflection and reasoning."[20] This further informs Bavinck's argument that even conscious thought can be unmediated by words: "there is also a kind of thinking, a consciousness, a sense, however unclear, which is non-verbal."[21]

Kuyper offers a discussion on this issue consistent with Bavinck's. When speaking about the emergence of concepts, Kuyper traces them back to unconscious impressions, using language almost identical to

---

19. Bavinck, *Beginselen der Psychologie*, 57, emphasis added. Dutch original: "Door het gevoel duiden wij, zooals Schopenhauer terecht zeide, al die onmiddellijke, rechtstreeksche, aan alle denken en reflectie voorafgaande kennis aan, welke tegen de kennis in abstracte begrippen en redeneeringen overstaat. Zoodra ons iets verteld wordt, voelen wij instinctief, dat het waar of onwaar is. Maar daarmede is dan ook beslist, dat het gevoel in dezen zin geen bijzonder vermogen is, maar eene bijzondere werkzaamheid van het kenvermogen."

20. Bavinck, *Beginselen der Psychologie*, 57–58, emphasis added. These claims are related to Bavinck's understanding of revelation as received *prior to* innate and acquired knowledge, creating impressions and intuitions, in his RD 2:68–73.

21. RD 1:377.

Bavinck's and betraying the Romantic roots of his thought while deploying further organic imagery:

> Speaking, therefore, in the organic sense, this "conception" [*begrip*] was already present *in its germ* in the first impulse that worked in us from the unconscious world of thought; this conception *germinated* in the impression [*besef*]; it *matured* into the idea; it directed us in our practical actions; and finally objectified itself in our forming of the conception. If, on the other hand, you take the "conception" as you grasped it in its completed form, then of course it became observable only at the end of this process of thought, and to you it had its birth at that moment only in which you plucked it.[22]

Notice the organic motif at work in order to describe the incremental progress of a concept's emergence. Impressions in the unconscious world of thought are the seeds of ideas, and ideas are then consciously clarified and matured into concepts. Practice and impression precede conscious conceptual representation.

Bavinck and Kuyper, then, claim that there is an unconscious knowledge that is felt rather than articulated—an immediate awareness that is known by the body not reducible to the forms of justified true belief. One might come to know God, then, without thinking it—knowledge of God remains ubiquitous and universal, rendering all humankind without excuse in a manner not contingent on explicit forms of conceptual thought.

These claims, taken from works that predate and postdate *Reformed Dogmatics*, reveal a strongly Romantic strand in Bavinck's thinking on general revelation. Revisiting his claims in *Reformed Dogmatics* in light of the above analysis would thus prove illuminating, while also providing a fuller picture of his dogmatic thought. In *God and Creation* he follows the classical Reformed understanding of general revelation: that God reveals himself through nature and the human conscience. Bavinck goes on to argue that this revelation has both an objective and a subjective side.[23] On

---

22. *Encyclopedia*, 25; Abraham Kuyper, *Encyclopaedie der Heilige Godgeleerdheid*, 2nd ed. (Kampen: Kok, 1908), 1:26, emphases original.

23. This coheres with Bavinck's emphasis on the correspondence between subject and object throughout his works: "All life and all knowledge is based on a kind of agreement between subject

the objective side, rational agents "get to know things because they exist and after they come into existence … from the world to God." On the other hand, he argues that the objective side of revelation "only highlighted one side of the truth" and requires an analysis of the subjective side of revelation. This includes affirming the classical understanding that humans are born equipped with the apparatus required to reason unto God: "we possess both the capacity (aptitude, faculty) and the inclination (*habitus*, disposition) to arrive at some firm, certain, and unfailing knowledge of God." But, more so, in the subjective side of revelation Bavinck also affirms that God reveals himself primordially and internally, arguing that there is an "'interior impact of revelation upon [humanity's] consciousness" that "precedes" both the implanted and acquired knowledge of God. God exerts a "revelatory pressure."[24]

It is this revelatory pressure that forms the basis for all cognitive acts. "Accordingly, the innate knowledge of God is not opposed to the acquired knowledge of God, for, in a broader sense, also the former can be called acquired. In fact, *God's revelation precedes both*, for God does not leave himself without a witness."[25] This revelation creates impressions (*indrukken*) and intuitions in a manner that correlates with Bavinck's comments on feeling in his analysis of the psyche. These impressions, then, are cognized and thematized by the conscious workings of the mind:

And humans, having been created in the divine image, were gifted with the capacity to receive the impressions [*indrukken*] of this revelation and thereby to acquire some sense and knowledge of the Eternal Being. The innate knowledge of God, *the moment it becomes cognition and hence not only cognitive ability but also cognitive action,*

and object" (RD 1:586). For more on the subject-object relationship in Bavinck, see van den Belt, *Authority of Scripture*, 229–99.; Sutanto, "Herman Bavinck and Thomas Reid," especially 124–31; and Brock and Sutanto, "Herman Bavinck's Reformed Eclecticism."

24. RD 2:69–73.

25. RD 2:73. Though Wolterstorff cites this passage, he makes no notice of this statement and focuses instead only on the immediately formed beliefs of which Bavinck speaks. See Wolterstorff, "Herman Bavinck—Proto Reformed Epistemologist," CTJ 45 (2010): 139. Insofar as Wolterstorff and Plantinga focus solely on knowledge as involving warranted (or justified) true belief, Bavinck's articulation of feeling as knowledge remains elusive. Indeed, if feeling is an activity of knowing, then Bavinck is open to the possibility that knowledge can be had without there being an explicit proposition to be believed. Romantic presence is irreducible to propositional belief.

*never originated apart from the working of God's revelation from within
and without, and is to that extent therefore acquired.*[26]

In a manner consistent with his *Beginselen der Psychologie* and
Philosophy of Revelation (and Kuyper's *Encyclopedia*), Bavinck's *Dogmatics*
contained a strand of Romanticism in his understanding of general revelation alongside the preservation of classical Reformed lines of reasoning
on this dogmatic locus. Though Bavinck included both nonconceptual
and conceptual awareness under the definition of "knowledge," it might
be useful to refer to the former as a kind of *phenomenological* awareness
that precedes explicit conceptual forms of knowledge for clarity's sake.[27]

Conceptually, we suggest that Bavinck's understanding of revelation
as that which precedes the act of reasoning develops Franciscus Junius's
distinction between implanted principles (which he calls "simple intuitive knowledge") and acquired knowledge, with particular sources within
the German Romantic traditions.[28] This use of Romantic philosophy to
recover a proper doctrine of general revelation explains the comment by
Bavinck in which he (whether rightly or not), judges that, after Calvin,
Protestant orthodoxy became a prelude to rationalism, echoing a similar
point made in the citation from Kuyper at the beginning of this chapter:

> Soon, however, Protestant theology started taking the road of ratio-
> nalism. Whereas natural theology was initially an account, in the
> light of Scripture, of what Christians can know concerning God
> from creation, it soon became an exposition of what nonbeliev-
> ing rational persons could learn from nature by the power of their
> own reasoning. ... Voetius still discerned the difference between

---

26. *RD* 2:73; *GD* 2:51. Bavinck expresses this same thought consistently in his Stone Lectures:
"For revelation always supposes that man is able to receive impressions or thoughts or inclinations
from another than this phenomenal world, and in a way other than that usually employed" (*PoR*, 175).

27. For more on the distinction between Bavinck's account of general revelation and the ones
on offer in the period of Reformed scholasticism, see Michael Baldwin, "A Theological Evaluation
of the Views of Herman Bavinck on Natural Theology" (MTh diss., Union School of Theology,
2021). Baldwin also includes a critique of Richard Muller's reading of Herman Bavinck on this issue.

28. Franciscus Junius, *A Treatise on True Theology*, trans. David C. Noe (Grand Rapids:
Reformation Heritage Books, 2014), 148.

this rationalistic argumentation and the Reformed doctrine of natural theology, but later theologians progressively lost sight of it.[29]

Bavinck is thus suggesting that this proper distinction between the affective character of general revelation as meaningful but nonconceptual and prior to active cognition is an appropriate recovery and updating of the older "Reformed doctrine of natural theology."

JOHAN BAVINCK ON GENERAL REVELATION

If Herman Bavinck argued that revelation is initially received in the psyche, known by way of feeling rather than cognition, Johan Bavinck, too, articulated general revelation along these lines.[30] God's general revelation does not imply that humanity ought to know him by the "natural light of reason" alone.[31] In this regard, he argues one must "disentangle" general revelation from the "abstract philosophical accretions" that attended its articulations and set it "in terms of biblical reality."[32] Thinking, reasoning, observing,

---

29. *RD* 2:78. Bavinck cites Francis Turretin, Petrus van Mastricht, and J. H. Alsted here. See Petrus van Mastricht, *Prolegomena*, vol. 1 of *Theoretical-Practical Theology*, trans. Todd Rester, ed. Joel Beeke (Grand Rapids: Reformation Heritage, 2017), 83. It is remarks such as these that stimulate Henk van den Belt's reflections on Bavinck's discontinuity with the Reformed orthodox tradition: "The question arises why Bavinck suggests continuity with the Reformed tradition and does not make the discontinuity explicit. It is possible that he is not fully aware of the discontinuity because he interprets the Reformed tradition from the perspective of modernity and finds a tool in the distinction of the *principium externum* and the *principium internum* to deal with the subject-object dichotomy. It does not seem very likely, however, that Bavinck who is so familiar with Reformed orthodoxy, is completely unaware of the discontinuity. ... In his concept of the *principia* Bavinck fences his position from subjectivism, but the *principium internum* enables Bavinck to give the religious subject a positive place and acknowledge an element of truth in Ethical theology" (*Authority of Scripture*, 249). Muller himself notes that Bavinck's *Certainty of Faith* "follows a line of nineteenth-century scholarship that identifies Reformed orthodoxy as a prelude to rationalism." See Muller, "Kuyper and Bavinck on Natural Theology," *BR* 10 (2019): 25n74. Indeed, Bavinck's remarks there go along with Bavinck's rather offhand critique of the Reformed orthodox here and imply that he continued to uphold this line of reading through to the *Dogmatics*, despite his Reformed orthodox commitments otherwise. See also Bartholomew, *Contours of the Kuyperian Tradition*, 285.

30. This reception of general revelation, it should be noted, is due wholly to the reliable and dynamic action of God as the subject, rather than the human agent.

31. This is not to claim reason ought to play no role in articulating those beliefs. Indeed, the neo-Calvinists argued that reasoning had an appropriate place—the point, however, is that revelation is a primordial feature of creaturely existence precisely because God never leaves himself without a witness, and in a manner that is precognitive.

32. J. H. Bavinck, "Religious Consciousness in History," in Bolt, Bratt, and Visser, *J. H. Bavinck Reader*, 238.

and conscious reflection are not "where God meets" humankind. Rather, "the meeting point of general revelation," J. H. Bavinck writes, is "first of all in the problems inherent in being human, that is, in being a fallen human being."[33] In his reflections on the matter, he surveys a few biblical texts before honing in on the classical locus of Romans 1.

Commenting on Psalm 19, J. H. Bavinck observes that general revelation is paradoxical precisely because God reveals without words: "This passage is all about speech without words, witness without words, that makes an impact on people with invisible force and against which they have no defense because it engulfs them all around in its silent majesty." From Amos 4:13, he argues that there is a direct revealing act of God on what he interprets to be the self-consciousness in human beings. If God "makes known his thoughts to men," then, he reasons, something "of God also exists in the great mystery of that double effect on our self-consciousness. It is directly connected to God."[34] In Psalm 139 and Job 33:14–17, he surmises, revelation is intrinsically personal—an encounter that pervades the individual's conscience. Acts 17, further, teaches that this "language without speech" is intended by God to evoke a response—the universal religious consciousness that produces the pagan religions form precisely that response to general revelation when special revelation is rejected or unavailable.

Finally, J. H. Bavinck argues that Romans 1 declares that God makes himself "manifest" through "voiceless speech."[35] General revelation occurs not so much in the propositions that philosophers infer from an active reflection on nature, but is more primitively related to the relations that image bearers have with their environment and one another, along with the direct workings of God in their consciousness. Accordingly, the meaning of God making it plain (Rom 1:19) to all of humankind is, for J. H. Bavinck, that God "grips them in their inner lives." That this revelation is described to be understood (Rom 1:20) indicates that God's revelation truly penetrates into every human being: "The apostle wants to show

---

33. J. H. Bavinck, "Religious Consciousness and Christian Faith," in Bolt, Bratt, and Visser, *J. H. Bavinck Reader*, 279.

34. J. H. Bavinck, "Religious Consciousness in History," 235–36.

35. J .H. Bavinck, "Religious Consciousness and Christian Faith," 277.

clearly here that it is not only possible, but that it actually happens." This, in turn, renders intelligible why humanity is said to be without excuse. The reason general revelation does not produce true worship, then, is not due to a failure of individual humans to reason unto God such that they are ignorant of him, but only because they suppress this unconscious knowledge in a similarly unconscious fashion. This "repression," J. H. Bavinck reasons, is psychological in nature and irreducible to erroneous epistemological inferences that lead to false beliefs. Suppression "need not be understood as a conscious action. It can develop in total silence in the human heart. I am inclined to understand this in the sense of repression, as the concept of repression has been developed in recent psychology. As a rule, repression occurs unconsciously, but that makes it no less real."[36]

To be sure, J. H. Bavinck's appeal to psychology is not meant to suggest that he adopts uncritically a kind of Freudian emphasis according to which the act of repression so submerges a particular subconscious state or memory such that one can be totally unaware of it. The categories of unconscious knowledge and suppression here are used precisely to argue that it is a real suppression by the sinful psyche—the innermost being of the image bearer. As such, it is a responsible suppression and repression of that which is clearly revealed. Knowledge of God actually happens because God's revelation is penetrative and pervasive—suppression's unconscious character emphasizes not our lack of responsibility but exactly our culpability. Suppression has become so second nature that its occurrence needs no conscious action.[37] In this, Johan Bavinck's analysis of the psyche complements his uncle's, especially as the latter judges that the unconscious is to be related to the soul. A "theory of the unconscious finds support in Holy Scripture insofar as it definitely takes the view that the soul is much richer and deeper than the consciousness ... and it posits this thought as basic to the doctrine of sin."[38]

---

36. J. H. Bavinck, "Religious Consciousness in History," 242, 244.

37. For a recent philosophical exposition of unconscious knowledge and knowing via a kind of second nature compatible with the sketch I offer here, see, for example, Andrew Inkpin, *Disclosing the World: On the Phenomenology of Language* (Cambridge, MA: MIT Press, 2016).

38. Bavinck, "Unconscious," 197.

This emphasis on the holistically personal character of revelation's encounter with the human psyche brings into view the primordial relationship that image bearers have with the created world around them. There is a bond that connects subject and object—a bond through which general revelation comes. General revelation "must be understood more existentially."[39] Speaking in a romantic fashion, Johan Bavinck writes:

> General revelation occurs in the living connection between people and the world around them, in what one could call the symbiotic relationship between people and the world. Older philosophy was once inclined to isolate people too much from the world and to consider humanity in isolation. *It regarded humanity as a subject over against the world. And when it made humanity the object of its study, it placed primary emphasis on humanity's observational and thinking relationship to the world.* We need to keep in mind that humanity exists in an unbreakable and living relationship with the world and that it can never be isolated from it for even one moment.[40]

The upshot seems clear: humanity's reception of general revelation is not contingent on its active use of reasoning, nor is it contingent on its developing an active *habitus* so that people can infer the existence of God from contingent things.[41]

---

39. J. H. Bavinck, "Religious Consciousness and Christian Faith," 278.

40. J. H. Bavinck, "Religious Consciousness and Christian Faith," 278, emphasis added. Visser, in the introduction to the reader, observes that J. H. Bavinck's doctoral thesis argues that "the processes of thinking and learning, far from occurring autonomously, are closely tied to an intuitive apprehension of given reality. It is precisely the operation of this feeling in the process of human reasoning that points to the influence of the human self" ("Introduction," 8).

41. J. H. Bavinck regards this to be in tension with the thought of Roman Catholicism (see especially "Religious Consciousness in History," 256–58). Matthew Levering's description of Thomas Aquinas seems relevant: "Unlike Anselm, then, Aquinas does not think that the fool is actually, in the strict sense, a fool; the fool's statement is not, as Anselm thinks it to be, logically nonsensical. Rather, the fool, due ultimately to the effects of original sin, lacks the speculative *habitus* that would enable him to reason to God from contingent things." See Levering, *Scripture and Metaphysics: Aquinas and the Renewal of Trinitarian Theology* (Oxford: Blackwell, 2004), 59. J. H. Bavinck further suggests that the Reformed account of missions and general revelation are thus different from that of Thomas. In Bavinck's interpretation, Thomas "clearly distinguishes between truths that can be understood through the natural light of human reason and those that must be revealed to humans as mysteries of faith. He proposed that missionaries should first build on general concepts that could be derived from natural theology when they encountered paganism and then seek ways to teach the mysteries of faith from this foundation." See J. H. Bavinck, "General Revelation and the Non-Christian Religions," in Bolt, Bratt, and Visser, *J. H. Bavinck Reader*, 97. It might be illuminating here to consider the neo-Calvinists

IV. Revelation and Reason

As Paul Visser notes, this does not rule out an appropriate place for conscious reflection; "the structured religions demonstrate this reflection" on divine revelation. It does, however, resist a conflation between revelation and the conscious use of natural reason. A focus is then placed on the relational and holistic accounts of knowing that might be eclipsed by an emphasis on explicit awareness and reflection. Image bearers "have a permanent fellowship with God, *even when we are not aware of it*. Human life consists of a continual dialogue with God, a conversation that God continues to initiate. This I-Thou relation comprises the core of our existence." Visser notes that J. H. Bavinck, too, was influenced by Schleiermacher in his account of humanity's religious response to God: "Bavinck had serious reservations about much of Friedrich Schleiermacher's theology. Yet he was influenced by Schleiermacher's notion of religion as the 'feeling of dependence' and wholeheartedly agreed with Schleiermacher's rejection of the rationalistic construct of *religio naturalis*, adopting this as a point of departure for his own work."[42]

The Romantic tinge established by the two Bavincks echoes Kuyper's characterization of the implanted knowledge of God as a result of general revelation. On this, Kuyper writes:

Knowledge of God is implanted, infused into man. It is inseparable from his nature. He cannot shake it off. ... The infused knowledge of God is not something that man possesses. It radiates from God from moment to moment as the steady impression on man's heart of God's omnipresent power. God has made of man's heart a mirror. That mirror may be split and broken but it still reflects God's radiance, though not His true image. The *human heart*, though fallen, remains open to knowledge of God. Our philosophers may talk proudly of our capacity for knowing God, but the Church speaks of the majestic impression of the Lord that bears down on all men.

Thus, the natural knowledge of God is not acquired through training or study. It is infused into all men. That is why all people

---

as upholding a (Romantic) mixture of what Lydia Schumacher has described as the *concursus* and *influentia* models of divine illumination. See especially her *Divine Illumination: The History and Future of Augustine's Theory of Knowledge* (Oxford: Blackwell, 2011), 142–78.

42. Visser, "Introduction," 34, 44–45, emphasis added.

share in it. It is inseparable from human nature and belongs to man as a human being.[43]

This description is consistent with Kuyper's rather lengthy analysis of the innate (or, rather, implanted) knowledge of God in his *Encyclopedia*. There, he further argues that God's manifestation of himself in our being, prior to our "logical action" working in us, only produces "nothing in me beyond perceptions, impressions, and feelings." Indeed, "the seed of religion must unfold the flower-bud in the *word*."[44] Hence, James Bratt is right to observe that Kuyper characterizes the knowledge of God Romantically. Though often suppressed due to the entrance of sin, the knowledge of God in Eden was an "immediate intuition," impinging on the hearts of God's image bearers—here, "Kuyper's Romanticism was also at work again."[45]

REASON WITHIN REVELATION

Returning to Herman Bavinck's account of the nature and function of natural-theological proofs, with the previous section in view, proves illuminating. Two facets pertaining to the structure of Bavinck's thought, however, ought to be kept in mind as we do so. First, though Bavinck distinguishes between general revelation and rational reflection, thereby subordinating the latter and not endowing it with revelational authority, Bavinck does see a place for the diligent exercise of renewed reason to render that knowledge in more explicit forms. Attending to the soul as the subject of conscious and unconscious life, Bavinck argues that representations arise from the intuitions and impressions gathered in ordinary living.

Representations are not the first and the primary thing in the conscious life of the soul. There are also sensations, impressions

---

43. Abraham Kuyper, "The Natural Knowledge of God," trans. Harry van Dyke, BR 6 (2015): 75, emphasis mine. These comments go well with Kuyper's account of the prereflective life of the individual and society in his 1908 political address, *Ons Instinctieve Leven* (Amsterdam: W. Kirchner, 1908). English translation: Abraham Kuyper, "Our Instinctive Life," in Bratt, *Abraham Kuyper: A Centennial Reader*, 255–77 (see especially 276–77). Kuyper's account of the "common" and instinctive life of the people, it is worth noting, is more Romantic than Reidian. See George Marsden, "The Collapse of American Evangelical Academia," in *Faith and Rationality: Reason and Belief in God*, ed. Alvin Plantinga and Nicholas Wolterstorff (Notre Dame, IN: University of Notre Dame Press, 1983), 250.

44. *Encyclopedia*, 269, emphasis original.

45. Bratt, *Abraham Kuyper: Modern Calvinist*, 209.

[*indrukken*], awareness [*beseffen*], intuitions, instinct, and so on. A representation is actually only the name for the product of a sensation or recollection, and cannot include all of the activity of consciousness.[46]

To be sure, he reminds his readers that this activity of the psyche is not to be confused with conscious thinking and willing. Representations are worked on by "the soul [*de ziel*], produced or reproduced, connected or distinguished," he writes, "consciously or unconsciously, with or without her will."[47]

The role of reason, then, is to work with these representations and to bring about concept formation. In short: "thinking is the processing of representations into concepts [*voorstellingen tot begrippen*], of judging and determining, of tracing in the world of perception the thoughts on which they rest, of the law according to which they are governed."[48] This is stated more explicitly in his *Philosophy of Revelation*, where Bavinck demarcates a clear line that distinguishes between the unconscious life of representations, on the one hand, and the conscious acts of thinking that forms concepts, on the other. He writes, "between perception and intellect, representation and conceptions, association of representations and conceptual thinking, there is a fundamental difference."[49]

Reasoning, therefore, plays a necessary function in the construction of science, and is itself a particularly *human* capacity that distinguishes them from all other creatures. As such, Bavinck can even claim that in a sense it is a "higher activity [*hoogere werkzaamheid*]" of the soul, in turning representations into concepts. Stated succinctly in an Aristotelian fashion, Bavinck claims that "reason is thusly a characteristic of humanity [*De rede is daarom een kenmerk van den mensch*]."[50] When claims like

---

46. Bavinck, *Beginselen der Psychologie*, 39. Dutch original: "Voorstellingen zijn lang niet 't eerste en het een en al in het bewuste leven der ziel. Er zijn ook gewaarwordingen, indrukken, beseffen, intuïties, instincten enz. Eene voorstelling is eigenlijk alleen de naam voor het product eener waarneming of herinnering, en kan niet alle werkzaamheden van het bewustzijn omvatten."

47. Bavinck, *Beginselen der Psychologie*, 40.

48. Bavinck, *Beginselen der Psychologie*, 104.

49. *PoR*, 56.

50. Bavinck, *Beginselen der Psychologie*, 98, 100. See also Bavinck's comments in *RD* 1:231–33. These comments should be balanced by Bavinck's assessment elsewhere: "Medieval scholasticism … owing to various causes held the writings of antiquity, especially of Aristotle, in excessive reverence"

these are situated within Bavinck's broader account of revelation and unconscious knowing, however, it is clear that the work of reason is not to *produce* knowledge, in a movement from ignorance to knowing. Rather, the work involves categorizing, thematizing, and bringing into explicit rational forms the already obtained primordial knowledge produced by the instinctive, intuitive, and relational connectedness that marks the lives of human beings.[51]

Second, Bavinck's comments on natural theology should also be read in light of his structural remarks on general revelation, as found in his *Prolegomena*.[52] There Bavinck argues against forms of dualism that tend to separate natural and supernatural revelation. He sees himself standing on the Reformational recovery of the intrinsic "bond between special and general revelation." Bavinck argues that the Reformed were responding to a dualistic structure in Roman Catholic prolegomena, according to which "knowing and believing, reason and authority, natural and supernatural revelation, occur dualistically side by side."[53] As such, the "Reformation took over this distinction between natural and supernatural revelation while nevertheless in principle assigning a very different meaning to it," for the Reformers insisted that Scripture and illumination were necessary to read general revelation properly.[54]

Further, because general and special revelation have the same source, namely, God, "all revelation … is supernatural."[55] Though Bavinck keenly

---

(*PoR*, 42).

51. Bavinck, again, is consistent with Kuyper on this point: "Still, we may never conclude that the instinctive life alone has value to us, as though reflection could safely be neglected if not eliminated. We have always had a different view of the matter, as is evident from the founding of the Free University. We have consistently stressed that a higher and more certain development of our conscious life calls for reflection, and that a political-social-religious group that neglects to arm itself with learning runs the risk of degenerating into a merely emotional undertaking" (Kuyper, "Our Instinctive Life," 266).

52. See also the fruitful critical engagement with Bavinck on natural theology in Duby, *God in Himself*, 112–16.

53. *RD* 1:304–5. Bavinck repeated this remark in opening of his Stone Lectures, but in relation to nature and grace: "The Reformation brought a change in so far as it endeavoured to transform the mechanical relation between nature and grace of Rome into a dynamic and ethical one" (*PoR*, 3).

54. *RD* 1:304.

55. *RD* 1:307. James Eglinton calls this "Bavinck's '*Nee!*'" (in parallel to Barth's *Nein*) to natural revelation (*Trinity and Organism*, 139).

affirms that Protestants and Catholics agree on natural revelation's insufficiency for salvific matters, he still believes that the Reformers improved Aquinas's account. In Bavinck's reading Thomas argues that "human beings can—without supernatural grace—know natural truths."[56] Bavinck thinks that the Reformed emphasis on common grace is theologically more fitting to account for the real presence of true beliefs in unregenerate creatures.[57] So Eglinton: "Medieval and neo-Thomism ... [Bavinck] claims, are riddled with a series of (what Bàvinck sees as unbiblical) dualisms: religion as *natural* and *supernatural*, doctrinal articles as *mixed* and *pure*, the human being *in a natural state* and *with superadded gifts* and so forth."[58]

Steven Duby summarizes Bavinck's concerns about natural theology well:

> Bavinck is critical of what he calls a "dualistic" account of the
> · natural knowledge of God in Thomas's writings and in Roman
> Catholicism. ... According to Bavinck, Roman Catholicism places
> the knowledge of God from nature alongside the knowledge of God
> from supernatural revelation without sufficiently integrating the
> two. This framework encourages a "rationalism in the sphere of
> natural revelation" that downplays the effects of sin on the human
> mind in its pursuit of God. It also implies that the knowledge gained
> from supernatural revelation so exceeds the human intellect (not
> merely the *fallen* intellect) that the result is (though Bavinck does
> not explicitly use the term here) a fideism about Christian dogma
> that would logically undermine rational exploration of the truth of
> supernatural revelation. In Bavinck's view, the Reformed tradition
> stresses the need for the illumination of the truths of natural reve-
> lation by God's revelation in Scripture and by the renewing work
> of the Holy Spirit. Thus, Reformed theology, at least in the earlier
> expressions of it in the seventeenth century, circumvents an auton-
> omous natural theology and places natural theology firmly under

---

56. *RD* 1:319. For the sake of emphasis, the question of whether Bavinck's interpretation of Aquinas is correct is a separate question.

57. *RD* 1:319.

58. Eglinton, *Trinity and Organism*, 40.

the tutelage of Christian dogmatics. It also insists that while the truths of supernatural revelation cannot be produced or legislated by reason, their content eludes or reproves not reason as such but only fallen reason in its hostility to the truth of God.[59]

One should keep these moves in mind when one comes to Bavinck's treatment of the natural-theological proofs in the second volume of his *Dogmatics*. The natural-theological proofs are not to be taken as natural truths erected in anticipation of supernatural truths. Rather, the Reformed "incorporated it in the doctrine of faith."[60] If it is God "who reveals himself in his handiwork," it "presupposes that it is not humans who, by the natural light of reason, understand and know this revelation of God."[61] This pattern of reasoning is consistent with Kuyper's:

> No conclusion can be drawn to the infinite, neither can a Divine reality be known from external or internal phenomena, unless that real God reveals Himself in my consciousness to my ego; reveals himself as God; and thereby moves and impels me to see in these finite phenomena a brightness of His glory. *Formaliter*, neither observation nor reasoning would ever have rendered service here as the principium of knowing.[62]

The conscious acts of reasoning concomitant to the construction of a natural theology that produces true theology (*theologia vera*) require special revelation. Further, in keeping with the first observation in this section above, rational reflection is a second moment that testifies to what all creatures know nonconceptually in their consciousness, turning that into articulated concepts. Proofs of God's existence are testimonies to the knowledge revealed in one's consciousness, and the moral proof is itself no exception: "Even the moral proof is the product of the moral consciousness inherent in humans. In both cases it is the complete revelation

---

59. Duby, *God in Himself*, 112–13. See also his response to Bavinck's concern on pages 124–25. His reading of Bavinck on Aquinas here is identical with Sutanto, *God and Knowledge*, ch. 4.

60. *RD* 2:78. Bavinck sets this in contrast to the "general view," according to which "one stood on a rational scientific foundation prior to and apart from faith. And to this day Rome and Roman Catholic theology still maintain the same rationalistic foundation" (*RD* 2:77).

61. *RD* 2:74.

62. *Encyclopedia*, 343.

of God that introduces the knowledge of God into our consciousness."
Scripture addresses those already addressed by God—it appeals not "to
the reasoning intellect but to the human heart and conscience."[63] It speaks
with power precisely because it invokes the knowledge that human beings
already feel in their consciousness and thus cannot be ignored. In the
same fashion, the proofs of God's existence as reinterpreted by Scripture
witness to and resonate with what creatures have long felt to be true.

These claims serve as the lens through which Bavinck went on to consider the strengths and weaknesses of the proofs of God's existence. The
upshot of his discussion is that none of the proofs are logically unassailable, but nevertheless they are useful insofar as they are considered as
expressions produced by faith of that which is primordially felt in one's
ethical and religious consciousness. In other words, the intellect takes
that which is impressed on consciousness and gives it conceptual form.
Summarizing eloquently, Bavinck wrote this:

> Faith attempts to give an account of the religious *impressions* [*indruk-
> ken*] and *feelings* [*aandoeningen*] that we humans receive and carry
> with us in our soul [*ziel*]. That faith also exerts its influence on the
> intellect, which in turn seeks little by little to introduce some order
> in that chaos of impressions and notions [*indrukken en beseffen*]. It
> classifies them. ... Impressions come to us from the world of ideas
> (the ontological argument); from the world of finite, contingent,
> and mutable things (the cosmological arguments); from the world
> of beauty and harmonious design (the teleological argument); from
> that of moral order (the moral argument); from the speech and his-
> tory of all humankind (the universal consent and the historical argu-
> ment). However, although these impressions may be so classified,
> no one should ever think that the six proofs are the sole, isolated
> testimonies God sends us. ... Both from within and from without,
> God's witness speaks to us. God does not leave himself without a
> witness, either in nature or history, in heart or conscience.[64]

---

63. RD 2:74, 76.
64. RD 2:90; GD 2:72.

Bavinck's rather antiquated use of the word *aandoening*, coupled with the impressions (*indrukken*) received from the religious sphere, seems significant. The word, in this context, implies a particularly potent emotional stirring uncontrollable by the patient.[65] These religious feelings, in turn, are worked on by the intellect in order to produce a conceptualized articulation that forms the natural-theological proofs for God's existence. Christians, armed with the spectacles of Scripture, are equipped to reflect on this revelation precisely because the articulated proofs witness to "their own religious and ethical consciousness."[66] Scripture articulates and connects with that which is already felt.

Seen especially in light of Bavinck's analysis of impressions in one's consciousness and feeling as a feature of the knowing faculty in his *Beginselen der Psychologie* and his later Stone Lectures, general revelation is consistently located in the realm of the nonconceptualized, and rational reflection on that revelation is always a second moment. The result is a firm distinction between revelation and human cognition, along with a clear demarcation between general revelation and natural theology. Hence revelation is anterior to reason. Stating a truth about God is not revelation, but a response to revelation. The moment propositions or concepts are articulated to describe what one receives in general revelation, one moves into the realm of natural theology or reflections that arise from that revelation, unless those propositions are the ones themselves revealed by Scripture.[67]

One finds these same emphases in Kuyper and J. H. Bavinck. Kuyper describes natural theology this way:

> Natural theology has often been portrayed as a process whereby man calmly contemplates nature, observing its order, regularity and beauty, and from there ascends to a recognition of God's

---

65. We are grateful to Koos Tamminga and Marinus de Jong for bringing this to our attention.

66. *RD* 2:91.

67. While Mats Wahlberg argues that revelation necessarily involves propositional content against those who argue that revelation is essentially nonpropositional, it seems that the neo-Calvinists are arguing that revelation could be transmitted in both nonpropositional and propositional means. In other words, though revelation could contain, and indeed, is perhaps more clearly transmitted through, propositions, this is not necessarily the mode by which God reveals. See Wahlberg, *Revelation as Testimony: A Philosophical-Theological Account* (Grand Rapids: Eerdmans, 2014).

great power. Nothing is further from the truth. For ordinary man, such calm contemplation is an exception. Our constant contact with nature directly affects our life, our body, our struggle for survival. Not abstract reflection but restless, painful experience has acquainted us with the power of nature.[68]

The same themes are invoked: the positing of an opposition between intellectual contemplation and holistic recognition, a primordial "contact" with nature from a detached reflection on it, and so on. Kuyper's natural theology is a kind of whole-souled response to this ongoing and prereflective contact with nature. He explicitly locates the "natural knowledge of God" in the "unconscious" and states that natural theology is the attempt to "account for those *feelings and wonders* that is causing his *heart* to tremble."[69] Likewise, J. H. Bavinck writes:

If we wish to use the expression "general revelation" we must not do so in the sense that one can logically conclude God's existence from it. This may be possible, but it only leads to a philosophical notion of God as the first cause. But that is not the biblical idea of "general revelation." When the Bible speaks of general revelation, it means something quite different. There it has a much more personal nature. ... God's deity and eternal power are evident; they overwhelm man; they strike him suddenly. ...They creep up on him; they do not let go of him, even though man does his best to escape them.[70]

---

68. Kuyper, "Natural Knowledge of God," 78. Kuyper relates this notion of revelation to science in that it prevents scholars from presuming that academic inquiry is always necessary for human flourishing "by means of his revelation." He argues that humans in every age have "rich" knowledge "in their heart, in their soul" that bears the "mark of the eternal." "Scholars, then, must begin by being rich in that faith if they are ever to feel their heart stir with the holy impulse that drives them to engage in true scholarship." See Abraham Kuyper, *Scholarship: Two Convocation Addresses on University Life*, trans. Harry van Dyke (Grand Rapids: Christian's Library Press, 2014), 9.

69. Kuyper, "Natural Knowledge of God," 76.

70. Bavinck, *Church between Temple and Mosque*, 124. For an exploration of the implications of these dogmatic insights to a theology of religion, see Daniel Strange, *Their Rock Is Not Like Our Rock: A Theology of Religions* (Grand Rapids: Zondervan, 2015).

Once again, the neo-Calvinists argue that general revelation has affective dimensions that need to be taken seriously.

CONCLUSION

Some significant implications follow. First, general revelation, for the neo-Calvinists, produces an affective and implanted knowledge of God quite independently of the exercise of creaturely reason. Again, this is not to deny the importance of rational reflection in order to produce in more explicit forms what is already known by general revelation. Rather, such rational reflections are always second moments—they are always provisional and ought to be normed by special revelation.

Second, this chapter illumines Bavinck's self-conscious philosophical eclecticism, a point first made in the previous chapter. Throughout Bavinck's oeuvre, one encounters numerous passages in which he argues that theology is not bound to a single philosophical handmaiden, but is "not per se hostile to any philosophical system and does not, a priori and without criticism give priority to the philosophy of Plato or Kant or vice versa."[71] Precisely because philosophy is a subordinate reflection on general revelation, all philosophical explorations can be subject to revision and reconsideration. Every age grasps at truth. Calvinism, then, "is sufficiently pliant and flexible to appreciate and appropriate what is good in our [modern] age."[72] As emphasized earlier, the neo-Calvinists held that truth was approximated and developed by the philosophical and cultural milieus throughout a diversity of places and times. We submit that Bavinck's distinction between general revelation as preconceptual and a rational reflection of it as a secondary moment is what accounts for this neo-Calvinistic philosophical flexibility. This modus operandi is characterized by an openness, because no single philosophical handmaiden is invulnerable from reconsideration, and flexible, because other handmaidens can become organically connected to one's theology. Thus, for example, there is no need to choose between Herman Bavinck the Thomist or the

---

71. *RD* 1:609.
72. Bavinck, "Future of Calvinism," 21.

Romantic. He saw himself as free to use sources from both intellectual traditions while never subscribing to either as an "ism."[73]

Third and finally, an attention to the Romantic tinge of neo-Calvinism's doctrine of revelation allows us to retrieve the centrality of intuitions and affections for a robust theological anthropology. Though reasoning is indeed an important part of what it means to be human, the affections are no less so—a holistic anthropology and revelation emphasize the importance of both of these dimensions. Rather than suggesting that reasoning is reliable, while the affections are pliable and a source of confusion and uncertainty, we do well to suggest that the affections remain a way of knowing in congruence with, rather than in competition against, a diligent use of the intellect.

---

73. See especially Brock and Sutanto, "Herman Bavinck's Reformed Eclecticism."

V

Scripture and Organism

*That the treatment of the principium of Theology, i.e. of the Holy
Scripture, is given so much space could not be avoided. In all this
controversy the Holy Scripture is the question at stake, and the
encyclopedia that places itself unconditionally upon the Scriptures
as its basis cannot find a plan until the all-embracing question of the
Scriptures has been fundamentally solved.*

—*Abraham Kuyper*, Encyclopedia of Sacred Theology: Its Principles

W HILE NEO-CALVINISM AS a dogmatic standpoint is often associated
with the doctrine of common grace or eschatology, it is perhaps
surprising to some readers to note that, from the perspectives of Kuyper
and Bavinck, it is precisely the doctrine of Scripture in which they had to
do the most extensive work. Kuyper was prompted by the controversies
that surrounded this locus in his day concerning the reliability and his-
toricity of the narratives of Scripture and the use of Scripture in theology
and the other sciences. Bavinck, too, argued that the doctrine of Scripture
was one particular doctrine that they sought to defend and rearticulate in
light of the newer knowledge of the modern era.[1] Indeed, "Bavinck saw
the rise of modern theology's emphasis on the humanness of Scripture

---

1. Bavinck, "Modernism and Orthodoxy," 96. See also Eglinton on the context within which
Bavinck developed his doctrine of Scripture (*Trinity and Organism*, 161–68). Bavinck's doctrine of
Scripture has been the focus of much scholarly debate as well: see especially Eglinton, *Trinity and
Organism*, 155–58; Pass, "Upholding *Sola Scriptura* Today."

as a necessary response to pre-modern theology's inadequate handling of the topic."[2] They both saw the need, therefore, to show that Scripture properly belongs to and aids the university sciences, and that a recognition of Scripture's divine origins need not compromise appreciation for its human authors.

Bavinck argues that the historical investigations of the modern era correspond well with the opening words of the book of Hebrews: "God spoke to our forefathers at many times and in various ways."[3] These newer avenues of research prompt the responsible Christian scholar to give an account of the historical and psychological means by which Scripture is produced—to give an account of not merely divine authorship but the human instruments by which God authored Scripture:

> The preceding gives us the right and the obligation to research the psychological and historical conditions in which revelation, inspiration, incarnation, and regeneration have occurred and to cast light on the organic character of all these wondrous facts. All of Scripture preaches the unity of God, that is, the unity of the God of nature and of the God of grace, and therefore it cannot dualistically separate creation and recreation, for it always binds them organically and harmoniously together. Discerning and demonstrating this connection, therefore, belongs to the task of scholarly theology.[4]

In the rest of this chapter, we develop Kuyper and Bavinck's account of Scripture with particular attention to its unique construction. What, in their own view, were the distinct features of their doctrine? What makes, in their judgment, an *organic* account of Scripture, rather than a mechanical one? This involves at least two moves: investigating the relationship between theology and Scripture with the other sciences, and then unpacking the doctrine of the organic inspiration of Scripture itself.[5]

---

2. Eglinton, *Trinity and Organism*, 165.

3. Bavinck, "Modernism and Orthodoxy," 105.

4. Bavinck, "Modernism and Orthodoxy," 105.

5. On this former issue on the organic nature of theology, Kuyper locates the emergence of this understanding within his day: "in the sense in which we now interpret the domain of theological

This chapter shows that Kuyper and Bavinck defined Scripture as the *principium* of theology, without which the construction of true theology would not be possible. Though Scripture is not a manual for the other sciences, it remains authoritative for the other scientific disciplines as science ultimately forms a united organism. Scripture, in their understanding, is the book for humanity. This affirmation, however, must be coupled with a vital articulation of the organic character of scriptural inspiration. This chapter thus moves on to Kuyper's and Bavinck's articulation of the organic relationship among Scripture, theology, and the other sciences, and then to their articulation of organic inspiration.

SCRIPTURE'S AUTHORITY
AND THE ORGANISM OF SCIENCE

The starting point for understanding Scripture's authority, for the theology of Kuyper and Bavinck, is Kuyper's firm distinction between *the exact sciences* on the one hand and the *system* underlying them on the other. Attending to this distinction clears away possible misconceptions, particularly that the emphasis on Scripture's authority in the organism of science implies that Scripture is the only source through which all knowledge is derived. Rather, the authority of Scripture fits in the formation of a *system* or a worldview through which one interprets the deliverances of the exact sciences and places them into their proper places within the organism of knowledge. General and special revelation both serve as sources of knowledge, but special revelation is the means by which a Christian world- and life-system is constructed.

Kuyper introduces this distinction when discussing the common mistake that "all of our knowledge about nature and the world should be derived from Scripture." Emphatically, Kuyper argues that the objects of our study function as the sources for our knowledge of those objects—we learn about animals by studying animals, geology by studying the earth, and so on, and "it would be a sin of omission to delight in Scripture while closing the other book of nature and human life and pushing it aside."[6]

---

studies as one organic whole, the science of Theology has now been born in our century" (*Encyclopedia*, 292; see also 291–95).

6. *Pro Rege* 1:201–2.

Such a move, either closing the book of nature or relegating all knowledge to Scripture, would produce a one-sided dualism that is reducible to naturalism or biblicism. Kuyper's call, therefore, is for Christians to learn as much as they can from the deliverances of the world's scholarship.

Here Kuyper makes a firm distinction between the deliverances of that scholarship and the *system* that unbelievers often form beneath them: "In order to understand this, you need only to consider the distinction between what all these sciences offer as the results of strict research and the system that they construct on their own and make to rest upon conjecture and presuppositions."[7] The empirical data that these studies yield command one's agreement, but not so with the systems under them, or their interpretative frameworks. For Kuyper, Paul's warnings against the wisdom of the Greeks and the necessity of standing on the wisdom that comes from God are an antithesis between *systems* rather than one of empirical data:

> First, there were the results derived from strictly regulated research; second, there were the thought systems concerning world and life erroneously constructed upon conjecture. The Greeks offered the latter to the world, however, as their wisdom and their philosophy. Thus, when the apostle turned against the Greek's over inflated wisdom, he was not saying anything against strict science but rejected only whatever scholars and scientists presented about things concerning which they knew nothing.[8]

Hence the issue, for Kuyper, is not the good work that unbelieving scholarship generates, but that these scholars may *transgress* their jurisdiction and predicate on *systematic* matters that lie entirely beyond their domain: "Researchers in the exact sciences constantly allowed themselves into an arena that was not theirs, and they tried to construct all kinds of systems for which they simply lacked the support."[9] This tendency to move from the exact sciences to system building is explainable by

---

7. *Pro Rege* 1:203.
8. *Pro Rege* 1:204.
9. *Pro Rege* 1:207.

what James Bratt considers to be a "fundamental and recurrent axiom in Kuyper," namely, that "thought by its very nature tends toward system."[10] Kuyper, then, argues that Scripture produces a system antithetical to the wisdom of the world. The Christian world- and life-view is not set against the deliverances of the sciences per se, but accommodates and grounds the data that the researcher produces.

> What Scripture does address and attack as false science, as erroneous wisdom, as fake philosophy, is the illusion of certainty that unbelieving thinkers of that time imagined they could claim for a system resting on nothing but conjectures, suspicions, and assumptions. The object of the exact sciences is the visible, audible, and tangible world. This is their field of strength, and as long as they limit themselves to that and are based on accurate investigation, they deserve confidence, praise, and gratitude.[11]

The exact sciences, however, do not provide any insight on the "unifying plan," the telos, or the divine government behind all things.[12] Christians ought to reject the systems they raise and then supplant these with their own:

> Any time we come upon systems built on suppositions and assumptions that attempt to explain or discard spiritual questions about which there can be no knowledge without faith, we deny it the label of science that it has usurped for itself, and from our side we try to posit over against it the Christian life-and worldview based on what God has revealed to us.[13]

This, then, is the function of the authority of holy Scripture. The deeper the sciences push through to the reality of things, the clearer they encounter the divine origin of all things. Divine ideas undergird all of reality, and the Logos is the one through whom and in whom all things exist.

10. Abraham Kuyper, "The Blurring of the Boundaries," in Bratt, *Abraham Kuyper: A Centennial Reader*, 373–74. Bratt's comment is the note on this line, in 374n20.

11. *Pro Rege* 1:208.

12. *Pro Rege* 1:208.

13. *Pro Rege* 1:209.

"Scripture does not lock Christ up within the sphere of grace or within the world of humanity; it places all creation—the visible and the invisible, both on the earth and beneath the earth—in direct dependence on Christ."[14] Excluding nothing from the Son, Kuyper cites Colossians 2:3 to the effect that in Christ are "all the treasures of knowledge and wisdom": "All study of nature, as well as psychology, anthropology, ethnology, or anything else, is the radiance of a new glory that is hidden in Christ. ... This is because we see in it the sacred mark of its origin and because we know that it is only a small part of 'all the treasures of wisdom and knowledge' that are hidden in Christ."[15]

This distinction equips us to look back on Kuyper's construction in his *Encyclopedia*. There he describes the task of the encyclopedist to produce within one's consciousness an "*organism* of science" that replicates the organic reality of the cosmos. The ideal "Encyclopedist who is a man of science interprets that knowledge as a *system*, and understands it consequently as *science*."[16]

An articulation of the organism of science does not involve the mere collection and placement of facts or different academic disciplines side by side, but rather constructs an arrangement that traces the connectedness of each fact. Kuyper uses many colorful analogies to communicate this central point, distinguishing between a lexicon and an organic encyclopedia. While a lexicon merely observes limbs, flesh, and bones, an encyclopedia sees a body; while a lexicon organizes medicines by their uses and packaging (in bottles or powders), the encyclopedia "must enter upon the organic relations of this world of medicines and from this derive a principle for determining the arrangement."[17]

Hence, as a science of the sciences, an encyclopedist needs to discern the unity between all the different sciences and articulate the relationship of the parts with the whole. This means that while there exists a diversity of academic disciplines, all of these disciplines relate into a larger organism of science. The organism of science, then, depends on the nature of reality

---

14. *Pro Rege* 1:212.

15. *Pro Rege*, 1:213

16. *Encyclopedia*, 29, emphasis original.

17. *Encyclopedia*, 30.

itself as organic, as all things stand in organic relationship.[18] Kuyper's description here is worth quoting in full:

> Science, in its absolute sense, is the pure and complete reflection of the cosmos in the human consciousness. As the parts of all actually existing things lie in their relations, so must the parts of our knowledge be related in our consciousness. As a country is sketched on a chart, and we succeed even better, as cartography advances, in sketching the country upon the chart just as it is, so also must science convert the actually existing cosmos into the logical form. The further science advances, the easier it will be to reproduce the cosmos logically, and to make all its parts to be clearly seen, together with their several relations. And thus science divides itself, because in proportion as the logical reproduction becomes more accurate, it will image in a more organic way whatever exists organically. And so does science begin to show itself to us as an immeasurable field, in which all sorts of divisions and subdivisions must be distinguished, and upon which the mutual relations among these divisions and life is ever more clearly exhibited. It is this organic relation with which Encyclopedia has to deal. The field of our knowledge itself in its organic inter-relations as the object to be investigated by it.[19]

With this general sketch of science in view, Kuyper argues not merely that the encyclopedist is interested in the *scientific* character of theology, as theology necessarily presupposes that the object of its study—God— truly exists, but also that theology is an integral part of the organism of science. Theology, then, remains an independent discipline whose justification depends on its own subject matter, but it also stands in organic relation to the other scientific disciplines.[20] In Kuyper's own words: "the conception of Theological Encyclopedia consists in *the scientific investigation of the organic nature and relations of theology in itself and as an integral*

---

18. *Encyclopedia*, 64–66, 77–78. Kuyper couches this in terms of the subject-object relationship. While the subject engaged in science is humanity as an organic whole, the object of science is reality as an organism itself.

19. *Encyclopedia*, 39.

20. The analysis here is consistent with Bartholomew, *Contours of the Kuyperian Tradition*, 271–82.

part of the organism of science." Theology remains an independent science
amid the organism of the sciences, and it presupposes not merely that this
God exists, but that God himself has made himself known. Echoing the
classical Reformed orthodox commitments of Franciscus Junius, Kuyper
argues that God accommodated his revelation to the needs of finite creatures, producing an ectypal theology in order that rational creatures can
know him scientifically.[21]

This organic relation between theology and the other sciences brings
us to Kuyper's discussion of the necessity of Scripture for apprehend-
ing that organism of science. Grasping the whole and organic character of reality requires the efforts of the whole of humanity. As such, it is
impossible to grasp reality's unity precisely because the investigators of
science do not stand on the same subjective position: "since subjects are
not alike, since different points of departure prevail from one consciousness to another, and since not only differences but contradictions arise
time after time as a result, the illusion of a single science can no longer be
maintained."[22] Christians and non-Christians will thus inevitably produce
conflicting works of scholarship.

This does not mean that Christians and non-Christian would not
observe the same empirical phenomena and data such as counting, weigh-
ing, or measuring.[23] The noetic effects of sin, in other words, do not affect
the reception of *data* per se, but of the *system* that locates the place within
which that data fits within the whole. Hence, Kuyper gladly admires the
great learning, by common grace, of figures such as "Plato and Aristotle,
Kant and Darwin," but insists that their production of "true and essential
knowledge on the one hand" nevertheless "led to a life-conception and a
worldview utterly opposed to the truth of God's Word on the other." As
Kuyper summarizes: "the real darkening of sin is found in something completely different, in our having lost the gift to comprehend the true context,
the proper coherence, the systematic unity of things."[24] This observa-

21. *Encyclopedia*, 54, 211–19, 248, emphasis original.
22. Abraham Kuyper, "Common Grace in Science," *Abraham Kuyper: A Centennial* Reader, ed.
James Bratt (Grand Rapids: Eerdmans, 1998), 453, emphasis original.
23. *Encyclopedia*, 601–2.
24. Kuyper, "Common Grace in Science," 448–49.

tion, then, leads to Kuyper's oft-quoted understanding of two kinds of science stemming from the antithesis between unregenerate and regenerate humanity, respectively.[25]

Since science retraces reality in one's consciousness, science seeks to understand the divine ideas that are reflected within God's created cosmos. Hence, it follows that Christians, who are illumined by the Spirit and informed by Scripture, are better able to grasp that systematic unity through which the data of the empirical sciences are located. "If you agree that the Kingdom of God is not in the least limited to the institutional church but rules our entire world-and-life-view, then Jesus' saying means that only those who have received the inner enlightenment of the Holy Spirit are able to get a view of the whole that is in harmony with the truth and essence of things."[26] As Bartholomew notes, "Theology alone studies palingenesis and that in this regard other disciplines must lean on theology's insights."[27]

This illumination of the Spirit, in turn, enables believers to see the world in light of Scripture. Scripture speaks not merely about salvation, as it "affords certainty on the cardinal questions that govern our entire view of life, and these questions cannot be said to belong to the field of special grace." To the contrary, Scripture, "reveals to us the mystery of creation" and as such is necessary for the construction of a Christian science (meaning Christian scholarship).[28] Kuyper emphasizes this point:

> It is of highest importance to bring this clearly front and center. If special revelation were limited to what belongs strictly to the salvation for sinners and passed everything else by, then we would lack the data for building a temple of science on a Christian foundation. ... Even more, it does not place these two, the way of salvation and natural life, next to each other as in two ticket-lines but intertwines them and offers us a view of the world, its origin, its historical

---

25. *Encyclopedia*, 150–82. On the differences and similarities between Kuyper and Bavinck on this point, see Sutanto, *God and Knowledge*, 93–97.

26. Kuyper, "Common Grace in Science," 458.

27. Bartholomew, *Contours of the Kuyperian Tradition*, 273.

28. Kuyper, "Common Grace in Science," 458–59.

course, and its destiny in which the entire work of redemption fits as in an invisible matrix. With these fixed points in front of us, we are afforded the possibility of constructing an entire Christian science that frees us from idle speculation and gives us knowledge of the real condition of things, as it was, and is, and shall be.[29]

This nuanced understanding of Scripture not as a manual for the sciences yet necessary for the sciences corresponds to Kuyper's placement of theology within the organism of the sciences. While theology "is by no means called upon to arbitrate in every domain of science," it remains necessary to reckon with the fact that regeneration implicates one's construction of science, and it is theology's role to investigate this radical reality. Palingenesis (regeneration) remains the root of science: "real science is born only from the human consciousness that has been restored again to its normal self, and therefore cannot recognize as such the fruit of the working of the still abnormal human consciousness."[30] Hence, Kuyper insists that there is, indeed, a Christian treatment of each field of study, especially those that work more closely with unseen realities.[31] This goes closely with one of Kuyper's favorite images of the relationship between special grace and natural life. Grace is not like "a drop of oil upon the waters of our human life," but is an organic grafting that leavens the whole organism.[32]

The object of science "forms an organic whole," and it is sin that leads us to fail to see its organic character. The science "under the power of re-creation, since it includes theology," possesses "the *missing links*" that mark up the unity of science. To sum up, (1) theology remains an

---

29. Kuyper, "Common Grace in Science," 459–60. This corresponds to Kuyper's appeal to Scripture as a means of epistemologically justifying the corresponding relationship between subjective thought and external reality: "No explanation can ever suggest itself to our senses, of the all-sufficient ground for this admirable correspondence and affinity between object and subject, on which the possibility and development of science wholly rests, until at the hand of Holy Scripture we confess that the Author of the cosmos created man in the cosmos as microcosms 'after his image and likeness'" (*Encyclopedia*, 83).

30. *Encyclopedia*, 226, 602.

31. See, for example, *Encyclopedia*, 602, 613–14.

32. *Encyclopedia*, 397. Kuyper juxtaposes his understanding of Scripture over against Methodism and Rome on pages 403–4.

independent science with its own subject matter, namely, the revealed
ectypal knowledge of God; (2) theology, within the circle of regeneration,
provides the unity that locates the other sciences within the organism of
science; and (3) theology, though an organic part of science, has fixed
boundaries. Kuyper, then, desires no "subserviency of the other sciences
to theology as the queen of the sciences," and envisions a more reserved
relationship where theology takes the results of the other sciences seriously, even as it investigates the organic roots and links between them.[33]

That theology supplies the missing links between the sciences and
its organic shape is not surprising, as it is only sin that has caused the
appearance of division between the human sciences as well as the necessity of a twofold revelation, general and special. God, after all, is behind
both: "In God, who is and always will be Himself the principium of all
being (essential) and all knowing (cognition), nothing else is conceivable
than the unity of principium."[34]

As we turn now to Herman Bavinck, we will see some of the same
emphases. Bavinck's understanding of the organism of science and the
organic relationship among theology, Scripture, and other disciplines has
received more sustained attention and thus can be treated here more summarily and briefly.[35] We will focus on three salient aspects of Bavinck's
thinking in this regard: (1) the leavening role of Christianity for the sciences, (2) the precise way in which Scripture is related to the sciences,
and (3) the production of an organic view of science when conceived in
light of Christian faith.

First, then, Bavinck argues that Christianity not merely advances the
piety of individual lives, but leavens the entire natural order. This includes
the human vocations of marriage, society, art, and science themselves as
functions born of human nature. As commonly observed, Bavinck argues,

---

33. *Encyclopedia*, 602, 606. See also page 397, on the organic and thus universal significance of
the special *principium*.

34. *Encyclopedia*, 389.

35. See especially Sutanto, *God and Knowledge*, chs. 2–3; Wolter Huttinga, "'Marie Antoinette' or
Mystical Depth?: Herman Bavinck on Theology as Queen of the Sciences," in Eglinton and Harinck,
Neo-Calvinism and the French Revolution, 143–54; Michael Bräutigam and James Eglinton, "Scientific
Theology? Herman Bavinck and Adolf Schlatter on the Place of Theology in the University," *Journal
of Reformed Theology* 7 (2013): 27–50.

whether rightly or not, that this is a Reformed conviction, in distinction from both Roman Catholicism and Lutheranism, which, in varying ways, leave much of the natural life untouched by the gospel. One of the clearest passages on this is found in his article on catholicity:

Rome thus maintains the catholicity of the Christian faith in the sense that it seeks to bring the entire world under the submission of the church. But it denies catholicity *in the sense that the Christian faith itself must be a leavening agent in everything.* In this way an eternal dualism remains, Christianity does not become an immanent, reforming reality. This dualism is not an antinomy in which one of the realities annuls the other. Rome does not abolish the natural order in Manichean fashion but suppresses it. It leaves marriage, family, possessions, earthly vocation, the state, science, and art intact and even permits them, in their own place, a greater space and freedom than Protestantism tends to do.[36]

However, his passage is not meant to be read as a triumphalist advocacy of the successes of Protestantism in achieving its leavening ideals. Bavinck argues that the Reformed were "even less successful" than others "in Christianizing life." "Art, science, philosophy, political and social life never fully incorporated the principles of the Reformation. Although dualism was theoretically overcome it remained a practical reality in many areas of life." In broadly Protestant circles, Pietism and Methodism missed a "reformation in the genuine, true, full sense of the word. Instead, individuals are rescued and snatched out of the world—the world lies in wickedness—there is never a methodic, organic reformation of the whole cosmos, of nation and country." He thus laments that the "unbelieving results of science are rejected, but there is *no inner reformation of the sciences on the basis of a different principle.*"[37] It is passages such as these that inform the

---

36. CCC, 231, emphasis mine.

37. CCC, 243, 246, emphases mine. In another place, Bavinck argues that one can detect the lack of an organic reformation even in the encyclopedia of theology:

"Still we must remember that at one time the word *theology* suggested only dogmatics or dogmatic theology. Even when exegesis of Scripture or church history was mentioned, these were often placed separately, next to the theological disciplines, and were sometimes designated as auxiliary disciplines. There was no attempt to develop an organic arrangement of all the theological disciplines. There was

neo-Calvinistic suspicion against any form of dualism, coupled with a conviction that distinctly Christian sources can aid every area of natural human life.

What, exactly, does this "inner reformation" of science look like? It does include, at least, taking the doctrines found in Scripture seriously as resources to rethink the principles and the shape of science. But, like Kuyper, Bavinck qualifies this carefully. "Scripture is not designed to be a manual for the various sciences. It is the first foundation (*principium*) only of theology and desires that we will read and study it *theologically*." Likewise, "the created world is the external foundation (*principium cognoscendi externum*) for all science," and creaturely intelligence, illumined by the Logos, "is the internal foundation of knowledge (*principium cognoscendi internum*)."[38] This is an important qualification: Scripture does not tell us the details of how to conduct an empirical investigation, nor does it instruct us in the tools of modal logic, and to read it as if it is a direct source of these other sciences is a mistake. Yet, Bavinck is also clear that Scripture still plays a critical role for the other sciences, and even that the *principia* for all of life are found in Scripture.

Much misuse has been made of Baronius' saying: "Scripture does not tell us how the heavens move but how we move to heaven." Precisely as the book of the knowledge of God, Scripture has *much to say also to the other sciences*. It is a light on our path and a lamp for our feet, also with respect to *science and art*. It claims authority in *all areas of life*. Christ has [been given] all power in heaven and on earth. Objectively, the restriction of inspiration to the religious-ethical part of Scripture is untenable; subjectively the

---

virtually no comprehension of an encyclopedic system of theology. One can detect only beginnings and feeble attempts at such an arrangement.

It is even surprising how little the principle of faith that people confessed was developed in different directions or applied to various areas of life in the centuries of orthodoxy. After a time of struggle, when a firm doctrine was established, there soon appeared a traditional dogmatics. Later theologians simply agreed with the earlier pronouncements and naively copied them. Hardly anyone felt a need for development. They rested on the laurels that the fathers have achieved, keeping what they had, but they did not sufficiently consider continuing reformation. That is why in our century there is so much for Reformed people to do, not only academically but also practically." ("Theology and Religious Studies" in Bolt, *Essays on Religion*, 50)

38. *RD* 1:233, 444, emphasis original.

separation between the religious life and rest of human life cannot be maintained. Inspiration extends to all parts of Scripture, and religion is a matter of the whole person. A great deal of what is related in Scripture is of *fundamental significance* also for the other sciences. At every moment science and art come into contact with Scripture; *the primary principles [principia] for all of life are given in Scripture*. This truth may in no way be discounted.[39]

Hence, though Scripture is not a scientific textbook, it remains a resource that should be used in other scientific domains. Bartholomew's observation on this is apt: "Bavinck rightly resists both *dualism*—in which Scripture only addresses issues of 'faith'—and *biblicism*, according to which Scripture is seen as a manual for the sciences. He rightly notes that Scripture's orientation toward the world is authoritative for all of life."[40]

This is what makes the difference between Christian science (or critical scholarship) and non-Christian science. Bavinck's 1904 work *Christelijke wetenschap* (Christian Science) develops this point. Though Bavinck does not agree with Kuyper's characterization of two kinds of science traceable back to two kinds of people, Bavinck insists that there is a Christian understanding of science in contrast to a non-believing one: "Belief and unbelief, Christian and positivist conceptions of science stand diametrically against each other. Compromise is here not possible, but an obligation to choose definitively."[41] Accordingly, "faith and science stand in a relationship of conception and birth, as tree and fruit, as work and wage; the knowledge is the fruit and the wage of faith."[42]

For Bavinck, the connection between faith and science does not consist in the claim that the unregenerate will fail to do science, but that

---

39. *RD* 1:445, emphases added; *GD* 1:472. Dutch original: "Ieder oogenblik komen wetenschap en kunst met de Schrift in aanraking, de *principia* voor heel het leven zijn gegeven in de Schrift."

40. Bartholomew, *Contours of the Kuyperian Tradition*, 90.

41. Bavinck, *Christelijke wetenschap*, 9. Dutch original: "Geloovige en ongeloovige, Christelijke en positivistische opvatting van de wetenschap staan lijnrecht tegenover elkander. Vergelijk is hier niet mogelijk, maar besliste keuze plicht." Bolt also rightly notes that Bavinck affirms the conflict between Christian and non-Christian science (*Bavinck on the Christian Life*, 140).

42. Bavinck, *Christelijke wetenschap*, 16. Dutch original: "Geloof en wetenschap staan dus tot elkander in verhouding als ontvangenis en geboorte, als boom en vrucht, als werk en loon; het weten is de vrucht en het loon des geloofs."

they are lacking the resources to justify its pursuit or properly understand its character and place. They have a kind of atomistic knowledge.
True science, in Bavinck's judgment, continues to flourish in his day only
because it "in fact still rests in part on Christian foundations. But to the
same extent it seeks to undermine this, [science] labors also to her own
destruction."[43] Indeed, the "newer practice of nature and history, in her
noblest form, consciously or unconsciously presupposes the thoughts of
Christianity."[44] Eglinton and Michael Bräutigam's comment concerning
Bavinck's conclusions is appropriate: "Having claimed that the universe
cannot be coherently viewed without metaphysics, Bavinck turns the
reader toward the revelation of the Triune God."[45] Bavinck concludes
his treatment on Christian science with a reflection on how revelation
informs the believer of the true character of things, protecting the believer
from straying in science:

> Because there is in science, just as in everywhere else, much false-
> hood and counterfeiting, God gives to us in his revelation a guide
> and a signpost, which directs our steps in the practice of science
> and protects us from straying. Christian science is a science that
> examines all things in the light of his revelation, seeing, therefore,
> things as they truly are in their essence. In the eyes of the world
> this may be foolishness, but the foolishness of God is wiser than
> men, and the weakness of God is stronger than men. For we can
> do nothing against, but for, the truth.[46]

---

43. Bavinck, Christelijke wetenschap. 97. Dutch original: "Wel is waar staat de wetenschap heden ten dage op eene aanzienlijke hoogte; zij rust feitelijk voor een deel nog op Christelijke grondslagen. Maar in dezelfde mate als zij deze ondermijnt, arbeidt zij ook aan haar eigen verderf."

44. Bavinck, Christelijke wetenschap, 104–5. Dutch original: "Meer nadruk behoort nog hierop te vallen, dat de nieuwere beoefening van natuur en geschiedenis, in haar edelsten vorm bewust of onbewust de gedachten van het christendom onderstelt."

45. Eglinton and Bräutigam, "Scientific Theology?," 46.

46. Bavinck, Christelijke wetenschap, 130. Dutch original: "Maar omdat er in de wetenschap, evenals overal elders, zooveel schijn en namaak is, schonk God ons in zijne openbaring een gids en een wegwijzer, die bij de beoefening der wetenschap onze schreden richt en ons voor afdwaling behoedt. Christelijke wetenschap is dus zulk eene wetenschap, die bij het licht dier openbaring alle dingen onderzoekt en ze daarom ziet, gelijk zij waarlijk, in hun wezen zijn. In het oog der wereld moge dit dwaasheid zijn, maar het dwaze Gods is wijzer dan de menschen en het zwakke Gods is sterker dan de menschen. Want wij vermogen niets tegen, maar voor de waarheid."

Third and finally, a question: What is the product when viewing science and scholarship in the light of Scripture? Bavinck argues that what emerges is an *organic* view of science where science is ultimately a singular organism comprising a diversity of disciplines. He teases this out explicitly in numerous places, and for our present purposes, two texts are especially clear. The first is his posthumously published essay *"Christendom en Natuurwetenschap"* ("Christianity and Natural Science"), and the second is his 1902 inaugural address at the Vrije Universiteit of Amsterdam, "Religion and Theology."

In the former, Bavinck explicitly connects Scripture's influence as the ground for understanding the oneness of science:

Scripture ... frequently touches all the other mundane sciences. It is not dualistic: she distinguishes between the natural and the spiritual but she does not separate them. The one is connected to the other. ... Christianity has made us first to understand that the world, that humanity, that science is one. Therefore, revelation is not strictly limited to religious and ethical being, but also lets the mid-point of its light shed over the whole of natural life, heaven and earth, plant and animal, angel and man, over all of creation. And therefore the object of theology is not the bare knowledge of God, but also that of the creature insofar as it stands in relation to him and reveals him.[47]

Tying this language together, Christianity has laid the foundation "for the organic unity of science" precisely because it presents an alternative between pantheism and deism:

47. Herman Bavinck, "Christendom en Natuurwetenschap," in *Kennis en Leven: Opstellen en artikelen uit vroegere jaren*, ed. C. B. Bavinck (Kampen: Kok, 1922), 197. Dutch original: "Maar nu is het ter anderer zijde evenzeer waar, dat de Schrift, juist om ons eene zuivere 'geestelijke' kennis te geven, dikwerf met al die andere mundane wetenschappen in aanraking komt. Dualistisch is zij niet; zij onderscheidt wel het natuurlijke en het geestelijke maar zij scheidt het niet; het eene staat met het andere in verband; ethos en physis liggen niet gescheiden naast, maar grijpen telkens in elkaar; het Christendom heeft het ons 't eerst doen verstaan, dat de wereld, dat de menschheid, dat de wetenschap ééne is. Daarom kan de openbaring niet strikt tot het religieus-ethische beperkt wezen, maar laat van dit middelpunt uit haar licht ook vallen over heel het natuurlijke leven, over aarde en hemel, plant en dier, engel en mensch, over al het geschapene. En daarom is object der Theologie niet bloot de kennis Gods, maar ook die der creatuur inzoover zij tot God in relatie staat en Hem openbaart."

Each particular science is "sovereign in its own sphere." But as the objects of the different sciences are not separated side by side, all parts of creation, on the contrary, closely cohere; even God and the world are not deistically separated or pantheistically identified but in their duality are once again one, so are all the sciences closely related; *each fills the other, each is an integral part of the whole. Science is one, and therefore animated by a single highest principle.*

And what principle can or may that be other than the Christian one? On the ground there is but a choice between two principles, the theistic and the pantheistic. On the standpoint of polytheism, deism etc., there is no unity of science, no encyclopaedia of all sciences, no "scientific teaching" is possible. *Christianity, Christian-theism has first laid the foundation and paved the way for the organic unity of science.*[48]

In his 1902 address, he connects these ideas to the idea of a Christian university, with an ideal of an all-encompassing science:

To these factors that are peculiar to Christianity, we owe the notion of a singular, all-encompassing science. ... With this One and Only Son of the Father at the centre, with his Word as a light, on the foundation of monotheism, an *"einheitliche"* [united] worldview came into being, an all-encompassing science, which, in the university, the greatest creation of the Christian faith, found its embodiment.[49]

He goes on, drawing on the organic language of unity-in-diversity in order to show that the unity of science, once again, should not be used to compromise the diversity of disciplines:

---

48. Bavinck, "Christendom en Natuurwetenschap," 201–2, emphases added. "Elke bijzondere wetenschap is weer 'souverein in eigen kring.' Maar gelijk de objecten der verschillende wetenschappen niet los naast elkander staan, alle deelen der schepping integendeel ten nauwste samenhangen, God zelfs en wereld niet deistisch gescheiden noch pantheistisch identisch zijn, maar in hun tweeheid weer één, — zoo zijn ook alle wetenschappen ten nauwste verbonden; *de eene vult de andere aan; elke is een integreerend deel van het geheel. De wetenschap is ééne, en daarom door één hoogste beginsel bezield.*"

49. Herman Bavinck, "Religion and Theology," trans. Bruce R. Pass, *Reformed Theological Review* 77 (2018): 114–15.

Certainly, science is one, but this unity is no uniformity; it does not exclude diversity, just as all manner of diversity exists in the cosmos, of matter and spirit, things visible and invisible, so too the one science subdivides into various particular sciences, which all proceed from a particular presupposition in accordance with their special objects, practice a unique research methodology, and possess a variable degree of certainty.[50]

These remarks, while showing a measured confidence in the resources within Scripture and its theological content to aid in the practice of science, do not erase difficult questions when it comes to application. Theologians and scientists at the Vrije Universiteit of Amsterdam continued to wrestle with what it means to do science under Reformational principles in practice: What happens when the information in one field (e.g., natural science), for example, directly conflicts with the center of the organism (theology)?[51] While Bavinck insists that theology ought to be a "servant-queen" of the sciences,[52] it is often unclear how asserting these principles alone answers these difficult questions.[53]

With Scripture's importance as an authority for theology and as an aid for the other sciences, then, we do well to turn to Kuyper's and Bavinck's treatments of the doctrine of Scripture, as well as their attempt to articulate its organic character. Observing their treatments of this doctrine will highlight the continuities and discontinuities in their respective accounts.

KUYPER ON THE INSPIRATION
OF SCRIPTURE

Kuyper's arguments concerning Scripture itself are rich, and for our present purposes we will observe primarily those sections in which the organic

---

50. Bavinck, "Religion and Theology," 121.

51. For a summary of some of the issues that emerged on this topic, see Sutanto, *God and Knowledge*, 71–73.

52. Herman Bavinck, *De wetenschap der H. Godgeleerdheid: Rede ter aanvaarding van het leeraarsambt aan de Theologische School te Kampen* (Kampen: Zalsman, 1883), 33–36.

53. This is chronicled in Arie Theodorus van Deursen, *The Distinctive Character of the Free University in Amsterdam, 1880–2005: A Commemorative History*, trans. Herbert Donald Morton (Grand Rapids: Eerdmans, 2008). See also Sutanto, *God and Knowledge*, 71–73, 177–80.

motif and Scripture are treated together. As we will see, the motif informs Kuyper's account by providing the categories of unity-in-diversity and center and periphery as serviceable to describe Scripture's form, authority, and purpose.

Kuyper's discussion of the attributes and inspiration of Scripture within his *Encyclopedia* comes after the discussion of the special principium's (grace) relation with the natural principium, namely, that this gracious act of God adds nothing substantially new to what is natural, but rather restores it, coming alongside it as an auxiliary aid. As such, Kuyper invokes one of his oft-used negative metaphors to depict their relationship: not as "a drop of oil upon the waters of our human life, and we maintain, on the contrary, that the need of such an auxiliary principium is *universally human*; that in its organic working this principium bears an *universally human* character; and that in the final result towards which it directs itself, it has an *universally human* significance."[54] This emphasis on its organic connection with what is universally human shields Kuyper from what he thought to be the dangers of dualism, according to which grace and nature are simply put alongside one another, or as if grace were a second layer on top of nature.

Scripture, Kuyper argues, is included within this special principium, which includes the "whole plan of redemption." The special principium includes the work of the Spirit in vitalizing the knowledge of God, including the works of illumination and of perpetuating the work of sacred ministry. Just as these works have in view regenerate humanity, and thus have the aim not of individuals here and there but of the human race, so too Holy Scripture is addressing "those nations as an organic unity, as *cosmos*."[55] The Spirit attends to its production and its reception within our consciousness, and this universal aim of Scripture informs Kuyper's discussion of the attributes of Scripture.

What becomes clear, then, is that though Scripture and theology ought organically to touch all of natural knowledge and life, Scripture continues to have its own unique function, namely, to produce the saving knowledge

---

54. *Encyclopedia*, 397, emphasis original.
55. *Encyclopedia*, 398, 400–401.

of God and to be the ground of true theology. Though Kuyper argued that a "believer of the nineteenth century knows much more than a believer of the tenth or thirteenth century ... that additional knowledge is ever dug from the selfsame goldmine; and that former generations stood behind in wealth of knowledge, can only be explained by the fact, that in those times the working of the mind was not so far advanced."[56] Provocatively, Kuyper likens the believers of these earlier centuries to children and the church in the present to a full-grown man.[57] But one should not read this as an endorsement of a simple developmental theory of tradition, according to which later believers are taken to be more mature because they have grown past their need for Holy Scripture. Rather, Scripture's authority relativizes the difference between past and present believers, as both are seeking to ascertain the depth of Scripture's meaning. It is at the end of this discussion, then, that Kuyper argues that "the Holy Bible itself is the proximate and sole cause (*principium proximum et unicum*) for our knowledge of God."[58]

This is not surprising, as Kuyper emphasizes before that theologians are "in an absolute sense" dependent on the will of God to reveal himself. "Only when the wondrous God will speak, can he listen. And thus the Theologian is absolutely *dependent* upon the pleasure of God, either to impart or not to impart knowledge of Himself." This is true not only of special revelation, but also in general revelation, as it is still *revelation*: "From the finite no conclusion can be drawn to the infinite, neither can a Divine reality be known from external or internal phenomena, unless that real God *reveals* Himself in my consciousness to my ego; reveals himself as *God*; and thereby moves and impels me to see in these finite phenomena a brightness of *His* glory. Formaliter, neither observation nor reasoning would ever have rendered service here as the principium of knowing."[59]

---

56. *Encyclopedia*, 402.

57. For the philosophical background of Kuyper's and Bavinck's developmental claims here, see Pass, *Heart of Dogmatics*.

58. *Encyclopedia*, 405.

59. *Encyclopedia*, 251, 343, 405, emphasis original. Kuyper's comment here relates well with our chapter "Revelation and Reason."

Kuyper introduces the attributes of Scripture not by following what has become the standard terms for a Protestant doctrine of Scripture. While traditionally the terms "sufficiency," "necessity," "authority," and "perspicuity" identify the attributes of Scripture, Kuyper instead uses the terms "durability, catholicity, fixedness and purity."[60] This is not to suggest that Kuyper would disagree with the former terms—we have just seen that Kuyper wholeheartedly affirmed Scripture's authority and necessity—but Kuyper's chosen terms do indicate differing emphases. The chief emphases that emerge in Kuyper's discussion are Scripture's written form, its universal trustworthiness and scope within a pluralist global reality, and the consciousness that technological advancement has improved Scripture's spread.

The durability of Scripture stems from its written form. Speech is impermanent, and memory is short—writing overcomes these two limitations. "Writing tries to do the same thing that the photograph does, but by attaching a meaning not to sound, but to root forms." Writing preserves accuracy and approximates divine reality: "By writing, human thought approaches the eternal, the enduring, and, to a certain extent, impresses upon itself a Divine stamp."[61] As such, written revelation is fitting, and the entrance of sin has only intensified the need for its written form.

As a written text, revelation thus also transcends the text's location and time, reaching the human race: "Only by this written form could it be a revelation to our race *as a whole.*" Reflection on Scripture's durable and written form, then, leads Kuyper naturally to its catholic and universal character. If God intends his church to be universal, for humanity as a single organism, so must revelation too have a catholic character: "Writing lends wings to thought. It neutralizes distance of time and space, and thereby puts upon thought the stamp of eternity and of omnipresence."[62] This focuses the point that divine revelation in human words rightly takes the form of holy Scripture.

---

60. *Encyclopedia,* 405. The original Dutch terms Kuyper uses are "het *duurzame,* het *katholieke,* het *vaste* en het *onvervalschte*" (*Encyclopaedie der Heilige Godgeleerdheid* 2:359).

61. *Encyclopedia,* 406–7.

62. *Encyclopedia,* 408–9.

Kuyper goes on to treat fixedness and purity together, and pits these scriptural attributes against the limitations of human memory, specifically to our "*multiformity* and *untrustworthiness*."[63] The multiform and untrustworthy character of human memory entails that tradition, too, will be mired with "injurious multiformity." Here Kuyper adduces examples from the oral traditions of the world, from the differing traditions between the Eastern and Western churches, and the diversity of traditions that stem from other religions. In every "highly developed form of religion" in Islam, India, and China, there is a desire for "a basis of fixedness" in a written text.[64]

Kuyper then qualified what he means by Scripture's purity, as the written form can only guarantee its purity in a limited sense against the sinful tendencies of human interference. While he concedes that printing would have further ensured Scripture's purity were it available during Scripture's production, handwriting is still a better guide "against falsification" over oral transmission. Nonetheless, printing aids in the spreading of the Scripture and "liberates men from men and binds them to God." Printing does allow the Scriptures to reach into its "fullest mission of power," over against what Kuyper believes is the Roman desire to suppress the "spread of the printed Bible."[65]

At this point, Kuyper articulates, in great detail, the nature of and relationship between Scripture's inspiration and the other works of God, especially in providence and miracles. We will focus on the organic motif specifically, as Kuyper weaves this motif substantially within his account. Kuyper argues that inspiration has to be understood in connection with God's other works and that the production of Scripture was aimed at humanity as an organism. Inspiration is thus different from the mystical utterances of the religious, where a specific revelation is given for private devotion and passes by transiently, disconnected from the rest of life. He goes on to articulate inspiration within the scope of God's plans. God decrees redemption and wills humanity to come to know his purpose.

---

63. *Encyclopedia*, 410. It is worth noting that in other contexts, as we have shown, Kuyper (and Bavinck) treats multiformity as a positive reality, rather than a hindrance.

64. *Encyclopedia*, 410–11.

65. *Encyclopedia*, 412.

The organic idea comes to the fore once again, and with it comes the distinction between *center* and *periphery*, unity and diversity: "here, as with all organisms, distinction *must* be made between that which *centrally* directs itself to all and that which *individually* limits itself to single persons." In this particular context, Kuyper argues that the inspiration of Scripture is that which hits the center of the organism of humanity and hence "*must* appear in that objective form in which it would continue from age to age and spread from nation to nation."[66] This prompts Kuyper to articulate the distinction between inspiration and illumination as two periods within the organism of revelation:

> Considered, therefore, from this point of view, it lies entirely in the organic character of revelation, that it passes through two periods, the first of which brings it to its complete measure, and the second of which allows it, having reached its measure, to perform its work. And this is what we face in the difference between inspiration and illumination. Inspiration *completed* the revelation, and, appearing in this completed form, the Revelation now performs its work.[67]

This organic character of revelation's process explains why inspiration took so long to complete, while also helping Kuyper to make a sharp distinction between the inspired revelation of God and the illumination that was then given to the church, while maintaining the connection between the two. If revelation is not merely intellectual, but appears "in life itself," then inspiration is linked to the drama itself that led to the incarnation, completing the process of inspiration, before then entering into the "ecumenic appearance of the church"—that second stage, not of inspiration but of illumination.[68]

The distinction between center and periphery also continues in Kuyper's discussion of inspiration in relation to miracles. Miracles can either be central or peripheral: the central miracles have to do with the center of the organism of redeemed humanity, Christ himself, and the

66. *Encyclopedia*, 418, emphasis original.
67. *Encyclopedia*, 418–19.
68. *Encyclopedia*, 419.

periphery have to do with the signs that attest to God's working in Christ. "The incarnation is the centrum of this entire central action, and all miracles which belong to this category tend to inaugurate this incarnation, or are immediate results of it, like the resurrection." Central miracles are incarnation-related, whereas "typical miracles [belong] in the periphery."[69]

Inspiration belongs to the *central* category of miracles, taking place spiritually and psychically, and then manifesting itself physically. While the incarnation is primarily a physical miracle, inspiration is a psychical miracle—and the two go hand in hand: "as the incarnation brought life into the centrum of human *being*, inspiration brings the knowledge of God into human *knowledge*, i.e. into the central consciousness of our human race. From this special principium in God the saving power is extended centrally to our race, both by the ways of *being* and of *thought*, by incarnation and inspiration."[70] Both have their aim in the redemption and consummation of the organism of the human race.

It is at this point that Kuyper emphasizes that inspiration does not stand above or contradict the laws of nature, but rather goes along with it: "that which you call natural power or natural law is nothing but the *immanent* power of God and the *will* of God immanently upholding this power, while both of these depend upon his transcendent counsel." This is in contrast to a mechanical view, according to which a miracle is defined as a disruption into an otherwise self-enclosed cosmos-machine. The laws of nature are simply scientific descriptions of the ordinary ways of God's sustaining and directing providence. Behind both creation and redemption is the single decree in the mind of God: "there is no twofold counsel, so that on the one hand the decree of creation stands by itself, to which, at a later period, the decree of salvation is mechanically added; but in the deepest root of the consciousness of God both are one."[71]

There is thus a profound unity undergirding Scripture's production, located in God's decree and effected by the Spirit as the primary author of Scripture. Kuyper's exegetical arguments from Scripture itself concerning

---

69. *Encyclopedia*, 424.
70. *Encyclopedia*, 425.
71. *Encyclopedia*, 425–26.

Scripture's inspiration and authority attest to this conviction that the Bible forms an organic unity. This explains why it is legitimate for the authors of the New Testament to cite Old Testament texts in a modified form, for here the "Holy Spirit ... the same primary author ... *quotes himself*, and is therefore entirely justified in repeating his original meaning in application to the case for which the quotation is made, in a somewhat modified form, agreeably to the current translation."[72] Likewise, Kuyper argues that one cannot maintain faith in Christ and hold that the Scriptures can be mistaken, both with respect to so-called holy or *innocent* matters. Admission of mistakes in Scripture, or of Christ's testimony, impugns on Christ's character, Scripture's self-testimony, and the unity between Christ's self-consciousness, person, and mission within God's redemptive plan. "He who breaks in principle with that ancient view of the Scripture cuts the cord of faith, which bound him to that Christ as his Lord and his God."[73]

Kuyper does, however, nuance this point later on by arguing that attending to Scripture's genre as history does require us to expect "no notarial acts" but rather a writing that expresses "the impressionistic certainty of life." Scripture is not to be measured as a scientific textbook in the modern sense of the term. Rather, it is history written in ordinary language, according to ordinary experience. Our certainty of faith cannot be identified with a certainty of the intellect, and as "soon as it is thought that the holy ore of Scripture can be weighed in the balance with mathematical accuracy, the eye of faith becomes clouded, and the gold is less clearly seen."[74]

It is only from the perspective of this unity, therefore, that one can discuss the multiformity of Scripture. Starting with unity affords a proper understanding of Scripture's diversity. Beginning with diversity cannot lead one to Scripture's divine unity. By diversity, Kuyper has in view

---

72. *Encyclopedia*, 450, emphasis original. Kuyper's high view of God as the primary author of Scripture should thus carefully nuance Bartholomew's comment that "Scripture becomes the Word of God only when the Spirit facilitates God's address to one in and through Scripture" (*Contours of the Kuyperian Tradition*, 86). The Spirit does illumine Christian readers in order to understand and accept the text as God's word, but the text was authored by the Spirit, and as such is the word of God to humanity.

73. *Encyclopedia*, 456, 456.

74. *Encyclopedia*, 549–50.

the various genres and forms of discourse in Scripture, along with the inspiration of its various human authors. Behind these human authors is "the consciousness of God, and He it is, who in His time has so created each of these writers, so endowed, led and impelled them, that they have contributed what He wanted, and what after His plan and direction was to constitute His Scripture."[75] Appeals to the writing of Scripture as the ethical byproduct of a naturalistic process are impossible—it is not that God selects certain fallible human texts and puts them into service—he superintends their production and is the primary author of Scripture. In another place, Kuyper links this organic view of inspiration to Scripture's *infallibility*: "Hence inspiration is the name of that all-comprehensive operation of the Holy Spirit where He has bestowed on the Church a complete and infallible Scripture. We call this operation all-comprehensive, for it was organic, not mechanical."[76]

The all-encompassing operation of the Spirit that sustains the authorship of Scripture leads to an appreciation, rather than a negation, of the human authors of Scripture. In order for us to take this diversity seriously, Kuyper uses the analogue of the incarnation: "As the Logos has not appeared *in the form of glory*, but in the form of a servant, joining Himself to the reality of our nature, as this had come to be through the results of sin, so also, for the revelation of His Logos, God the Lord accepts *our* consciousness, our human life *as it is*."[77] The phenomenology of reading Scripture, therefore, parallels closely with perceiving Christ. Just as a mere phenomenological observation of Christ's body and blood may not lead us to conclude that this was the divine Son who took on flesh, so might those who investigate "the human phenomena in the Holy Scripture's" may not engender "the impression of faith."[78] It is when one stands back and looks at the whole that one can see this diversity undergirded by the reality that it is, in its entirety, the word of God. Just as one ought to look

---

75. *Encyclopedia*, 474–75.

76. Abraham Kuyper, *The Work of the Holy Spirit*, trans. Henri de Vries (Grand Rapids: Eerdmans, 1946), 76.

77. *Encyclopedia*, 479. For a detailed analysis of this incarnational analogy in Kuyper and Bavinck, see Richard B. Gaffin Jr,. *God's Word in Servant-Form: Abraham Kuyper and Herman Bavinck and the Doctrine of Scripture* (Jackson, MS: Reformed Academic Press, 2007).

78. *Encyclopedia*, 480.

at the image of a painting and not lose sight of that image when looking at the individual brushstrokes, so must one return back to the unity of the Scripture's conception when its diversity is studied.

This leads Kuyper to a lengthy discussion of the instruments and forms of inspiration. The human authors of Scripture can be moved by God through internal or external addresses, by an influencing motion, by dreams and visions of varying intensity. God communicates redemption by way of miracles and ultimately reveals himself in the incarnation.[79] Crucially, Kuyper again deploys the distinction between center and periphery. The Spirit might work through the center of the human author's consciousness, as in a dream or a trance, "as is the case with most of Ezekiel's visions,"[80] or through the periphery, by a subtle influence that proceeds to penetrate the heart of the author.

Just as God providentially orders all things and we have our being and movement in him (alluding to Acts 17:28), God also "selected the most suitable persons. ... He Himself caused these men to be born for this purpose, predestined them for it, and caused them to spend their youth amid such circumstances and surroundings, that in His own time they stood in readiness as suitable instruments." In God's providence he leads them toward their suitability and provides the grace necessary for them to produce precisely the writings that God ordains. As genuine agents under God's inspiration, the human authors imprint their writings with their own personalities and character. It is within this context that Kuyper discusses the reality of "degrees of inspiration" with regard to Scripture: "As a 'virtuoso on the violin' can only exhibit a part of his art on a violin of two strings, and only on the full-stringed instrument can bring all his powers into play, so the holy playing of inspiration that sounds in our ears, is entirely different, far richer, and infinitely more intensive, when God makes use of a David or a Paul than when Nahum comes from the woods or James's epistle is unrolled before us."[81] However, the "degrees of inspiration" here has to do not with their content (for Kuyper has already

---

79. *Encyclopedia*, 481–504.
80. *Encyclopedia*, 506.
81. *Encyclopedia*, 514–20.

made clear that Scripture cannot err), but with its *effect*. The affective reception of Scripture varies according to the different human authors God chooses to use.

Analogues of the more *direct* influences, where "the human spirit appears as little more than a phonograph," Kuyper argues, are found in the Romantic examples of the impulse toward poetic expression, enthusiasm for certain ideas, and the "stimulus of genius": "our consciousness is not a boat propelled by the oar-stroke of our own exertions, but that it may likewise carry a sail which may be filled by winds over which we have no control."[82] Hence, while Kuyper avoids a *mechanical* view of inspiration, he was not averse to a doctrine of inspiration according to which the Spirit does, in a myriad of ways, influence the human authors directly. He defends this by suggesting that such influences are by no means abnormal to the human situation. Human beings do not normatively make decisions by way of calm, rational contemplation and by conscious deliberation, but are rather driven toward action through external influences often outside their control. Far from undermining the genuineness of their action, they enhance it.

BAVINCK ON THE INSPIRATION
OF SCRIPTURE

As commentators have observed, Bavinck believed that premodern theology grasped the divine origins of Scripture but did not take sufficient account of its humanness and its organic connection with general revelation.[83] The rise of modern biblical criticism led him to better appreciate the psychological mediation of God's inspiring work and the human authorship of Scripture. Hence, while in many ways Bavinck does stand on classical and Reformed convictions concerning the attributes of Scripture, Bavinck's own position does not fit neatly "either with the

---

82. *Encyclopedia*, 506–7.

83. Eglinton, *Trinity and Organism*, 165. Bartholomew, likewise, observes: "He [Bavinck] notes that awareness of the historical and psychological mediation of Scripture is a fruit of modernity so that a mechanical view of inspiration has rightly made way for an organic one. Far from an organic view detracting from the Bible as Scripture, it enables Scripture to come more fully on its own" (*Contours of the Kuyperian Tradition*, 90).

modern theologians or in his own *gereformeerde* context."[84] As we will see, for example, though Bavinck maintained the classical emphases on the sufficiency, necessity, authority, and clarity of Scripture (as opposed to Kuyper's creative rearticulation of these as Scripture's durability, fixedness, catholicity, and purity), Bavinck more fully articulated an organic account of inspiration and utilized distinctions such as center and periphery in his own creative way.[85]

Bavinck's concession that modern theology takes more seriously the humanness of Scripture is thus not a capitulation to modern theologians' overall worldview, but is theologically motivated by a desire to envision a more capacious understanding of revelation and inspiration. Instead of conceiving the Bible as a book disconnected from the rest of God's revelation and creation, he insists on the divine origins of Scripture and thus the need to connect it to the rest of God's revealing work: "The word of God in nature, in Israel, in the NT, in Scripture may never even for a moment be separated and abstracted from him. God's revelation exists only because he is the Logos. He is the first principle of cognition, in a general sense of all knowledge, in a special sense, as the Logos incarnate, of all knowledge of God, of religion, and theology (Matt. 11:27)."[86]

As such, Bavinck articulates a high doctrine of Scripture. Scripture is an organism—a manifold diversity united as a singular whole by God's intent: "The revelation that Scripture discloses to us does not just consist in a number of disconnected words and isolated facts but is one single historic and organic whole, a mighty world-controlling and world-renewing system of testimonies and acts of God." It is "the eternally ongoing speech of God to us."[87] Before he gets to a discussion of the *organic inspiration* of Scripture, having in view the relation between divine authorship and human authorship, he emphasizes that Scripture "was not only "'God-breathed' at the time it was written; it *is* 'God-breathing.'"[88] Summing up the New Testament's teaching on the Scripture, Bavinck traces the organic

84. Eglinton, *Trinity and Organism*, 182.
85. Van Keulen, *Bijbel en Dogmatiek*, 163–64.
86. *RD* 1:402.
87. *RD* 1:340, 384.
88. *RD* 1:385, discussing 2 Tim 3:16.

unity of Scripture to God's primary authorship: "though composed of various parts and traceable to various authors, [Scripture] actually formed one organic whole whose author was God himself."[89]

It would be a mistake to suggest that Bavinck's insistence on the humanness and diversity of Scripture implies believing in its errancy.[90] Bavinck's use of the incarnation as an analogy to Scripture's divine-human content includes the perfect sinlessness of Christ's human nature. Though Bavinck does nuance this point—as we will see later—he insists that just as Christ's human nature remained sinless, so too, is Scripture pure. Scripture is the word of God in servant form.

Bavinck's organic account of inspiration thus stands in continuity with Kuyper's and is deployed in order to preserve the fullness of human authorship while maintaining the Spirit's primary authorship:

> The activity of the Holy Spirit in the writing process, after all, consisted in the fact that, having prepared the human consciousness of the authors in various ways (by birth, upbringing, natural gifts, research, memory, reflection, experience of life, revelation, etc.), he now, in and through the writing process itself, made *those* thoughts and words, *that* language and style, rise to the surface of consciousness, which could best interpret the divine ideas for persons of all sorts of rank and class, from every nation and age. Included in the thoughts are the words; included in the words are the vowels.[91]

If these observations highlight the fundamentally orthodox character of Bavinck's doctrine of Scripture, Bruce Pass has shown that Bavinck's organic account, however, displays creative elements, especially seen in the way in which Bavinck leaves out the word "infallibility" in his doctrine

---

89. *RD*, 1:394.

90. *RD* 1:438; Eglinton, *Trinity and Organism*, 178; Gaffin, *God's Word in Servant Form*, 56. However, note Bruce Pass's nuance: "Gaffin stands on firm ground when he corrects Rogers and McKim for suggesting that Bavinck advocates anything short of plenary verbal inspiration. Inspiration in Bavinck embraces not only the words of Scripture but even the vowels. Gaffin's identification of Bavinck with inerrancy as it is described in the Chicago statement, however, is problematic" ("Upholding *Sola Scriptura* Today," 530).

91. *RD* 1:438.

of Scripture, and in his implicit charge that older orthodox accounts of the doctrine were mechanical. As Pass summarizes:

> The term "infallible" is conspicuous in its absence in Bavinck's own account of the inspiration of Scripture. … First, the term "infallibility" (*onfeilbaarheid*) was not at all unfamiliar to Bavinck. Kuyper employed the term repeatedly, as did Warfield, and Bavinck was familiar with their writings. Second, the term "infallibility" appears with some frequency in the passages of *Reformed Dogmatics* both before and after Bavinck's account of inspiration. In these passages the term is used almost exclusively in connection with the authority of tradition in Roman Catholicism. Third, in Bavinck's historical recount of the doctrine of Scripture, where it is reported that the church Fathers, medieval scholastics and magisterial Reformers held that the Bible is without error, one finds a pregnant statement. In his historical recount Bavinck opines "Occasionally one can discern a feeble attempt at developing a more organic view of Scripture." … Bavinck may well have identified the term "infallible" with the mechanical character of the view of Scripture upon which he sought to improve.[92]

Pass's argument is thick, taking into account other sources that trace the development of Bavinck's thought on Scripture's inspiration. For our present purposes, we will summarize his observations that trace Bavinck's argument in the *Dogmatics*. This involves observing Bavinck's distinction between (1) center and periphery, (2) form and content, and (3) Christ's sinlessness and technical scientific precision. The point here is not to argue that Bavinck believed in Scripture's humanness as fundamentally entailing the presence of errors, but rather that "the inability to demonstrate the coherence of the available archaeological [evidence] and the biblical text need not overturn a well-versed inerrancy."[93] Attending to Bavinck's argu-

---

92. Pass, "Upholding *Sola Scriptura* Today," 520–21. Pass is citing *RD* 1:415.

93. Pass, "Upholding *Sola Scriptura* Today," 533. Earlier, on page 524, Pass puts it this way: "For Bavinck, every single word of Scripture is inspired. Some of these words, however, are peripheral to Scripture's soteriological purpose. By differentiating between words that are closer to and further away from the centre, Bavinck seeks to abolish the perceived necessity of securing what is irreplaceable by defending what is trivial."

ment here serves not to sever him from his orthodox Reformed tradition but to display the detailed granularity with which he articulated his doctrine of inspiration. In Bavinck one sees no naive doctrine of inspiration that fails to acknowledge the complexity of Scripture itself.

Bavinck's distinction between center and periphery takes it into a rather different direction from Kuyper's *Encyclopedia*. As we have shown, Kuyper deploys this distinction in order to discuss the *modes* of inspiration primarily. Bavinck, however, discusses this distinction in relation to Scripture itself as an organism:

> Inspiration has to be viewed *organically,* so that even the lowliest part has its place and meaning and at the same time is much farther removed from the center than other parts. ... In Scripture, as well, not everything is equally close to the center. There is a periphery, which moves in a wide path around the center, yet also that periphery belongs to the circle of the divine thoughts. Accordingly, there are no kinds and degrees in "graphic" inspiration. The hair of one's head shares in the same life as the heart and the hand. ... It is one and the same Spirit from whom, through the consciousness of the authors, the whole of Scripture has come. But there is a difference in the manner in which the same life is present and active in the different parts of the body.[94]

The distinction between center and periphery, therefore, cannot be identified as an inerrant center with errant peripheries. The centrifugal character of an organism dictates that the whole organism shares the same life, and thus every part of Scripture is inspired. It does, however, mean that the center and periphery play different roles, with varying degrees of importance. As such, Bavinck identifies Scripture's central purpose as "religious-ethical through and through." It is not a scientific text for other sciences, but "is the first foundation (*principium*) only of theology and desires that we will read and study it *theologically.*" This does not mean, as we have seen, that Bavinck thinks that Scripture has no bearing on the other sciences: "A great deal of what is related in Scripture is

---

94. *RD* 1:439. See also Pass, "Upholding *Sola Scriptura* Today," 523.

of fundamental significance also for the other sciences." But it does mean "*that* [in the theological] purpose Scripture offers us all the data we need. In *that* sense it is completely adequate and complete."[95]

This involves acknowledging that Scripture presents not "exact knowledge." "This is a standard that may not be applied to it." Like Kuyper, Bavinck argues that the prophets and apostles "uses the language of everyday experience" rather than "the language of the academy." Furthermore: "Its purpose is not to tell us precisely all that has happened in times past with the human race and with Israel but to relate to us the history of God's revelation. ... Sacred history is religious history." Bavinck argues that the so-called failure of Scripture to meet the "standards of secular history" does not compromise its identity as God's word. In this regard, however, he concedes that Scripture presents a lesser degree of precision than we might wish: "Holy Scripture bears witness to the fact that it follows a direction of its own and aims at a goal of its own. In its determination of time and place, in the order of events, in the grouping of circumstances, it certainly does not give us the degree of exactness we might frequently wish for. The reports about the main events, say, the time of Jesus' birth, the duration of his public activity ... etc., are far from homogenous and leave room for a variety of views."[96]

It is in this context that Bavinck invokes the distinction between form and content, the second distinction. In Bavinck's words: "Even in the case of historical reports, there is sometimes a distinction between the fact that has occurred and the form in which it is presented." While secular standards of exact history demands precise historiography that narrates events in terms of photographic and strictly sequential ordering, the authors of Scripture describe events in accord with their religious-theological purposes. Even though the authors of Scripture have not sought to present the event in accord with "the rules of historical criticism," they still offer a true account.[97] In Pass's words, though "organic inspiration

---

95. *RD* 1:444–45.
96. *RD* 1:444, 446–47.
97. *RD* 1:447–48.

does invoke a distinction between form and content ... form cannot be played off against content."[98]

Finally, care should be taken in precisely defining the analogy between Scripture's divine-human authorship with Christ's divine-human natures. Bavinck draws the analogy to clearly draw a line between Christ's sinlessness and Scripture's human authorship: "The recording of the word, of revelation, invites us to recognize that dimension of weakness and lowliness, the servant form, also in Scripture. But just as Christ's human nature, however weak and lowly, remained free from sin, so also Scripture is 'conceived without defect or stain;' totally human in all its parts but also divine in all its parts."[99] Just as orthodox Christology puts a priority on the divine nature of Christ taking on a contingent and created human nature, so does Scripture's divine origin and unity take precedent behind the human authors. And just as Christ was sinless, so is Scripture without stain.[100]

Though the analogy should indeed indicate that Scripture is without error just as Christ was sinless, this should be qualified carefully. "Scripture never intentionally concerns itself with science as such. Christ himself, though free from all error and sin, was never, strictly speaking, active in the field of science and art, commerce and industry, law and politics." In volume 3, Bavinck's comment concerning Christ's knowledge is relevant, as it echoes these comments from volume 1: "Granted, Jesus did not give instructions in any human science, nor did he come on earth for that purpose. He came to make known to us the Father and to carry out his work. ... This was knowledge not of a purely scientific but of a religious nature, one that was of the greatest importance for the faith of the church."[101] Hence, though Bavinck clearly affirms that Jesus did not err with respect to what the Father willed to reveal through Himself, "Bavinck neither affirms nor denies this possibility" that "Jesus did in fact err in other areas," Pass writes. In sum: "The incarnational analogy in Bavinck ... is less capacious. Bavinck refrains from speculating as to whether Jesus erred in any area beyond

---

98. Pass, "Upholding *Sola Scriptura* Today," 524. Pass clarifies this comment in contrast to Roger and McKim.

99. *RD* 1:435.

100. See also Eglinton, *Trinity and Organism*, 173–78.

101. *RD* 3:313, 445.

the exercise of his prophetic office. Rather, the correspondence between Jesus' words, and, by extension, the words of Scripture, to the truth they represent is determined by their soteriological purpose."[102]

CONCLUSION

This presentation of Kuyper's and Bavinck's doctrine of Scripture, paying attention specifically to Scripture's relationship to theology and the other sciences, and its inspiration, presents a complex picture with various tensions. On the one hand, Scripture plays a role in the leavening of the other sciences, and yet the sciences enjoy a relative degree of independence from Scripture. Scripture is divine and without error, and yet there is still a distinction between center and periphery, such that there might be a difference in the effects of particular portions of Scripture as opposed to others (Kuyper), and a distinction between the historical events that took place and the form in which they are represented in Scripture (Bavinck).

While the organic motif does help explain the humanness of Scripture without negating its divine character and origins, Kuyper and Bavinck do not deny that real complexity exists when one attends to the diversity of Scripture's content. Further, though organic inspiration also frees one from having to explain difficult tensions in the periphery in order to maintain the central parts of Scripture, this may not satisfy the studious historiographer who does indeed want to trace the text to particular events. Nonetheless, the organic way in which Kuyper and Bavinck have represented Scripture itself and its relation to the sciences represents a sophisticated and orthodox account that "could be profitably put to constructive use."[103]

---

102. Pass, "Upholding *Sola Scriptura* Today," 529–30.
103. Pass, "Upholding *Sola Scriptura* Today," 536.

VI

Creation and Re-creation

*In the powerful mind of the French Reformer [Calvin], recreation
is not a system that supplements Creation, as in Catholicism, not
a religious reformation that leaves Creation intact, as in Luther,
much less a radically new creation as in Anabaptism, but a joyful
tiding of the renewal of all creatures. Here the Gospel comes fully
into its own, comes to true catholicity. There is nothing that cannot
or ought not to be evangelized.*

—Herman Bavinck, "The Catholicity of Christianity and the Church"

THE RELATIONSHIP BETWEEN creation and salvation is one of the
most prominent and tenacious matters appearing in the whole of the
neo-Calvinist theological tradition. For Kuyper and Bavinck, the relationship between nature and grace (read: God's work of creation and
redemption) remained an eye-catching motif across both corpuses. In
their logic, the nature-grace relation is a supreme concern of Scripture
and is therefore central to their dogmatics. For Kuyper, we must "trace
our whole confession of the Son and Holy Spirit back to the Father," as he
draws from the example of the Apostles' Creed. And in the church "our
whole preaching of salvation ... must be brought back again to God the
Father, and with it back to creation and to the re-creation of all things."[1] As
stated prior, Kuyper and Bavinck follow their forebears in stating clearly

---

1. CG 1:127.

that the object of theology is God, and when one focuses on God in his revelation, the two striking realities of history are God's chosen bookends: creation and re-creation.

Since theology has God as its object, from the earliest publications, these fathers of neo-Calvinist theology focus especially on the Triune God's economy, particularly how Scripture speaks of his agency in the world. God's blatant, self-expressed identity pronounces that God is the Creator and the Redeemer of the world. God is the Maker of heaven and earth (nature) and the Remaker of heaven and earth (grace). Kuyper and Bavinck's turn-of-the-century focus on creation and re-creation has reawakened a theology of continuity between God's two activities for more than a century following. One might say that the continuity of God's work in the nature-grace relation is the key insight of neo-Calvinism.[2]

To be specific, despite the fact of human guilt and creaturely corruption that reared its nasty head in the early moments of creation history, there is, for Kuyper and Bavinck, an organic unity between these two operations. In brief, neo-Calvinism accents an essential theological commitment: that the *goal* of salvation is not an entirely new idea, even post fall, because the goal of re-creation is the end of creation yet by different means. Re-creation's end is creation's original end: that God would make his dwelling place with humanity, the Immanuel principle. When we speak in this way, we mean that God's determination of the human terminus in his creative work is his purpose in his redemptive work. So Kuyper: "It is and always shall be, the world which God Almighty has created, which He, in spite of all the sins ... will so bring out to a perfect form of life, that it will perfectly correspond to His purpose of creation."[3]

---

2. Spotting the neo-Calvinist emphasis on the continuity between creation and re-creation is no new undertaking. Previous scholars have noticed and suggested that "grace restores nature" is *the* theme of first-generation neo-Calvinism. Eugene Heideman in 1959 wrote that the nature-grace relation "may be called the central thought of Bavinck's theology." Bartholomew suggests that Kuyperianism understands the "gospel to be the healing power that restores creation, in line with God's original design and toward its originally intended consummation." Wolters, in *Creation Regained*, assumes that "grace restores nature" or the restoration motif was the center of both Kuyper's and Bavinck's projects. See Eugene Heideman, *The Relation of Revelation and Reason in E. Brunner and H. Bavinck* (Assen: Van Gorcum, 1959), 191; Bartholomew, *Contours of the Kuyperian Tradition*, 69; Wolters, *Creation Regained*, 10–11.

3. Abraham Kuyper, *The Revelation of St. John*, trans. John Hendrik de Vries (Eugene, OR: Wipf & Stock, 1999), 344.

Therein, re-creation is not a repristination of the Edenic life, but oriented toward the goal of original Edenic life: God with us.

Neither Kuyper nor Bavinck treats the continuity of God's creative and salvific purposes as a novel idea. Kuyper claims to be restating according to the "superior theologians" that in re-creation one sees the unity of the Spirit's work across history.[4] Kuyper and Bavinck turn to Augustine and Calvin to argue for the unity of God's actions in his determination to bring about creation's original goal by means of special grace. Both theologians brought this Calvinistic theological principle to bear on the modern moment, suggesting that the grace of God in regeneration (of the self), renewal (of culture), and re-creation (of the world) is not bounded by the realm of the ethereal alone. Indeed, while God re-creates human beings from the inside out, the application of the gospel will also extend to the boundaries of the material order, and this future reality can even be witnessed in shadow in the time between the now and not yet. As Bavinck concludes: "Not only the church but also home, school, society, and state are placed under the dominion of the principle of Christianity."[5] Then, *at the heart of neo-Calvinism is God's action of recreation as the essence of Christianity and the meaning of world history.*

Bavinck, in his essay "The Essence of Christianity," argues in fact that Christ's gospel is not the "full content" of Christianity but the starting point and center. Yet, the incarnation, death, and resurrection of Jesus Christ is not the "final destination"—he points to the future, "where God will be all in all." He describes the essence accordingly: "Christianity is no less than the real, supreme work of the Triune God, in which the Father reconciles his created but fallen world through the death of his Son and re-creates it through his Spirit into the Kingdom of God."[6] For Kuyper, in what he calls the "dispensation of grace," God condescends and applies a bandage to "the injured part of the body," thereby emphasizing that it

---

4. "Thus Following the Sacred Scripture and the superior theologians, we reach a confession that maintains the unity of the Spirit's work, and makes it unite organically the natural and the spiritual life, the realm of nature and that of grace," Kuyper, *The Work of the Holy Spirit*, 46.

5. CCC, 238.

6. Bavinck, "Essence of Christianity," 46–47.

is creation that needs to be healed in re-creation.[7] The order of grace in salvation history has come to serve the creation order.

In this chapter, we take up a detailed investigation of this principle by (1) focusing on the dogmatic logic in three sections and then (2) addressing a growing conversation related to the creation/re-creation dynamic in neo-Calvinism in the fourth. By considering the end of creation and re-creation, the problem of creation, and the the nature of re-creation, we will uncover a robust theological account of both Kuyper and Bavinck's understanding of the relation between creation and re-creation. There is so much agreement between the two that we will consider them jointly. Then we will deal with a criticism particularly applied to Bavinck's concept of re-creation in the section "Re-creation and the Vision of God." The criticism appears in the form of a summary question: Does neo-Calvinist theology (Bavinck in particular) sacrifice the classical confession that salvation is ultimately the vision of God by making too much of the material goods of re-creation? Neo-Calvinist theologies have been reprimanded for maximizing the extent of salvation and consequently minimizing the God of salvation. Instead of salvation as communion with God, perhaps neo-Calvinist thought overeternalizes creaturely desires and earthly goods at God's expense.

THE END OF CREATION AND RE-CREATION

Creation is the "foundation of all revelation," and so also the "foundation of religious and ethical life." Pronouncements such as these are manifold in Bavinck and Kuyper, and with them began a theological emphasis on the meaning of creation that would pour into all the streams that broke from the neo-Calvinist current of the last century. The word "creation" in their Reformed theology is load-bearing with multiple implications. It is the confession that the one God brought the world forth out of nonbeing. It implies that there is a Creator, from whom all creation is entirely distinct. Bavinck even suggests that the idea of creation is a real "consolation in suffering." The doctrine of creation, he claims, is not first a product of

---

7. *Encyclopedia*, 369.

mere natural reason, but a God-revealed fact.[8] To speak of creation is to say that God is absolute sovereign and humanity absolutely dependent.

Yet, what is the point of creation? What is the end of creation, its highest good and final cause? How should the two realms of creation, heaven and earth, relate? As Bavinck states above, creation is the first revelation and foundation of all revelation, and is therefore also the establishment of religion, a relation between God and the human creature. This means creation has a religious purpose: creation exists so that creatures would cast their eyes on the glory of its Creator foremost. God's purpose in making is to make (for himself) a free relationship and (for us) an absolutely dependent and necessary relationship. So, from the perspective of the creature, Bavinck persistently deals with a closely related question. He states emphatically that "one of the most difficult problems that exists" is relating "earthly goods" (nature) to "heavenly goods" (grace). The relationship between "this life and the life to come," he proclaims, is "very challenging."[9] What is the relationship between the embodied human and the spiritual life, and how does it serve the end of creation according to the will of the Maker?

In the nineteenth century, Kuyper and Bavinck both lamented that segments of academia and the populace had attempted to solve the conundrums of origin and the relationship between the visible and invisible by capitulating to a novel abstraction of modernity: insisting the spiritual does not exist at all and subsequently retreating to the simplicity of a mere materialist order.[10] The materialist current beneath modernity's feet led both theologians to continually ask questions concerning the relation between the beginning and end, the earthly and heavenly.

Both, *sed contra*, contended for the catholic, Christian faith's insistence that the relation between creation and re-creation, as well as the relation between the visible and invisible, is one intended for organic union. In the former, God's will to glorify himself by renewing the realm of creation is the unifying end of God's revelation in his creative and re-creative

8. RD 2:407–8.
9. KGHG, 134–35.
10. See, for example, the introduction to CW, the introduction to Kuyper's *Lectures on Calvinism*, and WWG, 527–28.

agency. Re-creation is the theological concept that satisfies the relationship between all earthly ends and spiritual ends as well. It is the answer to the question of the nature-grace relation: grace restores and renews nature into the kingdom of God, where the two realms of creation are united, the product of re-creation. Neo-Calvinist theology understands that, in Scripture, the kingdom of God is the telos of creation and re-creation, and the organic union between the visible and invisible.[11] Specifically, one of the first and most significant points that the neo-Calvinist fathers urged on their readers was that this kingdom, only capable of being established cataclysmically by God, was the end of creation *before* it was the end of re-creation. Eschatology precedes soteriology.

The kingdom, in other words, is not merely a novel result of God's gracious action. When Christ comes announcing the kingdom, he does so in order to recover creation's goal. God's work of creation was unto the kingdom of God prior to his work of grace. It is true that Kuyper, starting his theological reflection on the foundation of God's absolute sovereignty, understood well that the plan of the Triune God was eternally unchanged— that God from eternity has determined that grace should restore nature, God being unmoved by history. Simultaneously, if one looks carefully at the end of creation itself and particularly at the purpose of humanity in relation to the covenant of works, one finds the kingdom of God implicitly framed in the perfecting union of the Edenic temple and the cultural mandate of Genesis 1. It is this logic that offers the classic neo-Calvinist dictum "grace *restores* nature" to its original end: God making home with humanity on earth.[12] Kuyper makes the point of God's unified work: "the Savior of the world is also the *Creator* of the world; indeed he could become its Savior only because he was its Creator."[13] Kuyper even extends this logic to Christian action before the coming of the kingdom in Christ's second advent:

---

11. For the interested reader, Bavinck develops his theology of the kingdom in contrast to Albrecht Ritschl's this-worldly kingdom, wherein God establishes the perfectly moral religion in Jesus Christ (Bavinck, "Theology of Albrecht Ritschl").

12. Bavinck uses the phrase "grace restores nature" in *RD* 3:577.

13. Abraham Kuyper, "Common Grace," in Bratt, *Abraham Kuyper: A Centennial Reader*, 169–70.

Christ does not undo the work of creation, but joins himself to that creation and builds upon it. This same truth applies to Christian society. If the foundation of society is provided in creation, and if sin has deformed the edifice of society, then Christ comes not to establish an entirely new kind of society alongside it, but his kingly authority rather extends in order to restore the original, to correct what has become deformed, to perfect the unfinished construction.[14]

If one asks, then, "What is the highest good?" and "In what life does creation find its true fulfillment?" or "What manner of creaturely life makes most of the glory of the Triune God?" then the answer is also to see God in the garden-temple, the city of God, the kingdom of God, or as it is put in Ephesians 1, the presence of God in the union of heaven and earth. Bavinck wonders then about all manner of secondary goods: Is the ultimate good individual freedom or communal harmony? Is it sensual or spiritual? Was Plato correct to suggest that the release from sensation and individuality into the ideal is humanity's chief end?[15] As the chief dogmatician of the neo-Calvinist movement, Bavinck placed intense attention on the biblical concept of the kingdom of God to do the work of uniting individual and communal, sensational and spiritual, earthly and heavenly, history and eternity.

THE GOD OF CREATION'S END

Before all else, for both Kuyper and Bavinck (and we will come back to this point in the final section of this chapter), the kingdom of God is God's kingly presence on earth with his people. In this presence, the body of Christ is fulfilled, satisfied, and finally joyous. But there are other goods at play in this discussion, including holiness, virtue, happiness, prosperity, wealth, honor, eternality, peace, rest, and reward. Eternal life, says Bavinck, is fellowship with God, fellowship with God's people, and fellowship with God's land.[16] All goods are rooted in the fact of being in the presence of God, who is condescended in the union of heaven and earth, the kingdom.

---

14. *Pro Rege* 3:23.
15. KGHG, 135.
16. WWG, 529.

Since Kuyper and Bavinck placed so much weight on the theological concept of the re-creation of original creation, and particularly so as God's presence on earth, following their fathers, neo-Calvinist theologians continue to advance the exegetically established theological hope that the kingdom of God, (or as Kuyper often says: the kingdom of glory) is the end of re-creation, as well as the meaning of history. Indeed, Bavinck understood his work on the theology of the kingdom and re-creation to be aiding in a recovery of the kingdom concept that was vibrant during the era of Reformation and missing at varying degrees in the centuries following. Bavinck is well-known for his central focus on the kingdom as the pearl and leaven: the kingdom of heaven is a pearl of great price—one sells everything to buy it. "The kingdom of heaven is a mustard seed that grows into a tree. The kingdom of heaven is leaven and God sows that leaven until the whole lump is leavened; until all sin is eschewed and the whole world is the object of God's loving work."[17]

One might summarize the whole logic with this quote from Bavinck: "As creation, being a work of wisdom, points back to generation, it also points forward to revelation ... and revelation has salvation as its goal. ... Although revelation has this soteriological content, it is a restoration, and not an annihilation, of God's creative work, which was corrupted by sin. Revelation is a work of reformation."[18] God's work of revelatory grace serves the end of creation itself and then, because of sin, must be a work of *reformation.* The twentieth-century evangelical theological renewal on the nature of salvation as re-creation is due in some measure to these emphases. Several important points of dogmatic theology pertain.

The doctrine of God is the starting point for theological reflection on creation and its end. For Kuyper and Bavinck, even making metaphysical sense of history and science is a matter of faith in the Triune God just as much as it is for the discipline of theology. If there is a unity and organizing principle to all the events of the space-time continuum, then it has to be found in reflection on the invisible, rather than in studying the events themselves. Faith compels a comprehensive world- and life-view that gives rise to a

17. CCC, 224.
18. CW, 114.

philosophy of revelation, including a philosophy of history. This logic is part of an organic worldview.

For example, confessing the "unity of God" is the "foundation" of a true view of both "history" and "nature."[19] Bavinck goes on and makes the possibility of a unified, meaningful existence contingent on the fact of the oneness of God's being and the unity of God's consciousness. The unity of a creaturely organism depends on the absolute unity of its maker. Because *one* mind and will created the world rather than a pantheon or impersonal fate or chance, history can be *history*, not the just the collision of atoms causing uninterpretable events across time.

Then, Kuyper and Bavinck both rely on the doctrine of God to find the meaning of creaturely life in every way. For instance, in 1881, a twenty-seven-year-old Bavinck described God cheekily as "an entirely perfect system" in order to make the point that life in contemporary society could never reach its potential without the widespread confession of the Triune God, which informs the analogous creaturely systems of human existence: the moral, juridical, social, and political.[20] All persons must proceed on the basis that life is systematic, teeming with unity in diversities, and all persons act on the typically unconfessed basis that a *Word* is the foundation of everything. Kuyper argues too that "when the focus is on Christ, the focus is on God himself and our soul finds rest only when it surveys and summarizes the whole course of history from paradise to the return of the Lord under one perspective."[21]

To understand creation, one first must understand that God was and is entirely blessed within himself apart from creation. Kuyper emphasizes that we must not think of "the creation, the world, the universe, things visible and invisible, angels and humans, body and soul" without saying that these things came into being apart from God's "self-sufficient and blessed" life within himself from all eternity. Only that which is in God is essential, he argues. God creates only because it pleases him to "make the reflection of his own glory radiate in this overwhelming abundance of his

---

19. *PoR*, 111.

20. Herman Bavinck, "The Pros and Cons of a Dogmatic System," trans. Nelson Kloosterman, *BR* 5 (2014): 92.

21. *CG* 1:267.

own creative power." All of this is the case precisely because God is triune and not mono-static. A singular, rigid unity cannot enjoy a beatific state, he argues. Yet, God "possesses within himself the full life of personality."[22] God's triunity makes creation possible. If creation were a need, then God would be something other than absolute and thus unable to share from the abundance of his own being.

Further, one of the significant initial points Kuyper and Bavinck emphasize is that all of what God does in pouring forth contingent being is the work of the one God. The one God, being one in mind and will, displays one plan for the one history of the world. That history of the world is above all marked by creation and re-creation: "It is always one and the same God who acts both in creation and re-creation." The Father creates and re-creates all things *through* the Son and *in* the Spirit. The unity of God in God's agency toward the world is derivative of the fact that the Trinity is one. Father, Son, and Spirit are one in nature, with the same attributes, unity in Trinity and Trinity in unity. All the works of God *ad extra* are the works of the one God unfolding into being "through the cooperation of the three persons."[23]

Appealing to Athanasius and Ephesians 4:6, Bavinck argues that "as Father God is *above* us all, as Son he is *through* all, and as Spirit he is *in* all, and that the Father creates and re-creates all things *through* the Son *in* the Spirit."[24] All proceeds from God the Father. All is accomplished by the Son. All is completed by the Holy Spirit. "Thus, the entire cosmos was created and arranged according to a fixed plan ... [where] all things were oriented unto each other... exist together in an unbreakable connection ... provid[ing] glorious insight into the systematic, ordered, and teleological nature of the creation."[25] In creation, the Son is mediator and Spirit perfecter, as is the case with redemptive re-creation. The goal and work are unified. Likewise, so says Kuyper on the "ingoing and outgoing" works of God: "We begin with the general distinction: That in every work effected by Father, Son, and Holy Ghost in common, the power *to bring*

---

22. *CG* 1:468–69.
23. *RD* 2:318–19.
24. *RD* 2:319; Athanasius, *Letter to Serapion* 14; 28; 2.6, 7.
25. Bavinck, "Pros and Cons," 90.

forth proceeds from the Father; the power *to arrange* from the Son; the power *to perfect* from the Holy Spirit."[26]

Bavinck even argues that there could be no creation at all unless God were triune. He explains: the eternal generation of the Son is the first communication of God in an absolute sense. God first generates the Son and communicates himself fully to the Son, who is God. Eternally, God communicates his full image. Contingently, God communicates his image to creatures in creation. Bavinck argues that the "two are connected. ... If in an absolute sense God could not communicate himself to the Son he would be even less able in a relative sense to communicate himself to his creature."[27] This insight highlights the uniqueness of the Christian doctrine of creation, wherein God is not a monadic prime mover but eternally intrapersonal and communicative. Likewise, in *Wonderful Works of God*, he argues that because humanity is the image of God, God is shareable, shareable absolutely within himself in the communicative nature of the divine persons and shareable relatively outside himself in creation.[28] Bavinck places particular emphases on the possibility of creation, incarnation, and re-creation grounded in the fact of eternal generation.

Turning to God, then, as the starting point of creation's end is merely a part of the broader Calvinist logic mentioned prior that God's glory is the point of creaturely existence. Kuyper emphatically and persistently declares throughout his corpus that the glory of God is key to the meaning of history, which is ultimately found in the union of heaven and earth. For example, his work on the *Revelation of St. John*:

> The Apocalypse returns to the starting point of Gen. 1:1—"In the beginning God created the heavens and the earth." In keeping with this, the final outcome of the future, foreshadowed in the Scriptures, is not the merely spiritual existence of saved souls, but the restoration of the entire cosmos, when God will be all in all in all under the renewed heaven on the renewed earth. ... [This] restoration is and ever will be the salvation of that which was first created.[29]

---

26. Kuyper, *Work of the Holy Spirit*, 19.
27. *RD* 2:420.
28. *WWG*, 306.
29. Kuyper, *Revelation of St. John*, 344.

The teleology of creation, then, for Kuyper and Bavinck, results from a logic that believes in the unity of God's consciousness, from which God brings forth a creation order that is analogous to his image, striving toward a creaturely organism that displays a creaturely unity in diversity. In beginning its dogmatic arguments with God in himself and then moving to the organism of creaturely telos, neo-Calvinist theology emphasizes the point Kuyper called the "mother-idea" of Calvinism, as mentioned in chapter 2: "It is not God who exists for the sake of His creation; the creation exists for the sake of God. For, as the Scripture says. He has created all things for Himself."[30] This analog of organism does not suggest that God's consciousness is an organism, a unity of parts, but that the unity of parts in both creation and the kingdom of God was and is to image God in himself. *"Our God creates and re-creates everything in his own image by his Word."*[31]

THE SPIRIT OF CREATION AND RE-CREATION

In Kuyper's corpus especially, there is immense attention given to the work of the Spirit, with special reference to both creation and re-creation. Kuyper argues that the Father as King determines the kingdom, the Son builds it, and the Holy Spirit finishes. This is a way of speaking not merely about the redemptive work of God but about the work of creation. The Spirit's work has always remained the same: "Wherefore the Spirit's work leading the creature to its destiny includes an influence upon all creation from the beginning. And, if sin had not come in, we might say that this work is done in *three* successive steps: first, *impregnating* inanimate matter; second, *animating* the rational soul; third, *taking up His abode* in the elect child of God."[32]

The Holy Spirit's work in creation is to "kindle and bring forth all life"[33] by germinating, animating, and making home with the children of God. The work of the Spirit, as Kuyper puts it, is to bring creation to its

30. Abraham Kuyper, *Calvinism: Six Lectures Delivered in the Theological Seminary at Princeton.* New York; Chicago; Toronto: Fleming H. Revell Company,1899, 52.

31. Herman Bavinck, "Eloquence," in *On Preaching*, trans. James Eglinton (Peabody, MA: Hendrickson, 2017), 32.

32. Kuyper, *Work of the Holy Spirit*, 24.

33. Kuyper, *Work of the Holy Spirit*, 109.

destiny, to finish the work, to realize creation's end. For this reason, all
that the Spirit has done in creation's history since that power of privation (sin) entered the material realm is to bring humanity to said destiny.
The evil principle and power aims to keep creation from its goal, and the
Spirit is the paraclete (the one who comes alongside creation) in order
to complete creation.

Then, as Kuyper describes, the Holy Spirit first "antagonizes sin," and
he shall "annihilate it." "Redemption is therefore not a *new* work *added*
to that of the Holy Spirit, but it is *identical* with it. He undertook to bring
all things to their destiny either *without* the disturbance of sin or *in spite
of it.*" The Holy Spirit hovered on the teeming waters as the giver of life,
and the organizer of order, in the beginning. The Spirit's work between
sin and salvation or between the beginning of the age of antagonism and
the annihilation of sin is to preserve creation order, "save the elect," and
then in the end "restor[e] all things in heaven and earth."[34]

On the re-creative work of the Spirit, Kuyper states emphatically
that the glory of Jesus in re-creation depends on the finishing work and
immense weight laid down in the agency of the Spirit in bringing about
the glory of the Son in re-creation. The Spirit is Christ's Spirit and the perfecter of Christ's work. And so Bavinck as well: "This same divine wisdom
that created the world also re-creates it, and this same divine energy that
makes things that exist persist also leads them to a firmly established conclusion." Here, Bavinck argues that Christ mediates the re-creation of the
world as the divine Wisdom himself and that the same "divine energy," the
Spirit, who gives life and persistence, leads creation to its conclusion. For
Bavinck, similarly, until the Son cataclysmically mediates re-creation, the
Spirit of God (1) maintains life in the current order and (2) brings about
the goods of the Son's work with a view to adding citizens to the kingdom
of God, because he is the Spirit of Christ. This is the Father's plan: "The
plan for salvation is sealed within the plan for creation."[35]

Thus, as argued, the work of the Holy Spirit bears the same character
in creation and re-creation, *which is to perfect the work of the Son.* "If we

---

34. Kuyper, *Work of the Holy Spirit*, 24.

35. *CW*, 113.

admit that He quickens life in that which is created by the Father and by the Son, what does He do in the re-creation but once more quicken life in him that is called of the Father and redeemed by the Son? Again, if the Spirit's work is God's touching the creature's being by Him, what is re-creation but the Spirit entering man's heart, making it His temple, comforting, animating, and sanctifying it?"[36] The Spirit's work of re-creation, for Bavinck and Kuyper, is the commissioned work of the Son.

THE PROBLEM OF CREATION

We will return to the distinctives of a neo-Calvinist treatment of sin and its effects in chapter 7. It is necessary here nevertheless to briefly elucidate the reason for the "re-" in "re-creation." Kuyper and Bavinck both repeatedly argue that one's perception of the relationship between creation and salvation depends on what one understands the problem to be that stands in the middle. So Kuyper: "the differences that keep Christians divided find their origins in the first chapters of Genesis." He goes on to note that the nature of re-creation is especially determined by the doctrines of the image of God, the relation between nature and grace, and the fall into sin. Whatever a theologian thinks about these matters determines their doctrine of salvation, so Kuyper and Bavinck repeat. The oppositions between "anabaptists and Calvinists" as well as the "Roman Catholic Church and the Protestant churches find [their] origins" in Genesis 1–3.[37]

Kuyper suggests, then, to take the logic further, that one's understanding of the problem of creation also depends on a take on the state of righteous creation. First, Kuyper points out that the focus of original creation is on the goodness of the garden of Genesis 2. For him, by "garden" the Bible simply refers to a place that bears the mark of design ("it cannot mean anything else"), one fit for human beings. While animals need no design, humans do. In this space, there was nothing that could hinder humanity's production or distress humanity's will. The flora and fauna opened themselves to humanity, offered their goods, and adorned the space with a beauty that enticed the eye beyond the imagination of the

---

36. Kuyper, *Work of the Holy Spirit*, 46.
37. CG 1:126.

current order. There was peace, and no "tormenting insect," as the name Eden expresses "all-round delight." Yet, this was not the height of the good life. The fountain of God's love poured over humanity while simultaneously they looked forward to the fulfillment of their life in God's presence. Kuyper's sharpest point is to reprimand the contemporary reader lest they "settle for less" than the "highest ideal" and therefore "*miss* less because [they] *desire* less." The God of the garden in the space of the garden is an "overabundance," and sin blinds us from seeing the depths to which we have really fallen.[38]

In the garden, then, we must suppose that the first humans would have transformed into a higher state without the mediation of death and that this higher state would have been the natural development of human life as God intended.[39] This is not to say, however, that the state of glory would have come because "glory was already present."[40] There was to be no shift in either the ethical or ontological state of Adam. It was not that humans were to become supernature, or that they were to transform to a higher state of righteousness, but that they were to mature in the order God had made them in already, according to their nature, filling the earth and then enjoying the condescended presence of God. The tree of life was the sacrament of that maturity (Rev 2:7); for the one who makes it all the way, God grants the tree of life as food, the depiction of the state of maturity. The tree of life signified the telos of everlasting human existence in the garden, but now does so only as an agent of future healing. As it stands now, the tree of life has become a tree of death, capturing its eater in the order of death.

Such logic depends on both Kuyper and Bavinck's emphasis on the covenant of works. Their understanding of the covenant of works is a critical component in the unity between creation and re-creation as well as the origin of the need for re-creation. Covenant is a prominent conceptual

---

38. CG 1:130–32.

39. These emphases are found as well in the exegetical work of Geerhardus Vos. See, for example, "The Eschatological Aspect of the Pauline Conception of the Spirit," in *Redemptive History and Biblical Interpretation: The Shorter Writings of Geehardus Vos*, ed. Richard B. Gaffin (Philipsburg, NJ: P&R, 1980), 91–125.

40. CG 1:143.

feature of Bavinck's dogmatics in particular. The Creator-creature relation itself, the most fundamental of all relationships, is covenantal and is also the foundation of the possibility of religion. Bavinck defines the concept of covenant in general as "reciprocal fidelity and an assortment of generally recognized moral obligations" between persons. And "in Scripture 'covenant' is the fixed form in which the relation of God to his people is depicted and presented." Bavinck was convinced that Hosea 6:7 offers significant proof of the covenant relation between God and Adam prior to Adam's sin. The verse compares Israel to Adam and states that "like Adam they transgressed the covenant." Bavinck makes plain that affirming the God-Adam covenant traditionally called the covenant of works "must never be surrendered" because "covenant is the essence of true religion." For Bavinck, God's act of creation is covenantal, and the product of making a creature in his image is the covenant of works, which bears the character of religion. It is not just that God is master and humanity his servants, but also that God has given birth to a relationship "of a king to his people, of a father to his son, of a mother to her child."[41] All relations, he argues, find their model in the relationship between Creator and creature.

Like Kuyper, Bavinck construes the covenantal relation between God and Adam as provisional with a view to maturation and a passing through to higher glory or through sin unto death by means of obedience or disobedience to the moral law and probationary command. The covenant of works seeks one ideal: eternal life, fellowship with God.[42] Here is the connection between creation and re-creation, one established by the same covenantal purpose, that in the covenant of works and the covenant of grace, "Scripture knows but one ideal," eternal life. The covenant of works is the covenant of creation itself, established in the Creator-creature relation in Adam, and the covenant of grace is the covenant of re-creation, established in the Creator-creature relation through Christ. So Bavinck:

> This is further reinforced by the parallel that Paul draws in Romans 5:12–21 between Adam and Christ. As the obedience of one man, that is, Christ, and the grace granted to humanity in him, brought

---

41. RD 2:569.
42. RD 2:564.

acquittal, righteousness, and life, so the one transgression and mis-
deed of the one man is the cause of condemnation, sin, and death
for humanity as a whole. The relation between us and Adam is
like that between us and Christ. We in fact stand to Adam in the
same relation. He is a type of Christ, our head, from whom guilt
and death accrue to us because of his transgression.[43]

The specific question within this discussion of the prefall covenant that
provoked Kuyper and Bavinck above all in their late nineteenth-century
context was that of the condition of humanity before sin. Both understood
the Reformation and their own theologies on the nature of humanity prior
to the fall to be directly contra their perceptions of the Roman Catholic,
particularly modern neo-Thomistic, prelapsarian anthropology. It was
in working against their understanding of this anthropology that Kuyper
and Bavinck developed their theology of creation and re-creation. So
Kuyper: "From the Roman Catholic side, the notion had been accepted
that man's original righteousness did not belong to our human nature by
virtue of creation, but was added as a supernatural gift of grace to our
natural gifts. ... By nature, not righteousness but conflict ruled." Even
for original humanity, the flesh battled the spirit. God, however, added
a "safety measure" by supernatural grace, the likeness of God "added
to his nature."[44] Without said likeness, the battle of the spirit would be
lost to the flesh.

Thus, in this take, in the garden of God, nature was set over against
supernature. Therein, righteousness was not the natural state of humanity, but was a supernatural grace that humanity needed even without sin.
For Rome, according to Kuyper, the problem of creation is ontic from the
very beginning. God made his most prized creature naturally inadequate
for the presence of God. Nature stood opposed to, or unfit for, supernature. The union of the two was not possible according to natural creation.
Kuyper makes the point using Robert Bellarmine: "Bellarmine argues

---

43. RD 2:565. Likewise in RD 2:570: "The covenant of works and the covenant of grace do not
differ in their final goal but only in the way that leads to it. In both there is one mediator, then, a
mediator of union, now, a mediator of reconciliation." Also, for a full discussion of the relationship
between covenant and re-creation see Mattson, *Restored to our Destiny.*

44. CG 1:156.

that within a human being there is by nature 'a conflict between his flesh and his spirit, between his reason and desire ... resulting from a certain condition of the material; and that God has therefore added 'original righteousness' to nature as a golden bridle.'"[45]

Bavinck likewise argues consistently throughout his corpus that "Rome replaced the antithetical relation of sin and grace with the contrast between natural and supernatural religion. Upon this latter contrast she erected a system that conflicted with the principles of apostolic Christianity."[46] For Bavinck, the Roman doctrine errs by misunderstanding that God created Adam merely earthly, sensuous, and then added to that man the "divine image" as a gift. While this natural man is fit for natural religion, he can never attain to the supernatural destination, the heavenly life. So, God adds his image to make him fit for the presence of God, as if humanity by nature were not the image of God already.[47]

Quite simply, the neo-Calvinist fathers reemphasized in contrast that "our nature became so corrupt" and all human desire came into conflict with the Spirit, not by human nature in itself, but by "the disobedience of our first parents."[48] The most important emphasis of both Kuyper and Bavinck on the problem of creation (which determines the nature of re-creation) is that the human rebellion against God and humanity's subsequent fall from the life of overabundance is an ethical, not ontological, problem. Nature was always fit for the presence of supernature prior to human sin. The separation between the two is not an issue of being but one of justice in the face of unrighteousness. Even in the era of sin, the separation is not absolute. God reveals himself, and the hosts of heaven are ministering spirits. The Christian system within Protestantism, Bavinck argues, is not one of supernatural elevation but divine condescension in the covenant of grace.[49]

---

45. CG 1:158.

46. Bavinck, "Common Grace," 45.

47. For a full explanation of Bavinck's understanding of this doctrine, see "Common Grace," 45–48.

48. Heidelberg Catechism, Lord's Day 3, A 7.

49. Bavinck, "Common Grace," 50.

Indeed, there is a distinction between creaturely beings, between nature and supernature. But, the distinction between nature and super-nature must not be taken dualistically. So, "through the fall we did not lose anything that had been added to our nature, but something that belonged to our nature itself. ... Reformed churches have never taught that through the fall humanity's essence was affected, so that a sinner would no longer be a human being." Sin did indeed change the nature of humankind, but "the essence ... remained what it was, and will remain so, even if it descends forever into the place of damnation."[50] Our nature is totally corrupted by sin, as is the order of the world, but human and creaturely being is good in itself, as God made it. Thus, it is human nature and the nature of the world that are to be restored by grace. Grace restores but does not destroy nature. For God said, "Behold, it is very good" (Gen 1:31).

God did not ordain creation to be inadequate for his purposes. Why would the good God create nature in his absolute power in order to augment that creation to fill the gaps of its insufficiencies? Kuyper argues that this view supposes that God needed a "safety valve" to provide himself a net from the danger of creation. Such a view, he supposes, is "mechanistic" and not "organic"—that original creation had a breach in its unity only to be glued together by affixing a so-called supernatural gift. Instead, humanity's nature, bearing the essence of humanness, was to become exactly what it is was to become "via normal development."[51] The conflict is not normal. The conflict of the flesh and spirit is the product of human sin, and the problem of creation is a problem of ethics.

THE NATURE OF RE-CREATION

THE CHRIST OF RE-CREATION

Unlike creation order, Kuyper argues, *"the work of re-creation has this peculiarity, that it places the elect at once at the end of the road."* Putting this logic in the metaphor of the traveler journeying home, he writes: "Of course, he did not run that road; he could never have reached the goal.

---

50. CG 1:159–60.
51. CG 1:163.

His Mediator and Daysman travelled it for him and in his stead."[52] The work of re-creation, in other words, turns to look directly at Jesus Christ, the incarnate God-man. Restoration in the neo-Calvinist theology is not repristination. Most basic to Reformed theology in general is the understanding that the glorified eschaton is distinct and greater than the glory of the Edenic life. The Edenic life was teleological and unperfected. It is the incarnation that stands between. "Christ gives more than sin took away."[53]

Jesus Christ is the mediator of re-creation because he, as the Logos, is the mediator of creation. In speaking of the Logos of Christ, the Word, Kuyper argues that creation, and likewise re-creation, is not a "creation of newly invented things." Rather, all that God makes is "organically related to his own being." This is not to suggest that God is an organism or forms an organic unity with creatures. Rather, creaturely life is an organic unity that contingently reflects the absolute unity of God—all of creation bears God's image. How so? Kuyper is implicitly appealing here to a doctrine of divine ideas, that God is not only the cause but also exemplar of all actuality, except the privation of the good that is itself the power we call evil. In a second move, he appeals to the mediation of the Son in bringing forth the divine ideas: "because everything is created through the Word and there is absolutely nothing among what has been created that is not related in its origin to that Word that was from eternity with God and that was God."[54]

Here he makes a prepositional distinction. It is not that all was created out of the Word—a scenario of invented, made-up, altogether new things without direct relation to God's own attributes. Rather, all is created *out of* the Father and *through* the Son. Therefore, there is no creature in which the Father has not imprinted the image of divine being through the mediation of the Son, and there is no creature that does not find its exemplar in the mind of God. By the Word, the creation stands in unbroken relation to God. Colossians 1:16–17 is the exegetical source. Kuyper argues: Paul uses *synestēken* to suggest that all things hold together by

---

52. Kuyper, *Work of the Holy Spirit*, 50.

53. Bavinck, "Common Grace," 59.

54. CG 1:469.

the Word. *Synestēken* is not suggesting merely that the Son is the source of life for each creature, but that the Word is that which holds the diversity of creaturely being together as a unity; the Son is the organic interconnectional power. "Were the Word to withdraw from it, the universe would fly apart like dust."[55] The Son of God descends all the way to the subatomic, to the deepest domains beyond what the science of chemistry will ever reach, in order to hold the substratum of being together. He is the light that gives life to all.

When sin entered creation as the power of dualism, Christ, the mediator of creation, came to give more than sin took away, as mediator of re-creation. Thus, particular grace is everything; the center and the pivot. Likewise, that means Christ is everything. As Kuyper puts it: "Christ takes first position here. He through whom all things are, and we through him."[56] All of creation revolves around the Son because all was created through him, and all created for him. Thus creation is the servant of re-creation. The end of creation is re-creation, the kingdom of God, and the end of the kingdom is Christ himself. For Kuyper explicitly, Jesus Christ is the end of re-creation. Re-creation is not for the glorification of humanity foremost, but only as far as humanity participates in the eschatological life of Christ, the God-man.

Bavinck makes a similar point by way of theological method. In *Reformed Dogmatics*, he states that while Jesus Christ is not the starting point of theology, he is the center of theology, as he is the center of history and redemption. All of theological reflection prepares for Christ or infers from Christ. Thus, Christ is the "heart of dogmatics."[57] In his person, as the God-man, he is the living organism that stands at the center of the organisms of theology and re-creative redemption. He is also the heartbeat of the Christian's religious-ethical life. For at its center is the "mystery of godliness," or the substitutionary work of Christ.[58]

To apply the centrality of Christ more specifically to re-creation, Bavinck states: "In re-creation the creation is restored in all its *formae*

---

55. *CG* 1:471.
56. *CG* 1:266.
57. *RD* 1:274. For a book-length treatment of this idea, see Pass, *Heart of Dogmatics*.
58. *RD* 1:274.

and *normae*: the law in the gospel, justice in grace, the cosmos in Christ."[59] In other words, Jesus Christ is the kingdom of God. In him, all is made whole. His presence and rule is the definition of re-creation and in the re-creative work of the King, the Christ, his creative glory is all the more manifest and restored to its creation intent. The benefits of re-creation that accrue to humankind are second. They only take shape in the established glory of the King.

Bavinck argues that in the threefold office of Christ as prophet, priest, and king humanity is given a prophecy of the original task and re-creative telos. "In his exercise of the three offices ... lay the purpose and destiny of man." Christ came to reimage the true image of God as a man and then, by participating (or being united) in Christ, bring humanity to its fullness. In their prophetic call, the proto-humans were to herald the glory of God to the world. In their priestly call, they were to be representative agents of God to the lesser creatures. In their kingly role, they were to rule the earth as stewards of God's gifts. Jesus Christ is the fulfillment of the threefold call. He proclaims God to us; he reconciles us to God; he rules and protects.[60] Christ the King is the king of the kingdom and the unifying agent in the organism of re-creation.

How does Christ accomplish this re-creation? For Bavinck, although the incarnation is the starting point of Christ's historical work of redemption, it is not its most important feature or its center. While the blessed life highlights the telos that is Christ's kingship, Bavinck repeatedly argues that the high-priestly sacrifice of Christ is the center of redemption as well as history. His death on the cross is of "infinite power and worth" and is "abundantly adequate for the reconciliation of the sins of the whole world." The neo-Calvinist fathers follow Scripture in its emphasis on the love of God for the world. In Christ's sacrifice, the love of God is exhibited for the world, for "it is the Father's good pleasure" that "just as the world was created by the Son, so also it is destined to belong to him as the Son and heir."[61] Kuyper encapsulates the whole of the work of the mediator of re-creation here:

---

59. *CW*, 113–14.
60. *WWG*, 316–17.
61. *WWG*, 312, 340.

Christ gives more than sin stole; grace was made much more to abound. He does not simply restore us to the *status integritatis* [state of righteousness] of Adam; he makes us, by faith, participants of the *non posse peccare* [being unable to sin] (1 John 3:9) and of the *non posse mori* [being unable to die] (John 11:25). Adam does not again receive the place which he lost by sin. The first man was of the earth, earthy; the second man is the Lord from heaven. Just as we have born the image of the earthy, so too after the resurrection shall we bear the image of the heavenly man (1 Cor. 15:45- 49). A new song will be sung in heaven (Rev. 5:9, 10), but the original order of creation will remain, at least to the extent that all distinctions of nature and grace will once and for all be done away with.[62]

THE NATURE OF THE KINGDOM

While the present humanity wears the "autumnal robe of fadedness and decay," theologians occupy themselves with the imaginings of a re-created order. It has been a hallmark of the neo-Calvinist tradition of the twentieth-century to describe life in the union of heaven and earth in innovative ways. Perhaps more than any other theological tradition, neo-Calvinism has helped churches rediscover the fact of eschatological bodily resurrection. The "spiritual imbalance" of imagining a merely ethereal life in eternity is "pressed so far that the resurrection of the flesh hardly counts for anything anymore," Kuyper complains.[63] What do the neo-Calvinist fathers have to say on the nature of re-creation?

Perhaps one of the more common emphases from both Kuyper and Bavinck is on the earthly nature of the heavenly life—or on the importance of the union of heaven and earth in the kingdom of glory. The biblical images include the new Jerusalem, a new earth and a new heaven, the inheritance of the earth, the city with foundations and gates, fruit-bearing trees, and the river of life, enriched with a banquet meal of fine meats and aged wine. Indeed, this is figurative language, but, as Kuyper points out, language that accompanies the fact of resurrection—the union of soul and body. For Kuyper, this entire world will die and perish, but from it a

---

62. Bavinck, "Common Grace," 59–60.
63. CG 1:137, 571.

germ will rise that manifests the constituent physical and spiritual parts
that is presently contains. In this resurrection, all that is "mechanical or
artificial" will cease. For organic life, all will be made new. While a building is destroyed and an entirely new one is erected, when a caterpillar
becomes a butterfly, there remains an organic continuity. The latter is like
the resurrection of the body and the renewal of the earth.[64] If the Lord
has a body, then the form of the heavenly life must indeed accommodate his form. Kuyper also notes that in the re-created earth, there will
be a dominion over the life of plants and animals that enhances what we
already see in Adam's dominion in the garden, which is also witnessed to
in Daniel's preservation and power among the lions in the Old Testament.

All in all, Kuyper argues that the eschatological life is an organism, a
living communion, a body with one head. There is true organic life in
the kingdom of glory, individual human beings, plants and animals, and
all of it taken together as an organism itself, the parts of existence unified under the head that is the living Christ. Kuyper appeals to the Greek
verb in Ephesians 1:10 often translated as "to unite" (*anakephalaiōsasthai*),
arguing that its basic sense is "to unite under one head."[65] For Kuyper,
this verb conveys the same idea as "organism," the fullness of the union
of constituent parts as a living being. So Kuyper:

> The entire world constitutes an organic whole. Meanwhile this
> organic unity broke apart through the curse and through the fall.
> As a result, earth and heaven, which belonged together as one organ-
> ism under one head, have been torn apart from each other. ... Christ
> will end this by means of his return. He will once again organically
> reconnect those disconnected members and parts of the one great
> organism. ... It is precisely this that is being expressed with the Greek
> word *anakephalaioo*.[66]

Bavinck likewise appeals to Colossians 2:10, where Christ is called the
"head of all principality and power," alongside Ephesians 1:10, where Christ

---

64. CG 1:571–73.
65. CG 1:575–76.
66. CG 1:577.

is said to "recapitulate all things under one head." Bavinck understands these terms to mean that Christ is the principle of organism, the "unifying principle of life," as well as the "sovereign and king."[67] All creatures, with none excluded, are his subordinates. In his relation to all, he is King of kings, and in his relation to the eschatological church, he is the organic Principle, the unifying Agent, the Mediator of life. The eschatological organism is the created artwork of the "supreme Artist," re-created again in Christ. For Kuyper and Bavinck, this means that the great mystery of existence is that the re-creation of the organism under Christ has always been the plan of God and is the fulfillment of his creative purpose. More specifically the secret is this: "the original plan of God was not neutralized but continues full of majesty. ... It is in the re-creation of all things that original creation triumphs."[68] And yet, both theologians emphasize the multilayered nature of re-creation, its progressive and cataclysmic elements. There are at least four marks of re-creation. Three occur in the age before parousia, and the fourth, re-creation in itself, in the second coming of Christ.

The first mark is the incarnation and resurrection. In the incarnation, God pronounces that "what is genuinely human may never and nowhere be snuffed out or suppressed. ... The genuinely human must be made an organ and instrument of the form in which the divine exists."[69] While the work of re-creation is not performed in fallen humanity independently of his original creation, the incarnation is the pronouncement of the re-created creation in the God-man Christ. The Spirit has sustained the natural life, with gifts and talents, with the common graces, but in Christ the goods of humanity do not remain as they are. Particularly in the resurrection, the body of Christ is re-created and all the elect of God united to that body. In the resurrection, Christ is justified, and so the elect are justified, and Christ is made an organic whole, in body and soul, as a human being, and so the elect are pronounced a re-created organism by the Father in the body of the Son. But in the humiliation of incarnation

---

67. *WWG*, 365.
68. *CG* 1:577–78.
69. *KGHG*, 147.

itself, as Bavinck argues, God establishes in Christ that flesh and matter are not in themselves sinful, that matter is of divine origin, and that matter will never cease to be.[70] Kuyper likewise points out three facts of Christ's incarnation that bear witness to re-creation.

First, says Kuyper, "the Triune God raised Him from the dead. St. Peter stated this clearly on the day of Pentecost: 'Whom God has raised up, having loosed the pains of death.'"[71] In the resurrection of the Son, God has wrought mighty power for his elect. So Bavinck: "The physical resurrection of Christ is not an isolated historical fact. It is inexhaustibly rich in meaning for Christ Himself, for the church, and for the whole world."[72] Second, God the Holy Spirit performed a peculiar work in the resurrection to bring Christ to life. Third, this means that if the Spirit of life who brought Christ from the dead dwells in you, then the Spirit of resurrection as re-creation dwells in you. "The nature of this work is apparent from the Holy Spirit's part in Adam's *creation* and in *our birth*. If the Spirit kindles and brings forth all life, especially in man, then it was He who rekindled the spark quenched by sin and death. He did so in Jesus; He will do so in us."[73]

The second mark is the re-creation of the self, which has both a now and not-yet aspect to it. Here Kuyper and Bavinck have in mind the fact of regeneration within the life span of a particular human, or the application of the victory of Christ to the elect. This doctrine depends on some creational concept of the general gifts of life and breath, the common graces, and the fact that sin has corrupted the created self: "the Holy Spirit, who imparts unto man born from above gifts necessary to sanctification and to his calling in the new sphere of life, has in the first creation endowed him with natural gifts and talents."[74] In the incorporation of all earthly goods into the kingdom, Christ's Spirit will not allow those goods to remain as

---

70. *WWG*, 307.

71. Kuyper, *Work of the Holy Spirit*, 108.

72. *WWG*, 349.

73. Kuyper, *Work of the Holy Spirit*, 108–9.

74. Kuyper, *Work of the Holy Spirit*, 46.

they are. They must be wrested "from the dominion of sin. ... Since it is spiritual in nature, however, it only employs spiritual weapons."[75]

The first act of Jesus Christ in his exaltation is the sending of the Spirit, which includes the pouring of the Spirit on the flesh of the church. Christ gives more than sin took away, as the Spirit actualizes the benefits of Christ in the particular, historical lives of his people. In this re-creation of the self, being born of God, or born again by the word of the gospel, the Spirit causes the self to be renewed, bringing forth subjectively the fruit of faith and repentance. On the objective side of this re-creation, God the Father justifies the born-again servant, conferring the fact of Christ's justification to this citizen of the kingdom, forgiving their sins, and giving them the right to eternal life.[76] The regenerated soul's ongoing sanctification, the work of the Spirit to renew the self unto God's holy law, is a witness to the glorification of the self in the re-creation that accompanies Christ's second coming. The Christian life, then, is itself for Kuyper and Bavinck a re-creation and witness unto re-creation.

The third mark is the re-creation of the goods of the spheres, which also have a particular now and not-yet aspect. Since Jesus Christ is the atoning sacrifice for the sins of the whole world, there is no sphere of life untouched by sin and no domain that Christ has not come to save. Kuyper famously shouted that Jesus Christ is sovereign over "every square inch," every domain of creation and human life in particular.[77] Bavinck calls this Christian "universalism"—not that all persons will be saved from their sins, but that the entirety of the domains of existence will be saved by finding their fulfillment in Christ, even if not the particular contents of each domain.[78] This re-created salvation of the spheres of life themselves manifest the possibility of change even in the temporal life prior to the parousia. The kingdom is the "destiny and goal of all those life spheres that exist in society," and so, until then, the Christian life is exhibited in the work to sanctify those spheres.[79] We will explore this doctrine also

---

75. KGHG, 146.

76. WWG, 443.

77. Abraham Kuyper, "Sphere Sovereignty," in Bratt, *Abraham Kuyper: A Centennial Reader*, 488.

78. CCC, 224.

79. KGHG, 155.

in chapter 9 as it relates to neo-Calvinist ecclesiology and the mission of the church. Here we will only describe its briefest contents insofar as they include the sanctification of the relationships within the spheres as a witness to re-creation.

The spheres in this discussion do not include every single aspect of societal life but, more acutely, the domains of human relationship where some good structure of authority or relation is established by God either directly or by good and necessary consequence. Bavinck refers to the "state, church, and culture" as well as the family.[80] Kuyper to more: family, church, state, and the various organizational units of a society's meta- and subcultures, such as an art studio, a charity, a school, or a business—any place that exercises vocation. In addition one might include other God-given relationships, such as friendship, or even persistent relations that occur because of a sinful world: that between socioeconomic classes, the rich and poor, for example. Kuyper has no interest in trying to exhaustively determine the overlapping spheres of human life. These domains and relationships of life exist as an outworking of creational ordinances and have developed extensively in the human response to a sin-stricken world, each fulfilling a purpose.

For both Bavinck and Kuyper, Christ claims the whole of creaturely life, and because godliness is of value in every way, the life of the re-created Christian can indeed serve the good of each of these spheres of existence, and they do so as a witness to the re-creation of these domains in the eschatological life. As Bavinck states in magisterial form: "Christianity knows no boundaries. ... Sin has corrupted much. ... The pollution that always accompanies it penetrates every structure of humanity and the world. ... The blood of Christ cleanses us from all sin, it is able to restore everything ... anyone or anything."[81] Indeed, organizations and relationships can be restored, they can be entities that walk in accordance with God's moral law, or against it, insofar as they move according to the spirit of their people. To be sure, these entities may do so only because they are the expression of human action and decision. The possibility of renewing

---

80. KGHG, 155.
81. CCC, 224.

change stands on the renewal of an individual Christian, exercising godliness with wisdom in particular relationships and vocational practices. A governmental entity can be corrupt, or less so, and the lessening of corruption can be the product of Christian action and corporate repentance due to the work of the Spirit in the life of the organic church.

These sphere-sanctifying possibilities stand as witnesses to the eschaton. How so? In the most general way, the kingdom of God enlists all the goods of human life, the moral goods and their expression in relationship and vocation. So Bavinck: "in itself the Kingdom of God is not hostile toward all those goods. Rather, the Kingdom of God is independent from all of those externalities; it exists above them, enlists them as its instrument, and in so doing returns to them their original purpose."[82] The family, state, church, and culture all find their ends in the kingdom of God as the perfection of family, the most basic of all relations. Family is the primary life sphere from which state, church, and culture emerge. The eschatological and organic kingdom of God is the family of God expressed ultimately as all three spheres. The kingdom is the Father's household, and his people are his children. Christ is the firstborn among many brothers and sisters. Thus the Christian family is, potentially, the greatest witness to re-creation in the earthly life.

In the Old Testament too, Israel's theocracy was a testimony to the shape of this coming kingdom of God particularly as it relates to the life spheres. All of life, every minutia, in Israel was governed by the law of God. "In Israel's theocracy there is a manifest unity between religion and the whole of the people, between the church and state, believer and citizen, nationality and covenant." And so, in the kingdom of God, the "kernel breaks out of the particular husk in which it was enclosed."[83] For neo-Calvinism, one's relationship with God matters for everything. There is no standpoint outside religion. The kingdom in Christ is a societal reality that extends from a particular ethnic people group to encompass the whole world.

---

82. KGHG, 142.
83. CCC, 223.

Indeed, when Christ established his church after his exaltation, Christianity established the church and its religious life as a unique sphere. Christianity is a new life "that can penetrate and enliven every sphere and life form." This in no way entails any concept that structural transformation is necessary for the coming of the kingdom. For these neo-Calvinist fathers, the witness of re-creation in family and culture is not necessary but possible, a biblical calling and pursuit. Because Christ calls his people to godliness, Christian character and ethics should have an influence on the fullness of human life in all its forms. Indeed, we can and should, Bavinck argues, "speak of a Christian society and a Christian school." While the church is a unique organization established by Christ alongside the state and culture, the kingdom of God can manifest as leaven in any domain. For the church is not itself the kingdom of God, but the means for preparing for, and witnessing to, the kingdom. Thus, the church sends the people of God as a consecrated people to the common, natural life, in its moral, civic, and political expressions. Indeed, Sunday must sanctify the other days of the week. The church is not satisfied with piety only within its walls.[84] As Bavinck emphatically states:

> Viewing nothing human as foreign but as spiritual in nature, the Kingdom of God is universal, bound to no place or time, embracing the whole earth and everything human, independent of nation and country, of nationality and race, of language and culture. In Christ Jesus what is legitimate is only what has been created anew, with no exceptions. This is why the gospel of the Kingdom must be brought to all nations, to all creatures, not only to people but to the entire creation (Mark 16:15). The Kingdom of God extends as far as Christianity itself. It exists wherever Christ rules, wherever he dwells with his Spirit. Everything earthly, insofar as it is cleansed and consecrated through Christ, constitutes the Kingdom of God.[85]

Christ takes hold of all that is earthly finally and cataclysmically in his second coming. Until then, Christ manifests his future kingdom in

---

84. KGHG, 157, 159.
85. KGHG, 148.

the agency of Christian godliness alongside the gathering of the institutional church, which is able to spread abroad to all the domains of temporal relationships through the ministry of Word and deed. This hope and command does not ignore the antithetical relationship between the kingdom of this world and the kingdom of God. For Kuyper and Bavinck, there is no naive assumption that the world will slowly and gradually be entirely won for Christ—no, the parousia is a supernatural, cataclysmic hope. And yet, the temporal re-creation of the spheres is a mere act of obedience to the scriptural call to love God and neighbor, even in the midst of losing battles.

The final mark is the re-creation of the cosmos in the coming of the King, the apotheosis of Christianity. For Bavinck, the concept of re-creation is built into the logic of the catholicity of the church. He derives from Cyril of Jerusalem the idea that Christianity provides a catholic cure for a catholic problem, a cure for every kind of sin, the satisfaction of every kind of human need. The kingdom of God is on a catholicizing project. "All dualism is eschewed in the unity of God's theocratic rule."[86] There can be no separation between religion and the rest of life. The kingdom of God is the union of heaven and earth under the coming of the King. The kingdom does not come progressively. "The Kingdom of God is a supernatural act that occurs by means of divine cataclysmic intervention."[87] "Re-creation brings to us that which is eternal, finished, perfected, completed; far above the succession of moments, the course of years, and the development of circumstances."[88]

Kuyper points out a number of properties in the prefall life, as well as the early moments of the postlapsarian world, that give indicators of the physical parameters of the fully re-created cosmos. For one, the vitality of human life was immense even in the years after human rebellion. Yet, in existence apart from sin, "the life force does not diminish at all." One of the more obvious facets, then, of re-created life is its enduring vitality, which one may describe as everlasting. Scripture teaches clearly, Kuyper

86. CCC, 221–22.
87. KGHG, 164.
88. Kuyper, *Work of the Holy Spirit*, 50.

and Bavinck argue, that death came into the world by sin (Rom 5:12). Second, the vitality of re-created bodies is the act of Christ to "transform our lowly body" (Phil 3:21)—to put on the state of glory and take off the state of death. Kuyper argues that the two trees of Eden are the trees of matter and spirit. The tree of life is the tree of the body, intended in its eating for the glorification of the body. The tree of conscience, as he puts it, is the sign of the life of the soul. These two trees represent all that exists; all that humans consist of is "mind and matter," "the visible and invisible," "soul and body."[89] The resurrection life must be the perfection of unity in the relation between soul and body, just as the union of heaven and earth is the union of the material and spiritual creaturely organism in total. "In general [the resurrection] means the victory in principle over death."[90]

Third, this state of glory will remain unperturbed. In "paradise there was no sin but sin could enter. ... In the kingdom of glory ... not only is there no sin, but any entering of sin is utterly inconceivable." The state of glory is "sin-proof, death-proof, and curse-proof." If the problem of creation is first ethical, then the state of glory is one of "unclouded purity." If original righteousness is wisdom, holiness, and being precisely what one was made to be, then re-created life includes intellectual wisdom, a holiness put on in the likeness of the character of God, and being in the right, or being the fullness of human nature.[91] We will return to this point on the chapter that considers the image of God, but re-created humanity is precisely and fully the image of God, thinking God's thoughts and acting in the order of God's character. Additionally, if one is made in the image of another, then to be that image one must turn toward the image giver. In the state of re-creation, humanity is absolutely dependent on God in both being and will, running ever toward God, not away. The end of re-creation is "that we might live with God in eternal happiness."[92] We will consider this particular hope in seeing God in the following section.

Perhaps, however, the most unique frame of reference with respect to eschatology that the neo-Calvinist tradition has pursued appears in this

89. *CG* 1:140, 204.
90. *WWG*, 349.
91. *CG* 1:143–44, 172, 181.
92. Heidelberg Catechism, Lord's Day 3, A 6.

question: "Will the fruit of common grace be destroyed forever, or will that rich multiform development for which common grace has equipped and will yet equip our human race also bear fruit for the kingdom of glory?"[93] Neo-Calvinists have regularly pointed out the consequences of answering this question. On the one hand, to suggest that nothing of this temporal life "passes into eternity" is to "leave us cold and indifferent" in the present. Yet if something remains, then the current common life has everlasting importance. Kuyper and Bavinck both reject outright any hypothesis of development with regards to the coming of the kingdom. In their late careers, the sciences of eugenics that would breed countless evils in a generation to come was quickly rising, and both theologians pointed to the misguided scientism, mixed with religious fervor, that suggested a vision of a scientifically guided utopia. Kuyper is emphatic to say that Scripture is clear that the elements of the world will be burned, likely a metaphor for a total renewal. The eschaton will emerge from some sudden catastrophe, he argues. Kuyper draws the necessary conclusion then that "not a single human writing, not a single human work of art, will transfer from the existing situation to the new one."[94]

With such a clear insight on the end of the works of common grace, how and why did the neo-Calvinist tradition develop its common claim that there is immense continuity between the present life and the kingdom? Kuyper suggests that the output of the life of common grace will indeed perish like the blossoms of the tulip in winter. Yet, like the tulip, with its bulbs safely stored until winter passes, the "germ of this common grace" will be replanted and blossom all the more. Revelation 21:24 does indeed suggest that "the kings of the earth shall bring their glory" into the new heavens and earth. Kuyper explains that this is not meant literally; no book or work of art from the present life will brought into the kingdom of glory. Rather, all these will perish (2 Pet 3:11). However, the "powerful germ" at their foundation will not perish, but will abide.[95]

---

93. CG 1:543.
94. CG 1:544.
95. CG 1:545, 550.

He claims here that the parts of human life, the constituent parts of human nature, and the endowments of human endeavors, just like the beauty of the earth, will remain. God will replant what we are and what we do, in order that it blossom more richly than the imagination allows. Yet, the concrete products of common grace that we now know will be no more. For example, the human body is planted and degrades into dust. The resurrection will reconstitute the body, not by carrying over the old body into the kingdom, but by remaking the lost body of the dead with all its former parts and reuniting the soul to that new body. The germ that originates our labors will be present in the kingdom too, but not the products of those labors. This, for Kuyper, offers an even more exhilarating prospect than one of radical continuity between the products of the present life and artifacts of the next because in the eschatological life, humanity will achieve a development wherein all the frustrations of our strivings will be extinct, and the fruition of one's hands will be inexhaustibly good. In this eternal Sabbath, labors will be exchanged for righteous fruition.

This argument only considers the external fruit of common grace, however. But for the regenerated sinner, there is an internal grace, a development reserved for the elect within their earthly lives—sanctification. Will then the "personal development" of each of God's children "follow them" into the eternal life?[96] Kuyper draws here from Revelation 14:13: "their deeds follow them." So Kuyper: what is achieved in this life in terms of spiritual development is borne by the elect in the life of the kingdom. Herein an individuality is preserved alongside a doctrine of reward.[97] This is not to say there are some with deficient lives of beatitude in the kingdom, no. Rather, there is distinction, development, and difference. The spiritual life is not merely one of deed and virtue, either. But Kuyper includes here the personality, the way of being in a person. Of course, one possesses a name and carries aspects of one's prior formation that regard the self as an ego. Death, he emphasizes, following Heidelberg Catechism Lord's Day 16, A 42, includes an act of sanctification. The self passes through death, being sanctified unto eternal life, and in that passing

---

96. CG 1:552.
97. CG 1:552–59.

carries with it the formation that has already occurred in the "works that were set before them" by God (Eph 2:10).

Yet, in this carrying over, does the extent of personal formation include all that common grace had to offer that individual in the earthly life? Will the farmer carry the skills of his hands? Will the scholar, the knowledge of her field? There is an immeasurable difference of degree between the intellectual, emotional, and spiritual capacities and the actual formation of individual people. Kuyper appeals to Paul's metaphor of maturation between the child and adult in 1 Corinthians 13:11 to argue that a similar maturation will occur in the entrance into the kingdom of glory. Just as the child carries so much of the child's self into adulthood in order to develop to new heights of maturity, so the individual will carry the individual's self into the everlasting life and begin a new age of development. Thus, the formation of our character and person are not incidental matters to God. "These do matter somewhat for eternity; in fact, they matter *a lot*. Nothing is lost."[98]

Most importantly, and at the center of the organism of the everlasting life, is the fleshly body of Christ, the King of the kingdom. The Lord's Supper testifies in the present to the parousia, the interim meal that will no longer be necessary when his body appears, as it becomes an embodied banquet feast. In the Supper, the church enjoys the union of the fleshly and spiritual in the flesh of the bread and the presence of the Spirit of Christ. But in the new existence the bread and the fruit of the vine are fulfilled in his earthly presence. When the church eats this meal, we confess with Christ that we do not want this world to pass away but rather to "cast off its blemishes." In the words of Christ, this is the regeneration of creation (Matt 19:28). "Christ's merit is and remains for eternity the foundation upon which the building of everyone's salvation will rest ... and [in the kingdom] nothing remains to be saved because everything is saved ... and God the Father will be triumphant in his saved and restored creation."[99] Much more may be speculated, as Kuyper and Bavinck sometimes do, yet for both the first word of eschatology is modesty.

---

98. *CG* 1:568.
99. *CG* 1:583, 585.

THE VISION OF GOD IN RE-CREATION

We have only briefly made note of the emphasis of re-creation theology in the neo-Calvinist fathers: "God, and God alone, is man's highest good." Indeed, Bavinck begins his magisterial and popular work of theology, *Magnalia Dei* (*Wonderful Works of God*), with this statement. He spends, across so much of his corpus, ample ink declaring that the human creature "cannot be satisfied with what the whole corporeal world has to offer." Hence, "all men are really seeking after God. ... Man is an enigma whose solution can only be found in God." At the high point of his Christology, he overviews the benefits of Christ, which "are so rich that they simply cannot be calculated or estimated at their just value. They comprehend no less than a whole and perfect salvation. They consist of ... the granting of the highest good, namely, the fellowship with God."[100] In 1904 he wrote: "Salvation ... is not a human act but only the work of God."[101] Bavinck bookends both his *Reformed Dogmatics* and *Magnalia Dei* with emphasis on the vision of God in Christ. For this reason, it is surprising that in recent literature, an indictment against Bavinck's concept of re-creation (and made in contrast to Kuyper's) has been popular.

The recent indictment, particularly by Hans Boersma, is that Bavinck's theology is creation-affirming to the point of glory-negating.[102] Boersma cites Bavinck as the catalyst of a neo-Calvinist failure: the concept that instead "of gaz[ing] eternally into the face of God, we will carry our cultural accomplishments over into the hereafter, and also in the eschaton we will be actively engaged in social and cultural endeavours of various kinds."[103] We could consider these claims as (1) disparaging the vision of the face of God, (2) carrying our cultural artifacts into eternity, and (3) and being actively engaged in social endeavors in the eschaton. Regarding (2), Bavinck, *sed contra*, follows Kuyper directly (in Bavinck's chapter that Boersma is referring to throughout his argument), stating that although

---

100. *WWG*, 1, 2, 6–7, 338.

101. *CW* 114.

102. *SG*. An earlier version of this section appears as Cory Brock, "Revisiting Bavinck and the Beatific Vision," *Journal of Biblical and Theological Studies* 6 (November 2021), 367–382.

103. *SG*, 33.

the accidents of the world will indeed perish, the substance of the world will not. The individual accomplishments of common grace will fade, but the germ will be re-born: "so also this world passes away in its present form as well, in order out of its womb, at God's word of power, to give birth and being to a new world." Again, Bavinck gives a more nuanced presentation than Boersma's claim (that we will carry our cultural accomplishments into the hereafter *simpliciter*): "the new heaven and the new earth will one day emerge from the fire-purged elements of this world."[104]

Regarding (1), Bavinck fully affirms the beatific vision in the face of Christ, as Boersma admits, and this is without considering Bavinck's corpus as a whole but with focus on one chapter in *Reformed Dogmatics* 4. And, regarding (3), it is odd to suppose that for a Reformed theologian, being engaged in social relations in the afterlife undermines the spirituality of that life. Kuyper could not affirm more clearly that social endeavors proceed in the afterlife, and we will consider all these claims below (and they have been articulated already in this chapter).

While Boersma argues that this naturalistic emphasis is the product of Bavinck's theology, not Kuyper's, he more specifically hones in on the fact that Bavinck was "sharply critical" of the doctrine of the vision of God, while Kuyper "warmly embraced the doctrine."[105] This reading participates in a much older reading of Bavinck. Eugene Heideman had already identified a "restoration" motif and "glorification" motif in Bavinck's theology. The former is creation-affirming and the latter creation-negating, as Jon Stanley puts it.[106] Heideman perceives a contradiction between the two in Bavinck's corpus that is eventually overwhelmed by the creation-affirming aspect of the nature-grace relation.

In this section, we claim that this thesis as it relates to Boersma's most recent argument against Bavinck, reading dualism into Bavinck's eschatology between the beatific vision and the material goods of the eschatological life, fails to fit the primary sources. For Bavinck, because the Bible

---

104. *RD* 4:717, 720.

105. *SG*, 33–34.

106. Jon Stanley, "Restoration and Renewal: The Nature of Grace in the Theology of Herman Bavinck," in *Revelation and Common Grace*, vol. 2 of *The Kuyper Center Review* (Grand Rapids: Eerdmans, 2011), 88–89.

draws no dichotomy between creaturely, earthly life and the glorified, spiritual life in the immediate presence of God, theologians should not either. Consider his explanation of the vision of eternal life in the Old Testament especially: "Life was not thought of in an abstract, philosophical manner, as a kind of naked existence. By its very nature, life comprised a fullness of blessings: the fellowship of God *first of all*, but then too, the fellowship of His people, and the fellowship of the land that the Lord had given to his people." In Christ, all is fulfilled. For Bavinck, there is no choice to make between creation and spiritual glorification. Eternal life for humanity includes "unity in his soul and body, unity with God and in harmony with his surroundings," which is precisely what Kuyper argues as well.[107] Nevertheless, it is important to show briefly what Bavinck did think of the vision of God in the eschatological life to establish what has already been mentioned in this chapter: Christ is everything.

According to Boersma, Herman Bavinck sidelined the doctrine of the beatific vision. His broader claim, however, is that in Bavinck, "we witness the modern decline of the plausibility structure of a sacramental ontology—and of the corresponding sense that the future telos of created objects is inscribed in their nature." This is an important claim to take note of. The claim is that in Bavinck (1) due to a modernization of the relation between nature/supernature, we witness the undoing of the plausibility structure that nature relates to supernature in a participatory manner or that nature is disassociated from supernature, thereby moving toward a natural end at the expense of a supernatural end; and (2) final causation (teleology) is thereby either denied or at least undermined. Therein, Boersma's broadest claim is that Bavinck undermined teleology, or a teleological account of creation, what Boersma calls the "sacramental metaphysic underlying the Christian tradition."[108] Boersma then uses Bavinck's so-called critique of the beatific vision to show how Bavinck aided in the undermining of teleology.

While Boersma does credit Bavinck with elements of a "participatory ontology" within his corpus, he laments that Bavinck "opted mostly to

---

107. *WWG*, 529.

108. *SG*, 14, 27–28.

criticize the tradition on this topic," meaning that he was "out of sync" with the metaphysic of the Christian tradition. Boersma argues that Bavinck was "sharply critical of the theology of the beatific vision in the Christian tradition." Again, after making such grand claims (that Bavinck is out of accord with the metaphysic of the Christian tradition and seemingly rejects the beatific vision), Boersma qualifies: "I should note that Bavinck did not oppose the notion of the beatific vision per se." This qualification is maximized a few sentences later: "Although he nowhere denies the future of our face-to-face vision of God, he was clearly not of a mind to dwell on it at any length."[109] The claim has migrated from asserting that Bavinck is one of two theologians (the other is Hans Urs von Balthasar) who caused a decline in the plausibility structure of the world's participatory relation to God, the concept of final causation, and the undermining of the beatific vision, to the claim that while Bavinck affirmed the *visio Dei*, he did not write about it enough.

Boersma also states clearly, however, that Bavinck, in *Reformed Dogmatics* volume 4, argues that the essence of blessedness is "contemplation (visio), understanding (comprehensio), and enjoyment of God (fruition Dei)." Bavinck states the highest end of humanity explicitly, the vision of God, which is for Bavinck, unsurprisingly, beheld in the face of Jesus Christ and includes the immediate presence of the Triune God in fellowship with his people. The problem, for Boersma, is that the discussion is brief and that it still "remains true that most of Bavinck's affirmations of the beatific vision are perfunctory."[110]

Boersma, in some manner, answers his own objection to Bavinck's critiques by showing that Bavinck was very specifically critiquing a presentation of the beatific vision per his understanding of the Roman Catholic context of his time. Boersma argues that Bavinck, while affirming the beatific vision, complained against a nineteenth-century Roman Catholic presentation of that doctrine in four ways. Bavinck wanted to emphasize (1) that believers cannot come to know the very essence of God in some manner of deification wherein there is a substantial union

---

109. *SG*, 34.
110. *SG*, 34.

with the ontological Trinity, (2) that the natural is not to be elevated to supernature by some superadded gift, (3) that we do not conceive of arriving at the vision of God by condign merit, and (4) that the notion of the beatific vision ought not to leave Christ aside and understand the vision in some sense apart from the coming of Christ. All of these qualifications of the vision of God are unsurprising for Bavinck's Reformed Protestant theology. Boersma accordingly acknowledges that Bavinck's critique of this nineteenth-century neo-Thomist scholasticism is "understandable"[111] and seems to register no strong disagreement with any of Bavinck's conditions except that Bavinck could have talked more about how there are nuances in the Roman Catholic tradition that avoid these pitfalls. Here, again, like in the section "The Problem of Creation" above, Bavinck critiqued the particular presentation of the *visio Dei* in his own context with which he disagreed, while, of course, affirming the doctrine of the vision of God fully.

Bavinck argues in volume 4 of *Reformed Dogmatics*, for example, that "eternal life is our portion here already and consists in knowing God in the face of Christ. ... Christ is and remains the way to the Father, the knowledge and vision of God. ... The Son is the mediator of union (*mediator unionis*) between God and his creation." Boersma's complaint, then, is that Bavinck does not unpack that claim, one with which Boersma registers no disagreement. Boersma laments that in that particular section Bavinck does not spend significant pages explaining in a positive way just what the *visio Dei* entails. The real issue, then, is the problem of not saying enough, and more specifically not saying enough in the eschatology section of the *Dogmatics*. Yet, Bavinck argues that one of the reasons for not speculating into the positive nature of the *visio Dei* in detail is his conviction that eschatology must remain a modest endeavor. One can only go where Scripture goes, in his Reformed-theological logic. Scripture does not give positive explanation of the eschatological vision. So Bavinck: "The end of things, like their origin and essence, is unknown to us."[112]

111. SG, 36.
112. RD 4:589, 685.

What we arrive at is that Bavinck affirmed the beatific vision emphatically and clearly and was simultaneously critical of some theological expressions of that vision, particularly the nineteenth-century neo-Thomist understanding present within his own context, as Bavinck understood it. One could claim that Bavinck misunderstood the neo-Thomist presentation of the *visio Dei*. However, that is a separate claim. Bavinck made distinctions between less biblical ways of rendering the idea and ones more attuned to the logic of Scripture.

Did Bavinck fail to understand that there are Roman Catholic presentations of the vision of God that are more attuned to his rendering? Perhaps so. But Boersma's original claim is that Bavinck undermines the premodern plausibility structure of participatory ontology by a thoroughgoing critique of the beatific vision and thereby undermines the notion of final causation. We submit that this claim is untenable and that while later aspects of the neo-Calvinist tradition may participate in overmaterialized eschatologies that downplay the immediate presence of God in the face of Christ as the only hope of humankind and its highest good, neither Kuyper *nor* Bavinck does. In other words, Boersma misses that Bavinck was critiquing merely one stream of theological reflection on the *visio Dei* and makes the untenable claim that Bavinck was deviating from the Christian tradition on this issue.

These conjoined assertions that Boersma presents are not appropriate even by Boersma's own presentation of Bavinck. Additionally, Boersma's argument against Bavinck depends on assertions that are not directly derivative of the logic of Bavinck's quotations. For example, after quoting Bavinck's claim that in the eschaton there is not a mere passive rest but a communion with God in activity as well, Boersma writes: "Bavinck seems more at ease with an eschaton that continues the regular work week than with an eschaton that celebrates Sabbath rest." This line is a hasty generalization and mere assertion that cannot be derived directly from the logic of the quote. It gives no attention to the ample remarks Bavinck makes about Sabbath rest throughout his corpus. Boersma uses phrases such as "Bavinck waxes eloquent," which slant the presentation critically before the reader arrives at the argument. Indeed, Boersma's final summary of Bavinck's failure is a psychologism: "Bavinck simply was too much interested in the hustle and bustle of human activity in the hereafter to give any real thought to a positive articulation of the beatific vision."[113] It is important to note the indefensibility of claiming that a person gave no real thought to a concept. Boersma's presentation of Bavinck as one who affirmed the beatific vision and qualified what he took to be its errone-ous expressions manifests the opposite claim: it is no simple interest in this-worldly hustle and bustle.

Further, toward the conclusion of Boersma's presentation of Bavinck, in stating that Bavinck overemphasized the this-worldly character of the new heaven and earth, he cites *Reformed Dogmatics* 4:715 to make the point.[114] Boersma quotes, however, not from Bavinck but from the added editorial summaries in the English version of the *Reformed Dogmatics*. The editor writes: "While the kingdom of God is first planted spiritually in human hearts, the future blessedness is not to be spiritualized. Biblical hope, rooted in incarnation and resurrection, is creational, this worldly, visible, physical, bodily hope." It is important to note the difference here with what Bavinck says in the chapter that follows this introduction. One can surmise that the editors were drawing their summary from the fol-lowing quote (and other arguments like it in this chapter), which has a strikingly different accent.

> Since Jesus's advent breaks up into a first and a second coming, the kingdom of God is first planted in human hearts spiritually, and the benefits of that kingdom are all internal and invisible: forgiveness, peace, righteousness, and eternal life. The essence of future bless-edness, accordingly, is also construed more spiritually, especially by Paul and John, as a being always with the Lord (John 12:26; 14:3; 17:24; 2 Cor. 5:8; Phil. 1:23; 1 Thess. 4:17; 5:10; 1 John 3:2). But this does not confine this blessedness to heaven. This cannot be the case as is basically evident from the fact that the New Testament teaches the incarnation of the Word and the physical resurrection of Christ; it further expects his physical return at the end of time and immediately thereafter has in view the physical resurrection

---

113. *SG*, 38–39.
114. *SG*, 40n89.

of all human beings, especially that of believers. All this spells the collapse of spiritualism, which if it remains true to its principle—as in Origen—has nothing left after the day of judgment other than spirits in an uncreated heaven.[115]

Note the balance in the quote above that is absent in the summary Boersma quotes. There is no dichotomy presented between the goodness of spiritual salvation as "always being with the Lord" and the fact that the incarnation and resurrection materializes the eschatological life. Spiritualism, for Bavinck, is essentially a denial of the resurrection. Yet the Bible, according to Bavinck's reading, presents a holistic view.

From early in Bavinck's career he defined the aim of theology as seeking the knowledge of God unto the glory of God. The object of God's revelation of his own self is the knowledge of God that glorifies God, he argues in *Reformed Dogmatics*.[116] Seeking the face of God, which is the object of theology itself, is the current on which his doxological dogmatics flows throughout his corpus and career. Bavinck does not downplay the beatific vision, but he often uses other biblical terms and imagery to describe the eschatological life in the presence of God, the most common of which is "fellowship" or "to dwell" with God, as well as often referring to "communion with God," each operating within the metaphor of being at home with God or friendship with God.

In *Magnalia Dei*, after opening his theological handbook by stating that the immediate presence of God is humanity's highest good, he appeals at the end to the Old Testament to argue that "fellowship with God is the first and most important benefit of the covenant."[117] For Israel, there is no joy except in fellowship with God. The Lord is the rock and fortress, the shepherd, and the fountainhead of living water—without the presence of God, the people have nothing, he states. For Israel, death could only fully be dealt with when the Lord came to dwell with his people, purge it of sin, and remain with them in the land he had chosen. All of this hope is fulfilled in Christ's first and second comings. Bavinck emphasizes that Christ, having

---

115. RD 4:718.
116. RD 1:213.
117. WWG, 530

laid the foundation, will bring the kingdom into completion when he comes. New covenant believers, then, he states, look forward with great longing to the return of Christ to this world. All hope and expectation are laid before him and with him. Bavinck believes that Christ will return to earth in a "great chariot of victory" through the clouds of heaven, just as he departed.[118]

He goes on to express in multiple pages the glory and majesty of Christ's return, subduing Satan, putting an end to the beast of death, wherein Christ is all in all, and his church with him. For Bavinck, the appearance of Christ is everything, in which the whole of the kingdom is comprehended. In *Magnalia Dei*, in fact, he spends very little time explaining the secondary benefits of life in the kingdom, only describing the bounty of material life in one short paragraph. His emphasis within remains on the "immediate presence of God," where "all the citizens in that city share in the fellowship of God." In the final paragraph of the same book, he reiterates: "For all the inhabitants of the New Jerusalem will behold God's face, and will bear his name upon their foreheads."[119]

In *Reformed Dogmatics 4*, as Boersma points out, Bavinck does indeed address spiritualism in the final chapter of his dogmatics. However, this appears after two hundred pages of eschatological reflection on a whole host of other topics, which are not addressed in the critique. Bavinck makes the point that "this renewal of the visible world highlights the one-sidedness of the spiritualism that limits future blessedness to heaven. In the case of Old Testament prophecy one cannot doubt that it describes earthly blessedness." Again, his point is not to limit emphasis on the presence of God, but to restate the basic exegetical insight that eternal life is not merely spiritual but also physical, as Christ himself is a man. He was addressing the error of denying the material reality of eternal life within his own day. It is odd to use this point to make the claim that Bavinck is a primary catalyst for the undermining of final causation and participatory ontology (particularly when his emphasis is on the union and compatibility of heaven and earth). One can see the nuance in his point here: "The essence of future blessedness, accordingly, is also construed more

---

118. *WWG*, 530–31, 534, 339.
119. *WWG*, 548–49.

spiritually, especially by Paul and John, as a being always with the Lord (John 12:26; 14:3; 17:24; 2 Cor. 5:8; Phil. 1:23; 1 Thess. 4:17; 5:10; 1 John 3:2). But this does not confine this blessedness to heaven." This cannot be the case, as is basically evident from the fact that the New Testament teaches the incarnation of the Word and the physical resurrection of Christ.[120] Again (and it is worth quoting in full):

> Scripture consistently maintains the intimate connectedness of the spiritual and the natural. Inasmuch as the world consists of heaven and earth and humans consist of soul and body, so also sanctity and glory, virtue and happiness, the moral and the natural world order ought finally to be harmoniously united. The blessed will therefore not only be free from sin but also from all the consequences of sin, from ignorance and error (John 6:45), from death (Luke 20:36; 1 Cor. 15:26; Rev. 2:11; 20:6, 14), from poverty and disease, from pain and fear, hunger and thirst, cold and heat (Matt. 5:4; Luke 6:21; Rev. 7:16–17; 21:4), and from all weakness, dishonor, and corruption (1 Cor. 15:42; etc.).

Yet, attention is not given in Boersma's critique to Bavinck's actual point and emphasis:

> Still the spiritual blessings are the more important and innumerably abundant: holiness (Rev. 3:4–5; 7:14; 19:8; 21:27); salvation (Rom. 13:11; 1 Thess. 5:9; Heb. 1:14; 5:9); glory (Luke 24:26; Rom. 2:10; 8:18, 21); adoption (Rom. 8:23); eternal life (Matt. 19:16–17, 29; etc.); *the vision of, and conformity to, God and Christ* (Matt. 5:18; John 17:24; Rom. 8:29; 1 Cor. 13:12; 2 Cor. 3:18; Phil. 3:21; 1 John 3:2; Rev. 22:4); and fellowship with, and the service and praise of, God and Christ.[121]

Here Bavinck summarizes his understanding of the benefits of eternal life, appealing to the beatific vision as the center, as he does in the partial quote above:

---

120. *RD* 4:717–18.

121. *RD* 4:720–21, emphasis added.

Contemplation (*visio*), understanding (*comprehensio*), and enjoyment of God (*fruitio Dei*) make up the essence of our future blessedness. The redeemed see God, not—to be sure—with physical
eyes, but still in a way that far outstrips all revelation in this dispensation via nature and Scripture. And thus they will all know
him, each in the measure of his mental capacity, with a knowledge that has its image and likeness in God's knowledge—directly,
immediately, unambiguously, and purely. Then they will receive
and possess everything they expected here only in hope. Thus con-
templating and possessing God, they enjoy him and are blessed
in his fellowship: blessed in soul and body, in intellect and will.[122]

None of these examples takes into consideration the many other
instances where he affirms the beatific vision throughout his corpus. In
the other volumes of *Reformed Dogmatics*, for example, he concludes: religion aims at nothing less than eternal blessedness in fellowship with God.
Earlier in the first volume, he states that in the heavenly hosts and the
blessed, the triumphant church, the people of God experience *theologia
visionis*—a theology of vision where the ectypal theology of the creaturely
consciousness is closely aligned with God's self-knowledge.[123] Bavinck also
makes much of gazing at and worshiping God in eternal life persistently.
When we behold the kingdom, he exegetes, "the song will flow from our
lips: every house is built by someone, but the builder of all things is God.
God himself is it Designer and Builder."[124] He qualifies the vision of God,
arguing that no creature can behold the ontological Trinity as he is in himself. For this reason, the beatific vision is beheld in the face of Christ. He
carries on a similar discussion in the most lengthy treatment of the *visio
Dei* in *Reformed Dogmatics* volume 2. He overviews the history of the doctrine and comes to the following conclusions: "modesty [concerning the
doctrine] is certainly in keeping with Scripture. The Bible indeed teaches
that the blessed in heaven behold God, but does not go into any detail,
and elsewhere expressly calls God invisible. The vision awaiting believers

---

122. *RD* 4:722.
123. *RD* 1:269, 214.
124. KGHG, 170.

is described by Paul as 'knowing as we are known.'" Again, "Humanity's blessedness indeed lies in the 'beatific vision of God,' but this vision will always be such that finite and limited human nature is capable of it."[125]

In "The Kingdom of God, the Highest Good," Bavinck argues that the kingdom of God is the kingdom *of God*. Christ is the head of this living body. The kingdom exists unto the glory of God. That is its first purpose. "In the Kingdom of God, God himself is the King-Sovereign." Accordingly, the goal of the individual is that one's essence be "reflected in the mirror of [one's] consciousness, and that [one] thus become like God, who is nothing but light and in whom is no darkness (1 John 1:5)."[126] In other words, the end of each person is that one be restored by grace to full humanity, to being in oneself the nature that God pronounced over his image bearers: fully dependent on God, and without any internal conflict between the law of God and the desires of the personality, to become like God in the presence of God.

As clearly displayed already in this chapter, for both Bavinck and Kuyper, there is no reason to draw a dualistic dichotomy between heaven and earth. Both saw salvation as the union of heaven and earth in the second coming of Christ. To speak merely of heaven without earth or earth without heaven is to miss the biblical emphasis on the eschatological life. Bavinck attempted to derive a balance in the fact of organic union that begins even in the Old Testament: in the covenant with Israel, "Salvation is expected on earth, not in heaven."[127] The Israelites were looking for Messiah to bring the rule of God fully and finally to earth, to a people in a land. In the new covenant, Bavinck explains, in *Reformed Dogmatics* volume 4, Christ is the center of eternal life and *the final cause* of creation. It is worth quoting him in full:

> Eschatology, therefore, is rooted in Christology and is itself Christology, the teaching of the final, complete triumph of Christ and his kingdom over all his enemies. In accord with Scripture, we can go back even further. The Son is not only the mediator

---

125. *RD* 1:310, 2:189–91.
126. KGHG, 149–50.
127. *RD* 4:654.

of reconciliation (*mediator reconciliationis*) on account of sin, but even apart from sin he is the mediator of union (*mediator unionis*) between God and his creation. He is not only the exemplary cause (*causa exemplaris*) but also the final cause (*causa finalis*) of creation. In the Son the world has its foundation and example, and therefore it has in him its goal as well. It is created through him and for him as well (Col. 1:16). Because the creation is *his* work, it cannot and may not remain the booty of Satan. The Son is the head, Lord, and heir of all things. United in the Son, gathered under him as their head, all creatures return to the Father, the fountain of all good.[128]

It is critical to point out as well that Kuyper wholly rejects a dichotomy between spiritual and earthly goods in the kingdom of God. He refuses to contrast the end of beatific vision with the facts of a renewed material order. Bavinck and Kuyper both eschew all dualism on this point. There is no reason to dichotomize, in their logic, because the Scriptures do not. So, Kuyper uses the "dying of the grain of wheat" as "the pregnant metaphor" for the renewal of the human body, but not only the body. "At the same time" he argues, "we have the indication as to how one day this entire world will die and perish, but in order to bring forth out of its germ a similar, much more glorious world—except that it is purified from all curse and pain. … The essence itself will emerge in new and more glorious forms." Here Kuyper is emphasizing the material nature of the world, which is the same as the human body. "The present world which one day will perish before the coming new world, will continue its essence in that new world. That new world will be of the same kind as this old world, and will be able to be explained in terms of it."[129] Yet, what will life be like in this world?

Kuyper displays his scriptural balance in his commentary on the book of Revelation, where he focuses on the *visio Dei and* life in the kingdom. He argues that in that city, "The whole reborn humanity stands before God as a holy unity that is athrob with life," and this fully redeemed humanity "does not remain on its knees in uninterrupted worship of God," but it

---

128.   RD 4:685.
129.   CG 1:572.

also engages in "new callings, new life-tasks, new commissions." The life of the future age *will be a full human life* which will exhibit all the glory that God in the first creation had purposed and appointed for the same, but which by us was sinned away."[130]

Nevertheless, the question remains: does Bavinck have a constructive, detailed account of the beatific vision? Boersma notes that Bavinck "suggests that the Son will continue to mediate our access to God in the eschaton...Unfortunately, Bavinck does not elaborate how this continued mediation relates to the vision of God or in what sense we may rightly claim that this vision is direct or immediate if it is also mediated by Christ."[131] And while that is true at least with regard to the section of *Reformed Dogmatics* that Boersma interacts with in that quote, one could begin to construct a more detailed presentation through Bavinck's implicit affirmation of John Owen on the *visio Dei*.

In RD 3.259, Bavinck cites John Owen's *Declaration of the Glorious Mystery of the Person of Christ God and Man*.[132] Bavinck does not provide a particular page reference or quotation, yet the signal towards Owen is astute. As other interpreters have shown, Owen sought to reform the beatific vision for Reformed theologians by keeping it in line with the modesty of the Scriptural witness and by providing a Christocentric lens for it. Suzanne McDonald puts it tersely: "The beatific vision signifies very specifically for Owen, to behold the glory of God in the face of Jesus Christ."[133] There is thus a continuity between the sight believers have of Christ in the last day and the faith they exercise in the present order – our faith in Christ now will become our sight of Christ in the eschaton. The specific focus is on the "hypostatic union"; again: "The beatific vision is the beholding of the glory of God, and to behold the glory of God is to behold it in the person of Christ, fully divine and fully human."[134]

---

130. Kuyper, *Revelation of St. John*, 331–32.

131. *Seeing God*, 37.

132. John Owen, "Declaration of the Glorious Mystery of the Person of Christ, God and Man," in William H. Goold, *The Works of John Owen*, vol. I (Edinburgh: T&T Clark, 1682).

133. Suzanne McDonald, "Beholding the Glory of God in the Face of Jesus Christ: John Owen and the 'Reforming' the Beatific Vision," in Kelly M. Kapic and Mark Jones, *The Ashgate Research Companion to John Owen's Theology* (Farnham: Ashgate, 2012), 146.

134. McDonald, "Beholding the Glory of God," 146.

This personal reformation of the beatific vision has several benefits (over what McDonald considers the Thomist or Roman Catholic account). Firstly, by focusing on the person of the Son, the human nature of Christ is not to be considered a hindrance to the beatific vision, but rather a very constituent part of it. His humanity is not per se the reason for worshipping Christ, but rather his divine person is, but his humanity remains united to his person and hence not an impediment to fellowship with the person. As McDonald observes: "For Owen, we must ensure not only that Christ remains at the centre of our thinking about the beatific vision. He is absolutely insistent that we must recognize that it is the person of Christ, in his ascended, glorified humanity, who is at the heart of the beatific vision itself."[135] Secondly, a focus of the person of Christ as the object of the vision can include the sight of the glorified creature's physical resurrected body. While "the vision of God is principally intellectual, precisely because it entails understanding the fullness of the person of Christ, it is not exclusively so. To Owen, to deny a place to our glorified bodily senses is scripturally and theologically wrong-headed."[136]

While Bavinck may not have given as much detail as Owen's account, he was clearly aware of the broader Protestant reshaping of the beatific vision and appealed to it in this crucial juncture, which puts to rest Boersma's claim that Bavinck never drew from the broader Puritan and Reformed accounts to give a positive account of the beatific vision. This reference to Owen should also be kept in mind when that oft-quoted passage in the fourth volume of the Dogmatics is considered on Christology as eschatology: "The Son is not only the mediator of reconciliation (mediator reconciliationis) on account of sin, but even apart from sin he is the mediator of union (mediator unionis) between God and his creation. He is not only the exemplary cause (causa exemplaris) but also the final cause (causa finalis) of creation."[137] In fact, Bavinck's overall description is consistent with Boersma's own summary of Owen's account: "(1) Christ in his human nature will always be the immediate head of the glorified

135. McDonald, "Beholding the Glory of God," 153. Emphasis original.
136. McDonald, "Beholding the Glory of God," 157.
137. RD 4.685.

creation; (2) Christ will forever be the means and way of communication between God and the saints (3) Christ in his human nature will be the eternal object of divine glory, praise, and worship – contemplation will lead to praise."[138]

CONCLUSION

For both neo-Calvinist fathers, Christ is the center of the glory of the kingdom. The vision of God in the face of Christ we see clearly and immediately in eternal life. Kuyper asks: "What end would be served by this bodily existence of our Savior if he would be dwelling in nothing else but a sphere of invisible spirits? ... We see ... that a purely spiritual kingdom could fit neither with our confession of Christ nor with our confession regarding our own future."[139]

The Christian religion does not, therefore, have the task of creating a new supernatural order of things. It does not intend to institute a totally new, heavenly kingdom such as Rome intends in the church and the Anabaptists undertook at Munster. Christianity does not introduce a single substantial foreign element into the creation. It creates no new cosmos but rather makes the cosmos new. It restores what was corrupted by sin. It atones the guilty and cures what is sick; the wounded it heals. Jesus was anointed by the Father with the Holy Spirit to bring good tidings to the afflicted, to bind up the broken-hearted, to proclaim liberty to the captive and the opening of prison to those who are bound, to proclaim the year of the Lord's favor, and to comfort those who mourn (Isa. 61:1, 2). He makes the blind to see, the lame to walk; the lepers are cleansed and the deaf hear; the dead are raised, and the gospel is preached to the poor (Matt. 11:5). ... He was Jesus—that is, Savior. But he was that totally and perfectly, not in the narrow Roman Catholic, Lutheran, or Anabaptist sense but in the full, deep, and

---

138. Boersma, *Seeing God*, 326. Bavinck's agreement with Owen here suggests that his Christological account improves on Kuyper's account of the vision, which, as Boersma notes, leaves Christology behind in the eschaton as believers are considered to directly behold the essence of God. See Boersma, *Seeing God*, 340, 343.

139. *CG* 1:573.

broad Reformed sense of the word. Christ did not come just to restore the religio-ethical life of man and to leave all the rest of life undisturbed, as if the rest of life had not been corrupted by sin and had no need of restoration. No, the love of the Father, the grace of the Son, and the communion of the Holy Spirit extend even as far as sin has corrupted. Everything that is sinful, guilty, unclean, and full of woe is, as such and for that very reason, the object of the evangel of grace that is to be preached to every creature.[140]

Despite the fact of human guilt and creaturely corruption that reared its nasty head in the early moments of creation history, there is, for Kuyper and Bavinck, an organic unity between these two operations. In brief, neo-Calvinism accents an essential theological commitment: that the *goal* of salvation is not an entirely new idea, even post fall, because the goal of re-creation is the end of creation, yet by different means. Re-creation's end is creation's original end: that God would make his dwelling place with humankind, Immanuel, God with us.

---

140. Bavinck, "Common Grace," 61–62.

VII

Image and Fall

That is why God destined his only Son to enter the life of this world;
to take on our human nature; to gather, as the Head of humanity, the
split, divided, and scattered world into a unity once again and to unite
it in one body. This Son was to destroy the world's sin through his blood
so that it no longer stands guilty before the Holy One, and thereafter
to raise up in his own person the kingship that humanity had lost.

—Abraham Kuyper, Pro Rege

THE PURPOSE OF this book is to introduce readers to some of the more salient and distinctive theological contributions of neo-Calvinism. Though it is beyond the scope of this chapter to highlight all of the ways in which Bavinck and Kuyper articulate their theological anthropology, we will highlight what we consider to be some of their most significant contributions in this area, especially that the image of God in humanity is an image of the *Trinity*. Hence, precisely because God is triune, humanity, too, will be shaped by the pattern of unity-in-diversity. To Bavinck and Kuyper, human beings are a single organism, and the federal representation of Adam comprises the unity that underlies the diversity of that organism. Hence, while Bavinck, for example, clearly follows well-trodden lines of argumentation within the Reformed tradition—arguing, for example, for a dichotomy of soul and body rather than trichotomy of soul, spirit, and body, for creationism over traducianism, for the body as an instrument of the soul—his emphasis on the application of organic language not merely to the individual but to corporate humanity stands out as a distinctive of neo-calvinist theological anthropology.[1] From there, one can derive sustained reflection on social, ethical, and corporate dimensions of humanity's responsibilities.

Additionally, the organic emphasis, for Kuyper, was foundational for his biblical-theological anthropology, sketching a holistic narrative of the kingship of humanity in Adam and Christ. This chapter will begin by sketching Bavinck's understanding of humanity as an organism, while noting its implications for the doctrine of original sin and ethics. It will then move on to consider Kuyper's articulation of the human organism expressed in its royal calling from God, both in Adam and in Christ.

BAVINCK AND ORGANIC ANTHROPOLOGY

In this section, we first consider Bavinck's broader understanding of the relationship between the Trinity and his creation and the image of God in humanity. Second, we discuss the way in which that relationship implicates Bavinck's doctrine of original sin and theological ethics.[2]

TRINITY AND ORGANISM

Fundamental to Bavinck's articulation of the God-world relation is the strict distinction between the Creator and the creature. An ontological chasm exists between the two as "between the Infinite and the finite, between eternity and time, between being and becoming, between the All and the nothing." Mystery is the starting point of all dogmatic reflection because of its distinctly transcendent subject matter. In revelation God accommodates and creates for the human an ectypal theology, a self-communication on the basis of his (ultimately incommunicable) archetypal theology appropriate to the level of finite creatures. This confession that God is known only by virtue of analogical and ectypal communication from the divine subject eschews both rationalism (or univocity) and

---

1. *RD* 2:556, 559, 582–83.

2. Parts of this first section are adapted from Nathaniel Gray Sutanto, "Herman Bavinck on the Image of God and Original Sin," *International Journal of Systematic Theology* 18.2 (2016): 174–90, and Sutanto, "Egocentricity, Organism, and Metaphysics: Sin and Renewal in Herman Bavinck's *Ethics*," *Studies in Christian Ethics* 34.2 (2021): 223–40.

equivocism. Humans can know God because creation bears the imprints of who he is and because of God's voluntary act of revelation, yet this knowledge is "only a finite image, a faint likeness and creaturely impression of the perfect knowledge that God has of himself."[3]

An emphasis on God's incomprehensibility therefore is consistent with an affirmation of his communicability. Creation reflects the Triune Creator, and God's archetypal being is the basis for the patterns exhibited in creation. As such, Bavinck appreciates the attempts of Augustine and other theologians of the past to find vestiges and triads in creation that serve as analogues of the Triune Creator known after the contemplation of special revelation. Nonetheless, he ultimately judges these attempts to be increasingly speculative and calls for greater reserve. Thus, Bavinck prefers to articulate the reflections of creation's triune shape in terms of a nonnumerical unity and diversity on the basis of the Creator's archetypal unity and diversity: "In God, too, there is unity in diversity, diversity in unity [*eenheid in de verscheidenheid, verscheidenheid in de eenheid*]. Indeed this order and this harmony is present in him absolutely. In the case of creatures we see only a faint analogy of it." In creatures the diversity is not united in a simple or perichoretic manner, as it is in the Godhead, yet the unity can be discerned by a "profound physical unity [*physische eenheid*]," and also, in human beings, a "moral unity [*zedelijke eenheid*]."[4]

This marks a significant recalibration of the dogmatic reflections of the ancient and medieval theologians: "It represents the neo-Calvinist redemption of the 'marks of the Trinity' concept." In doing so, Bavinck shows that one can be wholly against natural theology and wholly for the *vestigia trinitatis*."[5] Though the Triune God is not like everything else,

---

3. RD 1:233; 2:30, 110. The distinction between archetype and ectype has a strong pedigree within the Reformed tradition; it is articulated in Franciscus Junius, *A Treatise on True Theology*, trans. David C. Noe (Grand Rapids: Reformation Heritage, 2014). See also Willem J. van Asselt, "The Fundamental Meaning of Theology: Archetypal and Ectypal Theology in Seventeenth-Century Reformed Thought," *Westminster Theological Journal* 64 (2007): 289–306; Mattson, *Restored to Our Destiny*, 27; Eglinton, *Trinity and Organism*, 106.

4. RD 2:322–27, 329, 331, 333; GD 2:344.

5. Eglinton, *Trinity and Organism*, 89. To nuance this point, Bavinck preferred the term "general revelation" over "natural theology," though accepted a limited use of the latter as long as that enterprise was set within the bounds of revelatory theology and its limits were well understood. See chs. 4 and 8 for more detailed analysis.

everything else is like the Triune God.[6] Unity and diversity is the particular expression of the triune shape of creation as an organism, both in its
parts and as a whole simply because creation *comes from* an archetypal,
wholly other One-in-Three. This pattern marks not only creation's being
but also Bavinck's theological epistemology. For Bavinck, there are ultimately two worldviews: the organic and the mechanistic. God's revelation constitutes an organic unity[7] such that its assimilation into human
knowledge will form a single organism of scientific knowledge in which
knowledge of the whole precedes the parts, with theology as the unifier
of the diverse fields of inquiry.[8] This organic concept is not unlike the
concept of cosmos in much Greek philosophy of old. Yet, the guarantee of
the organic and systematic character of epistemology and the sciences is,
again, rooted in the Triune God, who "himself provides us with an even
infinitely higher and richer and more glorious system. ... He who is one
in essence, in three persons ... the entirely perfect system: origin, type,
model, and image of all other systems."[9] As a result of this, Christians can
see the world organically in a way that "the world cannot see."[10]

The culmination of the above observations includes the insight that "for
Bavinck, a theology of Trinity *ad intra* requires a cosmology of organism
ad extra."[11] Eglinton offers a definition of the organic motif, as summarized in Bavinck's *Christelijke Wereldbeschouwing*.[12] First, because God is
a Trinitarian being, creation will display both unity and diversity as an
organic whole. Second, there is a priority on the unity, as it precedes diversity. Third and fourth, reality's unity and diversity will share a common

---

6. Eglinton, *Trinity and Organism*, 89, 112.

7. *RD* 1:44. See also Eglinton's observation that Bavinck mutes the organic motif when discussing general revelation apart from special revelation (*Trinity and Organism*, 150–52).

8. Bavinck, "Pros and Cons," 90–94. See also Huttinga, who argues that, for Bavinck, every science is theological ("Marie Antoinette or Mystical Depth?," 143–54).

9. Bavinck, "Pros and Cons," 92. Bavinck does not believe that God is literally a system. He confesses the simplicity and unity of God as absolute.

10. Robert Covolo, "Beyond the Schleiermacher-Barth Dilemma: General Revelation, Bavinckian Consensus, and the Future of Reformed Theology," *BR* 3 (2012): 53n55.

11. Eglinton, *Trinity and Organism*, 68. For the implications of this to Bavinck's theological epistemology, see Sutanto, *God and Knowledge*.

12. Eglinton, *Trinity and Organism*, 67–69.

idea and goal: the glory of the Trinitarian God, with the Logos as Christ in its center.[13]

   With the centrality of the organic motif in view, we can further clarify the significance of what it means for human beings to be made in the image of God. For, while "all creatures display *vestiges* of God, only a human being is the *image* of God." Indeed, with creation bearing the organic imprints of God's triune character, it is significant that Bavinck asserts the created nature of humanity as the "epitome" of all creation: "a micro-divine being."[14]

   With that phrase, the human being as a micro-divine being imaging the triune God, Bavinck appeals to some of the Greek fathers, who used the term "micro-theos" to define the human. Bavinck also treats the human individual as exhibiting patterns of unity-in-diversity within oneself. One has various faculties of knowing and willing, and they are united under the heart—that "seat and fountain of man's entire psychic life, of emotions and passions, of desire and will, even of thinking and knowing."[15] He further applies this organic articulation of humanity as a polemic against what he perceives to be a Roman Catholic anthropological commitment to nature-grace dualism, according to which the fall entails nothing more than the loss of a superadded gift of grace from God, leaving the moral and epistemic integrity of human nature intact.

   In contrast, Bavinck argues that the Reformed distinction between broad and narrow aspects of God's image is a more appropriate articulation of the human individual as made in the image of God in an organic unity.[16] The two aspects make up the image of God, and the narrow aspect is so intimately "bound up" with the broader sense of the image of God such that with the entrance of sin the former is lost while the latter is

---

13. On Schelling's influence on Bavinck on this point, see the chapter "Chalcedon and Modernity," in Pass, *Heart of Dogmatics*, 89–130.

14. *RD* 2:555, 562.

15. *RD* 2:556–57. For a more thorough examination of Bavinck's faculty psychology, see Sutanto, *God and Knowledge*, ch. 7.

16. *RD* 2:554. These comments may shed light on Bavinck's short remark on Aristotle in another place: "After all, just like Plato, Aristotle also ascribed more than one soul to human beings, and just like his predecessor, he did not succeed in combining these souls into one organic unit" ("Unconscious," 180).

ruined.[17] Consequently, grace restores one's nature fundamentally, having "the greatest significance for his or her whole life and labor, also in the family, society, the state, art, science, and so forth."[18] The natural person is lost, depraved, and distorted in sin, and cannot appropriately function without supernatural grace even in so-called natural affairs; sin marks the distortion of humanity's imaging essence and not merely a loss of a supernatural gift from God.[19]

Yet, precisely because the Triune God transcends the finite goodness of image bearers in his simple and infinite perfections, it follows that the image of God is too rich to be confined to the individual or even to the human family. Bavinck's corporate understanding of humanity is a macro-perspective in which he applies the organic language of unity and oneness to theological anthropology. Zoomed in, the individual is considered to be a single organic entity, and zoomed out, the image of God in its entirety (as every human being who has and will live) is a single organism—a diversity of organic individuals are considered together as a larger organic unity. In his words, the image of God

can only be somewhat unfolded in its depth and riches in a humanity counting billions of members. Just as the traces of God (*vestigia Dei*) are spread over many, many works, in both space and time, so also the image of God can only be displayed in all its dimensions and characteristic features in a humanity whose members exist both successively ... and contemporaneously side by side.[20]

The appeal to the vestiges of God signals Bavinck's dependence on the classical conviction concerning the divine perfections as the ground for creation's manifold diversity. While the divine perfections exist simply and absolutely in God, a finite creation can only reflect the glory of its Creator by a multitude of diverse objects. These ideas lend themselves

---

17. *RD* 2:554. See also *WWG*, 185–88.

18. *RD* 2:554.

19. In a discussion on the pollution of sin, Bavinck sets the Reformed view over against the mechanistic anthropology he discerns in Roman Catholicism again: "The image of God is not an external and mechanical appendage to us but integral to our very being, it is our health" (*RD* 3:174).

20. *RD* 2:577.

well to Thomas's classical articulation that "goodness, which in God is simple and uniform, in creatures is manifold and divided and hence the whole universe together participates in the divine goodness more perfectly, and represents it better than any single creature whatever."[21] Far from being a hindrance to appreciating the diversity within creation, then, the doctrine of divine simplicity (i.e., the negative deduction that God is not composed of parts and that all that is within God is God) undergirds it. Further, readers sensitive to the ways in which more recent developments associated with social Trinitarianism have modified classical Trinitarian metaphysics in order to use this doctrine to motivate an ethical program should note Bavinck's continuity with the classical Christian metaphysical tradition here. Bavinck did not see it necessary to modify classical Trinitarianism in order to derive social implications from the doctrine.

Bavinck is not offering what is called today social Trinitarianism, which does modify the classical doctrine of God. To suppose so would be anachronistic and conceptually false. The Trinity, for Bavinck, is absolutely mysterious, and dogmas constructed about the Trinity are done so with attention to the fact that the theologian does not comprehend who God is in himself but only reflects on God's self-disclosure. It is, however, true that his organic language is used in a similar fashion (the language of unity-in-diversity) by Stanley Grenz and others. Yet, the conceptual background is not the same.

To be clear, for Bavinck, creaturely being as diversity is not a reflection on God in himself in a manner that suggests God is a determined unity between three diverse beings with three distinct centers of consciousness and will. Rather, organic creaturely ontology is derivative of God as one in essence and three in person with a single divine consciousness in the most qualitatively absolute way. God has, in his creation, shown forth his image to the world and chosen to create a cosmos that reflects his image. Bavinck's doctrine of God is utterly opposed to anthropological projection and tritheism and is committed to a doctrine of the vestiges of the Trinity in creation order, following Augustine. For Bavinck, one does not have to draw a dichotomy between classical Trinitarianism and the image of

---

21. Thomas Aquinas, *Summa theologica* I.47.1.

the Triune God in vestige—he feels free to confess the classical doctrines of divine simplicity, aseity, and so on while also seeing deep implications of God's triunity for human relations. While creation is like the Trinity insofar as God is its ultimate source and principle of being, the Trinity is not like anything.[22]

Bavinck expands on these classical convictions for anthropology by giving them a covenantal and organic tinge: because of the diverse perfections of the simple God and his Trinitarian processions, human beings are created to mirror him in a single organism comprising a unity-in-diversity in creaturely form. While we are indeed a diversity of individuals, we are united together under a federal head in Adam or in Christ. As such, part of what it means to be made in God's image is precisely to be in *ethical solidarity*. We are God's image bearers not simply as individuals, but as a *corporate and ethical unity*—a single organism.

ORIGINAL SIN AND ETHICS

We can now explore the way in which Bavinck's organic anthropology implicates his account of original sin and theological ethics. Following Thomas McCall's recent discussion, an organic whole theory of theological anthropology is typically also an "organic whole realist" account, according to which humanity is somehow a single entity.[23] Interestingly, however, Bavinck eschews organic whole realism and opts for what we may call an *organic whole federalism*. Tied to the doctrine of original sin, a realist account argues that human beings inherit Adam's guilt or corruption because humanity really was, in some way, *in* Adam. Bavinck, however, was critical of a realist account, for reasons that would take us beyond the scope of the present chapter.[24] While he does identify the whole of humanity as a single organism, he does not argue that humanity was a singular metaphysical entity with individuals merely processing

---

22. This paragraph appears in an alternate form in Brock, *Orthodox yet Modern*, 39. On the classical contours of Bavinck's doctrine of God, see Sutanto, *God and Knowledge*, ch. 2.

23. Thomas McCall, *Against God and Nature: The Doctrine of Sin* (Wheaton, IL: Crossway, 2019), 185. McCall identifies specifically the views of Jonathan Edwards with this account.

24. For a discussion on Bavinck's critique of realism as a way of accounting for original guilt and corruption, see Sutanto, "Herman Bavinck on the Image of God," especially 184–87, and McCall, *Against God and Nature*, 168–70.

as extended parts of that single entity. Rather, human beings make up a unity-in-diversity, and what binds them is not that they share a meta-physical identity, as if they were numerically one thing, but their *ethical* relations. This ethical unity that binds the diversity of individuals into a single organism is precisely why the covenantal representation of Adam and Christ is fitting: their federal representations are proper to the organic shape of the human race and cannot be reducible to legal fictions. A key passage here from Bavinck's *Dogmatics*:

> The covenant of works and the covenant of grace stand and fall together. The same law applies to both. On the basis of a common descent an ethical unity [*etische eenheid*] has been built that causes humanity—in keeping with its nature—to manifest itself as one organism and to unite its members in the closest possible way, not only by ties of blood but also by common participation in blessing and curse, sin and righteousness, death and life.[25]

In other words, Bavinck imbues an ontological significance to ethical relations. Human beings are those for whom ethical relations are ontolog-ically constitutive. To be ethically related is essential to be a human being, and Adam's headship follows fittingly given humanity's design. That fallen human beings inherit Adam's guilt and corruption is thus not an arbitrary claim, but rather a correlate of the organic makeup of the human race.

Let us turn now to the *Ethics*. Under the section on the essential human nature, Bavinck emphasizes that image bearers are individuals in rela-tionship with God. Humanity, however, cannot be divided up and merely considered individualistically as "atoms or numbers,"[26] but must be con-sidered collectively as a unity. Though individuals truly are made in God's image, individualism, Bavinck argues, is a product of revolutionary and antitheistic thought.

> This atomistic view was the error of the French philosophers like Rousseau and is the fundamental error of revolutionary thought. The term "individual" belonged to the revolution and expressed

---

25. *RD* 2:579; *GD* 2:624.
26. *RE* 1:49.

its all-consuming character. Our fathers did not know the word "individualism" because for them there were no more individuals; to be human was always to be the image of God, a member of the human race. For the revolution, humanity is an aggregate mass of individuals who can be arbitrarily combined, like the random collision of Epicurus's atoms, into state, society etc. The revolutionary view is false. We have to be understood in the *relations* in which we stand, naturally and historically.[27]

Humanity's eschatological perfection, then, is not displayed by exhibiting virtues or good works individually, as if one's character could be properly developed or adjudicated in isolation. "The highest good is not individual moral perfection but the moral perfection of humanity. In fact, the one cannot be achieved without the other." This leads Bavinck to recognize not only the extension of humanity across space but also its extension across *time:* "in its successive generations is a unity, an organism to which we are related."[28] Each individual is responsible for the other, as husbands and wives care for one another and their children; as each individual, local church is part of the larger catholic church; as each past king or presidential rule implicates the future of their respective countries. Bavinck's identification of egocentricity as the organizing principle of particular sins, and his subsequent critiques of Pietism, Methodism, and asceticism, follow logically from this broader corporate understanding: these are traditions that emphasize that sanctification involves primarily (or exclusively) the formation of the individual in isolation—whether manifesting in the pursuit of private devotional practices or in the separation of the church from culture and society.[29]

In distinction from animals, human beings have ethical responsibilities, ties, and obligations, and these consist precisely in, with, and toward

27. *RE* 1:49–50, emphasis added.

28. *RE* 1:61, 230.

29. For a fuller discussion of this critique, see Sutanto, "Egocentricity, Organism, and Metaphysics," esp. 10–18.

relationships. "Animals form no family, society or state," Bavinck writes.[30] By way of contrast:

> For people, the physical, natural relation is also the first, and also passes away; but *ethical* [*ethische*] relationships develop out of and on the basis of the physical. Although the natural relationship is first, the moral and spiritual relationships follow. People remain in relationship to each other until the end of their lives. Those ethical ties are many and manifold.[31]

Human life is essentially a *moral* life. Hence, to be moral is never an issue of mere individual piety but to live in accordance with this corporate reality. Bavinck writes in no uncertain terms: "People are moral when they live according to the human standard—or, somewhat more profoundly, according to the notion of humanity—in all these relations."[32]

After sketching the essence of humanity, Bavinck turns to humanity under sin. At the outset of his discussion, he reminds readers that it would be a mistake to include the entire doctrine of sin under ethics.[33] He presupposes his discussion of the "origin, essence, and nature of sin ... [and the] guilt and punishment of sin" in the *Reformed Dogmatics* and notes that what must be discussed under ethics is "what we have become because of that sin," that is, the "the effect of sin on humanity in all areas of life."[34] Here we suggest that Bavinck is drawing on the classical distinction between originating sin and the sin originated as the twin aspects of original sin.[35]

---

30. *RE* 1:60.

31. *RE* 1:60; *GE* 1:71, emphasis original.

32. *RE* 1:61, emphasis original. This makes logical sense of Bavinck's comments concerning the relationship between religion and morality: love of God and love of neighbor are distinct but never divorced (*RE* 1:70–75).

33. "Vilmar includes the entire doctrine of sin in his *Ethics*, which is incorrect" (*RE* 1:79). Bavinck is referring to A. Vilmar, *Theologische Moral: Akademische Vorlesungen* (Gütersloh: Bertelsmann, 1871), 1:119–392.

34. *RE* 1:79. Later on, before classifying sins and identifying the organizing principle of sins, Bavinck writes this: "Here we are not discussing what sin is—that is, in relation to God, which is how we can first determine the nature of sin. Here, that issue is being assumed from dogmatics" (*RE* 1:100).

35. See *RD* 3:101. Despite redefining these terms considerably, Schleiermacher's comment on originated sin remains helpful: if originating sin has its origin within the human person, originated sin focuses on the entrance of sin into an individual from an extrinsic source. "Until then, and only to that degree, original sin is rightly called 'originated' because it has its cause outside the

Originating sin refers to that first sin by the first human beings, while originated sin refers to the impact or effects of that first sin to the rest of humanity. Under *Ethics*, the sin *originated* rather than originating sin is the point of discussion.

The sin originated is nothing short of pervasive. It affects every faculty of the human being. It signifies not merely the loss of original righteousness (again, contra Rome) but the distorting of the human nature. It is an animating principle that turns the whole self against God and neighbor. The heart, the *I*, the "very core" of our being, is "corrupt," and "this is why all human capabilities are also corrupt." The sin originated thus affects not merely the human's "spiritual life, our fellowship with God (Rome's view). But precisely because of that loss, the natural life in all its forms and dimensions is corrupted as well."[36]

This corruption takes the form of a division within one's internal life, as the faculties now war against one another instead of working together in harmony. "The mind has been loosened from the will through sin; it has become immoral, one capability alongside others rather than within them. It is torn loose from life; the heart that is dead also kills the mind." Sin is an atomizing force; it detaches the faculties from one another.[37] Analogously, and as a consequence, sin blinds us such that we now grasp only partial, isolated truths rather than the whole: "Thus, we do have some knowledge of individual verities, but we do not know *the* truth, the system, the unity of all truth in God."[38]

When sin entered into the world through Adam, an atomizing force created disorder within the faculties of the self and within the organism of humanity. Sin loosens and atomizes. Egocentricity, as the organizing principle of actual sins, is thus the means by which the organism of

---

individual." See Friedrich Schleiermacher, *Christian Faith: A New Translation and Critical Edition*, trans. Terrence N. Tice, Catherine L. Kelsey, and Edwina Lawler, ed. Catherine L. Kelsey and Terrence N. Tice (Louisville: Westminster John Knox, 2016), §71.1.

36. *RE* 1:88, 93.

37. This is consistent throughout Bavinck's corpus. It is crisply stated in his early essay, "The Kingdom of God, the Highest Good": "Understanding and heart, consciousness and will, inclination and power, feeling and imagination, flesh and spirit, there are all opposed to each other at the moment, and they compete with each other for primacy" (KGHG, 143).

38. *RE* 1:100, emphasis original. See also Sutanto's discussion of the distinction between mechanical and organic knowing in *God and Knowledge*, 93–100.

humanity is torn apart—it has ontological significance. If sin is an agent of division and atomization, regeneration by the Spirit is an agent or reunification and binding. Fittingly, regeneration produces a reuniting of one's self into a harmonious whole and a renewal of one's fellowship with God and others—it produces a life force that redeems the self and necessarily turns us *toward* others, restoring the spheres of state, science, art, culture, and family. The human individual is filled with gaps and disharmony—our wills conflict with our minds, our deeds with our conscience, and so on, but the spiritual life gives us a new, organizing principle of life:

> For the foundational principle of the spiritual life is the love of God in Christ poured out through the Holy Spirit ... and this principle now flows into all of life, into all the thoughts and deeds of the spiritual person. Love of God gives stature and form to the spiritual life; it organizes and inspires it, turning it into one beautiful organic whole which functions as the foundational *life-force*.[39]

If sin loosens and atomizes, the Spirit renews and rebinds. This life force, crucially, is outward-looking. It drives one's self into fellowship with others and thus reverses the atomizing powers of egocentricity. The spiritual life manifests itself precisely in the new bonds that are recreated with fellow believers precisely as believers are drawn toward God: "Because love for God is its foundation, spiritual life itself consists of fellowship with God, with Christ, and with fellow believers. Love strives after and *is* fellowship, a fellowship that is only possible through and in love. Hatred separates; love binds."[40]

Fellowship too, then, has ontological significance. When Christians reconcile and bind ourselves in ethical ties with one another, we are not only obeying God's commands—we are becoming more *whole*. Indeed, we

---

39. *RE* 1:248.

40. *RE* 1:248. As Ziegler also notes, fellowship with God and with other believers go together: "Reformed sources will regularly speak in related terms of a 'glorious and perfected *fellowship*' of believers with God and one another: when this tradition comments on the eschatological *state* of human being it does so chiefly with affective terms befitting this relational scenario, speaking of joy, blessedness, glory, and a 'full and pleasant sense of God's favor.'" See Philip G. Ziegler, "'Those He Also Glorified': Some Reformed Perspectives on Human Nature and Destiny," *Studies in Christian Ethics* 32.2 (2019): 165–76.

are witnessing to the work of God that renews and reconnects together the organism of humanity. Love binds the organism of redeemed humanity together, uniting it under a single head, and maturing it toward an eschatological telos. Crucially, Bavinck specifies egoism and isolation as twin dangers against the organism of spiritual life, and cooperation as an essential part of it:

> The genuine, normal condition.—that is, the health, of an organism consists in the following: (a) A vital principle animates from its center and controls and regulates everything. (b) no organs, parts, or members of an organism, animated from that center, isolate themselves from each other; rather, they cooperate with each other. This should happen in such a way that each member confines itself to being what it is supposed to be and actually is what it is supposed to be, arrogating nothing to itself (egotistically) [*egoïstisch*] but also not withdrawing itself (isolation) [*isolement*], such that the hand is the hand and nothing more, the foot is the foot, etc. (c) All members together, through the one vital principle, work toward one goal and consider themselves instruments for achieving the one task of life.[41]

More precisely, the organism of humanity does not deny the real individuality of each person, but rather recognizes that renewed humanity is a unity of diverse individuals and personalities. It embraces diversity and refuses one-sidedness, refusing to privilege one temperament, faculty, or attribute for another. Bavinck argues that this is already signified by the differing personalities of the apostles: John, Peter, Paul, and James each have differing modes of expressions, emphases, and strengths, yet none overrules the others, and they work complementarily. "Indeed, variety

---

41. *RE* 1:417; *GE* 2:279. This understanding of the spiritual life as *organic* life applies not only to renewed humanity as a whole but also to the individual Christian: "The very *I* of a new person dies and lives with Christ (Gal. 2:20); in the regenerated person there arises immediately a new consciousness, will, feeling, spirit, soul, and body; albeit all of these in principle. The spiritual life is an organism. But the new person is not one perfected in stages; we are perfected, but never perfect here on earth. The new life thus reveals itself like all organic life on earth, as a 'formative drive,' 'a creative drive.' For the Reformed, the organic life of those who are born again cannot be terminated, contrary to the Lutherans, who deny the doctrine of perseverance" (*RE* 1.346–47, emphasis original).

must continue so that humanity may be a single organism in which one member is different from and complements the other."[42]

Once again consistent with his *Reformed Dogmatics*, Bavinck's emphasis on the whole of humanity as the image of God is not meant to eclipse a proper expression of individuality.[43] The imitation of Christ, likewise, means following Jesus with our own uniqueness intact: "We must imitate him in everything, albeit in our own way, with our own individual personality, status, social class, and calling."[44] Bavinck's construction is typical of the neo-Calvinist tradition's emphasis on the social and corporate dimensions of anthropology—yet without sacrificing the emphasis on the freedom of conscience, and the authenticity of personal expression.

KUYPER AND THE NARRATIVE
OF ROYAL HUMANITY

Kuyper likewise prioritizes the unity of humanity in Adam, the organism. Insofar as Adam "represented our entire race, [he] was no individual."[45] Prior to Bavinck, Kuyper had emphasized the organism of humanity to some degree and did so early in his theological career, but he spent more ink collectively on the uniqueness of the *imago Dei*, which is humanity, per its ability to know God and according to its role in the "program of creation." Kuyper, in his later career especially, developed his anthropology in narrative form, focusing on the redemptive-historical through the logic of the kingship of the first and second Adam. Unlike Bavinck, however, Kuyper never completed any systematic, focused, and full-orbed treatment of anthropology. H. J. Lemkes wrote Kuyper in 1893 asking that Kuyper write a manual of human psychology and theological anthropology: "You who have pondered everything of importance, surely you have an anthropology in your head and heart which I urge you to share with us. It is my conviction that there is a *demand* for it in our time, and that you will not take it ill of me that I have taken the liberty to write you

---

42. *RE* 1:420.

43. "Every human being, while a member of the body of humanity as a whole, is at the same time a unique idea of God, with a significance and destiny that is eternal" (*RD* 2:587).

44. *RE* 1:339.

45. *Encyclopedia*, 186.

this."[46] Yet, Kuyper never did write a treatise on anthropology in itself. Bavinck instead took on this role in both in his *Reformed Dogmatics* and *Beginselen der Psychologie*.[47] Nevertheless, Kuyper's reflections on anthropology and sin are dotted persistently across his corpus and intertwined with his understanding of theology as a whole and the redemptive narrative especially. In works such as the *Encyclopedia*, *Common Grace*, and *Pro Rege*, Kuyper unveils a magisterial, exegetically based anthropology with a focus on different practical points in each of these works.

Kuyper's doctrine of humanity is filtered through the logic of the kingship of Jesus Christ as the fulfillment of the kingship of humanity itself, given as a gift to the pinnacle creature in the garden of God. The kingship of humanity includes dominion over the cosmos, expressed specifically in the call to name the animals, and in the blessing and mandate of Genesis 1:28–30. Additionally, in Kuyper's hierarchy, while humans were created and set (for a little while) lower than the angels in the hierarchy of rule, God's expressed plan was that humanity should be elevated above the heavenly hosts as rulers of a united heaven and earth in addition to their dominion over the ground. The glorification of humanity, the realizing of the Immanuel principle, and the extension of the Edenic temple across the cosmos also included the establishment of the kingship of humanity over the creatures in perpetuity, including over the hosts. Thus, the point of creation per humanity in Kuyper's logic is that, as servants of God, humans were made to be the king-stewards over the entire creaturely realm.

This narrative of kingship depends on the essential reality of organism. Kuyper argues that while creation consists of differing parts, the parts cohere as one. And "the unity of that coherence comes to expression in humanity as the creature that *gathers* everything else—all other creatures—under its dominion, so as to moreover consecrate, in a priestly fashion, the entire creation to God, and to dedicate it to him, in a kingly fashion, forever." This gift of dominion, as representative organism amid the *cosmos*, is derivative itself of the fact of *imago Dei*. Because humanity is from God, in his likeness, it alone can be the "holy dwelling place of

---

46. Abraham Kuyper, "Lemkes' Wish," in *On Education*, ed. Wendy Naylor et al., Abraham Kuyper Collected Works in Public Theology (Bellingham, WA: Lexham, 2019), 402–3.

47. See Kuyper, "Lemkes Wish," 403n2.

God," a true temple—"God would be in humanity and humanity in God."
God determines, then, that humanity is vice-regent of God in creation,
and its true and final rule must be progressively realized. This, in brief,
is what Kuyper calls the "program for creation."[48] That program is eternally focused in God's elective will on the hidden fact that Christ would
be the king and take hold for humanity of this kingship that Adam would
forfeit. Humanity in Adam and then in Christ, nonetheless, takes a lofty
position in the program.

The program is born, as must be stated in every loci, of God's plan for
God's glory. One of Kuyper's central anthropological emphases returns to
the mother idea of neo-Calvinism, which permeates all theo-logic: God
"created man *for his own sake*." While humanity is intended as the kings
of creation, that kingship is realized only as a gift of God and as royal
calling in absolute subordination to God's kingship. Thus, humanity is an
instrument for the glory of God. Humans "are created for God's use" so
that the definitions of what a human is and what a human is *for* depend
on God's speech.[49]

This lofty position and program God has given humanity is due to
the fact that, for Kuyper, humanity is the ectype of God, borrowing the
concept from Junius, as we observed above. The language of archetype/
ectype is not merely reserved for theological knowledge, but also, for
Kuyper, pertains to what humankind is. "As man stands as ectype over
against God, the archetype, man's knowledge of God can therefore be
only ectypal. This is what we meant when we called Theology a *dependent* knowledge—a knowledge which is not the result of an activity on our
part, but the result of an action which goes out from God to us: and in
its wider sense this action is God's self-revelation to His creature."[50] For
Kuyper, this means that humans are the richest revelation of God himself
to the world. They are a link, a gathering center.

Kuyper argues that Adam was created in a single moment in time, as
an adult, and because he is ectype, as the midway point between God

48. *Pro Rege* 1:474, emphasis added.
49. *CG* 1:168.
50. *Encyclopedia*, 256.

and the rest of creation.[51] In accordance with Bavinck's position, if one asked Kuyper to define the essence of the image, he would answer that the image is human nature, the ectype of God, the link between God and the rest of creation: "In so far as our nature is created after the image of God in original righteousness, this excellency could be lost and our nature become depraved; but not our creation after God's image so far as it pertains to its essence (*quod ad substantiam*). Our human nature is unassailable."[52] While human nature is corruptible, it is essentially the image of God, which means that the image of God cannot be lost.

Therein, humanity is the culmination of creation, in a hierarchy from the ground to plants to animal life to human beings. For one, human beings "epitomize the whole world," yet the essence of Adam is that God chose to mirror himself in humankind.[53] For "if the cosmos is the theatre of revelation, in this theatre man is both actor and spectator. This should not be taken in the sense that, in what is revealed in him, he adds one single drop to the ocean of cosmical revelation, but rather, that man himself is the richest instrument in which and by which God reveals Himself."[54] Kuyper ties together the concepts of humanity as ectype, the image of God, and the high and holy calling of humanity to image God to the world by way of conscious knowledge of God and its position in the program of creation.

Kuyper argues that, prior to sin, humanity as the mirror of God knew God by way of general revelation to a degree that is now impossible. "Adam possessed in himself, apart from the cosmos, everything that was necessary to have knowledge of God." Adam and Eve, apart from sin, were capable of learning of God from each other, from the animals, and through their own development, always obtaining "an ever richer revelation of God."[55] Again, Kuyper speaks not of an absolute denial of such knowledge after the fall, but of the clarity of the general knowledge of God before. By way of both self and world, to return to our chapter on

---

51. *CG* 1:226.
52. *Encyclopedia*, 507.
53. *CG* 1:226.
54. *Encyclopedia*, 264.
55. *Encyclopedia*, 186.

revelation and reason, Adam knew God both instinctively and by way of acquisition:

> But apart from all this acquired knowledge of God, he had in himself the capacity to draw knowledge of God from what had been revealed, as well as a rich revelation from which to draw that knowledge. Our older theologians called these two together the "concreate knowledge of God"; and correctly so, because here there was no logical activity which led to this knowledge of God, but this knowledge of God coincided with man's own self-knowledge. This knowledge of God was given eo ipso in his own self-consciousness; it was not given as discursive knowledge, but as the immediate content of self-consciousness.[56]

Without "further action of the logos within us" (reason) there was an "equally immediate knowledge of God," a consciousness born of the fact of being in his image. This knowledge was "much less experienced in words," which "Calvin called [the] seed of religion," an "ineradicable property of human nature" even after temptation and sin. This does not mean, for Kuyper, that Adam was created "with some sort of catechism in his head." Rather, in awakening to self-consciousness, Adam necessarily arrived at what Kuyper calls "original theology" from that which was in him.[57] While it is true that theology is the product of logic, with Adam this logic took place immediately.

Thus, humanity was made to be knowers of God. This is true both for the human organism entirely and for the individual. There is a collective ectype and an organic individuality wherein humanity and the particular human were made to know God. In fact, like we saw with Bavinck, the organic concept extends cosmos-wide. Creation is an organism; humanity is an organism; the individual human is an organism as well. Arguing against the practical realities of a separation between family life and educational life in his own circumstances, Kuyper emphasizes, for example, that "the child cannot be fragmented into various pieces, representing an intellectual side, a moral side, a religious side, a character-shaping side,

56. Encyclopedia, 186.
57. Encyclopedia, 187, 189.

and a practical-skills side. The child is a unity and must be formed in the recognition of that oneness."⁵⁸ Kuyper makes space, then, for speaking of the capacities of individual persons as details of the image. While humanity in itself is the ectype, the image of God, certain properties shine forth as a demonstration and consequence in persons, who are in themselves an organic whole, participating in the organism that is humanity. For Kuyper, the most important of these capacities is the logos in humanity, because humans are principally knowers of God. For "by his logos he appropriates revelation to himself, and in his logos reflectively (*abbildlich*) reveals something of the eternal logos."⁵⁹ Kuyper calls this deep-seated self, revealed in consciousness, the *pneumatical* aspect of personhood, which reaches its functional climax in knowing God.

Also among the properties Kuyper notes of Adam and Eve, the image of God means that original righteousness belonged to the nature of humanity and was not a superadded gift. Human nature, as created by God, is good in itself, not deficient or prone to concupiscence. Kuyper contrasts this Reformational view with Bellarmine, as noted earlier, who argued that the desire for the flesh or sinful desire was an aspect of being natural, or material, necessitating the likeness of God as an added gift to human nature.⁶⁰ For Kuyper, *sed contra*, this would require one to say that the fact of the material creation has some power over God that God had to overcome. It implies that the material is no mere creature but some pre-existent force that has the ability to turn good natures toward the evil, as if God were not creator of both spirit and matter. To be in the image of God, rather, includes humanity as a material, natural agent, possessing spiritual righteousness by human nature.

Thus, apart from sin, "humanity would have developed in terms of [this] unique essence." Humanity would have placed the spirit world under its feet. And if humanity would have subjected itself to God in full obedience, all of heaven and earth, all of creation, would have united in lifting up "hallelujahs to the Triune God."⁶¹ Kuyper notes repeatedly that

58. CG 3:454.

59. *Encyclopedia*, 264.

60. CG 1:164.

61. *Pro Rege* 1:474. This would not pertain, however, to Satan and the fallen hosts. They would have been destroyed.

this mirror of God (humanity) included at creation original righteousness, an unhindered body, and the perfections of wisdom and holiness, while yet facing a "moral battle" through which he could be brought to the fullness of life.[62] For Kuyper, humanity was created to mature, to grow into the knowledge of good and evil by way of a different form from through the power of temptation and sin. It is not as though humanity were intended to be guarded from evil forever. It was to face evil, but in the right time and through the right means, and with God to destroy the works of Satan. Becoming like God was to be the developmental conclusion of being like God, his ectype.

This means that Adam was made to know good and evil as God knows, but in a form that is eternal life, the repellent and destruction of all satanic evil, not by way of acquiring death. To be in the image of God, then, is to image God by knowing the world as God knows: to understand fully the boundaries of the good, to accept creation as God created, and to disavow forever any attempt to establish any other order than that which God determined.[63] The full maturation of humanity required walking through the knowledge of good and evil, but led by God, not tempted to sin by Satan. The promise of progressive understanding, stipulated on the ground of the covenant of works, ought to have culminated in a holy harmony of relations between self, world, and God. The image of God means that original humanity would reach

> a higher insight ... in order now to do everything not only according to the instinct of their creation, but also knowingly honoring God as King, Lawgiver, and Judge. In this way [Adam and Eve] would also have entered in into the highest fellowship with the truly moral life. They then would have done the good, not only because it was thus imprinted on their heart, but now also knowing that it was so, and why. Their moral existence would have fused with their religious existence into a higher harmony, and eternal life would have been bestowed precisely in this.[64]

---

62. CG 1:227.
63. CG 1:232.
64. CG 1:233.

Kuyper places the weight of the fall on Satan, the murderer from the beginning (John 8:44). Throughout his corpus, Kuyper draws a sharp dichotomy between Christ and Satan in order to protect the essentially human and creaturely from the claim that humanity is malformed in itself. For humanity would not fall, he supposes, without an external temptation. In distorting the order of creation, Satan, for Kuyper, does not appear as himself but takes control over an animal, a higher being making use of the "breathing, the throat, the tongue, the lips, the teeth ... the animal's organs to accomplish through that animal what the animal itself cannot do." The animal manifested in both speech and content an "alien, mysterious, hitherto unknown power."[65]

The power of Satan and the power of sin as a corruptive force within humanity (and cosmos) are distinct. Namely, humanity did not and could not fall "in the same way that Satan did." For Kuyper, the spirit world was not a domain under development like the human world. Since the spirits were not in the process of becoming, their decision to rebel prevents the corruption of the spirit world from a process of recovery. Their choices are final. Satan rather chooses to battle against the life of the world because Satan knows of the developmental nature of the creation, that it is in the process of becoming and thus still redeemable even after the fall. His war is not finished in the introduction of sin but only in his full dominion over creation, when it is no longer redeemable. Satan, then, needs the second Adam to walk through the trial of Adam, the temptation to sin, and to bow the knee to Satan's dominion if Satan is to finally prevail. Satan seeks throughout all of human history and in the life of Jesus Christ himself to "draw humanity further away from God; while God conversely displayed an all-surpassing compassion in order to draw the human race back to himself, to free it from Satan's embrace, and to carry out and complete his plan for humanity."[66]

The consequences of the temptation unto sin are immediate and apparent: paradise lost; the curse of childbearing, of the ground, and of death; the disease of the human heart and its permeation of society; the loss

65. CG 1:229–30.
66. *Pro Rege* 1:475.

of fellowship with God; humanity's glory devoured; division amid the human race; weakness against the power of sin—all under the dominion of Satan.[67] In the pneumatical self, the fall introduces a "breach of conscience." The moral conscience exists only as an aspect of human consciousness because of sin and is, at the same time, a sign of God's power over Satan as one of the first elements of the scaffold of common grace. For Kuyper, conscience is the "manifestation of the majesty of the Lord with which he, as God Almighty, maintains the true, moral world order over against the dishonest conceit of the sinner."[68] Apart from temptation and sin, humanity is morally upright by instinct, with no moral conscience. But after sin, God gives to humanity the moral conscience as judge. Thus, God immediately preserves the pneumatical self by way of common grace for the sake of the royal call.

Thus, the image of God (human nature) is not lost in the fall, but this is only because of common grace. "This is what our churches confessed when they spoke of sparks (scintillae) or remnants (rudera) which still remained of the image of God, which did not mean that they have remained of themselves, as though sin would not have extinguished those sparks or destroyed those remnants had it been able to do so; but that by 'common grace' God has restrained and curbed for a time the destructive power of sin."[69] Kuyper's postfall anthropological emphases include all that humanity still possesses and is capable of regaining. While sin is deadly, the imago still retains its integrity due to common grace. Even after the fall,

The capability of having consciousness, which is the distinguishing mark of the pneumatical, has not been lost, and in this lies man's openness to inspiration (Inspirationsfähigkeit). Hence, inspiration can work in the unconverted as well, as was the case with Balaam and Caiaphas, and though it generally occurs in connection with conversion, it is by no means dependent upon this. The creation of man as a pneumatic being opens the possibility of communion

---

67. Pro Rege 1:476.
68. CG 1:233.
69. Encyclopedia, 279.

between his spirit and the Spirit of God, by which the thoughts of God can be carried into his thoughts. To which is to be added, in the third place, that man is created, not as one who is always the same, but as a self-developing being, and that it is his end (τέλος) that God shall be in him and he in God, so that God shall be his temple (Rev. 21:22), and he a temple of God (Eph. 2:21). This, likewise, offers the means by which the influence of the Spirit of God upon his spirit can be supremely dominant.[70]

All in all, God "continues with his original creation plan," and in the unfolding of special revelation, one learns that this was the program of creation all along.[71] The program of creation is that humanity, not Satan, rule the world in the union of heaven and earth. So God will see to it, but not by the power of the fallen human race.

That is why God destined his only Son to enter the life of this world; to take on our human nature; to gather, as the Head of humanity, the split, divided, and scattered world into a unity once again and to unite it in one body. This Son was to destroy the world's sin through his blood so that it no longer stands guilty before the Holy One, and thereafter to raise up in his own person the kingship that humanity had lost.[72]

Kuyper's anthropology culminates in the second Adam, in what Christ means for the first Adam. "Even if [God's] creation is disrupted, his counsel is not undone. ... The original plan of creation will still be executed as God had ordained it." Yet, by the moment of temptation, it becomes clear that the program of creation will not be realized by "humanity drawing near to God, but only by God himself drawing so near to humanity that, in the Son, God united himself with the human race by assuming our human nature." Christ the king takes the place of the failed kingship of humanity. In his work of victory over sin and Satan, he comes to restore the royal calling of the human race, fulfilled in himself as King of creation.

---

70. *Encyclopedia*, 507–8.
71. *Pro Rege* 1:476.
72. *Pro Rege* 1:476.

For Kuyper, Christ's kingship is "entirely the same" as Adam's vocation
in that he came to constitute a "dominion over nature and over the spirit
world; that dominion makes creation into a unity so that as Priest he presents it to God and as King he subjects it to the Triune God."[73]

The point of creation also remains the same: that God's holy temple
"be manifest in humanity" and that all things be "delivered to God so that
he may be all in all."[74] The neo-Calvinist emphasis is perpetually that God
loves the world and so Christ's coming is no "foreign element;" for Christ
the human came for the life of the world. For Kuyper, creation's plight
demanded the coming of Christ for the realization of its essence, to be
the temple of God, and to subject the spirit world to humanity. Kuyper
even states that "God does not love individual persons, but the world."[75]
In the electing love of God, he does not abandon humanity and its world,
but saves.

Thus, for Kuyper, Christ is humanity. "If all of our race [the human
race] are not saved, it is because they who are lost are cut off from the tree
of humanity."[76] He argues that damnation is the denial of the organism, the
ultimate judgment unto individualism. This means that Kuyper understands that there is no human without humanity, no individual without the
organism. But, in Christ, "there is no aggregate but the 'body of Christ.'"
For Kuyper, the body of Christ is the original organism of humanity, the
elected humanity. Because Christ is second Adam, he takes the place of
Adam as the whole of the human race. In the eschatological life, for Kuyper,
regenerated humanity is humanity. Christ makes fully human. He ties this
claim directly to the knowledge of God in the life of this world.

> Hence [the body of Christ] is not something else nor something
> new, but it is the original human race, it is humanity, which, recon-
> ciled and regenerated, is to accomplish the logical task of taking up
> subjectively into its consciousness this revealed ectypal Theology,
> and to reflect it from that consciousness. Whatever a man may be,

---

73. *Pro Rege* 1:474–75, 477.
74. *Pro Rege* 1:475.
75. *Encyclopedia*, 209.
76. *Encyclopedia*, 209.

as long as he does not share the life and thought of this regenerated humanity, he cannot share this task. "The natural man receiveth not the things of the Spirit of God: for they are foolishness unto him: neither can he know them, because they are spiritually discerned" (1 Cor. ii. 14).[77]

Regeneration revives a person as a creature of God, denying mere individuality. Individualism separates persons into communities of aggregated individuals. For Kuyper, like Bavinck, such modernist individuality denies the fact of the organism. But Kuyper goes on to say that persons outside Christ, in the end of their days, are given precisely the individuality they desire and are cut off from the organism of humanity, which is only found in the regenerate humanity, the organic church. Bavinck speaks of becoming fully human in Christ, and Kuyper of being a member of the eschatological human. However, Kuyper does state that common grace has curbed the individualizing force of sin for life in this age. Thus, being cut off from humanity altogether is only an aspect of damnation after final judgment and not one of unbelieving persons while living on earth.[78] All human persons remain human in this life.

In Christ then, humanity is given back its vocation as royal stewards, with dominion over the life of the world under the rulership of Christ. By common grace, God witnesses to this vocation in the vocational stewardship of the life of the world in every age. But, in Christ, humanity will triumph. "After the end of all things, it will be clear not only that the disruption caused by Satan was entirely unable to undo God's ordination, but in fact, the effect of Satan's work was that God's virtues shone in even greater glory and final triumph surpassed what paradise had promised."[79]

The triumph of humanity, which is due entirely to the glory of Christ, is manifest in the life of Christ on earth. Christ exhibited his dominion over nature, over the spirit world, over disease, disaster, and death. Kuyper notes that the Gospel of Mark is symbolized by the lion, pointing to Christ's power as true humanity over nature and spirit. His speech is

---

77. *Encyclopedia*, 209.
78. *Encyclopedia*, 210.
79. *Pro Rege* 1:477.

authority and his deeds are power. In all this, he reveals the dominion of Adam. In him, "humanity's kingly authority over all creatures was restored; and humanity's complete union with the Triune God was realized."[80]

CONCLUSION

For both these neo-Calvinist theologians, creation reflects the Triune Creator, and God's archetypal being is the basis for the patterns exhibited in creation. For them, humanity is the ectype of God and the link, the *mikro-theos*, the royal steward, the climax of creation order. For Bavinck, though the Triune God is not like everything else, everything else is like the Triune God.[81] Unity and diversity is the particular expression of the triune shape of creation as an organism, both in its parts and as a whole simply because creation *comes from* an archetypal, wholly other One-in-Three. While "all creatures display *vestiges* of God, only a human being is the *image* of God." Indeed, with creation bearing the organic imprints of God's triune character, it is significant that Bavinck asserts the created nature of humanity as the "epitome" of all creation: "a micro-divine being."[82] For Kuyper, the same holds true. Yet, Kuyper's focus is specifically on the vocational imaging of the image of God in the life of the world as kings of creation. While in Adam that kingship is forfeit, in Christ humanity triumphs. In Christ, the mystical body, humanity knows God and rules all things. "Hence [the body of Christ] is not something else nor something new, but it is the original human race, it is humanity, which, reconciled and regenerated, is to accomplish the logical task of taking up subjectively into its consciousness [the] revealed ectypal Theology, and to reflect it from that consciousness."[83]

---

80. *Pro Rege* 1:478.
81. Eglinton, *Trinity and Organism*, 89, 112.
82. RD 2:555, 562.
83. *Encyclopedia*, 209.

VIII

Common Grace
and the Gospel

All "special" revelation, as it is commonly though not altogether correctly called, postulates common grace, i.e., that act of God by which negatively He curbs the operation of Satan, death, and sin, and by which positively He creates an intermediate state for this cosmos, as well as for our human race, which is and continues to be deeply and radically sinful, but in which sin cannot work out its end.

—*Abraham Kuyper*, Encyclopedia of Sacred Theology: Its Principles

KUYPER, IN HIS *Lectures on Calvinism*, and Bavinck in *Philosophy of Revelation*, both suggest that one determines one's world- and life-view in one's understanding of the three relations between God, self, and world.[1] For Christians, God is the sovereign first in all of these relations. God determines the nature of the human self. God creates the world. God

---

1. For Bavinck especially, a world- and life-view, or worldview, is not to be thought of as a religious or philosophical position one adopts that enables one to see the rest of reality correctly in some automated fashion. Bavinck resists the notion of worldview as a deductive enterprise. The metaphor of rose-tinted spectacles has often been used to describe this mistake. Worldviews are not like spectacles that enable the wearer to see everything clearly. Rather, for Bavinck, worldview is like the boundary of a map, formulated and drawn over time by inductive research. Worldviews answer questions such as "What am I?" "What is the world?" and "Why am I in the world?" and so on. They then give guidance to the knower on how to conduct life under the sun, as both scientist and artist, investigating and creating, while not transgressing the critical boundaries of reality in intellect and moral action. For more, see *CW*.

212

restores his relationship with humankind by Christ's mediation. God made all things and tells all things what they are and how they must be. If God to self and God to world are determined by God, then God also tells us how the self is to relate to the world, or how people are to relate to people, to the land, and to all of creaturely life. This final relation (that between a person and the world), however, is the most difficult to understand within the Christian worldview, as the church awaits the re-creation to come.

Differing perspectives on the relation between the Christian and the world abound and are famously summed up by H. Richard Niebuhr's five relations between "Christ and culture," all of which seek to fulfill the John 17 mandate (that one be in the world but not of it) with significantly differing emphases.[2] For the neo-Calvinist fathers, following John Calvin, common grace is a necessary concept corresponding to an empirical reality that mediates the possibility of the John 17 mandate in a polluted world. On the one hand, in the relationship between a Christian and the surrounding culture, an antithesis stands insofar as Christians participate in the reality of the uneven war between Christ and antichrist that extends into the relationship between the church and the world. On the other hand, "total depravity by sin does not always tally with [our] experiences of life."[3] The natural life, while corrupted by sin, retains truth, goodness, and beauty. Thus, while an antithesis stands between the Christian and culture, God's grace is ubiquitous, wherein "its tiny roots and fibers everywhere penetrate into the joints and cracks of the life of nature,"[4] enabling a livable life in the midst of the corrupted ground.

Simply put, then, for Kuyper and Bavinck, God's common grace is God's general favor that sustains the creation order despite sin. Common grace is distinct from special grace. God's special grace restores, renews, and recreates creation order as the kingdom of God. The former serves and anticipates the latter. There are indeed multiple possibilities for defining common grace that may place emphasis on differing aspects of its total relation to all of theology. Here is a fuller definition in brief: *God's*

---

2. H. Richard Niebuhr, *Christ and Culture* (New York: Harper and Brothers, 1956).

3. Abraham Kuyper, *Lectures on Calvinism* (Grand Rapids: Eerdmans, 1931), 122.

4. CG 1:173.

common grace is the fact of his loving patience in preserving both humanity and the creaturely cosmos despite human rebellion and its polluting corruption for the sake of redemption.[5] Common grace marks an era between the curse of the world and the second advent of Christ wherein God gifts moral, epistemic, and natural goods to the world, maintaining in high degree an organic creaturely unity despite the curse.

One of the related key emphases of the first-generation neo-Calvinists included continually pointing out the ubiquity of revelation. God reveals himself universally, in consciousness and nature, in the "I" and "thou," in subject and object—and he does so to every person who comes into the world. Kuyper and Bavinck both recovered the fact that the character of this universal revelation is dual. While revelation is both wholly gracious (in that God has chosen to speak) and the condemnation of human rebellion (in that God's justice is revealed in his speaking), God's determination to speak has two goals that do indeed display his favor to the world: (1) to preserve sinful humanity and the polluted cosmos, and (2) to chase after sinful humanity for the sake of the kingdom of Christ. Both of these serve the grand point of history: the glory of God in re-creation. Revelation's ubiquity and dual purpose unfold from God's grace as love into a dual grace of gifts. The ultimate gift is the work of the gospel: the redemptive grace of salvation in Christ. But the other grace is the manifold of gifts, which a human being experiences in every moment they draw breath. The gracious preservation of the cosmos in the gift of life itself is the servant of the end of grace: the redemption of the church. So Bavinck on special grace: in Christianity we see "God seeking man and coming to him again and again with mercy: 'I am the Lord your God!'"[6]

Neither Kuyper nor Bavinck regarded the doctrinal concept signified in that second gift, that God graciously preserves sinful humanity (or common grace), as novel. In their reading, Calvin considered common

---

5. Kuyper's work sparked a lineage of controversy surrounding the doctrine of common grace and whether or not the term "grace" can be attributed to those outside the domain of the church. Herman Hoeksema was a critical interlocutor in this debate. In 1924, the Christian Reformed Church affirmed the fact of common grace in a similar form to Kuyper's definitions: common grace is God's work in (1) the bestowal of natural gifts, (2) the restraining of sin in human affairs, and (3) the ability of unbelievers to perform acts of civic good.

6. Bavinck, "Common Grace," 42.

grace an aspect of God's all-encompassing providence, wherein he maintains human life and culture. For Calvin, this general favor of God upholds the goodness of creation in the face of humanity's radical depravity. This grace is the source of all human virtue and accomplishment, and even the source of the proper functioning of reason itself.[7] Calvin, Kuyper, and Bavinck confessed the fact of common grace not only because of its presence in Scripture but also because of the empirical tension that every thoughtful Christian feels between the biblical judgment that humans are unable to do good and the experience that they often do. There is so much that is true, good, and beautiful outside the domain of Christianity. Kuyper states the point provocatively: "The world turns out to be better than expected and the church worse than expected."[8] Bavinck asks the question accordingly: What is the "relation of Christianity to this wealth of natural life, which, originating in creation, has, under the law there imposed upon it, developed from age to age?" While Christianity is on guard "against paganism, it never despised or condemned natural life."[9]

One finds the resolution of this tension in the relation among creation, incarnation, and resurrection, where God declares his intention to keep the creaturely and human around forever in the body of Jesus Christ. Despite then the totality of sin's maneuvering into the crevices of the human consciousness, the benevolence of God arrests the potency of sin and preserves much of the goods of original creation unto the kingdom of God. This is the *generalem Dei gratiam*, general grace of God (according to Calvin), or *de gemeene gratie*, common grace (according to Kuyper).[10] Even in Calvin's underdeveloped doctrine of the general grace of God, there is an "untroubled acceptance," as Jochem Douma puts it, of the Bible's clarity regarding God's favor toward all that satisfies objections such as that of Klaas Schilder: "Only when something promotes eternal salvation can we truly speak of grace."[11] Kuyper and Bavinck both devel-

---

7. John Calvin, *Institutes of the Christian Religion* 2.2.3, 2.2.12–17.

8. CG 2:10.

9. Bavinck, "Calvin and Common Grace," 438.

10. Kuyper prefers *gratie* (grace) over *genade* (favor) because the Dutch term for "favor" bears the connotation of saving grace (CG 1:597).

11. Jochem Douma, *Common Grace in Kuyper, Schilder, and Calvin: Exposition, Composition, and*

oped this doctrine in the crucible of three witnesses: the biblical testimony, the empirical reality, and the pastoral need.

While Calvin taught Kuyper and Bavinck both the fact of the general grace of God, Kuyper notes that "in former times this subject never enjoyed separate treatment."[12] While many had noted a reality of grace in general, and especially so with regard to the virtues among the pagan philosophers, what is "neo" about neo-Calvinism in regards to this topic? It is that Kuyper (in particular) and Bavinck (to a lesser degree) offer the first-ever magisterial treatment of this doctrine. Kuyper thought that common grace was a distinct loci of dogmatic logic. In this chapter, we carry on the task of uncovering the distinctive dogmatic logic within these neo-Calvinist fathers with respect to common grace—a logic that can be summarized in three moves: (1) the fountain of common grace, (2) the revelation of common grace, and (3) the center of common grace. Finally, we end the chapter considering (4) common grace and natural law—a popular, controversial, confusing, yet important relation that has beckoned much consideration.

THE FOUNTAIN OF COMMON GRACE

Kuyper begins his enormous collection of newspaper articles on common grace (written over six years) with a clarion call: in the context of nineteenth-century (modern) Europe the Reformed community must recover the conviction that the grace of God in the gospel is particular, the "heart of our Reformed confession." God saves sinners unto eternal glory, and the heart of this heart is the "almighty sovereignty of God who elects whom he will."[13] Immediately, in the first article, Kuyper makes clear in brief

---

Evaluation, trans. Albert H. Oosterhoff, ed. William Helder (Hamilton, ON: Lucerna CRTS, 2017), xi.

12. CG 1:6.

13. CG 1:2. In the volume introduction to CG 1, Richard Mouw contends that "while Kuyper clearly operates out of a Reformed framework, his theology of common grace is not tied in any necessary manner to, say, specific doctrines about predestination and election" (xxii). Rather, Mouw argues, the doctrine flows from the confession of God's sovereignty. This suggestion, however, dissociates God's unified work from itself. Predestination and sovereignty are not separated acts of God's will. God's predestinarian decree is exercised in his sovereign rule. In Kuyper's logic, one can neither separate common from particular grace nor election and sovereignty, as he makes clear in the quote above. Kuyper makes precisely the opposite point with rigor in CG 2, ch. 13: "Common grace, no matter how fervently championed, gets lost again as long as we fail to include it in predestination or,

his Trinity-soaked logic that honors all three persons of the Godhead: God elects whom he will, the Son enacts God's will in covenant, and the Spirit brings the grace-restored individual into the community of the elect. The movement of particular grace is election (Father), covenant (Son), and community (Spirit).

Yet, this particularity of grace in the redemption of individuals does not take place in a vacuum but on the stage of the world in the lives of humans who are part of *humanity*. Grace does not separate the Christ-bought community from family, society, and nation outright. The believer who confesses "I have been saved by the grace of God" finds also another logic at work that maintains the bounds of the redeemed to the world and maintains humanity. Behind new covenant grace, there is another grace. Experientially, one confesses: I am renewed by the Spirit of God, reconciled by the Son of God, chosen by the Father, *and* have always been a child of creation, a creature among creatures, a human being— there is another grace within which the particularity of reconciling grace works like an actor on the stage; one cannot ignore the fact of the stage. In another metaphor Kuyper uses, he suggests that the fruit of the tree of particular grace in the cross of Christ was planted in a field, in a soil. The tree is particular, special, and fruitful, and the tree needs a place to be planted. Common grace is the act of God in providing the field.

If this second and grounding grace is a supernatural grace, a favor expressed toward creation where God is the subject of that grace and the world the object, then the perfections of the Triune God are the source of common favor. Kuyper notes that common grace magnifies God's forbearance, while God's holiness also condemns sin. If God were not patient in the midst of his holiness, then creaturehood would no longer exist. The transition from Genesis 2 to Genesis 3, for example, does not include death outright, but curse, law, and the mediation of a sacrificial system. Humanity does not "surely die," but one sees Adam preserved, Cain exiled, and justice postponed. Kuyper unveils the irony: "In that day [of sin] Adam would fully die, and behold, he lives nine times as long as

---

if you will, in the eternal decree. Only what has its roots in predestination can find its rightful place in the dogma of the church and in theologians' study" (112).

the oldest one among us, and reaches an old age of almost one thousand years. In this telling fact lies the redemptive thought that the majesty of God's justice works against sin and reacts to it by shifting, postponing, and delaying its effects." God deals "temporarily" with sin, Kuyper argues, and in God's bearing up "common grace is born."[14]

Thus, it is not the case that human nature is left naturally preserved after the fall of humankind into sin and death. Rather, the possibility and capability of human nature, and all other natures for that matter, are a "conferred good," as Douma puts it, summarizing Kuyper.[15] In restraining sin, there is a negative aspect of common grace—a constraint—and in the possibility of human development, of progress in the richness of human life and civilization, there is also a positive.

The confession of common grace for the neo-Calvinist fathers is not a concession to the tension of human experience first but an acknowledgment that before the face of God (*coram Deo*) sin is surely deadly, and yet we live, the just and unjust alike. God is patient and holy. God does not shirk his own nature in setting aside his justice but forbears and expresses a common patience to the cosmos, a stage-setting patience for the covenantal union between justice and mercy. On the one hand, they confess, humanity is entirely fallen, and simultaneously, life persists, beauty manifests, truth is known, and civilization develops. The answer in this tension is not the goodness of humanity but the patience of God, which is a favor or temporal grace with a first purpose of "the restraint of ruin that lurks within sin."[16] Common grace denies a widespread, modern notion that human progress and the general well-being of society is upheld by the fact that the majority of humans are essentially good, decent people.

Common grace, then, is dogmatic in that it is "an idea deduced directly from the sovereignty of the Lord, a doctrine that is and remains the root conviction for all Reformed people." The logic is clear:

If God is sovereign, then his lordship *must* extend over *all* of life, and it cannot be restricted to the walls of the church or within the

---

14. CG 1:7, 288.

15. Douma, *Common Grace in Kuyper*, 7.

16. CG 1:9.

Christian orbit. The non-Christian world has not been handed over to Satan, nor surrendered to fallen humanity, nor consigned to fate. God's sovereignty is great and all-dominating in the life of that unbaptized world as well. Therefore Christ's church on earth and God's children cannot simply retreat from this life. If the believer's God is at work in this world, then in this world the believer's hand must take hold of the plow, and the name of the Lord must be glorified in that activity as well.[17]

God's sovereignty means that not a single event in the processes of space-time unfolds apart from the decretive will of God. "Not a sparrow falls to the ground without the expression of the will of the Father of lights. Each moment, when we draw breath, we feel in our lungs the *a posteriori* evidence of the universal love of God." This patience toward sinful humanity and the sin-soaked ground is indeed a love, the love of God. God desires, after all, that none should perish. God loves the world, and while not mollifying his justice, he is patient. In his patience, common grace is no mere response to an unexpected turn, but the revelation of this dual grace is God's eternal will: "God did not have two plans for the world, one in case man remained standing and the other for the possibility that he fell. God's counsel is from eternity, not conditional but firm in itself, and it is *that* counsel of God which *alone* exists and will exist for eternity."[18]

By revisiting the doctrine of God, and specifically God's economy, as outlined in chapter 6, one can see the same logic applied specifically to common grace. In the economy of God's love expressed to the world, the Son of God bears up all things as mediator. "The world contains nothing, not a single thought, that has not been taken from the divine Being and brought about by the Word who himself is God. Therefore all that has been created corresponds to the being of God. It stands in indissoluble organic relationship with the being of God through the Word." The world does not possess life in itself, but in the Word there is life. The world "has life only because the Word is in that creation. The Word does not shine into the world, as if the world existed of itself and only now and then the

---

17. CG 1:xxxvi–xxxvii.
18. CG 2:124.

radiance of the Word would shine into it." Even when the life that the Word enlightens cracks and fissures in the chaos of sin, does the Word depart from the world? No. The Son of God, the eternal Word, as the light of life, has not allowed the darkness on earth to become "outermost darkness" (see 2 Pet 2:17; Jude 6, 13). The Eternal Word, the Son, shines in the darkness, and "that twilight in the midst of the darkness, those rays of light shining through the mists into the darkness—that is common grace."[19]

It is by the mediation of the Son, therefore, that God in the face of sin establishes the earth (Ps 93:1). God unveils his preserving love in the stability of the organism of creation. Why? For Kuyper, Satan introduced the toxic cancer of sin into the world. In that moment of descension to the dead, what would God do? Does his purpose stand? Would the world be released to Satan? Would humanity lose itself in the mire of chaos? No. God has blocked the corrupting power of sin with a greater power: common grace. "These are the three powerful dimensions of common grace that occurred. Absolute sin was curbed in *the human heart*. Complete death was curbed in *the human body*. The universal curse was curbed in *nature*."[20]

God's decretive will, expressed in the eschatology of the kingdom of God in Scripture as the "unity of heaven and earth" (Eph 1:10), remains the true end. If heaven and earth are to be unified in the Son of God, then earth must be maintained unto that end. This common grace is not the ultimate or the final cause of creation. It is the servant of the Christ-centered unity of heaven and earth. Before the incarnation, the Son mediates the ongoing establishment of the heavens and earth, of the human and animal, of reason and vocation, for the sake of the Son, who will unite the heavenly temple with the earthly.[21]

As God the Father wills the maintenance and preservation of the creaturely realm, and God the Son mediates that establishment as an expression of God's love, the Spirit of God distributes God's love as gifts to the world. God's Spirit is the Spirit of completion, of bringing about the will

---

19. CG 1:470, 474.
20. CG 1:591.
21. CG 2, ch. 14.

of God in the world. Bavinck offers an excellent and pithy overview of the agency of the Spirit in his work on the ground. After sin,

> the economy of the divine forbearance and long-suffering begins (Rom. 3:25). The times of ignorance commence (Acts 17:30). God allows the nations to walk in their own ways (Acts 14:16), yet does not leave himself without witness (Acts 14:17). In him they move and have their being; he is not far from each one of them (Acts 17:27, 28). He reveals himself to them in the works of nature (Rom. 1:19). Every good and perfect gift, also among the nations, comes down from the Father of Lights (James 1:17). The Logos, who created and maintains all things, enlightens each man coming into the world (John 1:9). The Holy Spirit is the author of all life, of every power and every virtue (Gen. 6:17; 7:15; Pss. 33:6; 104:30; 139:2; Job 32:8; Eccl. 3:19).[22]

It is the Spirit of God who gives and maintains life, who provides the consciousness its unity, who witnesses to God in the revelation of nature and conscience, who is not "far from each one of them." God's common grace, his love toward common creation, unfolds in the giving of natural gifts, which is the Spirit's work.

Therefore, common grace is not first an ethical doctrine of public responsibility (though it offers the possibility of responsibility as a pastoral implication) but the confession of the love of the Triune God to the cosmos in toto. It is not the *call* to cultural engagement but its ground, confessing the fact of God's work to carry on a unity and commonality among the regenerated Christ-bought church and those outside the family of God despite the antithesis. In doing so, God never departs from his plan: to unite heaven and earth in the Son. Common grace is God's stage-setting love for a particular, eschatological redemption.

---

22. Bavinck, "Common Grace," 41.

THE REVELATION OF COMMON GRACE

COMMON GRACE REVEALED IN HISTORY

Nothing can be known of this supernatural grace unless God chooses to reveal himself. In his revealing, he reveals this common love and supplies the gifts discussed above by the revelation and activity of the Spirit. The key insight, particularly noted by Bavinck, is that both general and special revelation constitute common grace, which we will explore in detail below. One can neatly categorize neither special revelation as the sole domain of the unveiling of special grace nor general revelation as the sole domain of the common. General and special revelation together form an organic unity, as does the reality of common and special grace; each relies on and interpenetrates the other.

Bavinck points out that this difference between the covenant of works in the garden of Eden and the covenant of grace in the rest of redemptive history is not revelation, but grace. Creation is revelation. "Creation itself is the first, rich revelation of God, the foundation and beginning of every subsequent revelation."[23] For Bavinck (as covered above, and we will revisit this below in detail) this means that there is no natural theology per se, if natural theology is taken to be knowledge about God inferred apart from revelation by reason alone. Rather, general revelation produces a general theology precisely because revelation is prior to reason, and this is so from creation itself. After human rebellion, there is no change in the fact of God's revelation, but there is in its content: it is now a revelation of God's grace in the face of the privation of the good.

Indeed, Bavinck makes the unique argument in *Philosophy of Revelation* that prior to the Abrahamic covenant the distinction between a general and special revelation is nearly absent.[24] The precise distinction between the two forms of revelation is muddy because special revelation's primary quality is that it is marked off by the covenant of grace, by God's electing love unveiled in the covenantal promise to save a people. Yet, prior

---

23. Bavinck, "Common Grace," 39.
24. *PoR*, 155.

to Abraham, God's special revealing, his particular condescension and speech to individuals, bears the quality of restraining sin.

Revelation in that pre-Abrahamic season remains a revelation to all peoples on the earth, blocking and judging and protecting the world from the destruction of the path of human rebellion in a series of cycles—Adam and Eve, Cain, Lamech, the Sons of God, Noah, Ham, Canaan, and Babel. Bavinck argues: "The earlier view [of the duality of revelation], which exclusively emphasized the antithesis, no less than that now prevalent which has an eye only for the agreement and affinity [between the Church and world], suffers from one-sidedness."[25] Prior to the covenant of grace as the covenant of particular grace to a particular people, special and general revelation coincide closely. Therein, the distinction between special and general revelation is not one of mode but content. After the fall of humanity, revelation takes on the content of grace in a twofold form.

For Bavinck, God comes to humanity after Genesis 3 in a gracious and merciful manner—life, food, clothing, relationships—these are human property by way of gift, not right. When God comes to Abraham and sets apart a covenant people, we watch the historical development of God's special grace in distinction from his common grace, which was already glimpsed in episodes such as the choosing of Noah or the separation of Cain and Seth. While it is easy to recognize common grace revealed in the domain of general revelation, in the upholding of the human consciousness, in the fact of the unity of the cosmos, in God's law revealed to the conscience, in the fact of truth, goodness, and beauty, the pagan virtues, and in the growth of the crops, Kuyper and Bavinck both place significant emphasis on an underemphasized aspect of covenant theology: that the biblical revelation of the Noachian covenant is the historical, covenantal ground of God's common grace. The Noachian covenant is a covenantal administration of the covenant of grace, carrying forth the promise of Genesis 3:15 through the choice of Noah.

Simultaneously, this covenant gives shape and promise to the history of common grace. Though underrecognized and underemphasized, the Heidelberg Catechism, drawing from Genesis 8:22, states that God's

---

25. *PoR*, 155.

fatherly hand brings "herbs and grass, rain and drought."[26] For Kuyper, while Noah is not the second Adam (a covenantal head of the human race), he is the second representative, the "progenitor." Noah is the second peak from which all the streams of humanity flow. The covenant that God forms with Noah after the flood has no particular grace, no judicial forgiveness of sins, but is indeed God's special revelation and God's covenant with humanity.[27] Bavinck argues that "in opposition to the unrighteousness that had evoked his wrath [in the flood], God now, as it were, firmly grounds the being and life of the creation in a covenant with all of nature and with every living being. This life and being are no longer 'natural.' Rather, they are the fruit of a supernatural grace to which man no longer has a self-evident claim."[28]

Even the lineage of the curse, Ham and Canaan and early Babylonia, is the product of Noachian-covenanted grace. From the fall of humanity to Noah, the reader sees the world breaking: humanity is cursed, the thorns and thistles come forth, the human-animal relation is antithetical and wild, and natural cataclysm and new, more heinous sins are walking side by side. Yet, God witnesses to his love. God is patient. Following his judgment of the world in the flood, God reveals his gracious and common love toward creaturely existence: "I establish my covenant with you and your descendants after you" (Gen 9:9). Common grace began in the Edenic curse, but it is grounded in an explicit covenantal era in Noah, from the postflood establishment of nature unto the second advent of Jesus Christ. So Bavinck on recognizing the goodness of God in all the lineages of humankind: "There is thus a rich revelation of God even among the heathen—not only in nature but also in their heart and conscience, in their

---

26. Heidelberg Catechism, Lord's Day 10, Q&A 27.

27. CG 1:13.

28. Bavinck, "Common Grace," 40. Kuyper points out that others questioned the universal scope of the Noachian covenant: "In the meantime, we need to consider a serious objection concerning this Noachic covenant. Already in the time of our fathers, the question arose as to whether this covenant as well, since it bears the character of a covenant of *grace*, needs to be understood as established with believers only, such that it did not concern the world in general. In particular, Pareus, Perkins, and Mastricht understood it in this more restricted sense, and Rivet also uses an expression that seems to indicate that he was of the same opinion" (CG 1:21). Yet, Kuyper cites Calvin: "There is no doubt that it was the design of God to provide for *all* his posterity. It was not therefore a *private* covenant ... but one which is *common* to all people, and which shall flourish in all ages to the end of the world."

life and history, among their statesmen and artists, their philosophers and reformers. There exists no reason at all to denigrate or diminish this divine revelation. Nor is it to be limited to a so-called natural revelation."[29] God's commonly gracious action is an expression of his providence.

The Noachian covenant is the ground for the ongoing organic unity of the world. When God establishes this covenant, he gives unity to the world. This grace is extended to humans, animals, and every organism of nature. "Therein, God's common grace to the whole of the cosmos preserves the organic unity of creation between human life, animal life, and inorganic natural life. Surely, the curse between these relations is obvious. Yet, the organism is not deceased and demolished." Genesis 8:21 (stating that the human heart is continually evil) stands emphatically against locating the progress of history, the building of civilizations, and particularly the ongoing ingenuity of human culture in the nature of humanity left to itself. "The beast within man remains just as evil and wild, but the bars around its cage were fortified, so that it cannot again escape like it used to."[30] Development without common grace is impossible. Knowledge without common grace is impossible. The organization of a healthy society and functioning of human relations across the spectrum of religious, ethnic, and socioeconomic distinctions is impossible, without the grace of God. So Kuyper: "In the end, we may simply conclude that knowledge and learning are nothing but discovering and learning the mystery of the means of common grace that God has ordained and appointed for us."[31]

This fact of covenanted common grace is the biblical foundation for the neo-Calvinist concept of religion in general. For Bavinck in particular, pagan religion cannot be conceived as merely natural religion but must also be seen as the product of God's revelation, wherein God's revelation is taken hold of by humankind and twisted and suppressed by idolatry. The difference in the Christian religion and world religions is not in revealed religion versus natural religion. For Bavinck, truly natural religion could only be philosophy separated from theology altogether. Rather, religion

---

29. Bavinck, "Common Grace," 41.
30. CG 1:26.
31. CG 2:583–84.

(various theisms with their rites and practices) is derivative of revelation, not mere natural reasoning, inference, or affection. On the power of God's revelation in pagan religion, Bavinck builds his case from Calvin, and also Lactantius, "who says that though the [pagan] philosophers missed the 'sum of things,' viz., that the world was created by God so that man might worship him, yet each of them saw something of the truth." Noting Calvin's doctrine of election and reprobation, Bavinck writes that even "reprobation does not mean the withholding of all grace."[32]

For Bavinck, ethnographic study into the indigenous peoples and early societies has consistently established that religion is the source of the development of civilization, of the arts and sciences as well. Theologically, it is revelation that is the objective ground of all subjective religion. Religion is the fact of being in relation with God expressed in the feeling, knowledge, and practices of dependence on God. While all religion stands condemned before God as idolatry, it simultaneously contains a base element of truth because it is a human-distorted set of beliefs and practices standing on a real relationship between the true God and his common revelation to a common humanity. This fact is clearly attested to in Scripture. Therefore, "there exists no reason at all to denigrate or diminish this divine revelation. Nor is it to be limited to a so-called natural revelation. … Furthermore, the revelation of God in nature and history is never a mere passive pouring forth of God's virtues but is always a positive act on the part of God. The Father of Jesus works always (John 5:17). His providence is a divine, eternal, omnipresent *power.*"[33]

We must draw a specific conclusion from Scripture, and particularly from the fact of the Noachian covenant. The only "difference between the religion of Israel and the religions of the world cannot lie in the concept of revelation. This difference cannot be expressed through the opposition of a *religio revelata* [revealed religion] and a *religio naturalis* [natural religion]." Rather, all religions rest on revelation with the admixture of idolatry. "The true, material difference in question lies in *gratia; gratia specialis*

---

32. Bavinck, "Calvin and Common Grace," 453. See Calvin, *Institutes of the Christian Religion* II.2.17.

33. Bavinck, "Common Grace," 41.

[special grace] is something unknown to the heathen."[34] Revelation and idolatry produce religions in which humanity seeks after an unknown god by means of distorting the Creator-creature distinction. But in God's covenantal grace, "here we see God seeking man and coming to him again and again with mercy: 'I am the Lord your God!'"[35] Thus, in all religions standing on common grace alone we see humans seeking after God in order to find him, but in special grace, God condescends to humanity in order to save.

CLASSIFYING THE GRACES

Grace is not first a thing or substance, but God's favor expressed toward the world, an unmerited favor. The term "grace" indicates the love of God principally but also has a second meaning: the object God gives itself can also be called grace. Grace both is God's favor as a perfection expressed to the world and can refer to the gift. In common and particular grace, the graces (gifts) are distinct, while both spill over from God's love (grace).

Scanning across the corpus of both Kuyper and Bavinck, one finds a number of ways to classify the various common graces. Kuyper, helpfully, divides them at times between the internal and external graces.[36] He describes them accordingly:

[The internal:] civic righteousness, family loyalty, natural love, human virtue, the development of public conscience, integrity, fidelity among people, and an inclination toward piety permeates life. [The external:] The other part of common grace manifests its operation when human power over nature increases, when invention after invention enriches life, faster concourse between countries arises, the arts flourish, the sciences enrich our knowledge, the enjoyments and delights of life multiply, when a glow comes

---

34. Bavinck, "Common Grace," 41. "Rome replaced the antithetical relation of sin and grace with the contrast between natural and supernatural religion. Upon this latter contrast she erected a system that conflicted with the principles of apostolic Christianity" (Bavinck, "Common Grace," 45).

35. Bavinck, "Common Grace," 42.

36. CG 1:539.

upon every expression of life, its forms become refined, and life's common features grow in their attractiveness.[37]

But, in all the possibilities, we return to the doctrine of the Spirit. Locating the graces of common grace, the gifts of the Spirit, is a never-ending macro- and micro-level endeavor. The Spirit is the giver of being and life. This is true at every level of creaturely being: the human being and animal, the life of the sun and stars, the atomic and subatomic, the quarks, the galaxies, the physical and metaphysical.

If we focus on the human, the Spirit gives the possibility of right reason, of unity between subject and object (enabling the fact of truth perception, as well as the potency of the arts and sciences), and of the agreement between the moral law and the conscience that creates the possibility of civic order, of interhuman relations, of family and nation. So Calvin: "Therefore this evidence clearly testifies to a universal apprehension of reason and understanding by nature implanted in men. Yet so universal is this good that every man ought to recognize for himself in it the peculiar grace of God."[38]

The mind of man, Kuyper argues, is fallen yet, as Calvin puts it, "clothed with God's excellent gifts." How so? The Spirit of God is the "sole fountain of truth."[39] The Spirit is the Spirit of truth, goodness, and beauty. For Kuyper, God unveiled his common grace on humanity even when he shortened its life span after the Noachian flood, because arresting the span of life is arresting the girth of sin. After the fall, God still has a purpose for his creation, and the groundwork of this special purpose is universally manifest in human and civilizational development. In part, this is a necessary conclusion derivative of the empirical data.

What then? Shall we deny that the truth shone upon the ancient jurists who established civic order and discipline with such great equity? Shall we say that the philosophers were blind in their fine observation and artful description of nature? Shall we say that those men were devoid of understanding who conceived the art of

---

37. CG 1:539–40.
38. Calvin, *Institutes of the Christian Religion* II.2.14.
39. Calvin, *Institutes of the Christian Religion* II.2.15.

disputation and taught us to speak reasonably? Shall we say that they are insane who developed medicine, devoting their labor to our benefit? What shall we say of all the mathematical sciences? Shall we consider them the ravings of madmen? No, we cannot read the writings of the ancients on these subjects without great admiration. We marvel at them because we are compelled to recognize how pre-eminent they are. But shall we count anything praiseworthy or noble without recognizing at the same time that it comes from God?[40]

Perhaps the most important expression of common grace on which development is made possible is the human consciousness. In particular, both Kuyper and Bavinck appeal to Calvin's seed of religion. For Calvin, the image of God and the internal, abiding notion of the Godhead universally remain despite sin. This fact is derivative of the fact that God establishes and maintains the consciousness itself, despite sin. Humans still know right from wrong, truth from falsehood, and parents and children need not be forced to have love for one another. From this foundation, human potency is made actual in history. Humans grasp hold of and develop the many raw gifts of God: music, art, the sciences, the state, the culinary delights. Bavinck makes the point that it is not simply that these gifts are necessary, but for our delight.[41] These are all common gifts from the Father of lights, mediated by the one who gives life, and actualized by the Spirit.

Bavinck summarizes this programmatically when he argues that the possibility of natural theology, law, and virtue are best grounded not in creation *simpliciter* but in common grace:

From the fall onward, human life and humanity itself is not simply grounded in the order of creation. ... The fruit of common grace— being allowed to retain something of what we by nature possessed by Adam ... is a gift of grace. ... It is in this sense that we also speak

---

40. Calvin, *Institutes of the Christian Religion* II.2.15.
41. Bavinck, "Common Grace," 51.

of natural theology, natural morality, and natural law. ... This is better than seeing it under the purview of creation.[42]

THE CENTER OF COMMON GRACE

Kuyper and Bavinck never leave the common benefits of the Noachian covenant as an end unto themselves. The Noachian covenant, while common, remains today the servant of particular redemption. God preserves organic unity, but that organic unity is never fully realized until the kingdom of God. Without the common grace of Noah's covenant, "the mercies of God in his work of salvation would have had no arena for its manifestation. What people now call our humane, our Christian world, would never have existed."[43] In Christ, we find the unity of common and special grace. The movements of history wind their way in the fulfillment of history, the content of special grace, Jesus Christ, Immanuel. Special grace stands on its feet in the uniqueness of Christ's church, uniting all the streams of humankind by grace into one body, purchased by the grace of Christ's death, which is the supreme center of grace. Yet, the special grace of the cross cannot be viewed properly without its relation to common grace.

As already stated, common grace is God's action to plant the field in which the tree of redemption can grow. Common grace prepared the soil for the coming of Christ. As Kuyper argues, because Jesus Christ came in the "fullness of time," we understand that ages and epochs are not equal. Common grace bears the ultimate focus on the fullness of time. Common grace, then, is prevenient, preparing for the cross and its work of bringing the nations into a people. As Bavinck states: "[Christ] is the ultimate content of the *foedus gratiae*. In him all the promises of God are 'Yes and Amen.' He is full of grace and truth, pure *gratia;* no new lawgiver and no new law, but Immanuel, God with us, Yahweh fully revealed and fully given."[44] In God's common grace, he prepared the world for Christ. Even

---

42. *RE*, 149.

43. *CG* 1:35.

44. Bavinck, "Common Grace," 43.

in facts such as the spreading of the Greek language, and the preservation of the religious disposition of the nations, God was making the way ready.

We have already pointed out above how the Son is the mediator of creation and therein mediates the possibility of existence both before and after the fall. The God-man Jesus Christ, in his climactic work of redemption as the pinnacle of special revelation and special grace, also serves the common. In the incarnation, he is the Son of Man. That is, Christ takes on *human* nature, and in doing so, there is a universality—that Christ is for humanity. First, this means that Christ has come not only for Israel. He is second Adam, covenanting with human nature. The grace that is revealed in the gospel, that of Christ, is "intended for all men. ... For a time the *gratia specialis* dug a channel for itself in Israel, only to flow out into the deep, wide sea of humankind, which had been maintained and preserved for it by the *gratia communis* [common grace]."[45]

But also, second, while special and common grace had been separate for centuries in the distinction between Israel and the nations, now in Christ they "combine."[46] In other words, as the gospel flows to the peoples of the world, and more and more become Christians, we see the unity of the preservation of the nations with the hope of the world, on the one hand, and the widespread Christian witness is the leaven of the social order, on the other. Everyone benefits from the fact of the church, even in places where the church is under immense threat. For one, the witness of the church to Jesus Christ goes forth, and this is a good for the world. Wherever the church thrives, so society is enlivened as well. Godliness is profitable for all circumstances. In this way the work of Christ serves the common.

Thus, since Christ is the golden thread of all of history, his incarnation is indeed a common grace to all of humanity. For all the ages and peoples persist (the light shines in the darkness) because Christ was and has come into the world. As Bavinck argues, Christ is history. He is the turning point of the ages, and there is no history without his history. In him, one finds the solution to the tension between nature and grace. That is, in

---

45. Bavinck, "Common Grace," 44.
46. Bavinck, "Common Grace," 44.

the incarnation, God says yes to nature. Now God the Son has taken on human nature forever. The incarnation is the affirmation of the common, the affirmation of creation.

Kuyper developed an eschatology of common grace that included its eventual demise. The first arena of its decline is widespread and occurs anywhere persistent human idolatry is present. He argues that Romans 1:24, 26, and 28 teach that God withdrew his common grace from pagan nations in the ancient Near East, giving them over to their own depraved choices. Prolonged idolatry, which is the transgression of the first command of God, gives way to hearts that turn in on themselves, rejecting all moral goods. Thus, for Kuyper, God curtails his common graces in the face of the persistent exchange of God's glory with the likes of creaturely glory. That does not mean an entire removal of common grace, but rather a partial withdrawal. The demise of common grace in total would mean annihilation. God continues to gift life and breath, the crops and seasons. Yet God curtails the internal graces. For Kuyper, this form of decline occurred in the Roman Empire prior to the missionary journeys of the early Christians and again in pagan Europe. For this reason, common grace is at its height when working in harmony with special grace, not in its absence.[47]

Human idolatry, then, is a manifestation of the mystery of lawlessness (*anomia*), provoking God's withdrawal of the internal graces. Yet Kuyper interprets the arrival of *the* man of lawlessness according to 2 Thessalonians 2:1–12 as the final moment of the decline in common grace, which is also its dissolution. Kuyper brushes the broad strokes leading to the parousia by way of a widespread rebellion of spiritual darkness, which leads to the unveiling of the man of lawlessness. Lawlessness by way of tyranny is incarnate in this particular man. At the height of this darkness, Christ will return as judge. Paradoxically, Kuyper argues that the external aspect of common grace will reach its pinnacle in the man of lawlessness, and this will be the sign of its end.[48] External human advancements will increase, and yet the internal aspects of common grace, including virtue

---

47. CG 1:501–2, 505.
48. CG 1:520, 539.

and respect for the moral order, will maximally decline, and then the man of lawlessness will appear.

In the man of lawlessness there is no internal common grace gifts, and the time of the man of lawlessness brings precisely what would have happened in the era of the church if only particular grace functioned without the common graces. In general, there "would [be] a hell on earth ... one great physical and spiritual degeneration into the most hideous diseases and inhuman cruelties."[49] Thus, the manifestation of particular grace in a visible way (i.e., the worship of the church) requires a foundation of common grace for the world to function. But in the man of lawlessness the self-deification of humanity becomes absolute, and common grace diminishes to the point of evaporation. At the rise of Babylon, the external graces will have been used to establish a world power, for Kuyper, that signals the end. So Kuyper:

> The glory of the world power that will be defeated in the judgment will exist only in that [external] kind of development. The enriching of life's external features will go hand in hand with the impoverishing of life's internal qualities. The common grace that is at work in the human heart, human relationships, and in public customs will gradually shrink and become less, and only that other operation of common grace, the one that enriches and expands the human mind and human senses, will find consummation. It will be a most beautiful and white painted sepulcher, but for the one who opens it, full of dried and stinking bones of the dead.[50]

There is, in other words, a redemptive-historical and eschatological dimension to common grace, as God preserves an intermediate state where the antithesis between regenerate and unregenerate is curbed and not yet eschatologically manifested:

> All "special" revelation, as it is commonly though not altogether correctly called, postulates *common grace*, i.e., that act of God by which *negatively* He curbs the operation of Satan, death, and sin,

---

49. CG 1:527–28.
50. CG 1:540.

and by which *positively* He creates an intermediate state for this cosmos, as well as for our human race, which is and continues to be deeply and radically sinful, but in which sin cannot work out its end.[51]

The question that arises then is, Why would God preserve the world today by common grace, only to allow its devolution in the man of lawlessness? Also, do the external common graces assist in sin? As Bavinck asks: "But why should [God] continue to preserve such a sinful world by a special action of his grace? Does he squander his gifts? Is he acting purposelessly?" It is the gift of knowledge that gives rise to the most sinful expressions of power. Yet Bavinck gives this reason: "Is it not because natural life, in all its forms has value in his eyes in spite of sin's corruption?"[52]

While we cannot comprehend the mystery of God's purposes, at least some answer can be had in the eschatological hope of the kingdom of God. In common grace, God pronounces over the world that although his kingdom is not of this world, it is to be in it and for it. Common grace is the witness of God to his ultimate purposes in special grace, manifest ultimately in his kingdom. Common grace is united to special grace in the same way that redemption unites itself to creation. Thus, the fact of common grace includes the earthly, temporal calling—one that upholds the expression of the cultural mandate in life after the fall. For the Christian, Christ renews all the more his common calling, even if the man of lawlessness will one day appear, corrupting all the accomplishments of the external graces.

In the judgment of Christ over evil and death, the era of common grace will end. Although the germ of the internal common graces will resurrect with the eschatological saints, the external accomplishments will not (see ch. 6). Yet, when "a new song will be sung in heaven (Rev. 5:9, 10) ... the original order of creation will remain, at least to the extent that all distinctions of nature and grace will once and for all be done away with. Dualism will cease." The kingdom of God does not require a foundation of common grace, one in which God's Noachian covenant upholds nature despite nature. Rather, in the coming of Christ, "grace does not remain

---

51. *Encyclopedia*, 279.
52. Bavinck, "Common Grace," 60.

outside or above or beside nature but rather permeates and wholly renews it. And thus nature, reborn by grace, will be brought to its highest revelation. That situation will again return in which we serve God freely and happily, without compulsion or fear, simply out of love, and in harmony with our true nature."[53] Christ will take up all things into an organic unity with him being the head, the principle, and the agent of harmony. Grace will renew nature and nature will be good, one organism. While common grace has held together the broken pieces, when the fullness of God's presence comes in Christ, the work of grace is finished. "The ministry of grace will end, and the kingdom of glory will be the kingdom of the saved, glorified nature, the display of God's original creation in perfect splendor."[54]

COMMON GRACE AND NATURAL LAW

Like considering the question of the beatific vision in chapter 6, the topic of common grace, natural law, and neo-Calvinism has provoked much discussion and publication. Natural law and neo-Calvinism have often been named as alternatives in the domain of Christian ethics. It is impossible to identity and even summarize all that has been written on natural law in Christian theology even in the present century, and this is also true for the relation between neo-Calvinist theology and natural law. Our concern in this section is only to elucidate briefly some main points regarding Kuyper's and Bavinck's posture toward natural law and how it relates to common grace. Again, while there is a Kuyperian tradition that continues, in this work we define neo-Calvinism as a specific, historical movement of neo-confessional Calvinism in the Netherlands of the long nineteenth century. Much of the conversation surrounding neo-Calvinism and natural law has been focused on the Dooyeweerdian stream of neo-Calvinism and its North American currents.[55] Yet, in keeping with historical parameters of first-generation neo-Calvinism, we are concerned here with Kuyper

---

53. Bavinck, "Common Grace," 59–60.

54. CG 1:585.

55. For example, see David VanDrunen, *Natural Law and the Two Kingdoms* (Grand Rapids: Eerdmans, 2010), 4n4. VanDrunen cites Henry Stob, Cornelius Plantinga, Albert Wolters, Craig Bartholomew, and Michael Goheen as his examples of neo-Calvinism, stating that they follow the writings of Herman Dooyeweerd.

and Bavinck. We find it helpful even to bypass much of the conversation surrounding the relation between neo-Calvinism and natural law in order to get back to the sources.

Natural law has been defined both widely and narrowly by legal theorists, philosophers, and theologians, among many other disciplines. For our purposes here, we work with what is perhaps the most important theological presentation—that of Aquinas—and some Protestant definitions that follow in general agreement with Aquinas. Aquinas places natural law among a set of four types of law: eternal, natural, human, and divine.[56] The eternal law is God's administration of his providential governance of the universe. The human is the particular determinations of law, or positive law, based on God's law. The divine is in part a restatement of the "eternal," highlighting God's teleological governance of creation, directing it toward its supernatural end, which includes God's power to judge the hidden deeds of humanity, or the total of supernatural revelation.

For Aquinas, in the midst of these, natural law is the rational creature's participation in eternal law where it is inclined by God to the acts and ends proper to its nature. Thus, with respect to God, natural law is an exercise of God's providential care for the world. With respect to humanity, natural law is the practical inclination toward the good and awareness of the bad derivative of God's creation of human nature itself. In other words, the fact of natural law means that humans know and are inclined to seek out the good and avoid evil because God created them to do so. Because of natural law, humans use practical reason to determine the good and ill of action, responding to the inclinations of their nature, and applying reason to each circumstance.[57] The basic positive presentation of the natural law is the Ten Commandments.

Several contemporary Reformed thinkers have used Aquinas's treatment of natural law and its appropriation among the early modern Reformed to restate said definitions in ways that appeal to the present. While there have been many other presentations of natural law alongside Aquinas, his have been the most important for the development of the

---

56. Thomas Aquinas, *Summa theologiae* Ia2ae, q. 91.

57. Thomas Aquinas, *Summa theologiae* 1a2ae qq. 91.2; 94 a. 2.

doctrine. David VanDrunen simplifies the idea and argues that natural law refers to the fact that "God has inscribed his moral law on the heart of every person, such that through the testimony of conscience all human beings have knowledge of their basic moral obligations and, in particular, have a universally accessible standard for the development of civil law."[58] J. V. Fesko emphasizes the tradition's broader phrase "the light of nature" to describe subjectively a "divine imprint" that is God's image in humanity that apprehends natural law as well as the objective light or natural revelation in creation. The light of nature, then, includes natural law, which is manifest as common notions, which are innate concepts of God, and the knowledge of the moral and immoral.[59] Within this group of distinctions, there is the underlying duality between naturally revealed law in natural law and supernaturally revealed law in Scripture.

There is significant agreement between the aforementioned definitions of natural law and Kuyper's view of the ordinances of God manifest to the human subject. Yet, Kuyper does often use synonyms for "natural law" that highlight his own nuances of the tradition. For Kuyper, the phrase "natural law" most often refers to the physical laws of nature, and he reserves the language of "ordinance" for God's moral law. In the following quote, he refers to God's care over the stars with the language of "natural law": "God rules in the created order through his natural law and in all creatures through his ordinances. This means that, in the absolute sense, God must also rule in everything that humans or angels do or accomplish as a result of their own thinking and expression of will. Everything that does not conform to God's will in thought, word, or deed is sin."[60] This is nothing but a semantic difference between laws of nature as natural law and ordinances (traditional natural law). In other instances, natural law can mean the perverse instincts of fallen human desires. To some degree,

58. VanDrunen, *Natural Law and the Two Kingdoms*, 1.

59. J. V. Fesko, *Reforming Apologetics: Retrieving the Classic Reformed Approach to Defending the Faith* (Grand Rapids: Baker Academic, 2019), 13, 15. Fesko appeals to the Canons of Dordt in this particular instance for this definition of common notions, III/IV article 4. As noted in our chapter on revelation and reason, Bavinck's and Kuyper's account of general revelation include common notions but go beyond them, as they affirm the affective, preconceptualized, and intuitive dimensions of God's revelation in the psyche.

60. CG 3:158.

Kuyper understood the ethic of the French Revolution to be emancipation from God in favor of a natural law—one that meant the urges of sinful desire in abrupt dichotomy with the ordinances of God. "Natural law" means "natural desire" in this instance. In further instances, while referring to the laws of nature as "natural law," he refers to the ordinances of God simply as the "moral" or "spiritual law": "both these, the natural as well as the spiritual laws, forming together one high order, which exists according to God's command, and wherein God's counsel will be accomplished in the consummation of His eternal, all-embracing plan."[61]

Despite the semantics, in toto, Kuyper and Bavinck are in close agreement on the subject of natural law and do indeed agree with much of what is described so briefly above as a theology of natural law dependent on Aquinas. The first is that both authors affirm the fact of "nature." Of course, "nature" is sometimes used as a synonym for "creation," as in "grace restores nature." But there are also natures within nature. For example, Bavinck speaks of human nature, which is the image of God and a basically religious nature, as well as the natures of other creatures: "The supernatural is not at odds with human nature, nor with the nature of creatures; it belongs, so to speak, to humanity's essence. Human beings are images of God and akin to God and by means of religion stand in a direct relation to God. The nature of this relation implies that God can both objectively and subjectively reveal himself to human beings created in his image."[62] For Kuyper, God's creation of natures extends into the organic institutions of life possessing in some sense natures in themselves: "Whatever among men originates directly from creation, is possessed of all the data for its development, in human nature as such. You see this at once in the family and in the connection of blood relations and other ties."[63] For both first-generation neo-Calvinists, human nature as created does indeed participate in God's eternal law and is teleologically driven by God-given nature toward humanity's highest good: God himself. Natures, as created, have final causes and teleological purpose.

---

61. *Lectures*, 115, 243. See also CG 2:39.
62. RD 1:308.
63. *Lectures*, 117.

Also, for both these theologians, the moral order is real and is the presentation of God's own character in his created world. Rejecting a voluntarist presentation of the ordinances, Bavinck argues that "the *existence* of things, accordingly, depends on God's will, but their *essence* depends on his mind."[64] This means that the moral order is fixed, in accordance with God's character, and not subject to willful change even by God. Humans are given by God human nature, which includes the conscience, which accuses and excuses human action according to the law of God. Kuyper registers his agreement with the tradition in general in *Our Program*, simply restating the Pauline doctrine: "For when the Gentiles, which have not the law, do by nature the things contained in the law, these, having not the law, are a law unto themselves, even though they do not have the law. They show that *the work of the law is written in their hearts,* while their conscience also bears witness, and their conflicting thoughts accuse or even excuse them."[65]

Yet, Kuyper and Bavinck do indeed separate themselves from their tradition to a degree as relates to this subject. The neo-Calvinist logic makes revelation and common grace so central to all human agency in religion and knowledge, the activity of the sciences (for example), and theology itself, that it becomes more difficult to speak of natural law and natural theology without severe qualification. Bavinck critiques his own tradition with regard to its development of a doctrine of revelation that dichotomized the natural from the supernatural: "Later theologians, especially the scholastics, therefore devoted great care to the determination and description of the relation between natural and supernatural revelation ... but did not think deeply about the concept of revelation and only mentioned it in passing."[66] This particular comment is in reference to Aquinas's *Summa,* and he extends the argument to later Protestant theologians.

---

64. *RD* 2:237–38.

65. Abraham Kuyper, *Our Program: A Christian Political Manifesto,* ed. and trans. Harry Van Dyke, Abraham Kuyper Collected Works in Public Theology (Bellingham, WA: Lexham, 2015), §63, 76–77; see also §§29, 31, 327.

66. *RD* 1:287.

Both Bavinck and Kuyper place, unlike their forbearers, an equal weight on the subjective nature of revelation as much as the objective revelatory force of creation, which distinguishes both natural law and natural theology from their traditional meanings. As seen above, Bavinck argues that access to natural law is now to be grounded in common grace rather than creation. Consider also the quotation from Kuyper already mentioned in our discussion of revelation and reason:

> No conclusion can be drawn to the infinite, neither can a Divine reality be known from external or internal phenomena, unless that real God reveals Himself in my consciousness to my ego; reveals himself as God; and thereby moves and impels me to see in these finite phenomena a brightness of His glory. *Formaliter*, neither observation nor reasoning would ever have rendered service here as the principium of knowing.[67]

The Romantic tendency in both Kuyper and Bavinck is to speak of revelation more as God's free and ongoing activity than a mere static reality, as well as to emphasize the subjective dimensions of revelation as the necessary correlate of any appropriation of objective law or knowledge of God. They place less emphasis on the human's activity in determining a knowledge of God, and more on God's revelatory activity in the human consciousness. To posit, for example, that there is such a thing as natural theology that is the result of the ratiocinative process of human reason in distinction from revealed theology is to only describe a natural philosophy.

For the neo-Calvinists, the earlier Reformed tradition were less careful in ensuring that natural reasoning is always dependent on God's dynamic revelation. For example, Francis Turretin distinguishes between "that which may be known of God" by nature alone in distinction from super-nature.[68] Likewise, Petrus van Masricht talks about "natural theology ... a theology that arises spontaneously, *without any revelation, from the rational*

---

67. *Encyclopedia*, 343.

68. F. Turretin, *Institutes of Elenctic Theology*, trans. George Musgrave Giger, ed. James T. Dennison (Phillipsburg, NJ, P&R, 1992–1997), 1.2.7.

nature concreated in all."[69] For neo-Calvinism, theology is the product of revelation, and never reason alone. Neo-Calvinist thought rejects the dualism between nature and supernature as applied to the activity of theology as well as law. Human nature and natural law, and its use of practical reason insofar as practical reason agrees with the natural law, is never a product of nature in itself, but of God's supernatural work in the human consciousness. The possibility and capability of human nature, and all other natures, for that matter, are a "conferred good."[70] Neither human reason or nature, for that matter, operates autonomously. There is no such thing as mere reason or mere nature left to itself to operate in the world apart from God's consistent and constitutive agency. Rather, the natural law is a product of general revelation, the common communication of God to all creatures in distinction from the rescue call of special revelation.

Bavinck believes that this rejection of a dualism between the "natural" and "supernatural" is the most consistent rendering of the Reformation's theology:

> The Reformed taught that there was no point of religious or ethical doctrine after the fall that man could derive from nature pure and unadulterated. There is no *theologia naturalis* [natural theology]. Not only can sinful man not derive from nature the Trinity and incarnation, he cannot even come to know God in his oneness, his being, and his attributes. He also misconstrues God's revelation in nature and suppresses the truth in unrighteousness (Rom. 1:18).[71]

The fact of human nature and its corresponding natural law is not a mere leftover of the prefall life of humanity. Rather, what remains is only the product of a grace that was not present prior to the fall. Natural law as humanity's participation in eternal law is a product of God's gracious revelation entirely. Despite the corruption of the self, God continues by the Spirit to reveal Godself, to give to human beings the graces of the faculties, and even gives the fact of personal consciousness itself. The debate, then, if one is conversing with Kuyper and Bavinck as interlocutors, is not

---

69. Van Mastricht, *Prolegomena*, 83, emphasis original. See Bavinck's brief critique of Van Mastricht, Turretin, and Alsted in RD 2:78.

70. Douma, *Common Grace in Kuyper*, 7.

71. Bavinck, "Common Grace," 58.

between a theological philosophy that upholds common notions and one that does not. Rather, properly understood, Bavinck's epistemic emphasis in particular is on the ontology of epistemology and epistemological justification, or the "how and why" of common notions. For neo-Calvinism, to understand natural law and common rationality as the possession of every human being by way of mere human nature is to commit the error of late medieval and post-Reformation Roman Catholic anthropology. One can certainly take up in a separate discussion whether Bavinck's understanding of said Roman theology is accurate, but for purposes of this intra-Reformed discussion, Bavinck understands the nature-grace dualism of Rome with particular regard to anthropology as follows:

> God first created man as an earthly, sensuous, rational, and moral being *in puris naturalibus* [in a purely natural state]. To be sure, to this he added the divine image, the *donum superadditum* [superadded gift]; but this was soon lost through sin. Original sin thus consists entirely or almost entirely in the loss of the *donum superadditum* and in the reversion to the state of nature, *in puris naturalibus*. Apart from the harmful influence of his social environment, man is still born in a condition like that of Adam before the fall, and lacking the *donum superadditum*. For even concupiscence is not in itself sin but only becomes such when desire escapes the hegemony of reason.[72]

In respect to the operation of the mind, this natural human can operate on the earthly plane in the same manner as before Adam's sin. The intellect is not disturbed in its operations as pertains to the logical, the mathematical, and the ability of the subject to know the objective world correctly. "In a word, we can conceive of a man existing entirely within the sphere of nature and who within these limits conforms completely to his ideal essence."[73] Bavinck does, at times, note that for this neo-Thomism the fall "weakened" these natural operations, but the possibility of their ideal

---

72. Bavinck, "Common Grace," 45–46.
73. Bavinck, "Common Grace," 46.

functioning remains present.[74] To review what we argued in chapter 6, on Bavinck's understanding of this Roman theology (which he admits is not the sum total of all Roman Catholic theology but a development within that dominates), the biblical problem of sin is not presented as an ethical problem. The curse of Genesis 3 is not given sufficient weight, and the power of sin to penetrate all of the human faculties and deaden the operations of the consciousness is left to only a part of the self. Bavinck explains the Reformation view in brief:

> The image of God did belong to man's being, but it had been lost through sin. Now nothing good remained in fallen man; all his thoughts, words, and deeds were polluted by sin. The Reformers' condemnation of the natural man was much harsher than that of Rome. The "psychical man" ["unspiritual" or "natural," RSV] of 1 Corinthians 2:14 was conceived by them not *in puris naturalibus,* by nature unable to grasp the mysteries of the faith, but as a sinner who because of the darkening of his mind is unable to grasp spiritual realities. Luther raged against "reason" his whole life long as something that always "resisted God's laws" and was a "dark lantern."[75]

Yet, the empirical reality of these common operations of human rationality is evident. The question is not whether there is commonality. There exists "in paganism a continued revelation through nature and the reason, in heart and conscience—an illumination of the Logos, a speech from the wisdom of God through the hidden working of grace." How does the neo-Calvinist theology account for the unity between subjective representation and objective reality or the universality of a common logic, the natural law, evidenced in the civil law that makes societal life livable? Or: one might ask of the origin of the law of nations—which Bavinck and Kuyper both appeal to frequently—a manifest identical witness of

---

74. Also: "The natural man of 1 Cor. 2:14 is, according to Rome, not sinful man but man without the *donum superadditum.* This man is capable, through the exercising of his gifts, of completely attaining his natural destination" (Bavinck, "Common Grace," 47). On this logic, Bavinck also notes, the "rationalistic" theology of the Enlightenment is not a problem in itself, but incomplete without the aid of supernatural revelation and faith.

75. Bavinck, "Common Grace," 50.

law across space and time in the established justices of history. Bavinck's answer is as follows: "The good philosophical thoughts and ethical precepts found scattered through the pagan world receive in Christ their center and unity."[76]

Again, the difference is not in whether there is rational commonality but in why there is—an ontology of epistemology and epistemological justification. Bavinck follows Calvin, who, on the one hand, "considered man's sin to be so serious and profound as to render human nature incapable of good, in whatever sphere." Yet, on the other, "it would not do to deny the true, the good, and the beautiful that one can see in mankind outside of Christ."[77] Thus, for Calvin, there is a distinction within the graces of God: general and special. Both are enacted by the Spirit of God. Kuyper also: "Thanks to common grace, the spiritual light has not totally departed from the soul's eye of the sinner. And also, notwithstanding the curse that spread throughout creation, a speaking of God has survived within that creation, thanks to common grace."[78] If the answer to commonality is common grace, then the center or principle of natural law is Christ, who is the center of history and the telos of common grace.

Nevertheless, a key qualification arises here. The reason for the term "common" rather than "universal" in the doctrine of common grace is that this grace of general revelation, including its manifestation as natural law, is not equally and universally distributed. It is not some static object to which all have access by way of logical reflection. The diminishment of common grace is a reality wherein God leaves the idolater to their own desires, and the possibility of participating in the eternal law is nullified.

Notably, this neo-Calvinist nuanced position is in accord with Jerome Zanchi: "After the Fall, however, natural law was almost entirely blotted out as was any law that looks to God and the worship of him or to our neighbors and the just and fair relationship with them. ... If we ever see a sliver of this aspect of natural law again in a human being, we must believe that it was written in that person's soul a second time in its entirety by God

76. Bavinck, "Calvin and Common Grace," 440–41.
77. Bavinck, "Common Grace," 50–51.
78. CG 1:55.

himself."[79] Bavinck in particular understands the neo-Thomist position to be that natural law is a leftover of a prelapsarian order, a mere aspect of being in the image of God, only one without the superadded gift of fitness for supernatural life. Natural law as the human's capacity for participation in the law of God has been little affected between Genesis 2 and 3.

Bavinck and Kuyper's emphasis, then, is not as much a quibble with whether this commonality in human persons exists, but over the fact that this commonality is better described as supernatural law by the act of common grace, rather than merely natural. Humans are not rational creatures because they remain the same between Genesis 2 and 3 but because God has chosen to actively establish their rationality and life in the midst of their darkness. Indeed, apart from Christ, "man has no true knowledge of heavenly things. He is ignorant and blind as respects God, His fatherhood and His law as the rule of life."[80] But for and through Christ, even common grace is established.

To summarize, after the fall, the fact and maintenance of human nature, among the other natures, is due to the ongoing agency of God, to be revelatory and present in the gifting of the self and delivery of the law to the self. Using Paul, Kuyper summarizes this position, arguing that

> according to the testimony of the apostle, it is not that this darkening changed all at once into pitch-black night, and all religious and moral awareness was totally deadened in sin, but to the contrary, that this otherwise necessary final impact of sin has been restrained, and thanks to that restraining there remains in people a consciousness of good and evil, an awareness of justice and injustice, a certain knowledge of what God wants and does not want. However dense and heavy the mists may be in which people are enveloped as sinners, the light did not abandon the struggle but continued to penetrate those mists.[81]

---

79. Jerome Zanchi, *On the Law in General: Sources in Early Modern Economics, Ethics, and Law*, trans. Jeffrey J. Veenstra (Grand Rapids: CLP Academic, 2012), 12.

80. Bavinck, "Calvin and Common Grace," 451.

81. CG 1:55.

Likewise, for Bavinck and Kuyper, the emphasis on the ongoing activity of God in the fact of self and natural law returns attention to the agency of the Holy Spirit, the Spirit of Christ, who is the Spirit of life, of human consciousness, of human knowledge and the conscience—for in him we live and move and have our being. God is not far from every one of us. The Spirit restrains sin, compels humanity toward common virtue, and makes possible knowledge and the base human functions in spite of human corruption. There is a radical gap between the idea that humanity operates naturally in its natural capacities and what neo-Calvinist theology articulates. Without the universal work of the Holy Spirit as the Spirit of common grace, humans could not know anything. Bavinck argues that we can hold a robust view of non-Christian human capacity and reason because of the common operation of the Spirit. Thus the outcome: "Consequently, traces of the image of God continue in mankind. Understanding and reason remain, and he possesses all sorts of natural gifts. In him dwells a feeling, a notion of the Godhead, a seed of religion. *Reason is a precious gift of God and philosophy a praeclarum Dei donum [splendid gift of God]*."[82] Following Kuyper, then, one might say that natural law is better stated in reference to neo-Calvinist revisions as spiritual or graced law.

Additionally, Kuyper and Bavinck qualify the possibility of moral commonality more than many theologians in the Reformed and neo-Thomist traditions according to the fact of sin and the fact of cultural context. We mentioned above the difference in common grace and a notion of universal grace—that latter idea would provide for an equal and unqualified participation in eternal law at all times and places. Yet, common grace does not. This is a key difference with the tradition. While, for example, VanDrunen (while indeed noting the fact of total depravity) speaks of the possibility of common moral consensus according to natural law in the civil realm by inclination and reason in a relatively consistent manner, Bavinck and Kuyper both sharply question just how common the appropriation of natural law is. While God's ordinance is real, present, and a conferred good given by God, the world, the flesh, and devil do much in order to quell the work of the conscience and quench the general

---

82. Bavinck, "Common Grace," 51.

revelation of the Spirit. Indeed, by common grace, there is hope of consensus, and there is also the typical fact of livable societal relations. Yet,
Bavinck questions the possibility of a static moral consciousness within
the domain of subjectivity that corresponds neatly to a common, universal, natural law. "The content of our conscience," he writes, "is derived
mostly from outside and, therefore, *differs* amongst different peoples. And
even if the conscience does contain something 'common' or universal
'by nature' ... it is very difficult to identify which duties are specifically
necessary pronouncements of the conscience entailed innately and not
received from the outside."[83]

He adds: "We always know the conscience only concretely, as it is
historically formed within the family, state, and society, through religion,
art, and science by all the moral authorities of a people."[84] For Bavinck,
while the moral order and natural law are reality, the domains of historical
context, human desire, and sin restrict the epistemic possibilities for the
human conscience to receive said moral order commonly and correctly
due to the complexity of the embodied self. This qualification is first set
in antithesis to a Kantian-framed religion that appeals to a rational universal access to moral imperatives as duty. Per Bavinck, the moral consciousness develops more in the experience of cultures, in relation to the
contemporary movements of science and art, in the generalized rules of
discourse and language, and grows up within specific communities such
as the church or some other religious context. Thus, it operates according
to a plethora of situated logics.

It is one thing, therefore to affirm that there is a natural law, and
another to assert that the momentary moral consensuses of one's own
culture, tradition, and intuitions are the correct human articulations of
natural law. Bavinck also makes another categorical qualification about
human belief and action. When determining belief and moral decision
making, humans do not operate according to the intellect as much as
the heart. Desire and disposition overpowers the intellect in most cases.
Thus, public ethics is often a matter of public empathy more than mere

---

83. Bavinck, "Conscience," 122.
84. Bavinck, "Conscience," 122.

agreement or disagreement with moral law.[85] This does not negate the fact of natural law but partially quells its impact apart from saving grace.

Additionally, there is a similar balance in Kuyper's reflections on natural law between the persistent commonness of positive law as an expression of the work of common grace and that of the persistent abuse and abandonment of the moral ordinances of God. By common grace, humanity is not in the regimen of total moral confusion. The facts of the justice systems, philanthropic pursuits, and human solidarity in our societies testify to the reality of the common grace gift of natural law. Yet, as Matthew Kaemingk summarizes Kuyper's concerns regarding civil morality:

> While common grace provides hope that consensus can be found, it does not provide absolute and perfect certainty that it will be found. While Kuyper was extremely certain that the Holy Spirit was cosmically active in all faith and cultures, bringing them together for moments of consensus and cooperation, Kuyper was never certain of what those moments of consensus would look like or how long they would last. Moreover, moments of consensus and cooperation were always just that, moments. Interfaith and intercultural moments of cooperation were always tenuous, temporary, and unpredictable. They were, with the help of the Holy Spirit, possible—but not always certain. A Christian pluralist's work for interfaith cooperation was driven by an uncontrollable and unforeseen hope in the mysterious work of the Holy Spirit, not by a certainty in some sort of identifiable and universal human morality.[86]

The neo-Calvinist explanation of and hope for commonality, as well as for the more specific unity in the public square of a given nation or subculture, is not human reason's apprehension of the moral order in itself or human nature as such but the common operation of the Holy Spirit.

---

85. "Logical arguments cannot prove such a belief. Those who prefer to believe that the world only deserves to be destroyed cannot be convinced of the contrary by any intellectual argumentation. Now, if this is the case, we again face here the dilemma: illusion or reality? and thus, in principle, the choice between atheism and theism. And in making that choice it is not the intellect but the heart that clinches it" (RD 2:89).

86. Kaemingk, *Christian Hospitality and Muslim Immigration*, 148.

CONCLUSION

For Kuyper and Bavinck, God's common grace is God's general favor that sustains the creation order despite sin. Common grace is distinct from special grace. God's special grace restores, renews, and re-creates creation order as the kingdom of God. The former serves and anticipates the latter. *God's common grace is the fact of his loving patience in preserving both humanity and the creaturely cosmos despite human rebellion and its polluting corruption for the sake of redemption.* Common grace marks an era between the curse of the world and the second advent of Christ wherein God gifts moral, epistemic, and natural goods to the world maintaining in high degree an organic creaturely unity despite the curse.

In the judgment of Christ over evil and death, the era of common grace will one day end. Although the germ of the internal common graces will resurrect with the eschatological saints, the external accomplishments will not. Yet, when "a new song will be sung in heaven (Rev. 5:9, 10) ... the original order of creation will remain, at least to the extent that all distinctions of nature and grace will once and for all be done away with. Dualism will cease." The kingdom of God does not require a foundation of common grace, one in which God's Noachian covenant upholds nature despite nature. Rather, in the coming of Christ, "grace does not remain outside or above or beside nature but rather permeates and wholly renews it. And thus nature, reborn by grace, will be brought to its highest revelation. That situation will again return in which we serve God freely and happily, without compulsion or fear, simply out of love, and in harmony with our true nature."[87]

Christ will take up all things into an organic unity with him being the head, the principle, and the agent of harmony. Grace will renew nature and nature will be good, one organism. While common grace has held together the broken pieces, when the fullness of God's presence comes in Christ, the work of grace is finished. "The ministry of grace will end, and the kingdom of glory will be the kingdom of the saved, glorified nature, the display of God's original creation in perfect splendor."[88]

---

87. Bavinck, "Common Grace," 59–60.
88. CG 1:585.

IX

The Church and the World

If God is sovereign, then his lordship must extend over all of life,
and it cannot be restricted to the walls of the church or within the
Christian orbit. The non-Christian world has not been handed over to
Satan, nor surrendered to fallen humanity, nor consigned to fate. God's
sovereignty is great and all-dominating in the life of that unbaptized
world as well. Therefore Christ's church on earth and God's children
cannot simply retreat from this life. If the believer's God is at work in
this world, then in this world the believer's hand must take hold of the
plow, and the name of the Lord must be glorified in that activity as well.

—*Abraham Kuyper,* Common Grace: God's Gifts for a Fallen World

K UYPER AND BAVINCK were churchmen. They were officers in Christ's
body and dedicated themselves to the life of the local churches of the
nineteenth- and twentieth-century Netherlands. They were career theologians and ordained ministers and did not conceive of the possibility of theology apart from the church, both in its invisible and visible dimensions.
This is to say that to be a theologian for these men meant (1) being called
by the Spirit of Christ to think God's thoughts after him and (2) being
servants of the instituted body in their geography by thinking within the
domains of the creeds and confessions of God's people of old. Kuyper
argues: "No other inference is possible, than that theological science can
only exist in the Church of Christ. Outside of her pale ... faith is wanting

and the enlightening, and the fellowship of saints [is wanting]."[1] It is the church before the academy that makes a theologian.

Both Kuyper and Bavinck appealed to their confessions regarding their doctrine of the church. On the question of the nature of the church as well as its relation to the world, Kuyper and Bavinck constructed from the foundations of texts such as Lord's Day 21 of the Heidelberg Catechism and the Belgic Confession article 36. From Lord's Day 21, for example, Kuyper proclaimed with the theologians of old that there is no salvation outside the church.[2] The "church" here is not a reference to an incidental fellowship in some denomination within some nation, but the living body of Christ, the organism. Yet, simultaneously, Kuyper was a champion of the institutional church, leading a significant group of Christians (the Doleantie) out of the national church and into a free church. In 1892, Kuyper and Bavinck both helped lead a merger of two free-church movements into the newly established Gereformeerde Kerken in Nederland (Kuyper had embraced the separation of church and state in his early career). Indeed, a cursory scan over Kuyper's bibliography reveals that much of Kuyper's writings are correspondences concerning the details of the institutional church—from church property to doctrinal inspections to state relations. He wrote four articles in 1869 on the liberation of the church from the establishment. The conceptual groundwork for the Vrije Universiteit was that a free church needed a free university. Thus, the majority of Kuyper's nineteenth-century publications concern the church.

Kuyper and Bavinck's development of the doctrine of the church was surrounded by a dynamic modern environment that was distinct from even the generation prior. From the disestablishment of the *volkskerk* in 1848, to Kuyper being locked out of his own consistory, to the blossoming of the free-church movement, all in the midst of an unprecedented religious pluralism and a theological scene dominated by modernist suspicions of the future of the church, a new era required a recovery of ecclesial

---

1. *Encyclopedia*, 587.

2. Abraham Kuyper, "Lord's Day 21," in *On the Church*, ed. John Halsey Wood Jr. and Andrew M. McGinnis, Abraham Kuyper Collected Works in Public Theology (Bellingham, WA: Lexham, 2016), 319.

orthodoxy in a modern Europe.[3] They faced the "church question," as Kuyper put it, which included, as John Halsey Wood notes, the question of whether the church should exist at all. Further, what is the church's nature, and what is its role in society?[4] These were Kuyper's questions and are also the questions of this chapter.

In chapter 3, we considered a significant aspect of the neo-Calvinist ecclesiology in its emphasis on the catholicity of the church. Kuyper and Bavinck conceived of the catholicity of the church as a multiform unity, a unity-in-diversity, which is organic rather than mechanical. Its unity is neither located in an institution, nor found in a specific geography (the mistakes of both Rome and to a lesser degree establishment Protestantism). The catholic church is one by way of the Spirit. The scaffold of denomination and church officers is just that, a temporary structure that cannot be the essence (and thus the principle of unity) for the church of Jesus Christ.

Bavinck argues that catholicity refers "to the church as a unified whole in contrast to the dispersed local congregations that make up the whole and are included in it." True catholicity, in contrast to national, is that "the unity of the church [is] inclusive of all believers from every nation, in all times and places." As such, a proper definition of the catholic "embraces the whole of human experience." These defining features of catholicity presuppose the all-encompassing and universal character of the Christian religion precisely as a "world religion that should govern all people and sanctify all creatures irrespective of geography, nationality, place, and time."[5] Thus, Christianity is a catholic religion with a leavening power that extends beyond the boundaries of the human, and Christ's church is one, holy, and catholic by way of its mystical union with Christ himself.

In this chapter, we focus more resolutely on a reality intertwined with that of catholicity: the fact of the essence of the church as organism and what this means for the relation between the church and the world in the current order of existence. We will consider the first-generation neo-Calvinist theology of the church in two parts in order to answer two

---

3. For a robust presentation of both the history surrounding Kuyper's ecclesiological development and the theology itself, see Wood, *Going Dutch in the Modern Age*.

4. Wood, *Going Dutch in the Modern Age*, 13, 41.

5. CCC, 221.

questions: (1) What is the church? (2) How ought the church relate to the world? First, we will unpack Kuyper's and Bavinck's doctrine of the church itself, with significant attention to the organic and institutional duality. Second, we will consider then the unique neo-Calvinist conception of how the church does and should relate to the kingdoms of this world. As the church continues to grapple with the meaning and implications of secularity, and while noting the distinctive contextual circumstances of Kuyper and Bavinck's ecclesiology, a fresh encounter with a neo-Calvinist ecclesiology can add depth and perspective to the church in the contemporary world.

THE CHURCH

Although the concepts of "institute" and "organism" are well-known as an ecclesiological distinction on the lips of contemporary Reformed church discourse due to Kuyper, these concepts are more deeply embedded in Kuyper's ecclesiology and bear more weight than often acknowledged.[6] While the concept of organism applied to the church is usually taken to refer mainly to Christian people scattered among the various domains of life doing the work of Christ, this particular definition is only an aspect of the meaning of the organism of the church.[7] Using this as the sole connotation leaves one with a temptation of superficiality by failing to treat the concept as the load-bearing term it is. It is not unfair to say that all of Kuyper's dogmatic logic on the church can be unfolded from the distinction and duality of organism and institute. For Kuyper, "organism" and "institute" (and when put in the opposite order, as it sometimes is, there breeds some confusion) is synonymous with "essence" and "form." To use the distinction then is, for Kuyper, to define the church altogether. In particular "organism" as applied to the church is a multivalent notion that includes a multiplicity of meanings all derivative of the metaphor of a living plant. Early in Kuyper's career, for example, he argued that the

---

6. It is true that Kuyper did not use the organism-institute language perpetually after the 1860s, but Wood argues that the principles of this model continued to pervade his ecclesiology in the '70s. In the '80s and '90s, he added the concept of the visible organic church to the organic-institutional relation. See Wood, *Going Dutch in the Modern Age*, 65, 87–88.

7. Kuyper, "Lord's Day 21," 322.

church is the "body of Christ" in the fullest sense, "the rich organism in which not only his spirit, but Christ himself lives on."[8]

The duality of organism and institute appears mainly in the 1860s in Kuyper's writings, and much of his early writings regard ecclesiology, as noted above. He also makes clear in his early work that not only is the concept of "organism" a product of the idealist philosophical context but that his primary source for the concept of organism is the Bible. He derives the concept of the organic from the metaphors of Scripture: the body, the vine, the tree of life, the river flowing from the temple, the garden of God, and so on.[9] Likewise for "institute," he appeals to biblical metaphors as the backdrop of the idea: the church as mother, the cornerstone and temple, the house. The distinction, while inspired by the Bible, is also one that was made clearer by the modern moment. Modernity, as a marker of the long nineteenth century, includes a philosophical and sociological turn to the self, and a wrestling with the duality of the inner self and outer world, which is captured in Kuyper and Bavinck's emphasis on the relations among self, world, and God as the determination of worldview. Just as Bavinck included the *principium internum* (the Holy Spirit at work on the self) alongside the *externum* (Scripture) in his dogmatic sources, so the organism/institute distinction carries the Romantic move of paying attention to both inside and outside, the invisible and visible, the dual that rejects dualism. The distinction does appear in modern theologies before Kuyper, but is used differently.

For Kuyper, the organism of the church is the hidden foundation of the world church, which is just to say that the organism describes the essence of the church. For Kuyper, "the essence of the visible church is and always remains the invisible church," and "the invisible church is the body of Christ—that is, the organic connection of all the elect, through the

---

8. Abraham Kuyper, "De Menschwording Gods: Het Levensbeginsel der Kerk (1867)," translated and quoted in Wood, *Going Dutch in the Modern Age*, 53.

9. Schilder, *sed contra*, offers a critique that Kuyper's "organic" church was born of nineteenth-century philosophy rather than Scripture. See K. Schilder, *Dictaat Christelijke Religie. Over de Nederlandse Geloofsbelijdenis* (Kampen: Van den Berg, 1977), 87–99; Schilder, *De Kerk I* (Goes: Oosterbaan & Le Cointre, 1960), 303–445; Schilder, *De Kerk III* (Goes: Oosterbaan & LeCointre, 1965), 141–52, 251–86.

Holy Spirit, under Christ as head."[10] In his famous Stone Lectures in 1898, he puts it accordingly: "Regenerating and confessing individuals, who, in accordance with the Scriptural command, and under the influence of the sociological element of all religion, have formed a society, and are endeavoring to live together in subordination to Christ their king. This alone, is the church on earth—not the building—not the institution."[11] The church as organism is indeed the medium of public Christian action and witness and therefore is visible too, as Kuyper argued in the 1880s and '90s. But this aspect of the organic idea answers the question of how the church relates to the world, as well as how institutional forms of the church could wax and wane and the church remain, more than it addresses the essence of the church foremost.

What is the church? For Kuyper, it is the organism of Christ. When one looks across the whole of his corpus on the theology of the church, it is clear that this concept has manifold meanings, including the mystical union of Christ and his body, as the elect, hidden in the counsel of God's will, as those who have been called from darkness to light, as the people of God prior to and separated from the institution. For example, in Kuyper's development of the doctrine of election, "election began with Christ, then God elected the church in Christ, and, finally, he elected the individual as a member of the church."[12] The organism includes all the parts of the church, including those that have yet to be added, and is also a term for the *ecclesia*, the community of believers who present themselves by faith in their own time because of the work of the Spirit in the human heart. In 1870, at his pastoral inauguration in Amsterdam, Kuyper gave an address titled "Rooted and Grounded," which is perhaps the most significant presentation of the organism/institute ecclesiology. He works from the apostle Paul's language in Ephesians 3:17 to describe the church as rooted, a metaphor of the organism, and grounded, one for the institute. He, rather quickly in his address, provides the critical synonyms "essence" and "form" in order to transfer the metaphors into analytic prose.

10. "Tract," 111.

11. Kuyper, *Lectures on Calvinism*, quoted in Wood, *Going Dutch in the Modern Age*, 2–3.

12. Wood, *Going Dutch in the Modern Age*, 67.

To make sense of this ecclesiology, it is important to see that the logic of the organism and institute flows from Kuyper's wider emphasis on the life-principle, or what he would later argue for in his Stone Lectures, that Calvinism is the life system that fits reality best. In the threefold relations between God, self, and world, Christianity proclaims that God is the origin and first principle in determining these relations. While humanism prioritizes the self, and pantheism the world, Christian theism proclaims absolute dependence on God. Calvinism, or the Protestant principle, more specifically states that God's sovereignty, or election, is the mother idea of life in this world. God determines everything from the eternal counsel of his will, and thus all creatures stand *coram Deo* before God in all moments. This principle is embedded in the doctrine of creation—that because God is maker, there is a creational logic to creaturely existence, where God determines the essence and purpose of all the kinds of creation (nature). While God defines the essence of his creatures, he invites humanity to invest in the form of creation, to develop and subcreate as stewards of God's determined world.

In the church, there is essence and there is form. The essence is first determined by the elective will of God, to choose for himself a people. God executes his determinations and gives form to that people in history, in many epochs, and invites his creatures to participate in the development of that form in the institutional frame of the church. To be sure, this wide-view lens of the ecclesiological idea from the perspective of election develops in the midst of a very specific context, and mainly through that which Kuyper opposes.

Kuyper was wrestling throughout the nineteenth century with how to address the logic of a free church in the midst of a nation with a national church. He notes that, on the one hand, there was the popular rejection of the institute in favor of an organism by some in the Netherlands of his early career. In rejecting the national church, they preferred to think of a living body, people who "want the church to flow out into society" exclusively and rejected the framework of institution altogether. On the other hand, there was a voice, he notes, that said "Jesus' church must become for us not an organism, but above all an organization." In the former the body of Christ is diffused in the midst of the world entirely, and in the other the church is swallowed by the priorities of the state. Kuyper's solution is, rather, to be both organic and institutional, precisely because such an ethic flows from the essence and form demanded by Christ. A free church, for Kuyper, is one that preserves the good of the institution without losing the spirituality of the organism and is essentially an organic body, escaping "Rome's paralysis."[13]

Thus, Kuyper turns in this sermon to Ephesians 3:17 and Paul's metaphor "rooted and grounded in love" to find biblical justification for the organic (rooted) and institutional (grounded) aspects of the body of Christ. Let us examine the concepts more closely. "Rooted," for Kuyper, is a metaphor that captures the idea of the unity in freedom of the people of God, bonded together by Christ, and simultaneously growing branches of the tree—a body that comprises individuality and is yet one tree. Thus, the organism is one in many, pluriform unity. Further, as branches connected to a vine, the people of God live only as they remain connected. Kuyper explains clearly that the organism motif comes from metaphors in Scripture that pertain to life: the body, plants, yeast. In all these parts are bound together "by means of a power operating invisibly, one that refers to a natural growth occurring not through something added but to a force that comes to outward expression from the inside."[14]

Simultaneously, the church is grounded. Here, Kuyper appeals to the metaphor of the constructed house in Scripture. The church not only grows organically, but is built up, stone by stone. God employs human hands to work and to build. While the nature of the church is a living body, growing together in Christ, Christ provides organization by office and wisdom for the direction of the body. He invites humanity to take part in stewarding the form. In the organism, God does all the work. God plants like God planted Eden. In the institute, God uses humans to cultivate, to expand, to prepare and prune like the farmer. So the creational principle, that God makes everything and determines that humans should assist in its development—creation and cultural mandate—becomes the principle of the church as well. An organism is whatever God makes, and it grows

---

13. Abraham Kuyper, "Rooted and Grounded," in *On the Church*, 48–49.
14. Kuyper, "Rooted and Grounded," 50.

up of its own accord. An institute is what humans do to assist the life of the organism; they give the organism shape in form.

Kuyper uses another illustration to makes sense of the relation: The wild, growing acre of land is organic. The cultivated acre is its human development. Human life itself is organic—instinctive and operating at a level untouched by human desire or consciousness. Yet, it is also conscious, developing according to the desires and decisions of the human self. For Kuyper, the family, society, and state are organic in principle because they grow instinctively.[15] For this reason, family, society, and state take shape in similar forms throughout all of history and its geographies. Adding to the bare form, relationships, culture, and positive law add conscious, determined form to the essence of each sphere.

Thus, the organism and institute are not two churches but one, the essence and the form. "Scripture refuses to allow separation" between these two aspects of the church. If sin had not entered through the corruption and temptation of Satan, the essence of church, state, and society would all be wrapped up in the development of the kingdom of God in the life of the world. Thus, the path to an eternity of glory apart from sin was entirely natural—the necessary, organic maturation of the people as God made them. Thus, the church, as we regard it today, an agent of Christ in the midst of the kingdom of this world, is inconceivable apart from sin because, without sin, the church and world would be one.[16]

Yet, in life as it is, there is the church as organism and institute in the midst of the world. A church, Kuyper argues, "can never be manufactured," and so a polity and confession do not constitute a church. "The church cannot lack the institution for the very reason that all life among human beings needs analysis and arrangement." For as soon as there is the church, there is a group of people that requires organization. While there are moments in the history of the church that are more instinctive (such as in Acts 2) and less institutional, there is nevertheless still an organism with some semblance of organized gathering. Bavinck points out that the institution is not merely a necessary arrangement of convenience but is

---

15. Kuyper, "Rooted and Grounded," 51.

16. Kuyper, "Rooted and Grounded," 50, 60.

established by Christ himself in the offices: apostle, elder, and deacon. Kuyper and Bavinck both suggest that those who know Christ, and there-fore God the Father, have for themselves a mother, who is the institution of the church. Kuyper states it all clearly in one sentence: "The organism is the essence, but the institution is the form."[17]

Bavinck uses the same distinctions, although there is some difference between him and Kuyper in the semantic range of the duality. Bavinck critiqued Kuyper as early as 1883 for several of Kuyper's ecclesiological details. For instance, Bavinck writes that with Kuyper's emphasis on local congregations "he does not do justice to the unity and solidarity of all churches."[18] Bavinck states clearly what he considers to be the essence of the church:

> Now there is no doubt that according to Scripture the characteris-tic essence of the church lies in the fact that it is the people of God. For the church is a realization of election, and the latter is election in Christ to calling, justification, and glorification (Rom. 8:28), to being conformed to the image of God's Son (8:29), to holiness and blessedness (Eph. 1:4ff.). The blessings granted to the church are primarily internal and spiritual in character and consist in calling and regeneration, in faith and Justification, in sanctification and glorification.[19]

The church's essence, what it is, is the people of God united to Christ. Whereas Kuyper regards the invisible essence of the church by the term "organism," Bavinck regards the concept of organism as the visible mani-festation of the essential church, rather than a term describing its invisi-bility. The organism that is the essence of the church, for Kuyper, has both invisible and visible aspects. He argues that "on the basis of the authority of Holy Scripture, the essence of the church must be viewed from four perspectives." By the term "church," one could mean the church as it exists in God's counsel, the church as its life is hidden in Christ, the church as it

---

17. Kuyper, "Rooted and Grounded," 54–56, 58.

18. Bavinck, "Review of Tractaat van de Reformatie van de Kerken, by Abraham Kuyper," De Vrije Kerk 9 (1883): 554, quoted and translated in Wood, Going Dutch in the Modern Age, 104.

19. RD 4:298.

is realized among human beings on earth, or finally, the church as it will one day in glory sing praises before the throne."[20] Kuyper uses the term "organism" to describe all of these aspects.

The question then arises of how the organism/institute duality relates to the invisible/visible duality. Bavinck and Kuyper both understand that the origin and principle of the church is located in God's elective will and in the spirituality of its birth. Thus, the church is invisible in these ways: "(1) as the universal church because a given individual cannot observe the church in other places and other times; (2) as the gathered company of the elect, which will not be completed and visible until Christ's return; (3) as the gathered company of the elect and called, because in the church on earth we cannot distinguish the true believers." Bavinck adds other reasons for calling the church invisible: because it is not of this world; Christ is the head and it is his body, which is invisible; because at times the church is deprived of a visible institution and the means of grace as in ages of persecution; because the internal faith of the heart is not observable.[21]

For Bavinck, the organism of the church is the people of God, wherever they are, apart from and underneath the scaffold of the institution, the formal ministry of the Word. "Organism" is a term reserved for the "realization of election" rather than the hidden foundation that is election. Thus, the organism is the people of God prior to the institution, members of the regenerate, in whatever space they occupy, both militant and triumphant. "The gathered company of believers on earth is not only structured charismatically but also institutionally. It is not only itself the possession of Christ but also serves to win others for Christ. It is a gathered company (*coetus*) but also the mother of believers (*mater fidelium*); an organism but also an institution; a goal but also the means to that goal."[22] The distinction between him and Kuyper is that while Bavinck reserves the term "organism" for the visible manifestation of the children of God, Kuyper uses the term to describe the hidden essence, the mystical union

---

20. "Tract," 88.

21. *RD* 4:290.

22. *RD* 4:298, 303.

with Christ himself, all the way back into the eternal counsel, where the organism of Christ is the idea of God.

The invisibility of the church, then, for Bavinck refers to the elected church and the church catholic, among the other aspects of invisibility listed above, while "organism" is a term for the essential makeup of the visible church: the people themselves called by Christ prior to and apart from the institution. He states:

> From this it follows that the distinction between the church as institution and the church as organism is very different from that between the visible and the invisible church and may not be equated with it. For both "institution" and "organism" describe the church in terms of its visible aspect. In this connection, one must also not forget that the institution and the organism of the church, when they assert themselves in the visible realm, have an invisible spiritual background.

For example, Bavinck expresses the organism's invisible dimensions when speaking subtly against Schleiermacher's doctrine of the church. Bavinck argues that the church is not "an association of individual persons who first became believers apart from the church and subsequently united themselves. But it is an organism in which the whole exists prior to the parts; its unity precedes the plurality of local churches and rests in Christ. It is he who, continuing his mediatorial work in the state of exaltation, joins his churches together and builds them up from within himself as the head."[23] While for both theologians the invisible church is the elect church, for Kuyper, the elect church in the election of Christ and his bride is the organism, manifest in time in the form of the organized people of God in this world.

In total, Kuyper and Bavinck both place an immense weight in their Calvinistic logic on the elective dimension of the church from eternity: "The beginning of the church," Kuyper writes, "points back to that eternal act of the Triune God, by which he elected from the entire human race ... whom he destined to be incorporated into his elect troops." The

23. RD 4:282.

visible church is "simply an institution for the ministry of the word." It is not the "essential church ... but an institution established by the church and for the church."[24] The visible church, then, is wherever the ministry of the Word takes place. For how will they hear without a preacher? The invisible church is an object of faith, and the visible is an institution of the assembly on earth.

Despite the semantic distinction, both agree that the church is the organism that is persons united to Christ, which then becomes manifest in various locales under the ministry of the Word. The institution belongs to the "well-being" of the church, not to its essence.[25] Additionally, this means that the church's visibility is not first in the ministry of the Word, but in the presence of a person who is one of Christ's people. Kuyper claims, along with his Reformed heritage, that the church is *invisibilis* (invisible), *visibilis* (visible), and *formata* (formed as an institution). Thus, he means the church is elect from eternity, called in space-time, and instituted in various locales. In what manner is Christ the King of this church? Bavinck answers: "by his Word and Spirit he gathers and governs his own and protects and keeps them in the redemption acquired."[26] It is both the case that the fact and unity of the church is from the Triune God's predestinarian will and that Christ accomplishes that will through the institution of the offices and means. Every particular church in both its institutional and organic life is a product of God's counsel, Christ's mediatorial work, and the Spirit's agency.

To summarize, for Kuyper, the doctrine of the church takes a twofold shape, which he also describes with the metaphor of a child from birth. A child is born and then, for the rest of its maturation, must be fed. The birth happens once, but the feeding is perpetual. "Likewise, there is a twofold operation from God to his church: first, an operation by which he engenders his church, carries it within a secret place, and forms it into its true shape; and then a second, entirely different operation, through which he feeds the church first with milk and then with solid food."[27] The

24. Kuyper, "Lord's Day 21," 345–46.

25. Kuyper, "Lord's Day 21," 359.

26. *RD* 4:372.

27. "Tract," 86.

organism is carried "within a secret place" and the institute is fed with solid food by the Word.

A number of implications follow from this duality, but let us briefly consider three. First, the church is not coextensive with the kingdom of God. Both theologians reiterate this point throughout their corpuses. To suppose the church visible to be the totality of the kingdom is false and damaging. The manifest church in the life of this world is full of wheat and tares. Kuyper calls this idea of the church as the kingdom a delusion. The visible church, for Kuyper, is the scaffolding that stands outside the building while it is erected. When the building is completed, the scaffolding surrounding it is taken down and the building stands in elegance on its own. The scaffolding is the church on earth, "defective and misshapen" in appearance.[28] The builders (the organism) building the house are supported by the scaffold (the institute) until the glory should appear.

Further, it is also true that the church triumphant is not the kingdom of God either, but the glorified citizenship of the kingdom. The kingdom of God is the society of Christ, which encompasses the whole of the cosmos in its season, extending well beyond the boundaries of the human people of Christ. Thus, it is inappropriate to consider the church as equal to the kingdom, and much more dangerous to speak of the visible church as the kingdom. Derivatively, the language sometimes used for ministry as "building the kingdom" is also inappropriate. As we saw in chapter 6, the ushering in of the kingdom is not progressive but cataclysmic. Further, in the society of Christ's parousia, there is no sin and no death, and nothing will exist in the life of the world outside its bounds. The church is a visible witness to the kingdom, and the people of God, the regenerate, organic church, are indeed citizens of that kingdom, but do not make up the whole of the reign of Christ.

Second, while it is more obvious that the church is not the kingdom of God, it is also important to say that the church, both organic and institutional, is not coextensive with Christianity itself. As Bavinck argues, "For neither the institutional expressions of the church nor the underlying essence in the organic church is coextensive with Christianity. The Spirit of Christ works beyond the domain of church and into the being of

---

28. Kuyper, "Rooted and Grounded," 58–59.

creation entirely." Christianity is "truly universal," and there can only be "one religion that is ... capable of permeating and sanctifying all others." For "God so loved the world, the cosmos, that he sent his only Son, the one by whom all things were created." The cross and resurrection "casts its shadow over all of creation."[29] Further, the people of God have no way of knowing all that the Spirit of God does beyond the domains of the formal and informal ministry of the church. Christianity as a religion speaks of the work of the Spirit of Christ in space and time. Christianity as a power, the power of Christ, extends beyond the boundaries of Christ's church and into all the realms of creation.

Third, Bavinck calls his reader to choose between a "narrow" and "broad" ecclesiology. Such Christian universalism (that Christianity is universally permeating), or how one relates creation to re-creation (nature and grace), calls for a "broad" ecclesiology.[30] For Bavinck, broad ecclesiology does not refer to the degradation of theological standards, or the relaxation of exegetical claims for the sake of a larger denominational consensus, but rather a posture of spiritual fellowship toward Christ-believing peoples of the world despite the varying scaffoldings of institutional separation. Because the unity of the church catholic is spiritual, bonded together by the Spirit of Christ, branches grafted into the root, the foundational spirit of unity among the people of God exists prior to and apart from institutional distinction. This must lead Christians to a spirit of fellowship and a deep desire for unity in ministry.

Bavinck notes the intimacy between the churches that Paul planted and visited in the New Testament and how they sought to care for the poor in Jerusalem, even from great distance. Also, there was a pre-institutional bond across the churches of Christ in the New Testament, which was decades prior to the development of robust institutional frameworks for the early church. Such a spiritual care for the brothers and sisters of Christ is "a manifestation of the unity and catholicity of the church ... that is purer and more glorious than the most wonderful church order." Bavinck proclaims that such a spiritual bond flows directly as a gift "from the unity of God himself." One may, however, become "enclosed" in a

---

29. CCC, 221–23.
30. CCC, 221

small church, a conventicle, through a dead conservativism or a separatist mentality, denying the love and fellowship of the body of Christ across nation, people, and even confessions. "Such a person shortchanges the love of the Father, the grace of the Son, and the fellowship of the Spirit and incurs a loss of spiritual treasures."[31]

Likewise, Kuyper appeals to his reader to consider the "spiritual mystery" of the church rather than its outward adornments. The kingdoms of the world are far more impressive in size and accomplishment than the physical appearances of the churches of the world (excepting perhaps the monetary and architectural investments of Rome). That, for Kuyper, is precisely the point. The true church is the body of God's Son, "who still continually protects and maintains it," and "oh, then suddenly all the relationships are turned upside down. Then you can and will no longer value any denomination ... but behold the spiritual building itself."[32]

THE CHURCH AND THE WORLD

To speak of the church and world relation is to speak, in this context, both of how God orders the relationship in Scripture and of the ministry he gives the church. How does the church relate to the world, and what does the church do in the world? As Bavinck famously emphasizes, the call of the church is to be stewards of the pearl and treasure, the message of cross and kingdom. This message and ministry of the Spirit among God's people is a leavening agent, because "it is precisely this sinful world that is the object of God's love."[33] Bavinck famously proclaims:

Christianity knows no boundaries of race or age, class, or status, nationality, or language. Sin has corrupted much; in fact everything. ... The pollution that always accompanies it penetrates every structure of humanity and the world. Nonetheless, sin does not dominate and corrupt without God's abundant grace in Christ triumphing even more (Rom. 5:15-20). The blood of Christ cleanses us from all sin, it is able to restore everything ... anyone or anything.[34]

---

31. CCC, 226–27.
32. Kuyper, "Lord's Day 21," 323.
33. CCC, 224.
34. CCC, 224.

Herein we find Bavinck's visible organic church: when all of the edifices of the institution are not visible, and the people of God are witnessing to the kingdom of God in their daily lives, the organism is manifest. Thus, for Bavinck and Kuyper alike, the gospel is a "joyful tiding ... for the family, society, for the state, for art and science, for the entire cosmos, for the whole groaning creation."[35] The question, however, and one that has arisen continually in relation to the neo-Calvinist theological movement, is what precisely it means for the gospel to be a "joyful tiding" for the state, for art and science, for the spheres of life. This question stands on another: How does the church relate to the world? These questions must be answered in three ways. First, for neo-Calvinism, the church stands in antithesis to the world. Second, the church exists as a sphere within the world alongside the family, state, and culture. Third, the church is called to exist as a leavening agent that permeates the world for the sake of its renewal.

For the sake of understanding the whole and before unpacking these three claims, we can summarize in brief a neo-Calvinist theology of the church and world, a political theology, as it may be called, while acknowledging the diversity of possible definitions of the political theology enterprise. Drawing together the intersecting theologies of Kuyper and Bavinck in their general principles, we learn first that the kingdom of God is the origin and purpose of life in this world. All that exists finds its end in the kingdom to come. The kingdom is the meaning of world history. Christ is the King of the kingdom, and in the age before his parousia, when all will be gathered up in the new creation, he has determined to administer his rule through the many authorities that occupy the multiple spheres of creation. In each sphere God has granted an aspect of authority and a relative freedom from the authorities of the other spheres. Simultaneously, there are no hard borders between these spheres, but they working at their best are an organism of relations. Although neo-Calvinism is often misunderstood for seeking to Christianize everything by calling for a Christian state, a Christian business, Christian art, and so on, as Govert Buijs states, "for Kuyper, Christians active in public life should not strive

---

35. CCC, 224.

to Christianize public life but to bring it into line with its creational intentions, to re-create it."[36] In other words, to "Christianize" is to recover the true purpose, the God-given nature, of a particular cultural enterprise and act into it as such.

At a macro level above the spheres, Christ rules through the dispensation of both common and special grace. By common grace, God preserves the world through the many gifts, through the revelation of the moral order, and through the good institution of the family, the state, and culture. Additionally, the sphere of the church is born in the midst of a sinful world by way of special grace. Thus, in general, there are four meta-spheres of authority in human life: family, church, state, and culture, and from these many more follow. The work of special grace, through both the work of the Spirit and the agency of Christians in the life of the world, can penetrate and renew each of these spheres, but never fully and finally until Christ's cataclysmic return. Christians, as the organic body of Christ in the midst of the world, are called to faithfully engage in the ministries of Word and deed in order to seek first the kingdom of God in the midst of the kingdom of this world. For Kuyper, the Christian ministry is "confession" and "witness," and we will unpack these terms below. Finally, when Christ takes hold of this world in new creation, "in this Kingdom of God, full sovereignty is handed over to the Messiah, a sovereignty that had descended from him in the various life spheres and returns completely once more to God, who will be all in all. ... The history of the nations and of their states finds its principal idea and explanation to be the Kingdom of Heaven."[37]

THE CHURCH IN ANTITHESIS TO THE WORLD

From Pentecost forward, the small church of Christ was in the midst of a world hostile to it. The church knew well by its own experience the reality of the antithesis. Yet, it is important to define carefully the nature of the antithesis between Christ and the world, or—better said—between Christ and Satan, as Kuyper points out. What does the word "and" mean in the

---

36. Govert Buijs, "Volume Introduction: On Entering Kuyper's Cathedral of Everyday Life," in *Pro Rege* 2:xxv.

37. KGHG, 163.

"church and world" relation? For neo-Calvinism, the antithetical relation between the kingdom of Christ and that of this world is not ontological but ethical. Bavinck states that the antithesis is not quantitative but qualitative.[38] The enemy is sin, Satan, and the principle of the flesh at work in the hearts of human beings. The battle is not with the person per se but with the ethical permeation of the force of sin. The battle, then, is *for* the person and for the life of the world against death. As Wood describes it, reflecting on an essay written by Kuyper in 1892, "Kuyper's ecclesiology provided an ontological basis for the antithesis in his doctrine that the organic church was a human organism distinct from the rest of humanity due to its regenerate principle."[39]

Kuyper describes this antithesis through the lens of redemptive history accordingly: After the fall into sin and curse, a new seed had to be replanted that would grow in the fullness of time and refresh the dead body that was once a living organism—"a life whose seed descended from heaven."[40] That life is the human life of Christ, unaffected by sin, who broke into the world of curse to be the antithesis to that which the world had become in sin, of which the cross is the supreme evidence. For Kuyper, there are two streams that flow today, which describes his understanding of the two kingdoms. There is, on the one hand, the kingdom of this world, which is the kingdom of Satan, of sin and death. And there is the kingdom of Christ, the stream that has flowed from God's holy mountain. The mechanical life of the sin-soaked ground, the instinctive life of the earth as it is today (red in tooth and claw), is juxtaposed to the new stream that is spreading its tributaries throughout creation, in order to restore the organism of old and bring that organism into a consummated form.

Bavinck and Kuyper both make much of Roman Catholicism's failure historically to rightly distinguish between a metaphysical antithesis and an ethical one. The problem, again, returns to the nature-grace relation, and because we have explained the relation thoroughly in previous chapters, we will only highlight the point here. For these neo-Calvinist thinkers, the Roman principle is that grace enters the world "to make possible the

---

38. CCC, 229.

39. Wood, *Going Dutch in the Modern Age*, 161.

40. Kuyper, "Rooted and Grounded," 53.

attainment of the supernatural *visio dei*." Thus, "it is not difficult from this to see how it became necessary for Rome to set itself over against culture, the state, society, science, and art. According to Rome, Christianity is exclusively church. Everything depends on this. Outside the church is the sphere of the unholy. The goal had to be to bring about the church's hegemony over everything."[41] The Roman church sought to make sacred that which is profane. For example, common art must become ecclesiastical art, and thereby holy. Marriage is acceptable, but celibacy is sacred. Kuyper, and the neo-Calvinist tradition following, has often been charged with attempting to Christianize everything (and we will come back to this point shortly), but the manner in which this idea is often understood is precisely the nature of the condemnation that both Bavinck and Kuyper level against Roman Catholic theology. To Christianize art, in the neo-Calvinist logic, is to set it free from ecclesiastical bounds, "to free nature from hegemony of the [institutional] church."[42]

In distinction from Rome, as Bavinck develops, Protestantism does not seek a material difference between sacred and profane but allows Christ to matter for all of life, calling art and science, family life and business practice, to seek the holy rather than unholy. Christian art is Christian not because it is about religious matter but because it honors God and is derivative of an artistic heart that understands that beauty is God's gift and art God's calling to humankind. Grace renews nature, and thus Christian transformation of the self determines a transformation of the self with respect to the agency of common life. The Christian perspective on art helps lift up art that displays the gifts of God in common grace especially. Contra Rome,

> the natural is as divine as the church even though its origin is in Creation rather than re-creation and derives from the Father rather than the Son. It is for this reason that the reformers had such a thoroughly healthy understanding of Christianity. They

---

41. CCC, 229.

42. CCC, 236. Bavinck did not believe the post-Reformation societies were all that successful in this enterprise: "However, the Reformation, no matter how universal in its conception, was even less successful in Christianizing life. Art, science, philosophy, political and social life never fully incorporated the principles of the Reformation. Although dualism was theoretically overcome it remained a practical reality in many areas of life" (CCC, 243).

are ordinary, natural people but people of God; there is nothing peculiar, odd, exaggerated, or unnatural about them, nothing of that unhealthy narrowmindedness that so often disfigures even sincere Christians.[43]

For neo-Calvinism, the natural order is not unholy in itself, but made such by sin. Thus, like the human person, anything is capable of being purified in order to seek the fullness of the value of nature. This is the logic of the first line of the creed: "I believe in God the Father almighty, maker of heaven and earth." In Calvinism, Kuyper and Bavinck both saw the full application of the Protestant principle. "Here the Gospel comes fully into its own, comes to true catholicity. There is nothing that cannot or ought not to be evangelized. Not only the church but also home, school, society, and state are placed under the dominion of the principle of Christianity."[44] To bring the logic together, the Reformation sought a more thoroughly biblical ecclesiology, summarized well in the Second Helvetic Confession, chapter 17:

> And seeing that there is always but "one God, and there is one mediator between God and man, the man Christ Jesus" (I Tim 2:5); also, one shepherd of the whole flock, one Head of this body, and, to conclude, one Spirit, one salvation, one faith, one Testament, or covenant,—it follows necessarily that there is but one Church, which we therefore call CATHOLIC because it is universal, spread abroad through all the parts and quarters of the world, and reaches unto all times, and is not limited within the compass either of time or place.[45]

Because of the catholicity of Christianity in toto, and the fundamental reality that is the organism of the church that exists prior to the institution, neo-Calvinism calls not for asceticism and anabaptism, nor the incorporation of the world into the life of the institutional church from the perspective of Rome, nor that the body of Christ live in and alongside the world according to moral agreement based in natural law, nor that

43. CCC, 236.
44. CCC, 238.
45. Bavinck quotes this chapter in CCC, 238.

the organic body of Christ become diffuse in the midst of the world and unrecognizably blended. Rather, neo-Calvinism calls for the church to live through the power of Christ for the sake of the renewal of the small world that each Christian community occupies. For godliness is of value in all circumstances. The regeneration of individuals that results in their ethical obedience to God in every sphere of life is the means by which the various spheres are transformed.

The reality of antithesis as a conclusion of the nature-grace relation leads Kuyper to develop a significant motif appearing throughout his ecclesiological writings: the church is a "colony of heaven."[46] Heaven, for Kuyper is a shorthand for the Christian homeland, the heavenly country. Thus, Christians are citizens of a twofold fatherland: first the earthly, which persists on the ground of common grace and is more specifically the geographical home in the midst of the plurality of nations, "the fatherland." The plurality of nations is a necessary and temporary response to the curse of creation. While the logic of Genesis 1–2 leads toward a rich unity in plurality of people under the singular headship of God himself, life after the curse necessitates national pluralities because widespread uniformity leads to heightened forms of sin (e.g., Babel), which Kuyper calls the curse of uniformity.

The second homeland is that of the heavenly country, which is the presently invisible kingdom of God that is to come. The heavenly country at the second coming of Christ means the dissolution of all temporary fatherlands and the establishment of the one kingdom. The heavenly country exists in the now and not yet where Christ has been seated, in the presence of the church triumphant, and in the relation of heavenly citizenship in the earth-dwelling regenerate. Thus, in the kingdom to come, creation's original goal of unity in plurality under God as king is realized in Christ's union of heaven and earth. Grace restores nature. The life of the world, which is rebellion against God's authority, directly opposes the church. The world opposes the church because the church tries to "rein in the world's sinful nature."[47]

---

46. Abraham Kuyper, "Twofold Fatherland," in *On the Church*, 307.
47. "Tract," 85.

Due to the thoroughgoing corruption of sin and the fact of the antithesis between Christ and Satan, between rebellion and absolute dependence,
both the fatherlands of national citizenship and heavenly citizenship are
gifts of grace, one common and one special. Each serves as a battlefront
against the plight of de-creation unto chaos and satanic rule, one relatively and one absolutely.

THE CHURCH AND THE SPHERES

One then can turn to the way God governs life in this world through both
common and special grace, or for the Christian, from the perspective of
both fatherlands. We briefly introduced the logic of the spheres in chapter 6. Kuyper gave his famous address, "Sphere Sovereignty," in 1880 at
the opening of the Vrije Universiteit. Kuyper's sphere sovereignty is a
tradition all its own, developed on the groundwork of Calvin, Johannes
Althusius, and Groen van Prinsterer.[48] It is, in some sense, a full-orbed
political theory with an immense amount of twentieth-century commentary and development. Kuyper's earlier ideas of the relation of the spheres
developed throughout his lifetime into a public theology, evidenced in places
in his extensive works on common grace, for example. For our purposes,
we merely reflect on its basics for the sake of understanding the church
and world relation, in order to lead us to the logic of mission and renewal.
Bavinck develops his own understanding of sphere sovereignty dependent
on Kuyper in his article "The Kingdom of God, the Highest Good." For
Bavinck, there are four meta-spheres: family, church, state, and culture
(culture serving as a broad accumulation of many possible subsocieties).
Kuyper is less interested in determining a particular and final list of spheres
("there are in life as many spheres as constellations in the sky").[49] He recognizes the possibility of nearly endless differentiation. Nevertheless, the key
insight derivative of Calvin is that God is sovereign (absolutely authoritative) and that in his holy governance of the world in the temporal order he
has given relative authority and freedom to each domain of life, particularly
the family, state, church, and culture, as neo-Calvinism develops the idea.

---

48. For a detailed account, see James W. Skillen and Rockne M. McCarthy, *Political Order and the Plural Structure of Society* (Grand Rapids: Eerdmans, 1991)

49. Kuyper, "Sphere Sovereignty," 467.

Further, God has given all authority in heaven and earth to Jesus Christ, who is in himself the kingdom of God, to be the sovereign of these spheres.

For now, Christ has determined to administer his rule through multiple spheres of life, and preeminently through common and special grace. There are, then, the common spheres of family, state, and culture, and also the special sphere of the church, born of special grace. The work of special grace can penetrate any of the spheres of the common life so that they witness to the renewal of the kingdom that is to come because each of them is purposed for and fulfilled in the kingdom of God. The kingdom of God is the ultimate family, the final state, the hope of all cultural endeavor, and the glorification of the elect church of Christ. For neo-Calvinism, then, the visible church, particularly the institution, is one of the several spheres given by God in the life of the world that exists for the sake of the kingdom of God. Both Kuyper and Bavinck interpret the domains of life in the present order of the world in the light of the fact of the kingdom of God.

For example, "the state ... is not the highest good but finds its purpose and goal in the Kingdom of heaven. Anyone who misunderstands this will eventually end up denying the church her noblest calling and instead value the state itself, viewed as the creator of culture and caretaker of freedom and equality, as the initial realization of the Kingdom of God." Also, "family, church, culture, all the various spheres of rich human living do not owe their origin and existence to the state—they possess a 'sphere sovereignty'—but they do nonetheless owe to the state the possibility of their development."[50] The division of the spheres and the separation of authorities is God's work of preventing any human from possessing absolute power. God has created the world with norms and laws both in the arena of nature and in human relationships.

What, then, is the church's "noble calling" in the midst of the spheres? It is helpful to consider the calling of some of the other spheres in order to highlight that of the church. With regard to the state, God has given it to be the sphere of spheres, the arm of justice. At its best, it enables the other spheres to live according to their calling without one encroaching

---

50. KGHG, 159.

on the authority of another unnecessarily. At its best, the church reminds the state of its dependency on God but never pursues a Christian state in any official way. The work of the church is never coercive, and that means the state must not serve Christianity from the top down but be influenced by Christ from the bottom up. "The Kingdom of God does not demand that the state surrender its earthly calling, its own nationality, but demands precisely that the state permit the Kingdom of God to affect and to penetrate its people and its nation."[51] Bavinck offers a rather comprehensive list of the authority and calling of the state:

> The state is not redemptive. Nor may the state attempt to foster the free, moral, spiritual life. The state functions in terms of the law. But by holding that law in high esteem, by cultivating respect and reverence for the law, by upholding its majesty, by inculcating respect for the moral world order as the unconditionally valid moral order, the state can become a tutor unto Christ. In this sense the state can and indeed does have the calling to labor for the Kingdom of God. By providing space for the various life spheres to do their work, and by guaranteeing for each of its subjects the development of this full and variegated life of the personality, the state fulfills its own nature and works for that Kingdom, which itself is also a state wherein God Himself is the Lord and absolute King-Sovereign.[52]

In all these spheres and their God-given order, sin is present and corrupts. "Sin threatens freedom within each sphere just as strongly as State-power does at the boundary," but the fact and authority of these spheres are indeed the creational norms that God has given the world and that Christ governs.[53]

With respect to culture, it remains the common calling of the human race to take up the cultural mandate and to steward the world with the gifts God has given. Bavinck claims that there are only two ways to do this: through science and art. He uses these terms in the broadest sense,

51. KGHG, 160.
52. KGHG, 161.
53. Kuyper, "Sphere Sovereignty," 473.

which is critical to understand with reference to the question of evangelizing science or art. Science is the work of inductive investigation—seeking to know. This occurs from the smallest child to the most astute biologist. The child, awakening in self-consciousness, comes to an understanding of their own identity through external differentiations, by seeing their own hands and feet, by dependence on their mother. The biologist carries forward such inductive work into adulthood, discovering all that God has made. "In order to rule over nature in the broadest sense, its essence, operation, pathways, and laws must be known."[54] Art is the second operation in the cultural call: to know first and then to organize. Art takes the knowledge of human experience and organizes it by subduing nature to the human will. To subdue the earth, for Bavinck, is to be a scientist and artist by way of knowing the world and then organizing it through reading, farming, or biological theorizing, among a multitude of other possibilities. These operations must be done for a purpose, and thus all activity in this world either serves the purposes of God or not.

The sphere of culture is a meta-sphere, which registers so much of common human activity underneath its class. Its purpose is the stewardship of human life and that of the world God has made. It flows from the fact of the *imago Dei*, the law of culture, and the common-grace gifts God has given to the world. Special grace, in its fight against the corruption of sin, leavens and heightens cultural endeavor, first by reshaping the motivation of the actor for the sake of the holy and then by serving the common good. The farmer sows and reaps for multiple reasons, but if these reasons are according to a principle of mere selfish gain, then such cultural dominion does not serve the life of the common good or the glory of God, all the while using the gifts of common grace. For there is no determinative action that stands apart from the human will and therefore no stance outside the moral order.

If the state promotes justice, and in the cultural mandate God calls humanity to be human, the family is the foundation and model of the other spheres of life. The family is juridical, nurtures cultural pursuit, and is religious and moral. The fourth sphere of the church, born by special

---

54. KGHG, 162.

grace, is that which norms the human's relationship to God in the midst of a fallen world and seeks to point life in the other spheres to the fact of absolute dependence on the Triune God.[55] When speaking of the sphere of the church in the life of the world, we have to make a distinction. Christ introduced another sphere by his person and work, one that Kuyper calls the "power of faith." The power of faith "created a free sphere with a free sovereignty within the iron ring of uniformity. ... The sovereignty of faith [is] the deepest piling upon which all sphere sovereignty rests." This sphere includes direct relationship to God by way of the mediator Christ, and an eschatological liberation of the world, the telos of all freedom. Thus, the hidden sphere, the kingdom in itself, ensures a domain for the freedom of conscience. In other words, there is the sphere of the organic church, where each branch is fixed to the root that is Christ, called in the midst of the world, to live as a follower of Christ under the absolute authority of Christ, with no other mediator in view. Revelation and conscience are its guides. Kuyper mentions the "sovereignty of conscience, and of the family, and of pedagogy, and of the spiritual circle."[56] These are the spheres of the organic church, family, school, and church institution. Thus, while Kuyper does not spell out this distinction in detail, there is an inner logic at work that divides the sphere of the church itself in a twofold manner between organism and institution.

While many illustrious kingdoms of people have been established on the face of the earth, Kuyper argues, they were and are all part "of the life of the world." Yet, the kingdom of God is from above, established by the God-man, and is a foreign power in the midst of the order of this world. When this world has ended, the church "will remain eternally and rise in glory, simply because it is not of this world"—herein lies, as Kuyper proclaims, the beauty of the church.[57] He is not speaking of the mere visible gatherings of denominational bodies or of the local instantiations of distinct church buildings, but of the catholic church, the whole body of Christ, which is called together by the work of the Spirit of Christ. While

---

55. KGHG, 156.

56. Kuyper, "Sphere Sovereignty," 469, 472.

57. Kuyper, "Lord's Day 21," 322.

the denominations and buildings of the local bodies will fade away, the church, which is the body of Christ, will remain forever. Therefore, in the sphere of the organic body of Christ, one stands as citizen of heaven in direct relationship to Christ the mediator.

The visible, institutional church is an aspect of the life of this world and is an extension of the authority of Christ over the conscience through the ministry of the Word. While the institution is vital in the life of the world and instituted by Christ, it will cease. Its offices and courts will find their end in the kingdom. The organism of Christ abides forever, but the scaffold does not. The visible institution of the church, in this way, is not to be considered one of the two kingdoms of God as in a traditional two-kingdoms theology, or one of the two governments or ways in which Christ rules in the present order (often presented as the church and the state). Rather, it is the visible ministerial authority of Christ on earth and exists as one of the many ways Christ rules the world—one with a particular job. The institution has no power over the domain of the conscience except insofar as it declares the word of God to the people, calling on Christians to make disciples and learn all that Christ taught.

Thus, the institutional church is a distinct sphere of life, given by God, for the sake of worship, for the building up of the saints, for their encouragement, and for commissioning them each week into the life of the world. It is the mother of God's people, as Kuyper drew on the biblical metaphor. The institutional church sends and commissions, in the name of Christ, the organic body of Christ back into the spheres of the world to live as Christians in the family, in the public sector, and in the many other subcommunities we occupy to seek the common and particular good of each of the people in those domains. Bavinck speaks of the institutional church in possession of the gospel as the pearl of great price, on the one hand, and the organic as a leavening agent, on the other. The people of God as institution are called to proclaim the gospel as pearl, as the great treasure (Matt 13:45–46), the ministry of the Word. The body of Christ, changed by the gospel all the way down, is to be leavening agents in temporal society. "The kingdom of heaven is not only a pearl; it is a leaven as well."[58] Herein,

---

58. Herman Bavinck, "Christian Principles and Social Relationships," in Bolt, *Essays on Religion*, 141.

this neo-Calvinist public theology is a theology spoken for the people of God as the organism within public spheres. The institute as mother serves that organism in feeding it and equipping it for life in the world.

"To the extent that each of these various life spheres answers more and more to its essential idea, it loses its sharpness and isolation from the others and prepares the way all the more the coming of the Kingdom of God. For that kingdom, since it is the highest good, destroys nothing but consecrates everything." In this kingdom of God, "full sovereignty is handed over to the Messiah, a sovereignty that had descended from him in the various life spheres and returns completely once more to God, who will be all in all."[59]

THE CHURCH IN THE WORLD

This concept of leaven leads to the work of the organism in the life of the world. It is helpful to return to the outworking of the institute/organism distinction once more. Kuyper argues that the visible, organized church is "simply an institution for the ministry of the word." It is not the "essential church … but an institution established by the church and for the church."[60] The institute is wherever the ministry of the Word takes place. For how will they hear without a preacher? Kuyper notes that there are pitfalls on either side of failing to make this distinction between organism and institution. On the one hand, Kuyper notes the problem of churchism, which "treats the institution of the church as the real, essential church itself, and, therefore, wants to churchify the world" (both Rome and Anabaptism are in view). Here, the church owns scholarship, art, science, and eventually the state, whether that is at a national level or in a separated community where the spheres are confused. On the other, there is churchlessness, "the elimination of the church." Here, the ministry of Christ is often understood to be stalled by the institutional church, and so the focus shifts entirely to building the kingdom of God outside the church in the midst of the spheres of life only. This is the tendency of what today might be called something like parachurchism. But Christ has cut through these reductions by establishing the body of Christ, the elect ones, called by the Spirit

59. KGHG, 163.

60. Kuyper, "Lord's Day 21," 346.

to fight for the organism of this world. To that body he has given officers and the call to assemble and preach.

For Kuyper, the gathered, visible body is the army's camp, where they are fed, nourished, and prepared for battle in the midst of the world.[61] The invisible church of Christ is unmixed, perfected, and pure, while the visible is mixed with non-Christians. Yet, these are not two churches, invisible and visible, but one—the spiritually invisible and externally visible. The church of Christ "is not identical to the institution of the ministry of the Word." The essence of the church is not the ministry of the Word. Rather, the essence of the church is persons united to Christ, who then become manifest in various locales under the ministry of the Word. The institution belongs to the "well-being" of the church, not to its being.[62]

This distinction fits into the twofold operation of the church on earth as colony of heaven, the church that encourages the saints through the worship of God, and the church that seeks to witness to the kingdom and pursue renewal for the sake of God's glory in the spheres of human life by the external ministries of Word and deed. Thus, while the two fatherlands run their course, the heavenly country condescends in some manner into the earthly, persuading the earthly to reflect the heavenly in times and places in the same logic as that of the presence of special grace enhancing the domain of the common graces. The local church is the primary expression of the heavenly's manifestation in the earthly homeland, working at its best as salt and light in the midst of a national citizenship. Thus, the church is the "earthly colony of the heavenly country."[63] This earthly colony of heaven is called to witness to the heavenly, and to engage in the spiritual battle that is Christ against sin, against the curse, and against the principalities of darkness that fight to uphold the dominion of death.

---

61. One of Kuyper's oddest distinctions is between official ministry and service for Christ outside the domain of the institution. Kuyper uses the term "ministry" only for ordained men in the gathered church preaching the Word and administering the sacraments. Evangelism, teaching children the Bible at home, and serving the poor are not for him "ministry" in a technical sense. The term "ministry" contains, for Kuyper, a particular authority given by God to his officers (see "Lord's Day 21," 351). We, however, are using this term more broadly here to make the same point he makes regarding the work of the church in the world as "witness" described below.

62. Kuyper, "Lord's Day 21," 358–59.

63. Kuyper, "Lord's Day 21," 323.

This leads to a doctrine of church as institute and organism, because this fight is extended into all the domains of national life and requires public Christian action. For if the heavenly will one day unite to the earthly and the God-created spheres of earthly life will be perfected in God's purposes, does not the fight against sin and the witness of the light in the present include developing the spheres for God's purposes?

> If God is sovereign, then his lordship *must* extend over *all* of life, and it cannot be restricted to the walls of the church or within the Christian orbit. The non-Christian world has not been handed over to Satan, nor surrendered to fallen humanity, nor consigned to fate. God's sovereignty is great and all-dominating in the life of that unbaptized world as well. Therefore Christ's church on earth and God's children cannot simply retreat from this life. If the believer's God is at work in this world, then in this world the believer's hand must take hold of the plow, and the name of the Lord must be glorified in that activity as well.[64]

Kuyper, in his lecture "Rooted and Grounded," also describes the work of the church in the midst of the other spheres accordingly:

> We have such an institution that is itself thoroughly formed, that works formatively upon the individual, structurally upon the family, directively upon society, and that chooses the Christian school as her vestibule. An institution that calls into being, from the roots of its own life, a unique science and art, that strives in its confession for a more correct expression of the eternal truth and for an ever-purer worship of the Holy One.[65]

As Kuyper speaks of the sphere of the church working directively on society, Bavinck speaks of evangelizing everything. The institution equips and sends the organism of Christ's body into the world for such agency—these are descriptions of the work of the church easily confused. What do these theologians mean by "evangelizing art" or the work of the church

---

64. CG 1:xxxvi–xxxvii.
65. Kuyper, "Rooted and Grounded," 17.

for a "unique science"? As we have seen above, biblical Christianity first frees people from treating the realms of life outside the institution of the church as profane and in no way seeks to subsume them under the boundary of the institutional church. Evangelizing the realms of society refers primarily to pursuing the various human vocations in alignment with the order of creation itself. Neo-Calvinist theology does not confuse this age with the age to come. There is no possibility of building or ushering in the kingdom of God apart from Christ's parousia. Rather, Christianity calls the family, the public, and the state to walk in alignment with the creational norms reaffirmed by Jesus Christ.

What are some precise ways in which the organic body of the church in the life of the world exercises an ethic that makes holy the creation that has undergone corruption in the varying spheres of life? This list could be immense, but we can direct the reader to several ways. Before doing so, it is important to point out Kuyper's distinction between the church's calling to confess and witness. "The first personal duty that you owe your King is to confess him; the second ... is to be a witness to him."[66] Confessing is defining oneself as Christ's servant, with Christ as Lord. Confessing happens in the corporate worship of the church and in family worship. Witnessing is for the sake of the non-Christian, for the sake of the world. Its purpose is to persuade. Witnessing is not exclusively evangelism, but also martyrdom, good works, and working directively on society for its good with an intent to lift up the glory of God in the truth of Jesus Christ. Many duties we pursue as Christians are not distinctively Christian (such as speaking the truth) but are Christian insofar as their pursuit is a derivative of motive. For God is the God of all things and in every sphere, his glory must be our motive. So Kuyper: "God is then the Sovereign over his soul, the Sovereign over his body, the Sovereign over his family, the Sovereign over his occupation, the Sovereign over his homeland. ... They are all subject to the sovereignty of the Lord of Lords. ... There is nothing that falls outside it."[67]

---

66. *Pro Rege* 2:29.

67. *CG* 3:2.

Yet, there is for neo-Calvinism a distinctly Christian ethic. Jesus Christ calls his people to confession and witness. Christ calls his people to love God and the church more than family, than the state, than the earthly society. There are natural duties and there are Christian duties.[68] These are made clear by Christ's imperatives as resurrection imperatives. In addition to the more obvious ministry of the Word as the witness of evangelism, other ethical directives of witness follow. For Kuyper, the Christian life is a life of fighting against the darkness of the world, flesh, and devil.

First, the church serves the world by the intellectual work of ontological justification, reminding humanity of the fact of creation, moral order, and its dependence on God. Recall that the "mother-idea" underlying neo-Calvinist theology of this first generation, as Kuyper suggested, was the fact of creation *coram Deo*—that every human being lived life under the eye of the Creator of heaven and earth.[69] Everything, Kuyper argues, matters to God. For Bavinck, all theological reasoning, including attempts to know the objects of creation as created, "whether they concern the universe, humanity, Christ, and so forth—are but the explication of the one central dogma of the knowledge of God."[70] Brian Mattson comments on this particular sentence in Bavinck's *Reformed Dogmatics*: "Created things are not self-generating or self-sustaining. Everything is utterly dependent upon God for its existence. The implication of this, upon reflection, is staggering: not only is God relevant to everything, he is of *highest relevance* to everything."[71]

If theology is the science concerning God, or that discipline that seeks to know God, then public-theological reasoning includes knowing all things in relation to God, in whom they all relate absolutely. Every creature, Bavinck repeatedly suggests (borrowing Schleiermacher's famous dictum), is in a relation of absolute dependence on God. All things relate

---

68. See *Pro Rege* 2:84.

69. Christianity "does not seek God in the creature, as paganism; it does not isolate God from the creature, as Islamism; it posits no mediate communication between God and the creatures, as does Romanism; but proclaims the exalted thought that, although standing in high majesty above the creature, God enters into immediate fellowship with the creature, as God the Holy Spirit" (Kuyper, *Lectures on Calvinism*, 12).

70. *RD* 2:29.

71. Brian Mattson, "What Is Public Theology?," *Center for Public Leadership* (2011): 7.

to and matter to God. The public-theological work of first-generation neo-Calvinism aided the various publics in knowing *how* all things relate to God. The spirit of revolution attempted to banish theology from all public spheres, disallowing theology, or biblical reasoning, from informing the various domains of public life. For Bavinck, the majority of his works outside dogmatics address general issues in contemporary society through the medium of philosophical reasoning, or considering the moment in light of the timeless, which is for Bavinck always philosophical-theological.[72] In this method of public-theological reasoning, Kuyper and Bavinck both called on their fellow Christians and modeled as public intellectuals what it means to aid the public in understanding what it means to be human, to be part of creation, to think according to a principle that fits reality. Thus, Kuyper and Bavinck do not seek to Christianize everything as in the sense of Rome, but to witness and call people to see God's creational norms and to understand that Christianity fits reality best—for people to see themselves as thinking and living *pro Rege* in the world.

Second, the Spirit working through the people of God calls the world to seek a vocational holism under the banner of the Triune God. This point follows directly from the prior. If the church prophesies to the public of the origins and purposes of the human being in the midst of a created world, we can ask more specifically how this works for specific persons: What does Bavinck mean by "evangelizing" science, for example, as from the perspective of the scientist? He means that the Christian biologist must refuse to separate the inductive work of biological exploration from the Christian confession, that theology cannot be cordoned off to a small, discreet place but must remain the organizing principle of the sciences. Further, this biologist seeks to be a witness to the unity of reality in the midst of her field. The Christian must desire an "inner reformation of the sciences on the basis of a different principle" from scientism.[73] Kuyper mentions the difference in heart and mind when a doctor approaches the "sick mammal" versus the "person created in the image of God." In the case of the lawyer and judge, "Is the law a functionally developing organ

---

72. This paragraph appears in Cory Brock, "Bavinck as Public Theologian: Philosophy, Ethics, and Politics," *Unio Cum Christo* 6.2 (October 2020): 119.

73. CCC, 246.

of nature or a jewel coming down to us from God himself, bound to his Word?"[74] The Christian worldview matters for all cultural activity in the life of the world. As Bavinck writes: "'if the gospel is true, then it carries with it its own standard for the valuation of all culture."[75]

Third, the church has over centuries (and does still) aided both state and society in offering insights born of the Protestant principle, which benefits the whole. Since the gospel is not a matter of institutional coercion, Protestantism promotes pluralism, the freedom of religions. Since the biblical witness teaches the value of the individual in light of the organism of humanity, Protestantism promotes the democratic ideal. Because the Bible teaches that persons are religious by nature and that religion is fundamental to all aspects of human life, the neo-Calvinist principle rejects the privatization of religion, its banishment from the public sphere. Since all persons are created in the image of God, the Christian principle, attested to by the church, declares that every individual matters before both God and humankind. The church calls on the state to recognize its dependence on God, that it may govern with a subordinate justice, one given it by the absolute sovereign, in order that it may not take that title for itself.

Fourth, the church as organism renews the other spheres by the exemplary work of Christians seeking to love their neighbor and thereby living as the best of citizens in their locale. Bavinck, speaking to the modern Christians, notes that as citizens of an earthly fatherland "we attempt to alleviate misery, to reduce crime, to lower the mortality rate, to enhance health, to oppose public disorder, and to limit panhandling."[76] Indeed, because the organism of Christ's body diffused into the midst of the world is called to love, Christians seek to uphold the moral order preeminently by sacrificial service to others and derivatively promote the welfare of their given society and subculture. The evangelizing of everything does not involve the redemption of the spheres, as in Anabaptistic or Roman Catholic attempts to realize a kingdom, but aims that in every sphere of

---

74. Kuyper, "Sphere Sovereignty," 487.
75. *PoR*, 203.
76. *CCC*, 245.

life people would walk in accordance with the moral order *coram Deo* and that witness would be especially present in the lives of the organic church as individuals who obey God in every sphere because of the gospel. Bavinck summarizes it this way:

> The gospel gives us a standard by which we can judge phenomena and events; it is an absolute measure which enables us to determine the value of the present life; it is a guide to show us the way in the labyrinth of the present world; it raises us above time and teaches us to view all things from the standpoint of eternity. Where could we find such a standard and guide of the everlasting gospel did not supply it? But it is opposed to nothing that is pure and good and lovely. It condemns sin always and everywhere; but it cherishes marriage and family, society and the state, nature and history, science and art. In spite of the many faults of its confessors, it has been in the course of the ages a rich benediction for all these institutions and accomplishments. The Christian nations are still the guardians of culture. And the word of Paul is still true that all is ours if we are Christ's.[77]

Finally, and here is the most important for Kuyper and Bavinck, the church as organism seeks the welfare of humanity by the care of souls and the care of the body through the ministry of evangelism and the ministry of mercy. Christ, argues Bavinck, has given the church a twofold office of elder and deacon as exemplary of the twofold ministerial call that extends to all Christians: the ministry of Word and deed. While the formal ministry of the Word happens within the institute, the missional ministry of the Word extends into the life of this world. There is primacy in this missional call, to proclaim the message of Jesus Christ for the sake of the souls of humankind. This ministry not only serves the soul but then, by the power of the Spirit, is capable of transforming even large segments of society for the common good through regenerated hearts.

In particular, Bavinck's interest in evangelism and foreign mission grew throughout the course of his career but especially after his second trip to

---

77. *PoR*, 212.

America in 1908. In 1910 and following, he wrote about and promoted the missionary movement to the extent of being the primary catalyst in having a chair of missiology created at the Free University of Amsterdam.[78] Kuyper, although distinguishing evangelism as a subcategory, maintains that the Christian must be both confessor and witness to the gospel and that "someone who witnesses for Christ is not out for himself, but for the one on whose behalf he is acting. His purpose is to try and win others over for Christ, or to make them aware of what they are rejecting if they continue to oppose Christ and to prove that what they in their self-delusion call a lie is actually the truth."[79]

Likewise, and in subordination to the ministry of the Word, God has given the diaconal call to all Christians, the ministry of mercy. Both Kuyper and Bavinck make clear that this ministry is the job of both institutional and organic presentations of the church. Bavinck calls for the renewal of the diaconal office as one of mercy. He chides the Reformed tradition for mentioning the power of Word and sacrament and forgetting the diaconal call. He argues that one of the jobs of the deacons in the early church was to administer the food given by the rich at the agape feasts, one of which is spoken of in 1 Corinthians 11, to ensure that the poor had food to eat and also some to take away after the celebration of the Lord's Supper. Every Christian and every church community is at war with the world, flesh, and devil, he states. Their call to action is not only an aspect of the organism but also the institution. Bavinck, describing elders and deacons, calls these offices that of the "overseer and caretaker of the poor."[80]

Yet, there is also the "universal office of believers," because when two or three are gathered in the name of Christ, there is Christ's presence in the midst of a church, and each of those two or three has the Holy Spirit and his gifts. As little Christs, in the imitation of Christ, the office of believer is prophetic, priestly, and kingly (people who "declare the excellencies of God," "offer up their bodies as living sacrifices," and "fight the good fight, overcome sin, the world, and death").[81] This war is taken up in first order

78. See Eglinton, *Bavinck: A Critical Biography*, 255.

79. *Pro Rege* 2:29–30.

80. *RD* 4:346–47, 375.

81. *RD* 4:375–76.

in the ministry of Word and then the ministry of mercy. So Kuyper: "May the poor find the church to be a place of refuge."[82] Bavinck summarizes the entire picture of the work of the church:

> It never militates against nature as such but does join the battle— always and everywhere, in every area of life and into the most secret hiding places—against sin and deception. And thus it preaches principles that, by moral and spiritual but not by revolutionary channels, have their pervasive impact everywhere and reform and renew everything. While, in keeping with Jesus's command, the gospel must be preached to all creatures (Mark 16:15), it is "a power of God for salvation to everyone who believes" (Rom. 1:16), a two-edged sword that "pierces down to the division of soul and spirit" (Heb. 4:12), a leaven that leavens everything (Matt. 13:33), a principle that re-creates everything, and a power that overcomes the world (1 John 5:4).[83]

CONCLUSION

The neo-Calvinist ethic seeks a transformation of life in the midst of the world from the ground up toward the norms of creation, not for the sake of ushering in the kingdom, but because God demands a holy life according to the power of the gospel and because Christianity is good for the common life of the world. As we conclude this chapter and book, it is worth quoting Bavinck at length on this point because here he summarizes the neo-Calvinist ecclesiology and its derivative ethic in toto:

> But even greater, it seems to me, is the faith of the person who, while keeping the kingdom of heaven as a treasure, at the same time brings it out into the world as a leaven, certain that He who is for us is greater than he who is against us and that He is able to preserve us from evil even in the midst of the world. Now is this not precisely what the catholicity of our Christian faith requires of us? The Gospel is not content to be one opinion among others of

---

82. "Tract," 69.
83. RD 4:395–96.

the lie but claims to be the truth, the truth that by its very nature is exclusive in every area. The church is not just an arbitrary association of people who wish to worship together but something instituted by the Lord, the pillar and ground of the truth. The world would gladly banish Christianity and the church from its turf and force it to a private inner chamber. We could give the world no greater satisfaction than to withdraw into solitude and leave the world peacefully to its own devices. But the catholicity of Christianity and the church both forbid us to grant this wish. We may not be a sect, we ought not to want to be one, and we cannot be one, without denying the absolute character of truth. The kingdom of heaven may not be of this world, but it does demand that everything in the world be subservient to it. It is exclusivistic and refuses to accept an independent or neutral kingdom alongside of it. Undoubtedly it would be much easier to leave this entire age to its own devices and to seek our strength in quietness. But such a restful peace is not permitted us here. Because every creature of God is good and not to be rejected if it is received with thanksgiving, because everything can be sanctified by the Word of God and prayer, rejection of any one of His creatures would be ingratitude to God, a denial of His gifts. Our conflict is not with anything creaturely but against sin alone.[84]

Thus the Protestant principle is that grace comes into the world to renew the world and restore nature to the end for which God created. The problem with the world is not the fact of the naturalness of the world, but sin, the ethical corruption of the creation. The antithesis is not quantitative, but qualitative. The church exists as an enemy to the sin that has corrupted the world. The separation is that between sin and grace, between Christ and Satan. The church in the midst of the world, like little Christs, hears the call to be leaven, agents of renewal, by the life-saving, sin-demolishing work of the pearl of great price, the history of Christ and his message.

---

84. CCC, 248–49.

Neo-Calvinist ecclesiology brings together the whole of neo-Calvinist theology, in that both its adoption of the organism/institute relation and that between church and world is a product of the logic of the nature-grace relation. These theologians develop the nature-grace relation, that grace restores nature, in the twofold aspect of grace, common and special. For Kuyper, the neo-Calvinist logic that stems from Calvinism is a thoroughgoing system—the theological determinations are systematic:

> Thus understood, Calvinism is rooted in a form of religion which was peculiarly its own, and from this specific religious consciousness there was developed first a peculiar theology, then a special church-order, and then a given form for political and social life, for the interpretation of the moral world-order, for the relation between nature and grace, between Christianity and the world, between church and state, and finally for art and science.[85]

---

85. *Lectures*, 12.

X

16 Theses

THIS BOOK INTRODUCES many of the central dogmatic contributions of neo-Calvinism through a close reading of Abraham Kuyper and Herman Bavinck on the theological loci that, in their perspective, needed rearticulating and refinement. Far from being a public or philosophical enterprise first, we argued that neo-Calvinism presents a holistic *theological* project, and whatever public or philosophical interests that arose out of this tradition are rooted first in that theology. We also sought to convey that the diversity and sprawling trajectories of neo-Calvinism today invoke the need to go back to the primary sources, lest the theological contours and roots of this tradition become forgotten or inchoate. Further, in Kuyper and Bavinck we are reminded of neo-Calvinism's Reformed and catholic roots, dependent as they were on the ancient, medieval, and Reformed confessional theologians who preceded them. Indeed, we submit that neo-Calvinism is at its best not when it is presented as a movement that sought to reconstruct a new Christian worldview from the ground up, parasitic on its past, but rather as an impulse that seeks to stand on and move forward through its catholic commitments.

In that spirit, then, we clarify that what this book seeks to commend is not so much that theology needs a reduplication or repristination of Kuyper's and Bavinck's precise theological statements. Rather, the theology they articulated was situated within their own context and was the product of a certain set of postures and instincts worth emulating—instincts that we have highlighted throughout this book. While we should still continue to learn much from their dogmatic constructions, it is those instincts that we wish to emphasize for our present emulation in this conclusion. Let us highlight three of them, in a way that harks back to our summative comments in our introduction.

First, it is hard to overestimate how important it was for Kuyper and Bavinck to convey that orthodoxy and modernity exist in a reciprocal relationship. An emphasis on orthodoxy at the cost of the modern (the new) leads to a conservatism that forgets that our work as theologians depends on the very conditions that enabled us to be here in the first place, and that our contemporary milieu still enjoys the gifts of divine providence and common grace. There is much to be thankful for in the present age. As such, this instinct leads one to eschew a kind of nostalgic longing for a bygone golden age of theology, as if such an age ever existed, and fuels a patient optimism that rests on God's sovereign plan. As Bavinck often refrained, the God who saved us in Christ Jesus is the same God at work in history today. On the other hand, an emphasis on the modern at the expense of our confessional, scriptural (and very ancient) moorings forgets that our modern age continues to be indebted to the very theological and ethical culture that it rejects. This posture of looking to the past and future with thankfulness and hope produces the sort of culture-affirming yet sin-rejecting, hopeful but sober, posture that can continue to fuel present theologians. It protects us from a malformed, curmudgeonly spirit that may take the twofold form of either looking down at the past with chronological snobbery or total suspicion toward the present. This also presents theologians with a challenge: How might we continue to transmit and translate the older theologies of the past in the contemporary philosophical idioms of the day? How might we continue to accommodate the genuine findings of contemporary scientific scholarship without compromising the substance of our theological commitments? How do we not merely tell, but show, that the Christian faith continues to be relevant for our age and, indeed, for every age?

Second, the call toward holism is itself a posture that can lead theologians toward the strenuous effort to do justice to the rich and manifold aspects of reality. Various philosophies that fail to rest on revelation will produce false binaries and reductionisms that will seek to reduce the immaterial to the material, or the material to the immaterial, body to spirit, subject to object, and vice versa. We may no longer be wrestling with the particularities of the debates that Kuyper and Bavinck found themselves in during the nineteenth and early twentieth centuries, but this posture of seeking to resolve false binaries by finding a third way forward, of patient interdisciplinary reading that opposes syncretism and reactionary alarmism, is surely needed today. The doctrines of revelation, common grace, of the corporate character of humanity, the organism of the church, all lend themselves toward these holistic postures that we believe would produce intellectual virtues required for the dogmatic tasks ahead.

Finally, those same doctrines also led to neo-Calvinism's commitments to an articulation of the catholicity of the Christian faith that highlights its true *universality*. Christianity is a pearl—it is the gospel for all places and all times. Christianity is also a leavening power: it can take root in and influence all places and times, and in a diversity of ways. This emphasis on the unity-and-diversity of the Christian faith means a further commitment to philosophical *eclecticism*. Christianity does not need any one culture or philosophical handmaiden, but rather is pliable and intellectually versatile. It is free to use any philosophy or culture it finds, can reshape any philosophy or culture it encounters, and is not married to any single intellectual or cultural milieu. Too often presentations of Christianity can look awfully suspicious as a call to a conversion not to the universal claims of Christ but to an assimilation of a particular nation's culture or to another philosophical system. Neo-Calvinism makes a firm distinction, then, between the philosophies and cultures that Christianity has providentially been tethered to in the past, and Christianity in and of itself—the form may look different in each time and place, but the substance and revelation remain the same. Taking the clams of Bavinck and Kuyper seriously means adopting a posture of humble anticipation when believers (and scholars) from differing philosophical commitments seek to articulate the Christian faith in ways that might sound different from ours. Just as Bavinck argued that Christianity in America should not be expected to sound or look the same as Christianity in the Netherlands, so should we not confuse *our* Christian expression with the kingdom of God itself. The former is a finite expression limited to one time and space, whereas the latter is universal, diverse, and the highest good to which all Christian communities and confessions everywhere are mere approximations. The Christian tradition has never been monolithic, and this organic diversification is itself an implication of the truly catholic character of this faith.

These postures should develop a hopeful and prayerful disposition in us, and we pray that this book has helped modestly toward that end.

NEO-CALVINIST THEOLOGY: 16 THESES

With these three theologically motivated postures in place, we hope the reader is aided by providing these sixteen summative theses that capture the main emphases of the book.

1. Neo-Calvinism is a critical reception of Reformed orthodoxy, contextualized to address the questions of modernity.

2. Christianity can challenge, subvert and fulfill the cultures and philosophical systems of every age.

3. Neo-Calvinism rejects theological conservatism and progressivism. Instead it applies historic creedal and confessional theology to the concerns of the contemporary world.

4. The Triune God created the world and all creatures as a living unity in diversity, with a definite purpose and goal.

5. "Organism" and "organic unity" are fitting terms to describe creation's many unities-in-diversities, as it analogically reflects the Triune God.

6. The image of God is the pinnacle of creation's organic shape, referring to humanity collectively, male and female, and the self as a unity.

7. The problem with the world is not ontological but ethical, that sin has corrupted much, in fact, everything.

8. Out of the sinful mass of the organism of humanity under Adam, God elects to regenerate individuals into a new, sanctified organic humanity under Christ, thus positing a covenantal antithesis between the seed of the woman and the seed of the serpent.

9. By the Spirit's work in common grace, God restrains sin and gifts fallen humanity with moral, epistemic, and life-giving goods to enjoy, for the sake of redemption in Christ.

10. God has truly revealed himself to every person both objectively and subjectively. This implanted affection and knowledge of God is not a human determination as the product of reason (or natural theology), but God's general revelation by the presence of the Holy Spirit.

11. The Bible is God's revelation of himself, as the Spirit inspires a diversity of human authors to write all that God intends to communicate, which serves as the ultimate norm and agent of unity, though not the sole source, for the fields of knowledge.

12. The Triune God and his revelation matter for the whole of the human life because every person always stands before the face of God.

13. Humans are wise to pursue a Christian worldview: Christian theology should discipline the insights of both philosophy and the various sciences and Christians should conform their whole selves to the lordship of Christ.

14. Re-creation's end is brought about by divine agency alone and brings creation to its original goal: that God would make his dwelling place with humankind, in a consummated and sanctified cosmos.

15. Jesus Christ's Messianic dominion as King of the kingdom of God is the aim of God's work in history and the purpose of creaturely redemption.

16. The visible church exists as institute and organism: as an institute to preach the gospel and administer the sacraments, and as an organism of individuals bound together by the Spirit to witness to new creation.

Bibliography

Allen, Michael. *Grounded in Heaven: Recentering Christian Hope and Life on God*. Grand Rapids: Eerdmans, 2018.

Amos, Scott. "Martin Bucer's *Kingdom of Christ*." Pages 189–202 in *The Oxford Handbook of Reformed Theology*. Edited by Michael Allen and Scott R. Swain. Oxford: Oxford University Press, 2021.

Anema, Anne. *Calvinisme en rechtwetenschap: een studie*. Amsterdam: Kirchner, 1897.

Aquinas, Thomas. *Summa Theologiae*. London: Burns, Oates, and Washbourne, 1921.

Asselt, Willem J. van. "The Fundamental Meaning of Theology: Archetypal and Ectypal Theology in Seventeenth-Century Reformed Thought." *Westminster Theological Journal* 64 (2007): 289–306.

Athanasius. *Letter to Serapion*. Pages 564–66 in *Athanasius: Select Writings and Letters*. Nicene and Post-Nicene Fathers, Series 2. Edited by Philip Schaff. Reprint, Peabody, MA: Hendrickson, 1994.

Bacote, Vincent. *The Spirit of Public Theology: Appropriating the Legacy of Abraham Kuyper*. Grand Rapids: Baker Academic, 2005.

Baldwin, Michael. "A Theological Evaluation of the Views of Herman Bavinck on Natural Theology." MTh diss., Union School of Theology, 2021.

Bartholomew, Craig G. *Contours of the Kuyperian Tradition: A Systematic Introduction*. Downers Grove, IL: IVP Academic, 2017.

Bartholomew, Craig G., and Michael Goheen. *Christian Philosophy: A Systematic and Narrative Introduction*. Grand Rapids: Baker Academic, 2013.

Bavinck, Herman. *Beginselen der Psychologie*. Kampen: Bos, 1897.

———. "Calvin and Common Grace." Pages 99–130 in *Calvin and the Reformation: Four Studies*. Translated by Geerhardus Vos. Edited by William Park Armstrong. London: Revell, 1909.

———. "The Catholicity of Christianity and the Church." Translated by John Bolt. *Calvin Theological Journal* 27 (1992): 220–51.

———. *The Certainty of Faith*. Translated by Harrie der Nederlanden. Ontario: Paideia, 1980.

———. *Christelijke Wetenschap*. Kampen: Kok, 1904.

———. "Christendom en Natuurwetenschap." Pages 184–202 in *Kennis en Leven: Opstellen en artikelen uit vroegere Jaren*. Edited by C. B. Bavinck. Kampen: Kok, 1922.

———. "Christian Principles and Social Relationships." Pages 119–44 in *Essays on Religion, Science, and Society*. Translated by Harry Boonstra and Gerrit Sheeres. Edited by John Bolt. Grand Rapids: Baker Academic, 2008.

———. *Christian Worldview*. Introduced and translated by James Eglinton, Nathaniel Gray Sutanto, and Cory C. Brock. Wheaton, IL: Crossway, 2020.

———. "Common Grace." Translated by Raymond C. van Leeuwen. *Calvin Theological Journal* 24 (1989): 38–65.

———. *De wetenschap der H. Godgeleerdheid: Rede ter aanvaarding van het leeraarsambt aan de Theologische School te Kampen*. Kampen: Zalsman, 1883.

———. "Eloquence." Pages 21–56 in *On Preaching*. Translated by James Eglinton. Peadbody, MA: Hendrickson, 2017.

———. "Essence of Christianity." Pages 33–48 in *Essays on Religion, Science, and Society*. Translated by Harry Boonstra and Gerrit Sheeres. Edited by John Bolt. Grand Rapids: Baker Academic, 2008.

———. "The Future of Calvinism." Translated by Geerhardus Vos. *The Presbyterian and Reformed Review* 17 (1894): 1–24.

——. *Gereformeerde Dogmatiek*. 3rd ed. 4 vols. Kampen: Kok, 1918.

——. *Johannes Calvijn: Eene lezing ter gelegenheid van den vierhonderdsten gedenkdag zijner geboorte, 10 July 1509–1909*. Kampen: Kok, 1909.

——. "The Kingdom of God, the Highest Good." Translated by Nelson Kloosterman. BR 2 (2011): 133–70.

——. "Modernism and Orthodoxy." Pages 146–81 in *On Theology: Herman Bavinck's Theological Orations*. Translated by Bruce Pass. Leiden: Brill, 2021.

——. *Modernisme en Orthodoxie: Rede gehouden bij de overdracht van het rectoraat aan de Vrije Universiteit op 20 october 1911*. Kampen: Kok, 1911.

——. *Philosophy of Revelation: A New Annotated Edition*. Edited by Cory Brock and Nathaniel Gray Sutanto. Peabody, MA: Hendrickson, 2018.

——. "The Pros and Cons of a Dogmatic System." Translated by Nelson Kloosterman. BR 5 (2014): 90–103.

——. *Reformed Dogmatics*. 4 vols. Edited by John Bolt. Translated by John Vriend. Grand Rapids: Baker Academic, 2003–2008.

——. *Reformed Ethics*. Vol. 1, *Created, Fallen, and Converted Humanity*. Edited by John Bolt. Grand Rapids: Baker Academic, 2019.

——. "Religion and Theology." Translated by Bruce R. Pass. *Reformed Theological Review* 77 (2018): 75–135.

——. "Review of Tractaat van de Reformatie van de Kerken, by Abraham Kuyper." *De Vrije Kerk* 9 (1883).

——. "Theology and Religious Studies." Pages 49–60 in *Essays on Religion, Science, and Society*. Translated by Harry Boonstra and Gerrit Sheeres. Edited by John Bolt. Grand Rapids: Baker Academic, 2008.

——. "The Theology of Albrecht Ritschl." Translated by John Bolt. BR 3 (2012): 123–63.

——. "The Unconscious." Pages 175–88 in *Essays on Religion, Science, and Society*. Translated by Harry Boonstra and Gerrit Sheeres. Edited by John Bolt. Grand Rapids: Baker Academic, 2008.

——. *Wijsbegeerte der openbaring: Stone-lezingen*. Kok: Kampen, 1908.

——. *Wonderful Works of God: Instruction in the Christian Religion according to the Reformed Confession.* Edited by Carlton Wynne. Glenside, PA: Westminster Seminary Press, 2019.

Bavinck, J. H. *The Church between Temple and Mosque.* Grand Rapids: Eerdmans, 1966.

——. "General Revelation and the Non-Christian Religions." Pages 95–109 in *The J. H. Bavinck Reader.* Translated by James De Jong. Edited by John Bolt, James Bratt, and Paul Visser. Grand Rapids: Eerdmans, 2008.

——. "Religious Consciousness and Christian Faith." Pages 277–302 in *The J. H. Bavinck Reader.* Translated by James De Jong. Edited by John Bolt, James Bratt, and Paul Visser. Grand Rapids: Eerdmans, 2008.

——. "Religious Consciousness in History." Pages 233–76 in *The J. H. Bavinck Reader.* Translated by James De Jong. Edited by John Bolt, James Bratt, and Paul Visser. Grand Rapids: Eerdmans, 2008.

Belt, Henk van den. *The Authority of Scripture in Reformed Theology: Truth and Trust.* Leiden: Brill, 2008.

Beversluis, M. *De val van Dr. A. Kuyper: een zegen voor ons land en volk.* Oud-Beierland: W. Hoogwerf Az., 1905.

Bishop, Steve, and John H. Kok, eds. *On Kuyper: A Collection of Readings on the Life, Work, and Legacy of Abraham Kuyper.* Sioux Center, IA: Dordt College Press, 2013.

Boersma, Hans. *Seeing God: The Beatific Vision in the Christian Tradition.* Grand Rapids: Eerdmans, 2018.

Bolt, John. *Herman Bavinck on the Christian Life.* Wheaton, IL: Crossway, 2015.

Bowlin, John, ed. *Kuyper Center Review.* Vol. 2, *Revelation and Common Grace.* Grand Rapids: Eerdmans, 2011.

Bratt, James. *Abraham Kuyper: Modern Calvinist, Christian Democrat.* Grand Rapids, Eerdmans, 2013.

——. "The Context of Herman Bavinck's Stone Lectures: Culture and Politics in 1908." *BR* 1 (2010), 4–24.

——. "Introduction to Modernism: A *Fata Morgana* in the Christian Domain." Pages 87–124 in *Abraham Kuyper: A Centennial Reader.* Edited by James Bratt. Grand Rapids: Eerdmans, 1998.

Bräutigam, Michael, and James Eglinton. "Scientific Theology? Herman
    Bavinck and Adolf Schlatter on the Place of Theology in the
    University." *Journal of Reformed Theology* 7 (2013): 27–50.
Brink, Gijsbert van den. "On Certainty in Faith and Science: The
    Bavinck-Warfield Exchange." *BR* 8 (2017): 65–88.
Brock, Cory. "Bavinck as Public Theologian: Philosophy, Ethics, and
    Politics." *Unio Cum Christo* 6.2 (October 2020): 115–32.
———. *Orthodox yet Modern: Herman Bavinck's Appropriation of
    Schleiermacher.* Bellingham, WA: Lexham, 2020.
———. "Revisiting Bavinck and the Beatific Vision." *Journal of Biblical and
    Theological Studies* 6 (November 2021), 367–82.
Brock, Cory, and Nathaniel Gray Sutanto. "Herman Bavinck's
    Reformed Eclecticism: On Catholicity, Consciousness, and
    Theological Epistemology." *Scottish Journal of Theology* 70.3
    (August 2017): 310–32.
Calvin, John. *Institutes of the Christian Religion.* Translated by Ford
    Lewis Battles. Louisville: Westminster John Knox, 1960.
Chaplin, Jonathan. *Herman Dooyeweerd: Christian Philosophy of State
    and Civil Society.* Notre Dame, IN: University of Notre Dame
    Press, 2011.
———. *On Kuyper: A Collection of Readings on the Life, Work, and Legacy
    of Abraham Kuyper.* Edited by Steve Bishop and John H. Kok.
    Sioux Center, IA: Dordt College Press, 2013.
Clausing, Cameron D. "'A Christian Dogmatic Does Not Yet Exist':
    The Influence of the Nineteenth Century Historical Turn on
    the Theological Methodology of Herman Bavinck." PhD thesis,
    University of Edinburgh, 2020.
Covolo, Robert. "Beyond the Schleiermacher-Barth Dilemma: General
    Revelation, Bavinckian Consensus, and the Future of Reformed
    Theology." *BR* 3 (2012): 30–59.
"De toekomstige regearing." *Algemeen Handelsblad,* August 1, 1901.
Deursen, Arie Theodorus van. *The Distinctive Character of the Free
    University in Amsterdam, 1880–2005: A Commemorative History.*
    Translated by Herbert Donald Morton. Grand Rapids:
    Eerdmans, 2008.

Doornbos, Gayle. "Herman Bavinck's Trinitarian Theology: The Ontological, Cosmological, and Soteriological Dimensions of the Doctrine of the Trinity." PhD thesis, University of Toronto, 2019.

Douma, Jochem. *Common Grace in Kuyper, Schilder, and Calvin: Exposition, Composition, and Evaluation.* Translated by Albert H. Oosterhoff. Edited by William Helder. Hamilton, ON: Lucerna CRTS, 2017.

Duby, Steven J. *God in Himself: Scripture, Metaphysics, and the Task of Christian Theology.* Downers Grove, IL: IVP Academic, 2020.

Edgar, William. *Created and Creating: A Biblical Theology of Culture.* Downers Grove, IL: IVP Academic, 2017.

Eglinton, James. *Bavinck: A Critical Biography.* Grand Rapids: Baker Academic, 2020.

——. *Trinity and Organism: Toward a New Reading of Herman Bavinck's Organic Motif.* New York: Bloomsbury and T&T Clark, 2011.

——. "Vox Theologiae: Boldness and Humility in Public Theological Speech." *International Journal of Public Theology* 9 (2015): 5–28.

Fesko, J. V. *Reforming Apologetics: Retrieving the Classic Reformed Approach to Defending the Faith.* Grand Rapids: Baker Academic, 2019.

Gaffin, Richard B., Jr. *God's Word in Servant-Form: Abraham Kuyper and Herman Bavinck and the Doctrine of Scripture.* Jackson, MS: Reformed Academic Press, 2007.

Gordon, Bruce. *Calvin.* New Haven: Yale University Press, 2009.

Harinck, George. "Calvinism Isn't the Only Truth: Herman Bavinck's Impressions of the USA." Pages 151–60 in *The Sesquicentennial of Dutch Immigration: 150 Years of Ethnic Heritage; Proceedings of the 11th Biennial Conference of the Association for the Advancement of Dutch American Studies.* Edited by Larry J. Wagenaar and Robert P. Swierenga. Holland, MI: Joint Archives of Holland and Hope College, 1998.

——. "Herman Bavinck and the Neo-Calvinist Concept of the French Revolution." Pages 13–30 in *Neo-Calvinism and the French Revolution.* Edited by James Eglinton and George Harinck. London: Bloomsbury, 2016.

———. "'Land dat ons verwondert en betoovert.' Bavinck en Amerika." Pages 35–46 in *Ontmoetingen met Bavinck*. Edited by George Harinck and Gerrit Neven. Barneveld: De Vuurbaak, 2006.

Harinck, George, and James Eglinton, eds. *Neo-Calvinism and the French Revolution*. London: Bloomsbury T&T Clark, 2014.

Heideman, Eugene. *The Relation of Revelation and Reason in E. Brunner and H. Bavinck*. Assen: Van Gorcum, 1959.

Heslam, Peter. *Creating a Christian Worldview: Abraham Kuyper's Lectures on Calvinism*. Grand Rapids: Eerdmans, 1998.

Hoogenbirk, A. J. *Heeft Calvijn ooit bestaan?: kritisch onderzoek der Calvijn-legende*. Nijkerk: Callenbach, 1907.

Hunsinger, George. *Disruptive Grace: Studies in the Theology of Karl Barth*. Grand Rapids: Eerdmans, 1999.

Huttinga, Wolter. "'Marie Antoinette' or Mystical Depth?: Herman Bavinck on Theology as Queen of the Sciences." Pages 143–54 in *Neo-Calvinism and the French Revolution*. Edited by James Eglinton and George Harinck. London: Bloomsbury, 2014.

Inkpin, Andrew. *Disclosing the World: On the Phenomenology of Language*. Cambridge, MA: MIT Press, 2016.

Junius, Franciscus. *A Treatise on True Theology*. Translated by David C. Noe. Grand Rapids: Reformation Heritage Books, 2014.

Kaemingk, Matthew. *Christian Hospitality and Muslim Immigration in an Age of Fear*. Grand Rapids: Eerdmans, 2018.

Keulen, Dirk van. *Bijbel en Dogmatiek: Schriftbeschouwing en schriftgebruik in het dogmatisch werk van A. Kuyper, H. Bavinck en G.C. Berkouwer*. Kampen: Kok, 2003.

Knauss, Daniel. "Neocalvinism … No: Why I Am Not a Neocalvinist." *Comment*, June 1, 2006. https://www.cardus.ca/comment/article/neocalvinism-no-why-i-am-not-a-neocalvinist/.

Kooi, Kees van der. "On the Inner Testimony of the Spirit, Especially in H. Bavinck." *Journal of Reformed Theology* 2 (2008), 103–12.

———. "Over kerk en samenleving. Enkele opmerkingen bij de verschijning van Kuypers *Commentatio*." *Documentatieblad voor de Nederlandse Kerkgeschiedenis na 1800* 65 (November 2006), 20–25.

Kuyper, Abraham. "The Blurring of the Boundaries." Pages 363–402 in *Abraham Kuyper: A Centennial Reader*. Edited by James Bratt. Grand Rapids: Eerdmans, 1998.

———. "Calvinism: Source and Stronghold of Our Constitutional Liberties." Pages 279–302 in *Abraham Kuyper: A Centennial Reader*. Edited by James Bratt. Grand Rapids: Eerdmans, 1998.

———. *Common Grace: God's Gifts for a Fallen World*. Translated by Nelson D. Kloosterman and Ed M. van der Maas. Edited by Jordan J. Ballor and Stephen J. Grabill. 3 vols. Bellingham, WA: Lexham, 2015–2020.

———. "Common Grace." Pages 165–203 in *Abraham Kuyper: A Centennial Reader*. Edited by James Bratt. Grand Rapids: Eerdmans, 1998.

———. "Common Grace in Science." Pages 441–460 in *Abraham Kuyper: A Centennial Reader*. Edited by James Bratt. Grand Rapids: Eerdmans, 1998.

———. "Conservatism and Orthodoxy: False and True Preservation." Pages 65–85 in *Abraham Kuyper: A Centennial Reader*. Edited by James Bratt. Grand Rapids: Eerdmans, 1998.

———. *Encyclopaedie der Heilige Godgeleerdheid*. 2nd ed. 3 vols. Kampen: Kok, 1908.

———. *Encyclopedia of Sacred Theology: Its Principles*. New York: Charles Scribner's Sons, 1898.

———. *Lectures on Calvinism*. Grand Rapids: Eerdmans, 1931.

———. *Lectures on Calvinism*. Peabody, MA: Hendrickson, 2008.

———. "Lemke's Wish." Pages 399–403 in *On Education*. Edited by Wendy Naylor and Harry Van Dyke. Abraham Kuyper Collected Works in Public Theology. Bellingham, WA: Lexham, 2019.

———. "Lord's Day 21." Pages 315–371 in *On the Church*. Edited by John Halsey Wood Jr. and Andrew M. McGinnis. Abraham Kuyper Collected Works in Public Theology. Bellingham, WA: Lexham, 2016.

———. "Modernism: A *Fata Morgana* in the Christian Domain." Page 87 in *Abraham Kuyper: A Centennial Reader*. Edited by James Bratt. Grand Rapids: Eerdmans, 1998.

———. "The Natural Knowledge of God." Translated by Harry van Dyke. *BR* 6 (2015): 73–112.

———. *Ons Instinctieve Leven.* Amsterdam: W. Kirchner, 1908.

———. "Our Instinctive Life." Pages 255–78 in *Abraham Kuyper: A Centennial Reader.* Edited by James Bratt. Grand Rapids: Eerdmans, 1998.

———. *Our Program: A Christian Political Manifesto.* Edited and translated by Harry Van Dyke. Abraham Kuyper Collected Works in Public Theology. Bellingham, WA: Lexham, 2015.

———. *Pro Rege: Living under Christ's Kingship.* Translated by Albert Gootjes. Edited by John Kok and Nelson D. Kloosterman. Vol. 1. Bellingham, WA: Lexham, 2016.

———. *The Revelation of St. John.* Translated by John Hendrik de Vries. Eugene, OR: Wipf & Stock, 1999.

———. "Rooted and Grounded." Pages 41–73 in *On the Church.* Edited by John Halsey Wood Jr. and Andrew M. McGinnis. Abraham Kuyper Collected Works in Public Theology. Bellingham, WA: Lexham, 2016.

———. *Scholarship: Two Convocation Addresses on University Life.* Translated by Harry van Dyke. Grand Rapids: Christian's Library Press, 2014.

———. "Sphere Sovereignty." Pages 461–90 in *Abraham Kuyper: A Centennial Reader.* Edited by James Bratt. Grand Rapids: Eerdmans, 1998.

———. "Twofold Fatherland." Pages 281–314 in *On the Church.* Edited by John Halsey Wood Jr. and Andrew M. McGinnis. Abraham Kuyper Collected Works in Public Theology. Bellingham, WA: Lexham, 2016.

———. "Uniformity: The Curse of Modern Life." Pages 19–44 in *Abraham Kuyper: A Centennial Reader.* Edited by James Bratt. Grand Rapids: Eerdmans, 1998.

———. *The Work of the Holy Spirit.* Translated by Henri de Vries. Grand Rapids: Eerdmans, 1946.

Levering, Matthew. *Scripture and Metaphysics: Aquinas and the Renewal of Trinitarian Theology.* Oxford: Blackwell, 2004.

Marsden, George. "The Collapse of American Evangelical Academia."
    Pages 219–64 in *Faith and Rationality: Reason and Belief in God*.
    Edited by Alvin Plantinga and Nicholas Wolterstorff. Notre
    Dame, IN: University of Notre Dame Press, 1983.

Mastricht, Petrus van. *Theoretical-Practical Theology*. Vol. 1, *Prolegomena*.
    Translated by Todd Rester. Edited by Joel Beeke. Grand Rapids:
    Reformation Heritage, 2017.

Mattson, Brian. *Restored to Our Destiny: Eschatology and the Image of
    God in Herman Bavinck's Reformed Dogmatics*. Leiden: Brill, 2011.

———. "What Is Public Theology?" *Center for Public Leadership* (2011): 7.

McCall, Thomas. *Against God and Nature: The Doctrine of Sin*. Wheaton,
    IL: Crossway, 2019.

McGraw, Ryan. *Reformed Scholasticism: Recovering the Tools of Reformed
    Theology*. London: Bloomsbury T&T Clark, 2019.

Mouw, Richard. "Abraham Kuyper's *Lectures on Calvinism*." Pages
    328–41 in *The Oxford Handbook of Reformed Theology*. Edited by
    Michael Allen and Scott R. Swain. Oxford: Oxford University
    Press, 2021.

Muller, Richard. "Kuyper and Bavinck on Natural Theology," *BR* 10
    (2019): 5–35.

Niebuhr, H. Richard. *Christ and Culture*. New York: Harper and
    Brothers, 1956.

Parker, Gregory W., Jr. "Reformation or Revolution?: Herman Bavinck
    and Henri de Lubac on Nature and Grace." *Perichoresis* 15 (2017):
    81–95.

Pass, Bruce. *The Heart of Dogmatics: Christology and Christocentricism in
    Herman Bavinck*. Göttingen: Vandenhoeck & Ruprecht, 2020.

———. "Upholding *Sola Scriptura* Today: Some Unturned Stones in
    Herman Bavinck's Doctrine of Inspiration." *International Journal
    of Systematic Theology* 20 (2018): 517–36.

Puchinger, G. *Hervormd-gereformeerd, één of gescheiden*. Delft: W. D.
    Meinema, 1969.

Ralston, Joshua. "Editorial." *International Journal of Systematic Theology*
    18.3 (July 2016): 255–58.

Sanders, Fred, and Oliver Crisp, eds. *Divine Action and Providence.* Grand Rapids: Zondervan, 2019.

Schilder, Klaus. *De Kerk I.* Goes: Oosterbaan & Le Cointre, 1960.

———. *De Kerk III.* Goes: Oosterbaan & LeCointre, 1965.

———. *Dictaat Christelijke Religie. Over de Nederlandse Geloofsbelijdenis.* Kampen: Van den Berg, 1977.

Schleiermacher, Friedrich. *Christian Faith: A New Translation and Critical Edition.* Translated by Terrence N. Tice, Catherine L. Kelsey, and Edwina Lawler. Edited by Catherine L. Kelsey and Terrence N. Tice. Louisville: Westminster John Knox, 2016.

———. *On Religion: Speeches to Its Cultured Despisers.* Translated by John Oman. Louisville: Westminster John Knox, 1994.

Schumacher, Lydia. *Divine Illumination: The History and Future of Augustine's Theory of Knowledge.* Oxford: Blackwell, 2011.

Smith, James K. A. *Awaiting the King: Reforming Public Theology.* Cultural Liturgies. Grand Rapids: Baker Academic, 2017.

———. *Desiring the Kingdom: Worship, Worldview, and Cultural Formation.* Cultural Liturgies. Grand Rapids: Baker Academic, 2009.

———. *Imagining the Kingdom: How Worship Works.* Cultural Liturgies. Grand Rapids: Baker Academic, 2013.

Stanley, Jon. "Restoration and Renewal: The Nature of Grace in the Theology of Herman Bavinck." Pages 81–104 in *Revelation and Common Grace.* Vol. 2 of *The Kuyper Center Review.* Grand Rapids: Eerdmans, 2011.

Strange, Daniel. *Their Rock Is Not Like Our Rock: A Theology of Religions.* Grand Rapids: Zondervan, 2015.

Sutanto, Nathaniel Gray. "Bavinck's Christian Worldview: Classical Contours, Context, and Significance." *Reformed Faith and Practice* 5.2 (2020): 28–39.

———. "Divine Providence's *Wetenschappelijke Benefits.*" Pages 96–114 in *Divine Action and Providence.* Edited by Fred Sanders and Oliver Crisp. Grand Rapids: Zondervan, 2019.

———. "Egocentricity, Organism, and Metaphysics: Sin and Renewal in Herman Bavinck's Ethics." *Studies in Christian Ethics* 34.2 (2021): 223–40.

———. *God and Knowledge: Herman Bavinck's Theological Epistemology.* Edinburgh: T&T Clark, 2020.

———. "Herman Bavinck and Thomas Reid on Perception and Knowing God." *Harvard Theological Review* 111 (2018): 115–34.

———. "Herman Bavinck on the Image of God and Original Sin." *International Journal of Systematic Theology* 18.2 (2016): 174–90.

———. "Neo-Calvinism on General Revelation: A Dogmatic Sketch." *International Journal of Systematic Theology* 20.4 (2018): 495–516.

Turretin, Francis. *Institutes of Elenctic Theology.* Translated by George Musgrave Giger. Edited by James T. Dennison. 3 vols. Phillipsburg, NJ: P&R, 1992–1997.

VanDrunen, David. *Natural Law and the Two Kingdoms.* Eerdmans: Grand Rapids, 2010.

"Vergadering van Predikanten en Gemeenteleden der Evangelische richting." *Provinciale Overijsselsche en Zwolsche Courant,* June 1, 1899.

Vilmar, A. *Theologische Moral: Akademische Vorlesungen.* Gütersloh: Bertelsmann, 1871.

Visser, Paul. "Introduction." Pages 1–93 in *The J. H. Bavinck Reader.* Translated by James De Jong. Edited by John Bolt, James Bratt, and Paul Visser. Grand Rapids: Eerdmans, 2008.

———. "Religion, Mission, and Kingdom: A Comparison of Herman and Johan Herman Bavinck." *Calvin Theological Journal* 45 (2010): 117–32.

Vos, Geerhardus. "The Eschatological Aspect of the Pauline Conception of the Spirit," in *Redemptive History and Biblical Interpretation: The Shorter Writings of Geehardus Vos.* Edited by Richard B. Gaffin Jr. Philipsburg, NJ: P&R, 1980.

———. *Reformed Dogmatics.* Vol. 5, *Ecclesiology, the Means of Grace, Eschatology.* Edited and translated by Richard B. Gaffin. Bellingham, WA: Lexham, 2016.

Vree, Jasper. "Historical Introduction. Pages 7–66 in *Abraham Kuyper's Commentatio (1860): The Young Kuyper about Calvin, a Lasco, and the Church.* Leiden: Brill, 2005.

Wahlberg, Mats. *Revelation as Testimony: A Philosophical-Theological Account.* Grand Rapids: Eerdmans, 2014.

Wolters, Albert M. *Creation Regained: Biblical Basics for a Reformational Worldview.* Grand Rapids: Eerdmans, 2005.

Wolterstorff, Nicholas. "Herman Bavinck – Proto Reformed Epistemologist," *CTJ* 45 (2010): 133–46.

Wood, John Halsey, Jr. *Going Dutch in the Modern Age: Abraham Kuyper's Struggle for a Free Church in the Netherlands.* Oxford: Oxford University Press, 2013.

Zanchi, Jerome. *On the Law in General: Sources in Early Modern Economics, Ethics, and Law.* Translated by Jeffrey J. Veenstra. Grand Rapids: CLP Academic, 2012.

Ziegler, Philip G. "'Those He Also Glorified': Some Reformed Perspectives on Human Nature and Destiny." *Studies in Christian Ethics* 32.2 (2019): 165–76.

Name Index

A

Alsted, J. H., 83n29
Althasius, Johannes, 272
Amos, Scott, 41–42
Aquinas, Thomas, 86n41, 91, 92n59, 191,
    236, 238–39
Aristotle, 61, 89, 105, 189n16
Athanasius, 142
Augustine, 22, 26, 77–78, 135, 187, 191

B

Bacote, Vincent, 6
Balthasar, Hans Urs von, 171
Bartholomew, Craig G., 1, 3, 17, 106, 111,
    122n71, 125n82, 134n2
Bavinck, Johan H., 10, 72–73, 83–88,
    94–95
Bellarmine, Robert, 149–50, 203
Belt, Hank van den, 6, 83n29
Berkouwer, G. C., 1, 10
Boersma, Hans, 168–77, 181–83
Bratt, James, 3, 21n18, 24, 50, 75n10, 88,
    102,
Brink, Gijsbert van den, 17
Bucer, Martin, 42

C

Calvin, John, 11, 13, 16, 18, 24–31, 40–42,
    74–75, 88, 94, 203, 214–15, 229,
    246

Cyril of Jerusalem, 163

D

Darwin, Charles, 105
Dooyeweerd, Herman, 4, 5, 10, 235
Douma, Jochem, 215, 217
Duby, Stephen, 91–92

E

Eglinton, James, 6, 8, 90n55, 91, 112, 188
Epicurus, 194

F

Fesko, J. V., 237
Freud, Sigmund, 85

G

Grenz, Stanley, 191

H

Harinck, George, 18, 58
Heideman, Eugene, 134n2, 169
Henry, Carl F. H., 2
Hodge, Charles, 21–22
Hoeksema, Herman, 214n5
Hunsinger, George, 2

J

Junius, Franciscus, 82, 105, 187, 201

Subject Index

Scripture Index

OLD TESTAMENT

NEW TESTAMENT

KUYPER'S MAGISTERIAL WRITINGS NOW IN ENGLISH FOR THE FIRST TIME.

To order and learn more, visit
abrahamkuyper.com.